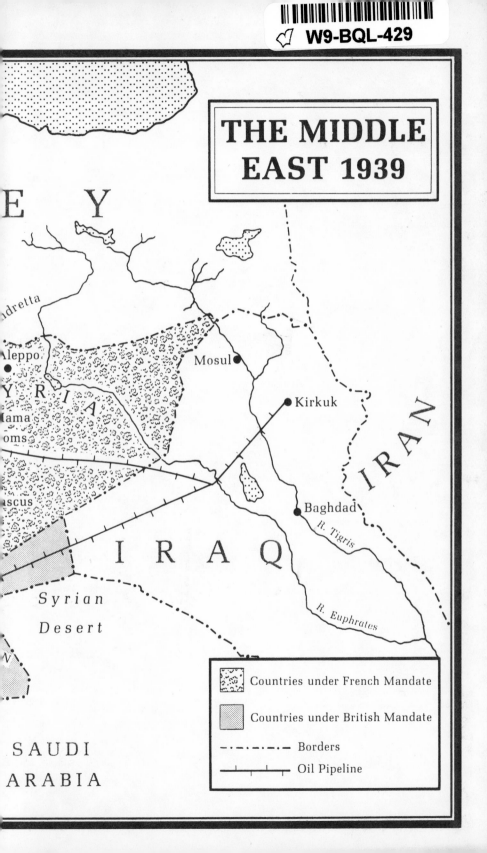

W9-BQL-429

THE MIDDLE EAST 1939

E Y

adretta

Aleppo

Mosul

Kirkuk

IRAN

Y R I A

ama

oms

scus

Baghdad

R. Tigris

I R A Q

Syrian

Desert

R. Euphrates

N

SAUDI

ARABIA

Countries under French Mandate

Countries under British Mandate

– ·– ·– Borders

├─┼─┼─┤ Oil Pipeline

THE
PALESTINE
TRIANGLE

NICHOLAS BETHELL

THE PALESTINE TRIANGLE

The struggle for the
Holy Land, 1935–48

G. P. Putnam's Sons ● New York

Contents

Illustrations

Between pages 320 and 321

Irgun barrel bomb, October 1947

Goldsmith Officers' Club, Jerusalem, after an explosion, March 1st, 1947 (*Associated Press*)

Lydda station during the evacuation of the British, February 1947 (*Imperial War Museum*)

Jewish refugees from *President Warfield* walking to trains in Hamburg (*Life Magazine* © *1947 Time Inc.: photo Walter Sanders*)

The end of the Mandate, May 1948 (*Illustrated London News*)

Azzam Pasha (*Associated Press*)

David Ben Gurion (*Radio Times Hulton Picture Library*)

Ernest Bevin (*Radio Times Hulton Picture Library*)

Harry S. Truman (*Radio Times Hulton Picture Library*)

Maps

Acknowledgements

Above all I have to thank Olwen Gillespie, whose three years of work in helping to research this book have produced results beyond all my expectations. As well as her other duties, she has found the energy to spend days in the Public Record Office, London, and long evenings typing up the results. I remain for ever grateful for her reliability and skilful detective work, originally in the vaults of Chancery Lane and later on the great computer at Kew, which has unearthed considerable hidden treasure.

I recognize too that my task would have been impossible without the help of Susan Hattis-Rolef, whose researches in Israel gave me access to much of the cream of Israeli archives, some of which she translated from Hebrew.

Among the many who lent me their personal archives describing their service in Mandatory Palestine, I particularly want to thank Tony Bailey, whose vivid contemporary account of the boarding of Jewish immigrant ships must be seen as a special contribution.

Several hundred Arab, Jewish and British participants in the Palestine drama have been kind enough to talk to me and share the memory of their experiences. I mention especially Musa el-Alami, Yigal Allon, Katie Antonius, Ike Aranne, A. J. Bailey, Evelyn Barker, Harold Beeley, Menachem Begin, Itzhak Berman, Isaiah Berlin, Robert Boothby, John Briance, A. Bruce, Ralph Capernerhurst, James Cassels, Richard Catling, Martin Charteris, K. Clifford Cook, Geula Cohen, Irene Collins, Alan Cunningham, Efraim Dekel, Abba Eban, Roy Farran, Bernard Fergusson, T. C. Foley, Hugh Foot, Richard Gale, Israel Galili, M. C. Gray, Nicol Gray, David Hacohen, K. P. Haddingham, Nicholas Hammond, D. J. R. Haslip, Adina Hay-Nissan, E. P. Horne, J. N. Hudson, Andrew Hughes-Onslow, William B. Jones, Bernard Joseph, Samuel Katz, George Kitchen,

Arthur Koestler, Teddy Kollek, Haim Landau, Arnold Lawrence, John A. F. Lawson, I. J. Linton, Malcolm MacDonald, Golda Meir, Rodney Moore, Geoffrey J. Morton, Robert Newton, Anwar Nusseibeh, John O'Sullivan, Micha Peri, T. A. E. Russell, John Rymer-Jones, Max Seligman, Itzhak Shamir, John Shaw, Colin Sundius-Smith, Eli Tavin, C. A. Wade, Dymock Watson, Ezer Weizman, W. J. Williamson, Ralph Windham, Yigael Yadin, Nathan Yalin-Mor, Yerachmiel Yaron.

1
The First
Four Thousand Years

WHO owns Jerusalem and the lands that surround it? No writer can shed light on this question without reference to its four thousand years of background. The burden of history lies heavily on the area, condemning it to continual strife throughout this century. People have tried to end the violence. Men whose decision-making lives last a mere five or ten years have been forced to address themselves to problems raised by four millennia. No wonder they have all failed.

The problem of Palestine and Israel is sharpened not only by history, but also by the intensity of emotion which the Holy Land arouses in hundreds of millions of people – Jews, Moslems and Christians. Many wars have been fought for control of the Wailing Wall, the Dome of the Rock and the Church of the Holy Sepulchre. As the influence of religion on political leaders has declined, reverence for the city which means so much to the three great faiths has survived, and nations with only half a claim to the coveted prize have succumbed to a dominating urge to grab it.

Some of the earliest records of these lands are in the Old Testament of the Bible, which describes their settlement, perhaps as early as the year 2000 BC, by the descendants of Jacob, son of Isaac and grandson of Abraham. The Bible tells how the followers of Jacob (or Israel) were taken into captivity by the Pharaoh of Egypt, from which they were led by the prophet Moses, who founded the laws of Israel's one-God religion. Scholars dispute how literally to accept the accounts of the lives of early Biblical figures – Aaron, Joshua, Samuel or Saul – but there can be no doubt that by 1000 BC Jewish tradition becomes historical fact. Israel was a kingdom and David was its king.

This kingdom of Israel lasted little beyond the reign of David and his son Solomon. First it became divided, then in the eighth century BC part of it was conquered by the Assyrian Empire. In 588 BC Jerusalem was destroyed by Nebuchadnezzar and its people taken to Babylon. At the end of the sixth century Cyrus the Great of Persia took Babylon and allowed the Israelites to return. The Holy Land changed hands again in 323 BC, when Alexander of Macedon defeated the King of Persia. It was then occupied by Ptolemy of Egypt and the Seleucid rulers of Syria. A successful revolt in the second century restored Jewish independence, but in 63 BC it was destroyed again by Pompey of Rome.

After the Roman conquest the Holy Land stayed under non-Jewish rule for nearly two thousand years. For some decades Jewish kings and procurators were appointed by Rome, the most famous being Herod the Great and Pontius Pilate, but by the middle of the first century AD the Jews were again in rebellion. Roman forces under Titus fought the rebels for several years before capturing Jerusalem and burning it in the year 70. A Jewish force still held out at Masada, a boat-shaped natural fortress on a hill on the western bank of the Dead Sea.

The story of Masada is important to our story, remembered as it is by Jews today as a most heroic and inspiring episode in their history. The defenders numbered about a thousand, including women and children. This puny force, by a combination of bravery and geographical good fortune, was able to hold off an entire Roman legion during the winter of 72–73 AD. The Romans were forced to spend many months building a huge ramp of earth up to a point on the west of the hill. Eventually, when it was clear that they were about to break into the fortress, the Jews under Eleazar ben Yair concluded that they would die as free men and women rather than as captives. They burnt their possessions and committed systematic suicide, killing one another group by group and individual by individual, leaving no one and nothing for the alien conqueror.

Further rebellions took place, inevitably followed by further massacres of Jews. In the repressions of the year 135, following the revolt led by Bar-Cochba, Jerusalem was totally destroyed and the Jews driven out of the Holy Land. From this date the Jews existed almost entirely in the diaspora, the scattering of their nation throughout the world. Their sacred places were burnt, their lands occupied by invaders, but through their religion and their Bible they were able to maintain a special identity and way of life over the centuries, in whichever country they lived as a community.

While some were ready to assimilate, most rejected intermarriage as a sure path towards their annihilation as a people, an abandonment of the certain hope that one day they would return to Jerusalem and the Land of Israel, which they still considered their own by divine gift. It was only by remaining thus aloof that they achieved the remarkable feat of surviving nearly two thousand years, often under cruel persecution, without a country, and emerging in this century as a recognizable nation.

Jerusalem remained a place of pilgrimage for Christians and began to flourish again in the fourth century, when the Roman emperor Constantine was converted to Christianity and constructed many more great buildings. But the Roman Empire was now in decline. In the early seventh century it was unable to resist the armies of the Persian Sassanid king Khosrau, who took Jerusalem in 614 and penetrated as far as Egypt. Under the emperor Heraclius much of this land was recovered a few years later. But this was already the lifetime of Mohammed the Prophet, whose flight from Mecca to Medina in 622 marked the beginning of the Moslem era. Yet another imperial power – the Arabs – was about to emerge and form lasting religious attachments to the Holy City.

The Byzantine armies were defeated by Muslim armies at the battles of Ajnadain in 634 and Yarmuk in 636. Two years later Omar ibn al-Khattab, the second Caliph, entered Jerusalem. Fifty years later the ninth caliph Abd-ul-Malik, built the Dome of the Rock, a great shrine on the site of the Jewish Temple, which Titus had burnt. It was from this site, Moslems believe, that the Prophet flew to Heaven on his magic steed, the 'buraq'. For them it is a very sacred spot, the third in importance after Mecca and Medina. For the Jews it is the most sacred spot of all, the site of their Temple, which the Romans destroyed. But ever since the seventh century it has been a religious centre for Arabs also, who lived in Jerusalem and cultivated the land around it. The only part of the Temple site to which Jews have from time to time had access is its western wall, known as the Wailing Wall.

Physically weak, but the proud possessor of leading shrines of the three monotheistic religions, Jerusalem was thereafter a magnet to invaders. The area was poor, much of the surrounding land being desert, and it was never able to support a powerful population, capable of making its own alliances and defending itself against the empires which from time to time cast covetous eyes upon it. When the Arabs declined, Jerusalem became a backwater, a place of pilgrimage but little more. It was when these pilgrim routes were cut, after the city fell into the hands of the Seljuq Turks, that European Christian nations conceived the idea of a campaign to recover control of their churches and, incidentally, some of the wealth and power of the Orient. In 1099 Jerusalem fell to the Crusaders, who set up a kingdom there similar in size and shape to the subsequent territory of Mandatory Palestine.

After about a century of Christian rule, Jerusalem was taken by Saladin of Egypt and had to survive various ruinous raids by the Mongol hordes of Hulagu Khan. In 1517 it was taken by the Ottoman Turks, in whose hands it remained for exactly four hundred years. It was only in 1914 with the entry of Turkey into the First World War on the side of Germany and Austro-Hungary that the ownership of the Holy Land could again be challenged.

It was natural for Great Britain and France, in their conflict with Turkey, to seek allies among those Arabs who were weary of the Ottoman Empire and anxious to rebel against it. Britain was at this point little interested in acquiring power in the Arab world. She was very interested in embarrassing Turkey. By the same token, certain Arabs were anxious to help Britain, if by doing so they could obtain their independence. Negotiations therefore took place by letter between Hussein, Sherif of Mecca, and Sir Henry McMahon, British high commissioner in Egypt. McMahon's crucial letter of October 24th, 1915, promised on Britain's behalf the independence of all Arab-populated areas of the Turkish empire with the exception of 'the portions of Syria lying to the west of the districts of Damascus, Homs, Hama and Aleppo'.

The Arabs assumed and maintain to this day that this promise included Palestine, which lies rather to the south of Damascus than to the west of it. On the other hand, Britain was to maintain that Palestine, administered by Turkey as the *vilayet* of Beirut and the independent *sanjak* of Jerusalem, was excluded by McMahon's letter. All sides agree that, as the Palestine Royal Commission explained in 1937, 'it was in the highest degree unfortunate that in the exigencies of war the British Government were unable to make their intention clear to the Sherif'.

The Arabs fulfilled their part of the bargain. In June 1916 the Sherif declared war against Turkey, overran many Turkish outposts in the Peninsula and with the help of the famous T. E. Lawrence harassed their lines of communication, especially the railway line linking the north with Medina. Arab forces supported General Edmund Allenby in his invasion of Palestine the following autumn, in which he defeated the Turks at Gaza in November 1917 and entered Jerusalem on December 9th. The word 'Allenby' is, when written, the Arabic word for 'the Prophet' – a bizarre coincidence which added to the conviction in many Arab minds that Britain had come to Jerusalem to restore the holy places of Islam to their rightful Arab ownership.

Meanwhile Jewish interest in the land of their ancestors grew in intensity, as cruel anti-semitism spread throughout Central Europe and Russia during the last years of the nineteenth century. Many tens of thousands of Jews were massacred in pogroms which the Tsarist government did little to prevent. Others were robbed, uprooted from their homes and exiled. In the face of such persecution Jews fled from Russia in huge numbers, perhaps as many as three million, to lands where anti-semitism was not so cruel. Many found homes in Britain and her Empire, but most went to the United States, where the Jewish population increased during the fifty years following 1870 from 250,000 to four and a half million.

It was these persecutions which gave initial impetus and urgency to Zionism, a movement much publicized by Theodor Herzl at a congress in Basle in 1897. A longing to return to Jerusalem had been deeply rooted in Jewish hearts for 1800 years, but now for the first time it was possible and necessary to put these aspirations into practice. During the decades of the exodus from Russia to America the Jewish population of Palestine also increased, though on a much smaller scale, from 25,000 to 80,000 in the years 1881–1914.

But there was a big difference in the attitudes of the two sorts of immigrant. Most Jews who crossed the Atlantic went in search of physical security and a decent way of life within a Jewish community, though in the context of American laws and customs. The immigrants to Palestine, those who were Zionists, had their sights set much higher. The Arab population they joined was poor and immature, politically and scientifically. Palestine contained no more than a few dozen Arab university graduates, almost all from Turkish universities. The Jewish newcomers felt no need to imitate their ways. Instead they would rebuild the Jewish cultural and religious institutions which had survived the diaspora. They would revive the Hebrew language. They would construct a land which was *theirs*, by historical and Biblical title, where the Jew was the owner rather than the tenant, the normal inhabitant rather than the stranger apart.

In Palestine, the Zionists hoped, Jews would live by right rather than on sufferance or by grudging courtesy of the gentile. No longer would they be confined to finance and small trade in the cities – work which had so often made them unpopular and persecuted. They would do normal jobs in the factories and fields. They would make Palestine a centre of civilization amid a desert of ignorance, a demonstration to all of what

Jews could achieve if they were allowed to flourish as a nation. They would provide a refuge for any persecuted Jew anywhere in the world and turn the territory into a Jewish homeland, or perhaps even – some time in the distant future – a Jewish state.

Originally based in Central Europe, the Zionist movement turned its eye towards Britain after she became Turkey's enemy. After some hesitation and after an offer of British East Africa (Uganda) had been seriously considered by many, the Zionists set their hearts on a return to Palestine, which they called Eretz Israel, the Land of Israel. But if they were to obtain it, Turkey would have to be removed. To achieve this aim their leaders Chaim Weizmann and Nahum Sokolow, who lived in London, formed close links with the government of David Lloyd George.

So Britain was lucky enough to find herself courted by the Zionists, who wanted Palestine, as well as by the Arabs, who wanted independence. All three nations had a common aim – the destruction of the Ottoman Empire. Britain grabbed the chance of embarrassing her enemy by making generous promises to both Jews and Arabs, promises which overlapped and were to cause all three sides much chagrin decades later.

In the autumn of 1917 Britain decided that a gesture in favour of the Jews would be of great benefit to her war effort. It would encourage the Jews of the United States, which had entered the war only on April 6th and were still unprepared for large-scale fighting in Europe. It would please Russian Jews, who were influential in the provisional government which had replaced the rule of Nicholas II in February, and encourage Russia to make more effort on the eastern front. It might even seduce the loyalties of the large Jewish communities in Germany and Austria.

The war was going badly and Britain was fighting for her life. The Russian army was weakened and the American army not yet ready. In April one quarter of the ships which left British ports were sunk by German U-boats. The Italians had lost the battle of Caporetto. Lloyd George, always a pro-Zionist, told the 1937 Royal Commission: 'The Zionist leaders gave us a definite promise that, if the Allies committed themselves in giving facilities for the establishment of a national home for the Jews in Palestine, they would do their best to rally Jewish sentiment and support throughout the world to the Allied cause. They kept their word.'

And so on November 2nd Britain produced her famous Balfour Declaration, named after Arthur James Balfour, the then foreign secretary. It expressed support for 'the establishment in Palestine of a national home for the Jewish people', adding that nothing would be done there 'which may prejudice the civil and religious rights of existing non-Jewish communities'. The Declaration was approved in advance by US President Woodrow Wilson and in 1918 by the French and Italian governments.

Neither the Arab leaders nor the Arab inhabitants of Palestine were consulted over the Balfour Declaration. It is therefore the Arab position that Britain and her allies had no more right to promise the Jews a home in Palestine than, say, Iraq would have had to promise them a home in California (see page 221). Arthur Koestler, himself a former Zionist, describes it as the promise by one nation to a second of the country of a third. Zionists and present-day Israelis, though, see it as a thoroughly justified act of restitution, the affirmation of the historical and, some would say, Biblical right of the Jews to return to the land from which they were driven by Roman invaders 1800 years earlier.

The text of the Declaration was a compromise and a disappointment to some Zionists, who had expected Britain to approve Palestine as *the* Jewish National Home, or even to refer to the possibility of a future Jewish state. The concept of *a* national home *in* Palestine was more vague and was soon the subject of controversy. What did it mean? Did it mean that the Jews were eventually to rule Palestine? Certainly those who drafted the Declaration did not mean this to happen immediately. They could not, because they were not sure that Jews would go to Palestine in enough numbers to become a majority and form a state. As yet they had witness only of the theoretical enthusiasm of the Zionists. They could not be sure that it would last, once Jews entered in sufficient numbers to discover the harshness of life there – the lack of water and the poor quality of the soil.

Some of those who drafted the document did envisage a Jewish state. Lloyd George, who was prime minister at the time, confirmed to the 1937 Commission that a Jewish state would not be set up immediately, but that if large-scale immigration led to a Jewish majority 'Palestine would thus become a Jewish commonwealth'.[1] In March 1919 Woodrow Wilson said that the Allies 'are agreed that in Palestine shall be laid the foundations of a Jewish commonwealth'. General Jan Smuts, a member of the Imperial War Cabinet when the Declaration appeared, told an audience in Johannesburg in November 1919 that he foresaw 'in generations to come a great Jewish state rising there once more'. Similar prophecies were made by other statesmen involved in the Declaration, including Winston Churchill.

But what of the Arabs? How could the promise of a Jewish National Home, with a possible future Jewish state, be reconciled with the promise that the rights 'of existing non-Jewish communities' would be preserved? Today the contradiction between the two promises seems to jump from the very page of the Declaration. Did Britain not realize what it was doing?

Lord Curzon was one of the first statesmen to raise the alarm. In January 1919, with Balfour at the Paris peace conference, he was in charge of the Foreign Office and he sent his Secretary of State (whom he was to succeed that autumn) several letters about Palestine. On January 16th he reported the view of Allenby and others that 'a Jewish *government* in any form would mean an Arab uprising, and the nine-tenths of the population who are not Jews would make short work of the Hebrews'. He had long felt, he added, 'that the pretensions of Weizmann and Company are extravagant and ought to be checked'.[2]

Balfour replied that, as far as he knew, Weizmann had never claimed the right to govern Palestine. He agreed that such a claim would be inadmissible and that Britain should promise no more than she had in the 1917 Declaration. Curzon replied that the term 'national home' might mean two quite separate things to Balfour and to Weizmann: 'He [Weizmann] contemplates a Jewish state, a Jewish nation, a subordinate population of Arabs and others ruled by Jews, the Jews in possession of the fat of the land and directing the administration.'

But in the complacent atmosphere of 1919 Curzon's voice did little to cloud the sunny mood of the Paris delegates. The evidence is that most of the victorious Allied leaders, if they thought about Palestine at all, believed that the Arabs would be persuaded to acquiesce in the construction of the Jewish National Home. After all, the Arabs themselves had received so much already. Had not Britain's help enabled them to gain their independence in vast Arab areas? Surely they would be suitably grateful and would fall in with Britain's plan?

Two statements delivered in London in July 1920 illustrated this belief. The first was a message by King George V to 'the people of Palestine', nearly ninety per cent of them Arab. It referred to 'the large part' played by British troops 'in freeing your country from Turkish rule' and promised that in future 'your country' would receive the peace and prosperity that had long been denied. It mentioned 'the gradual establishment' of a Jewish National Home, but followed this with the assurance that 'these measures will not in any way affect the civil or religious rights or diminish the prosperity of the general population of Palestine'.

On July 12th, five days after the King's proclamation, Balfour addressed a Jewish audience in London's Albert Hall. The whole question of Palestine would require tact and judgement from both Jews and Arabs, he said, but it was his hope that the Arabs 'will not grudge that small niche, for it is not more geographically . . . being given to the people who for all these hundreds of years have been separated from it'.

Balfour was one of the many British supporters of Zionism who believed that the National Home was not a gift to the Jewish people, but an act of restitution. The Jews were being given back something that had been stolen from them in the early years of the Christian era. This was the assumption on which all the claims of the Jewish leaders in Palestine were to be based in future years. As far as they were concerned, the basic argument of ownership was closed. As the decades passed, the National Home grew and tensions increased, they were to find it harder and harder to understand any British action which seemed to go against this principle.

Malcolm MacDonald, who as British colonial secretary in 1939 was the first man to face the full horror of the conflicting promises, wrote a Cabinet paper that January which contained harsh criticism of the Balfour Declaration: 'All this is very unsatisfactory, and we cannot avoid blame for the situation which has arisen. It is impossible to escape the conclusion that the authors of the various declarations made to Jews and Arabs during the war, which are really very difficult to reconcile, were rather confused about the whole business. I doubt whether they realized fully how many Arabs were already living in Palestine at the time when they made their promise to the Jews; they certainly cannot have foreseen how formidably that Arab population would increase after the arrival of Jewish capital and development and British administration; and they must have assumed in any case that these Arabs could be persuaded to acquiesce in the policy of the Jewish national home.'[3]

Also, one must remember, the year 1917 belonged to an age when most nations believed in the right of conquest. If a nation's armies conquered a territory in war, they thereby acquired possession of it and were entitled to do with it as they thought fit. The Balfour Declaration was the product of 1917, a particularly harsh year in an era of imperial power. Millions of men were killing one another in Europe. In such circumstances political leaders may have thought that if promises could save lives, they should be given, even if there was a risk that they would not be fulfilled and that a later generation of British leaders would be called to account for this failure.

After the war the victorious Allies dismembered the Ottoman Empire and independent kingdoms arose in the Arabian Peninsula. For certain other Arab-inhabited territories they devised the system of Mandate – a temporary trust to be held by one Allied country under the supervision of the newly established League of Nations. Iraq was under British mandate, but was organized as a semi-independent kingdom. Syria and Lebanon became a French mandate. Palestine, including the area across the Jordan (Transjordan), became a British mandate.

So it was that Great Britain became the last in a long line of imperial nations to gain control of Jerusalem and the Holy Land. Jewish organizations in the United States and elsewhere had particularly urged that Britain be selected by the League. Herbert Samuel, a well-known Jewish Englishman and former Cabinet minister, was appointed High Commissioner, instructed to rule Palestine not as a British colony but as a trust to be held by Britain under certain conditions. These conditions were laid down in a document dated July 22nd, 1922, which consisted of a Preamble and 28 Articles.

This Mandate document mentioned the Balfour Declaration and 'the historical connection of the Jewish people with Palestine'. It instructed Britain to recognize as a public body 'an appropriate Jewish agency' to advise the Administration in general economic and social matters and in 'close settlement by Jews on the land'. Article Six, the most controversial article, began with another promise which seems in retrospect impossible: 'The Administration of Palestine, while ensuring that the rights and position of other sections of the population are not prejudiced, shall facilitate Jewish immigration under suitable conditions. . . .' The 'other sections of the population' referred to must have been the Arabs, since at that time they were nearly ninety per cent of the Palestine population, but nowhere in this document or in the Balfour Declaration were the Arabs mentioned by name – a fact which seemed and seems to them an unforgivable humiliation.

Whatever the strict legal interpretation of these documents and promises, there can be no doubt that most Zionists took them as a go-ahead, a tacit assurance that Britain was sympathetic to their aim of an eventual Jewish state, and they were supported in this belief by many conversations with pro-Zionist British statesmen. It made sense, because at the time Zionism did seem to fit in with Britain's scheme of things. What could be better for Britain than the emergence in this crucial strategic area, a few miles from the Suez Canal, of a new, industrious, European-educated nation, friendly and grateful to Britain for the fact of its existence? The opposite argument, the fear that growing Jewish influence in the Fertile Crescent might damage Britain's relations with the Arabs, had not yet become politically significant. The Arabs as a whole were very weak and the Arabs of Palestine hardly seemed to exist.

Menachem Begin, who became prime minister of Israel in 1977, remembers the heady atmosphere of those days as a boy in Poland: 'I was brought up by my father to be an admirer of Britain. My father was one of the first Zionists and when the Balfour Declaration was proclaimed we saw in Britain the saviour of our people. And we always compared the Balfour Declaration to the Cyrus declaration. He was the king of Persia who let our people go from captivity in Babylon to return to Zion. And then they rebuilt the Temple. We thought that the great British people, with their sentiment for the Bible, were now making it possible for us to rebuild our state in the land of our forefathers. When Herbert Samuel was made the first High Commissioner, his picture was in all the shops in Eastern Europe and he was considered to be our prince, the first Jewish prince in the Land of Israel.'

This was the romantic idea created in the minds of many European Jews by the Mandate and the Balfour Declaration. The reality in the Palestine of 1922 was different. The Jewish population, swelled by 5514 immigrants in 1920 and 9149 in 1921, was only 83,000. It was still not certain how many Jews would want to come to Palestine or what institutions they would be able to build.

Slowly British officials were being forced to realize the self-contradictory nature of their policy and the practical problems it posed them. In January 1919 there was a moment of conciliation. Chaim Weizmann and the Emir Feisal, son of Sherif Husein of Mecca and a future king of Iraq, signed an agreement accepting the Balfour Declaration and encouraging Jewish immigrants to settle Palestine in the interest of both communities. At this point Feisal seems to have believed that the Jews would be content to enter Palestine in small numbers, bringing capital and expertise, and to help other Arab nations towards independence. But in April 1920, by which time such an outcome seemed less likely, there was the first serious outbreak of intercommunal violence. Five Jews were killed and 211 wounded. In May 1921 there was a worse outbreak, in which forty-seven Jews were murdered and forty-eight Arabs killed by British security forces.

Thomas Haycraft, Chief Justice of Palestine, wrote in his report on the riots that there was 'a feeling among the Arabs of discontent with and hostility to the Jews, due to political and economic causes and connected with Jewish immigration'. Already immigration was emerging as the great dividing issue. In February 1922 a delegation of Arab leaders told the

Colonial Office that the people of Palestine would not accept the Balfour Declaration or the Mandate. They demanded national independence in accordance with their interpretation of the McMahon pledge and Article 22 of the Covenant of the League of Nations, which 'provisionally recognized' all former Turkish provinces as independent. Mandatory rule, it said, was to last only 'until such time as they are able to stand alone'.

Winston Churchill, then colonial secretary, explained to the Arabs the British view that Palestine was not included in the pledge. He also explained frankly that independence could not yet be granted, because it would violate the promise given by Britain to the Jewish people. The Arab delegation now realized what this meant. What Churchill had said, they wrote, 'constituted the strongest proof that the Jewish national home is the cause of depriving us of our natural right'.

During 1922–6 the Jewish population of Palestine increased by 75,000. In five years it had almost doubled. In one year alone, 1925, 33,801 immigrants entered. Jewish funds from Europe and America were used to buy land, sometimes from improvident or absentee Arab landlords. Arab tenant farmers were being deprived of their land. These were the years when other Arab countries – Egypt, Syria, Iraq and Transjordan – were looking for progress to independence. Only in Palestine, it seemed, was no progress being made. The Arabs could see only one reason for delay. Britain was waiting for the arrival of more immigrants and would not hand over her Mandate until the Jewish community owned more land and was numerically stronger, strong enough perhaps to take control of the country.

These were years of great Jewish achievement. Young Jews fired with Zionist enthusiasm, mainly from Central and Eastern Europe but also from Holland, Yemen, France, Iraq, the United States and Britain, came to Palestine to cultivate land which had never been cultivated before, to make the desert bloom. Scholars from famous European universities came to be hewers of wood and drawers of water. Immigrant doctors set up medical services which could hardly be bettered anywhere in the world, to the benefit of the Arabs as well as the Jews. Groups of young people set out into empty spaces to find water, which was all they needed as the basis of a communal farm or kibbutz. They were industrious, dedicated and strongly motivated. They insisted that everything they were doing would be for the ultimate benefit of all Palestinians.

The Arabs were not convinced. In 1921 Herbert Samuel had appointed a certain Haj Amin al-Husseini as Mufti of Jerusalem and president of the

Supreme Moslem Council, the most powerful Arab office in the country. As such he disposed of considerable funds and these he had used to attract a political following and further his strong nationalist aims. The Husseini and Nashashibi families were already the two most influential in the country. Over the next decades the Mufti made the Husseinis stronger still, the leading hawks in the battle against Zionism. They felt that the Arabs were being swamped, with British connivance. To prevent this they were prepared to use any method and ally themselves with any foreign power.

The site of the Temple in Jerusalem, where the Dome of the Rock stands, is a most holy place to both Jews and Moslems. In September 1928 some Jewish worshippers, in violation of long custom and British law, brought a screen up to the Wailing Wall, the only part of the building to which the Jews have access. The purpose of the screen was only to separate men from women worshippers, but it caused the Mufti to launch a campaign accusing the Jews of planning a gradual encroachment upon the holy site, their eventual aim being to destroy the Mosque and rebuild the Temple.

It is hard to think of any idea more calculated to arouse emotion and hatred in the Middle East. Social discontent, nationalism and now religion were being used to persuade the Arabs of the dangers they faced and to provoke them into violence. During the second half of August 1929 133 Jews were massacred by Arab mobs roused to frenzy by speeches from religious leaders. In Hebron alone sixty-four Jews were murdered, and it was over the Hebron massacre that the British authorities were particularly blamed – for giving the Jews false promises of reassurance, for halfheartedness in attempts to control the murderous mob and for failing to send for reinforcements until it was too late.

The senior British police officer in Hebron, R. O. Cafferata, according to a Jewish author writing that same year, 'deprived us of the means of appealing for help and defence, betrayed us with empty promises, and gave the murderers and robbers their opportunity'.[4] The Arab killers were alleged to have set about their task crying: 'The government is with us!' The belief was growing among Jews that Britain was having second thoughts about her commitment to the Zionist enterprise, that there were some in the British administration, especially in the police, whose anti-semitism had allowed them to connive at a pogrom. The Arabs, of course, believed that Britain supported the Jewish side, that she was using Zionism to steal their country and thereby absorb it into her imperial scheme.

The Arabs too suffered fatal casualties, 116 in all, some through Jewish retaliation but mostly at the hands of the police. Three Arabs were hanged for murder. But the impact of the riots caused officials in London to consider Arab grievances and to conclude that there was some justification in their fears of being swamped by Jewish newcomers. In 1929–30 no fewer than three British documents were published, all of them newly sympathetic to the Arab point of view.

A commission chaired by Walter Shaw referred to 'the excessive immigration of 1925 and 1926'. Another inquiry by John Hope Simpson concluded that Arab interest demanded a temporary end to Jewish land settlement. He also addressed the problem of Arab unemployment. 'It is wrong,' he argued, 'that a Jew from Poland, Lithuania or the Yemen should be admitted to fill an existing vacancy, while in Palestine there are already workmen capable of filling that vacancy.' These views were supported in October 1930 by a White Paper authorized by the then colonial secretary, Lord Passfield (Sidney Webb).

The Zionists were deeply dismayed by these blows to the development of the National Home. The pro-Arab shift of policy seemed to them a surrender to religious extremism and mass murder. Weizmann immediately claimed that the 1930 White Paper was inconsistent with the Mandate and enlisted the support of his many influential friends in London to have it quashed. One of the men he approached was the future colonial secretary, who was later to play a great part in deciding Palestine's fate, the son of prime minister Ramsay MacDonald.

Malcolm MacDonald says: 'Weizmann and his friends came to see me through Lewis Namier, who had been one of my tutors at Oxford, and I took the matter up with my father. He arranged for a Cabinet committee under Arthur Henderson to review the matter and in the end Webb was persuaded to modify his policy. The Zionists were very grateful. They believed that I was on their side.' The outcome was a letter dated February 13th, 1931, from Ramsay MacDonald to Chaim Weizmann reaffirming that Jewish immigration would be limited only by Palestine's economic capacity to absorb them.

Jewish immigration declined from the high levels of 1924–6 and the violence seemed to cool down. But the violent events of the late 1920s damaged British authority in Palestine. Britain, it seemed, had inclined her policy in favour of the Arabs as a result of Arab rebellion. She had then changed it back in favour of the Jews as a result of parliamentary pressure at home. It all made both communities look sceptically at British policy and suspect that it had no clear direction, that it was based and would in future be based on the political demands of the moment rather than on any firm principle.

Then on January 30th, 1933, Hitler came to power in Germany. Within a few months Nazi laws were passed excluding Jews from German cultural life, farming, teaching and the civil service. As the pressure mounted many German Jews began to think of Palestine, their national home, where the Allies had promised that they could live 'as of right and not on sufferance'. In 1932 only 353 Jewish immigrants came from Germany. In 1933 the figure had jumped to 5392. Immigration overall rose from 9553 in 1932 to 30,327, then to 42,359, then to a peak of 61,844 in 1935, the year in which the notorious Nuremberg laws deprived Jews of German citizenship and penalized them in other cruel ways.

This was the prelude to the Nazi horror that was to destroy six million of the nine million Jews of central and eastern Europe. But it was also a time of alarm for the Arabs of Palestine. True, their fears were not of wholesale massacre, but, put at their highest, of wholesale expulsion from the land they considered their own. They were on a different level from those of the Jews of Europe. But they were none the less real and were based on unimagined social grievances.

For instance, David Hacohen, top director of Solel Boneh, the contracting agency of the Palestine Jewish trade unions (the Histadrut), remembers young pioneers (halutzim) coming to Palestine and using crude methods to stop Jews employing cheap Arab labour: 'The owner wanted to keep the Arab, because he paid the Arab 12 piastres a day, whereas our rate was 30, that was the union rate. So the halutzim stood by the gate and refused to let the Arabs in. Socialistically, it was not correct. We took a job away from a man who probably had a wife and children and we told the Jewish employer we'd beat him up if he continued to employ him.'

Hacohen had British friends, some of whom saw this going on and told him they disapproved of it. But at this stage Hacohen and the Jewish leaders who shared his views were prepared to put their ambitions for Jewish nationhood before their socialist beliefs. 'I know that socialistically you are right,' Hacohen remembers himself saying: 'but we want to build a Palestine for Jews as a whole, not only for Jewish capitalists. When we have our state, everyone will be unionized and the Arabs will be paid the same as ourselves.'

Jewish leaders like Hacohen realized that they were discriminating against the Arab. But they intended this to be only temporary. When they had achieved their political objective, they would make sure that the

Arab had equal rights, in every way, which meant that he would be materially better off than his brothers in other Arab countries. They hoped that the Arab would appreciate this and fall in with their plans.

Simultaneously the Jewish community was offering high prices to Arab landowners and finding willing sellers. Many of the sellers were absentees from Syria, but others were Palestinian. Land sales enabled the latter to acquire liquid wealth for the first time, then to turn this wealth into education, forming an elite which even today carries out much of the administrative work throughout the Arab world. But for the Arab tenant farmer the result was less fortunate. The new owners naturally required his land for cultivation by Jews. Sometimes he was provided with alternative land, but more often he was simply left landless. He was thrown off his land and not allowed to work it even as a hired labourer.

An example of this was seen at Wadi Hawarith by Hugh Foot, a young administrator who later became governor of Cyprus and other British colonies: 'It was a large stretch of land inhabited by Arabs in tents and shacks. Eventually, after long court cases, it was decided that they must be evicted. I had the dreadful job of going in with police, knocking down their tents and small structures and turning them off.' Great bitterness was aroused by such cases.

But the greatest Arab grievance was, as usual, immigration. The Arabs could easily work out that, if Jews continued to enter Palestine at the 1935 rate, they would very soon find themselves a minority community, and this in a land where in 1922 they had been nearly ninety per cent of the population. They were now down to seventy per cent, and their purchasing power was estimated at no more than twenty-five per cent of the country's total. Previously their complaint had been that of all Arab-inhabited countries Palestine alone was making no progress towards independence. Now their concern was that independence might indeed be granted in a few years, only not to them, to the newcomers from Europe who would outnumber them.

The stage was set for another outbreak of Arab violence. In mid-April 1936 a confused series of violent incidents led to Arab rioting in Jaffa and the death of sixteen Jews. But this time it was not a sudden outbreak, sparked off by a surge of emotion. It was a planned and coordinated attempt by the Mufti of Jerusalem and other Arab leaders to force various demands on Britain.

On April 21st these leaders declared a general strike. On April 25th an Arab Higher Committee was formed under the Mufti's presidency. The violence continued and Jews were assaulted in various parts of the country.

The British high commissioner unsuccessfully appealed to the Committee to help in the restoration of order. On May 8th the Arab leaders resolved to continue the strike and to withhold the payment of taxes until their demands were met. On May 18th Britain appointed a Royal Commission under Lord Peel to investigate the whole problem.

It was the Arabs themselves who paid the main financial price of the strike. It provoked the Administration to demolish a large number of houses in the old town of Jaffa, ostensibly as a sanitary measure, but in reality as a collective punishment, as was all but admitted when the matter came before the courts. Jaffa port was closed, so the Jews of Tel Aviv two miles up the coast lost no time in asking permission to build their own port, obtaining it and building a jetty which received its first ship a few weeks after the strike began. Arab boatmen and workmen thus lost a large part of their business for ever. Then as the strike dragged on through the summer, the question of the citrus crop became critical. If the strike lasted through the autumn, the crop would spoil. Thousands of Arab farmers and labourers would be crippled.

On September 29th, 1936, Auni Abdel Hadi, secretary of the Arab Higher Committee, went to see Emir Abdullah of Transjordan to suggest how the strike might be ended without loss of face. The result was a public appeal by Abdullah and two other Arab kings, Ghazi of Iraq and Ibn Saud of Saudi Arabia, asking their Palestinian brothers to end the revolt, relying on 'our friend Great Britain, who has declared that she will do justice'.[5] Lord Peel and his colleagues arrived in Palestine on November 11th to find peace restored and the Arabs back at work. At the end of this first stage of the revolt eighty-nine Jews had been killed, a handful of British and several hundred Arabs.

But as they took their evidence that winter, they could be sure of the threat implied even in this act of semi-surrender. The Arabs had ended their disturbances, they made clear, only to enable Britain to admit the justice of Arab grievances and fulfil Arab demands. Their leaders boycotted the Commission for all but its last few days in Palestine and their press kept up a strong attack. 'The Arabs of Palestine are looking at the Government with an eye of hate', wrote *ad-Difa'a* on December 21st. The Arab Higher Committee had called for an end to the violence and it had ended immediately. They were capable of restarting it just as quickly.

The Mufti finally agreed to give evidence before the Royal Commission. The Balfour Declaration, he said, was extremely prejudicial to Arab interests. It had enabled the Jews to acquire large tracts of fertile Arab land and would frustrate Arab plans for eventual independence. The ultimate aim of the Jews was the reconstruction of the Temple on the ruins of the Moslem holy places. Horace Rumbold asked him whether, in his opinion, Palestine was capable of assimilating and digesting the 400,000 Jews already there. Haj Amin replied with the one word: 'No.'[6] In that case, would some of the Jews have to be removed? 'We must leave all this to the future,'[7] was the Mufti's ominous reply.

He went on to explain that the Arabs had fought with Britain in the war so as to obtain their promised independence, not to put British rule in place of Turkish rule. In fact, the Ottoman Empire had not been so bad as many claimed, he said. In some ways the Arabs lived better then than they now did under the British. In short, the Balfour Declaration and the Mandate must be annulled and the sovereignty of Palestine transferred to an Arab body, after which the Arabs would 'deal with the Jews themselves'.[8]

Jewish witnesses, on the other hand, complained that Britain was in violation of Article Six of the Mandate in not allowing Jewish immigration up to the full absorptive capacity of Palestine. Immediate independence, they pointed out, and the Mufti's words seemed to confirm this, would mean placing the Jewish community under Arab domination and probably in physical danger. They urged Britain to do her duty by stamping out Arab terrorism and helping them to build the national home.

On March 12th, 1937, the Jewish case was further supported by the evidence of Winston Churchill, who had been colonial secretary at the beginning of the Mandate in 1922. The British government had not committed itself, he said, to making Palestine into a Jewish state, but it certainly *had* committed itself 'to the idea that some day, somehow, far off in the future, subject to justice and economic convenience, there might be a great Jewish state there, numbered by millions, far exceeding the present inhabitants of the country'.

Rumbold suggested that it would be 'harsh injustice' to subject the Arab 'indigenous population' to 'the invasion of a foreign race'.[9] Churchill replied that the Arabs had entered the area after the Jews, that their 'great hordes of Islam' had smashed the place up, turning it into a desert. 'Where the Arab goes, it is often desert,' he declared. In his view, *this* was the potential injustice, the idea of leaving the Holy Land as a desert, when it could be in the hands of men and women of energy and enterprise, who would plant it with orange groves.

Many pro-Zionists, Jewish and non-Jewish, likewise dismissed the Arab side of the case as an improper interruption in the inexorable march of cultural and economic progress. They believed that Britain was exaggerating the strength of the Arab nationalists, perhaps through ignorance of the true situation, perhaps with the cynical aim of stifling the national home, to which Britain was committed. The answer to the problem, they claimed, was a tougher line by the Palestine administration. Britain only had to demonstrate a little firmness and the rebellion would collapse like a balloon. The Arab masses would calm down, as soon as those few inflammatory leaders were removed, and would go along with the Zionist plans, from which they stood to benefit.

But the Arab masses showed little sign of calming down. In April two delegates of the Arab Higher Committee, Jamal Husseini (the Mufti's cousin) and Izzat Tannous, went on a mission to London to warn of the dangers of supporting Zionism. Tannous then went on to New York, where he told a hostile audience of pressmen that unless Jewish immigration to Palestine ceased at once 'there will be another uprising, far worse than the seven that have occurred'.[10]

The Mufti of Jerusalem was by now emerging as the clear national leader of the Palestine Arabs, as well as a significant leader of other Arabs, through his embodiment of their fears and resentments against Jewish immigration and land purchase. But his pure nationalism and single-minded patriotic fervour were darkened by the other side of his character, revealed not only in his ruthless opposition to political Zionism, which many considered a virtue, but also in his unscrupulous political methods – specifically his misuse of religious funds entrusted to his care and his frequent assassinations of Arabs who challenged his authority.

The invisibility of serious Palestinian political opposition to the Mufti was thus assured. But it was not only his physical vengeance that Arab leaders feared. They also feared the political extinction that would result from any less than wholehearted espousal of their cause in Palestine. For the simple fact was that almost all Arabs, Palestinian or otherwise, approved the Mufti's aims, even though they disapproved of his methods, and those few who dissented would never have either the courage or the means to admit as much in public.

Only in one respect were the Mufti and his party seriously challenged. This was over his policy of boycott and total opposition to Britain. The Nashashibi family and the National Defence party, led mainly by businessmen, believed that Britain could be converted to pro-Arab policies by argument and participation. It was the typical dilemma of a nation ruled by foreigners – to collaborate or not to collaborate. But it was complicated by being, as well as everything else, a blood feud between the Husseini and Nashashibi families. On June 30th, for instance, Fakhri Nashashibi was shot and seriously wounded in Jaffa by a Husseini agent.

On July 7th, 1937, the Peel Commission's report appeared. The solution it proposed was novel and radical, the partition of Palestine into an Arab and a Jewish state. The latter would be quite small, a strip of coastline running from south of Tel Aviv and widening south of Haifa to include Nazareth and the western shore of Lake Tiberias. Britain was to retain under permanent mandate the holy places – Jerusalem, Bethlehem and a corridor to the sea at Jaffa. The Arabs would take the rest.

An elegantly written work of some four hundred pages, the report remains one of the standard historical works on Mandatory Palestine. It pointed out that partition would give the Jews the state for which they clamoured, their own country where they would control their own immigration and where they would be free of the centuries-old curse of always being a minority. They would be able to bring in as many refugees from Nazi Germany as they wished. The only limit would be the country's capacity to absorb them – a criterion over which they would be the judge. The Arabs would achieve their long-sought goal – independence. True, it would only be in part of Palestine, but it would be in the larger part. And was it not in their interest to make this sacrifice in order to rid themselves of the fear of being swamped completely?

Lord Peel and his colleagues admitted that there had been British mistakes: 'We did not fully realize the difficulties of the task it [the Mandate] laid on us. We have tried to overcome them, not always with success.' There was no solution that gave both sides everything they wanted. But at least partition offered something, and 'half a loaf is better than no bread'. Imperfect though it was, partition was the only solution that offered 'the inestimable boon of peace'.

These proposals, however well argued, stood little chance of being fully accepted by either side. The London *Jewish Chronicle* immediately described them as 'a nightmare scheme' which 'will strike a chill into the hearts of Jews already oppressed with heavy cares'. The frontiers would be unworkable – 'a bewildering criss-cross, aggravated by enclaves and corridors'. The Report was a victory for Arab terrorism and the result of British weakness. A little more firmness, the *Jewish Chronicle* claimed, would result in 'a vigorous Arab movement for the reopening of Palestine to Jewish immigrants'.[11] Within a few days the slogan was coined: 'No Jewish state without Zion'.

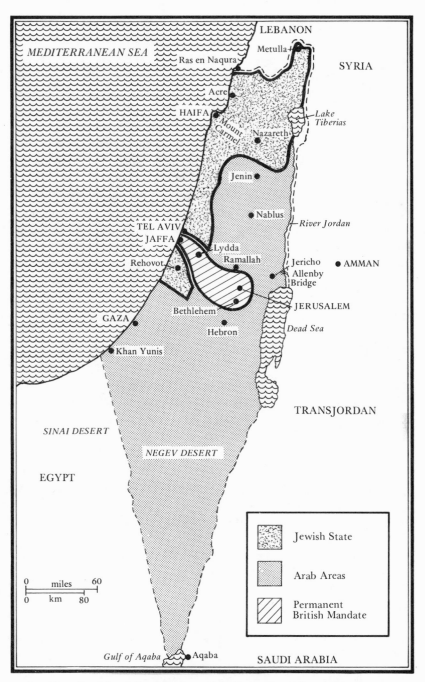

Partition: Provisional Frontier, from the Palestine Royal Commission Report,
July 1937

The Report earned the special hostility of the main Zionist 'opposition', the Revisionist party led by Vladimir Jabotinsky, whose programme demanded the 'revision' of Zionist policy and development of the National Home over all the Land of Israel, including Transjordan. He had said to the Royal Commission: 'A corner of Palestine, a canton – how can we promise to be satisfied with it? We cannot. We never can. Should we swear to you that we should be satisfied? It would be a lie.'

Like most Revisionists, Jabotinsky came from Eastern Europe, from Odessa in Russia. Others came from Poland, where the Jewish community was three million strong, about ten per cent of the population. 'We have got to save millions, many *millions*,'[12] he told the Commission. For him a Jewish majority in Palestine was a minimum demand, not a maximum, and he did not think this unjust to the Arabs, who had many states, while the Jews had none. His ideas seemed crazy at the time, to the Jewish 'establishment' as well as to the British and Arabs. Immigration on such a scale was simply impossible. It would mean chaos and starvation. A few years later, when almost all those Polish Jews had been murdered, his ideas seemed not so crazy.

Then after some days of reflection Jewish leaders came to wonder whether partition might not offer some hope. The proposed Jewish state was far too small, they all agreed, but at least it would give them a base from which to operate. 'If partition is accepted and goes through, I hope that the Jews will treat it merely as a stepping-off ground for further advance',[13] said Josiah Wedgwood, a pro-Zionist member of the House of Commons. Arabs took careful note of this comment.

This was the feeling that came to dominate the twentieth World Zionist Congress that August. The Negev desert, said Weizmann, was unsuitable for colonization, but in any case 'it would not run away'. David Ben Gurion was more precise. There could be no question, he said on August 15th, 1937, of giving up any part of the Land of Israel, but it was arguable that the ultimate goal would be achieved most quickly by accepting the Peel proposals. The Congress agreed by a majority to negotiate for frontiers favourable to a possible partition.

At the same time as the Zionist meeting in Zurich, four hundred Arab delegates met at Bludan in Syria and emerged unanimous in their fundamental objection to partition of any sort. In no way were they convinced by the British arguments. Their reply was that independence would benefit them little if it meant losing Jerusalem, Jaffa, Haifa and northern Palestine for ever. The idea seemed to them not a sensible compromise, but the violation of a principle, the simple and unchallengeable fact that Palestine belonged to *them*.

It was at this point that Nazi Germany woke up to the fact of turmoil in Palestine. Until mid-1937 their anti-semitism was expressed in a willingness to let Jews emigrate, to get rid of as many as possible. The Nuremberg Laws had induced about 120,000 Jews to leave Germany for ever, one third of them to Palestine, where under a system known as Haavara they were able to export part of their property.

But rumours of the proposals for partition caused alarm when they reached Berlin early in June. Foreign Minister Konstantin von Neurath pointed out in a telegram to London, Baghdad and Jerusalem that the prospect of a Jewish state might mean a change of German policy. The proposed state gave Germany the worst of both worlds. It would be too small to 'dump' many more Jews in. On the other hand, it would become a consolidating point for Jewish political influence, as the Vatican was for Roman Catholics or Moscow for communists. The time had come to support the Arab cause as a counterbalance to world Jewry and as a means of embarrassing Britain.

It was the beginning of a relationship which was to prove disastrous to the Palestinian Arabs. But at the time it seemed too good an opportunity to reject. The Jews had good relations with Britain, the United States and other important countries. But Arabs had no such influence in London, Paris or Washington. They too were looking for a counterbalance. On July 15th the Mufti called on Consul-General W. Döhle, the German representative in Jerusalem, to tell him that the Palestine Arabs were united in their rejection of partition and in 'sympathy for the new Germany'.[14]

The British government announced its acceptance of the Report and its resolve 'to give effect to a scheme of partition'. The Arab delegates in Bludan resolved that this would not happen. Palestine was quickly becoming the rallying point of Arab nationalism, the one issue on which they all agreed. Bludan was the beginning of an era, for it showed that if Arab unanimity was possible on this issue, it might be possible on other issues. The author of an Arab Office pamphlet wrote in 1947: 'It served as a focus for all the political energy of the Arab world and did more than anything else to encourage the movement for unity.'[15] British documents show that in London close attention was paid to the Bludan conference, especially in the Foreign Office, because it was one of the first real challenges to Britain's predominant position in the Middle East. Officials saw the Arab nations acting together, behaving like a political power in their own right. They were on their way to concluding that they would have to listen to Arab wishes more intently if Britain was to maintain her position.

Agents of the Mufti controlled the revolt from a headquarters in Damascus. They sent men round the towns of Syria and Lebanon, buying arms from the population with money from the extensive religious funds, about £60,000 a year, which the Mufti controlled in his official capacity. They showered the Arab world with pamphlets denouncing British imperialism, injustice and cruelty. They kept an assassination list of officials, details of which were sometimes leaked into Palestine and did no good to British morale. On June 13th they made an attempt on the life of Roy Spicer, Inspector-General of the Palestine police.

British officials began to live with the danger of murder and established their own rules of self-preservation. When they travelled it was with three armed policemen in the car and a 'pick-up' vehicle in front and behind, on the lookout for ambushes and landmines. They varied their time-tables and routes. Their offices were guarded and they never entered a room first, always after a policeman who checked the interior. Foot recalls: 'When I sat down to work at a desk, I'd take my revolver out and put it in front of me, and if I went out of the room for any reason I took it with me, carrying it in my hand. It's no good having a revolver in your holster. To be any use it's got to be in your hand.'

Yelland Andrews, District Commissioner for Galilee, was high on the assassination list because he had organized the Peel Commission's pro-gramme and was thought to have influenced it in favour of partition. He realized his danger and took all the proper precautions. Then on September 26th he telephoned Foot with the good news that the rebel command in Damascus had removed his name from the list and that he was going to church in Nazareth to celebrate. He and his bodyguard Peter McEwan were not on the alert as they entered a narrow lane near the Anglican church. Arab gunmen shot them both dead.

British opinion was outraged. A leader in *The Times* two days later reminded readers of the situation. Arabs were being murdered for refusing financial aid to the extremists or for advocating an understanding with the Jews. Two Arab landowners suspected of selling land to Jews had been murdered only a few days earlier. The Arab Higher Committee had con-demned Andrews's murder, but they could scarcely have done otherwise, said *The Times*, recalling the Peel Commission's view that the Mufti and his colleagues must bear a 'full share of responsibility' for the 1936 disorders.

On October 1st, 1937, the authorities, stung by allegations in London of weakness and timidity, arrested five members of the Arab Higher Committee, deported them to the Seychelles, strengthened press censorship and dismissed the Mufti from the presidency of the Supreme Moslem Council – the source of his large funds. The Mufti took sanctuary in the *haram esh-sharif*, the most holy shrine of Jerusalem, where no British soldier or policeman would enter, then escaped overland and by boat to Lebanon, probably with British connivance. About fifty suspects were arrested and detained in a camp at Acre, which already held 150 political prisoners. Mention of any of these events in the local press was forbidden. 'Better late than never. Andrews has not died in vain,' wrote Blanche (Baffy) Dugdale, a well-known pro-Zionist and Arthur Balfour's niece, in her diaries. 'This changes the whole situation, makes partition a certainty.'[16]

It seemed for a moment that British firmness had quelled the rebels. 'A week now has passed since the Palestine government took its drastic steps and the country has never been more peaceful,' wrote a correspondent of the *New York Times*, which generally supported the Zionist cause. At last action was being taken to isolate and destroy the 'small minority' who supported the Mufti's terrorists. Then during the night of October 14th Jewish colonies and buses were attacked, the oil pipeline was set on fire, a train was derailed and two British policemen were killed in an ambush. *The Times* blamed the new outbreak on weak leadership in the past, which had prevented the police from 'strangling disorder in its cradle'.

The revolt was on again, and on a greater scale than in 1936. Money was extracted from rich Arabs to replace the lost religious funds. Arab policemen and others who worked with the government were kidnapped, tried by kangaroo courts and killed. The rebels lurked in the hills, where there were few roads, descending on Jewish settlements and British posts, then riding back into the hills. Once again the Administration had lost control.

This time the British fought back hard. John Briance was one of a number of policemen who could dress, talk and almost pass as an Arab: 'We tracked them and out-guerrillaed them. We did searches and ambushes, but we needed intelligence. I would go into villages with six Arab policemen and talk to people. You had to establish your position, show them that you were sympathetic to their cause, but once they trusted you they would give you information.'

But as the situation deteriorated, the British police and army used tougher measures. Hugh Foot says: 'When we thought that a village was harbouring rebels, we'd go there and mark one of the large houses. Then, if an incident was traced to that village, we'd blow up the house we'd marked.' The death penalty was decreed for possession of arms and carried out on a rebel leader, Sheikh Farhan es-Saadi. By the end of January 1938 seven rebels had been executed.[17] The *New York Times* reported on January 26th: 'The hangman's black flag was hoisted three times today over Acre fortress as a grim token of British determination to stamp out terror in Palestine.' On February 1st a band of about a hundred rebels was surrounded on a wooded hill near Haifa and bombed from the air. Fifteen of them were killed or wounded.[18]

Collective punishment, mainly fines and curfews, became commonplace. A British senior policeman says: 'In those days there were no press around and we could exercise the law in a rough and ready way. There were so many pressures we could bring to bear – preventing a village's animals from grazing, preventing them from sowing their crops – that we hardly ever had to use brute force. Sometimes we billeted a police unit on a village, so that they had to feed and house it, making it clear that once the bad men were found the police would go away. Often when we'd brought sufficient collective punishment to bear, the community would bring their malefactors in handcuffed.'

These measures were not enough to crush the revolt, which drew part of its impetus from stories of British brutality. 'Their bombs were efficient, their landmines blew us off the road, their barricades stopped our patrols and in the end we had to withdraw from the countryside,' says John Briance. Hugh Foot's wife was evacuated and he was forced to move from his house into Nablus Fort: 'All ordinary administration ceased. Every morning I looked through a long list of disorders and destruction – telephones cut, bridges damaged, trains derailed, convoys ambushed and fighting in the hills.'[19]

Of course in any conventional encounter, whether with British forces or the Jewish Supernumerary Police (established by Britain in July 1936), the Arabs seemed to come off worse. They lost men often by a ten-to-one ratio. In 1938 there were sixty-nine British, 292 Jews and at least 1600 Arabs, rebels and others, killed in the fighting. But their enthusiasm for the holy war which the Mufti had proclaimed, their feeling of justified grievance and perhaps their hope of booty kept the revolt going in spite of these losses. On December 22nd, 1937, Colonial Secretary William Ormsby-Gore announced an improvement in the security situation, but all over the Christmas weekend 1500 British troops were involved in battles in the hills west of Tiberias.[20] The optimism was premature.

In January 1938 yet another Commission under Sir John Woodhead began to work out the details of a partition plan. Britain had accepted partition but was pausing before putting it into effect. High Commissioner Arthur Wauchope left Palestine a deeply disappointed man, assailed in the British and American press for allowing the situation to deteriorate, to be replaced on March 3rd by Harold MacMichael, an Arabic scholar who had served many years in the Sudan. On March 12th Hitler's armies invaded Austria and absorbed it into the Third Reich. Hitler's newspaper *Völkischer Beobachter* kept up a barrage of abuse against British brutality in Palestine, praising the Arab rebels as freedom fighters.

Orde Wingate, a British officer of strong pro-Zionist views, was leading his famous 'special night squads', mixed Jewish and British units, against the rebels, countering terror ruthlessly. His methods were successful, but unconventional. In Hugh Foot's opinion, he 'forfeited our general reputation for fair fighting'.[21] A further irritant to Arab opinion was the Tegart Wall, an eighteen-foot-wide barbed-wire entanglement built early in 1938 by order of security adviser Charles Tegart to keep out the rebels and arms smugglers. It cost £100,000 and ran along the entire Palestine–Syria frontier, dividing the two countries to great Arab annoyance. It did little to help security, because further south the frontier stayed open.

Weizmann was by now a firm partitionist. On January 25th he spoke up for it in Jerusalem and derided the Revisionists' idea of a large Jewish state.[22] The only alternative to fulfilling the Balfour Declaration in part of Palestine, he said, was stagnation and regression in the whole of Palestine. It was part of Weizmann's policy of 'maximum pressure for minimum demands'. And it seemed that it would be accomplished. On March 10th British Prime Minister Neville Chamberlain said to him: 'Why do you worry so much? Why are you so uneasy? We are committed to partition.'[23]

At the back of many Zionists' minds there was the idea expressed by Laurie Hammond, a member of the Peel Commission, that partition would be the Jews' first step towards getting back into the rest of the country.[24] But Weizmann's first priority was a Jewish state, even a small one, with control of its own immigration to allow the relief of European Jewry. His task was to persuade his many powerful British friends that this plan was in Britain's interest too.

His main supporters in the Cabinet were Walter Elliot, minister of health and a close friend of Blanche Dugdale, by now a powerful informal channel between the Zionists and the British, and Malcolm MacDonald, who had been so helpful over the Passfield White Paper. Great was their delight when on May 16th, 1938, MacDonald succeeded Ormsby-Gore as colonial secretary and became responsible for Palestine policy. Blanche wrote: 'I think this is probably the best appointment that would be made from the Jewish point of view.'

2

The Arab Revolt
and the White Paper

THREE weeks after assuming office MacDonald expressed his anxiety over Palestine to High Commissioner MacMichael: 'The weekly returns of outrages for the month of May indicate no improvement, but rather the reverse.'[1] Unless some progress was made against the terrorists, British prestige would suffer considerably. The French government were still permitting the Mufti to control the rebellion from his headquarters in Damascus. France had been asked to curb these activities, but she was Britain's rival in the Middle East and not inclined to be helpful. 'The Mufti had shown no signs of an incorrect attitude,'[2] was her reply. There were only two ways out – to crush the rebellion by force, which would be difficult and would risk a backlash from friendly Arab countries, or to find a solution which would cause it to subside. The problem was that any such solution was bound to involve yet another change of policy by Britain.

In June and July MacDonald had three long meetings with his good friend Weizmann and put to him certain arguments. He himself, he said, was still a supporter of partition as 'the least of the evils that we had to choose between'.[3] Weizmann had urged him to put partition into practice immediately, believing that once this was done Arab opposition would disappear and reputable Arab leaders would make terms with Britain and the Jews. But, MacDonald said, a host of experts in the Arab world were now advising him that this was pure wishful thinking.

MacDonald took upon himself the role of Devil's advocate in order to explain to Weizmann the Foreign Office's argument. The gist of it was that the whole Arab world was intensely and permanently opposed to partition. If Britain were to impose it against Arab wishes, she would win the undying hostility of Palestinian Arabs and have to keep large armed forces there indefinitely. She would lose the friendship of Egypt, Saudi Arabia, Iraq and Syria, thus putting vital alliances at risk. She would also cause dismay among the Moslems of India at a time of delicate negotiations over India's future. The result would be to weaken Britain diplomatically and to encourage Nazi Germany in further aggressions. And if Britain suffered, the Jews would suffer, because 'Great Britain was the principal friend in the world today of the sorely tried Jewish people'.[4]

The British government had given general approval to the Peel Commission's partition proposals. But if it now accepted the Foreign Office's gloomy forecasts as accurate, it would have to abandon partition. In the long run this would be in the Jews' interest as well as Britain's.

Weizmann replied that this picture was always being 'conjured up', but he thought it exaggerated. The Arabs had received ninety per cent of what they wanted after 1918 and would not lightly cast aside British friendship. If Britain were now to abandon partition, the Arabs would see this not as a mark of generosity, but as a surrender to terrorism by a weak and effete nation. It would not buy Arab loyalty, which was an uncertain quantity anyway, and it would destroy Jewish loyalty, which could otherwise always be relied upon.

If partition were abandoned, MacDonald continued hypothetically, he might perhaps propose an immigration schedule to bring the Jews up to forty per cent of the total Palestine population over ten years, to double the present Jewish population of 450,000, at the end of which the whole question would be re-examined. Weizmann replied that a few years ago he would have accepted this idea. Indeed, if he could be sure that MacDonald would remain in charge of Palestine policy for a period of years he would accept it now. But there had been too many vacillations and changes. The only solution now was partition and a Jewish state, which would be Britain's friend and ally under all circumstances.

It was not only his disillusionment with British policy that was hardening Weizmann's position. He was also having to face the fact that recent events had undermined his position as a moderate Jewish leader. The Yishuv, the Jews of Palestine, were demanding a tougher stance vis-à-vis Britain. Weizmann's unique place in the Zionist movement was based on his past achievements, especially the Balfour Declaration, all won by his policy of close cooperation with Britain. But there were now leading members of the Jewish Agency, for instance David Ben Gurion, who were questioning whether this policy was still valid, as well as leading members of the Revisionist party who had made up their minds that it was not.

On March 15th, 1938, three days after Hitler's occupation of Austria,

Britain had announced a six-month immigration quota of only three thousand – the smallest figure for years, and this at a time when the important Jewish community of Vienna was in mortal peril. Was this the policy of a friend? Jewish leaders were under pressure to speak out against the injustice of it. A few were by now convinced that diplomacy and politics would not be enough to achieve their Jewish state and save the Jews of Europe. They would have to fight.

This was the reasoning behind Irgun Zvai Leumi (National Military Organization), the military arm of Jabotinsky's Revisionist party. Around August 1937 they decided to abandon the principle of self-restraint (*havlaga*), laid down by the main Jewish leaders, and retaliate against the Arab community. In November, under the command of Moshe Rosenberg, they killed ten Arabs in a straight act of reprisal. The Jewish Agency, always bitterly opposed to the Revisionist movement, at once condemned the Irgun for 'marring the record of Palestine Jewry'.

After David Raziel had taken over as Irgun commander, there was the famous case of Shlomo Ben-Yosef, hanged in Acre fortress on June 29th for an unsuccessful reprisal attack on an Arab bus. Fellow Irgun members saw the execution as a cynical act of policy. The British authorities had hanged many rebellious Arabs. Very well, they would now hang a Jew, just to demonstrate their impartiality. Ben-Yosef became the first of the Irgun's martyrs. A few days after the execution they launched a series of bomb attacks on Arab-populated areas, killing five Arabs, in Jerusalem and Tel Aviv, then twenty-three in Haifa, then ten in Jerusalem, then thirty-nine in Haifa.

The Irgun were well organized in Poland, where most of them were born. The rightist Polish government gave them arms and training facilities, mainly because they shared the same basic aim as the Zionists – a large-scale exodus of Polish Jews to Palestine. Itzhak Shamir (Yzernitzky), who in 1977 became speaker of the Israeli parliament, says: 'It was a political agreement. They helped us for anti-semitic reasons. We explained to them, "If you want to get rid of the Jews, you must help the Zionist movement." ' Nathan Yalin-Mor (Friedmann-Yellin) takes a less harsh view of the motives of the Polish leadership: 'They saw us as fighters for the freedom of our people. And they thought that Zionism would bring an end to Polish anti-semitism. They believed that there would always be anti-semitism, as long as there were three million Jews in Poland. They were very helpful in issuing passports to Jews who intended to enter Palestine illegally.' Another Irgunist, born in the small Polish town of Suwalki, travelled between the two countries as the link man with the Polish government. He was a handsome young revolutionary, a linguist and a poet. His name was Abraham Stern.

At this stage the Irgun were a small group, rejected by most of the Yishuv as dangerous men who were harming their cause. Weizmann told MacDonald that he was 'very disturbed' by the July attacks on Arab areas. He had no doubt that the Revisionists were responsible for some of it. He had even heard, he said, that illegal shipments of Revisionists to Palestine were being financed by Nazis. The language he used showed the depth of his dislike of the Revisionists, who seemed to him to be threatening the basis of his life's work, his good relations with Britain. They were dangerous, crazy men. There was even, unbelievably, talk of their taking up arms against Britain.

In Britain the idea seemed quite bizarre. The Jews were tied to Britain and would never rebel. The possibility was not even taken into account in forming British policy, which was now moving inexorably towards the conclusion that partition would have to be abandoned. 'I thought it a proper precaution to prepare him [Weizmann] for this possibility,'[5] wrote MacDonald on August 21st, 1938. Partition was still at this stage official policy, but MacDonald was being encouraged, under the pressure of the Arab revolt, to discuss other possible solutions with Arab and Jewish leaders in the faint hope of finding common ground.

On July 29th Muhammed Mahmoud, prime minister of Egypt, banged another nail into partition's coffin. He told MacDonald that the Arabs would never agree to the Jews' reaching forty per cent of Palestine's population and might not agree to thirty-five per cent. He added that, if partition was imposed, Britain would never have peace. She would lose her valuable friends in all the Arab world and in India. On August 19th Izzat Tannous, at the time the head of the Palestinian office in London, told him: 'The Arabs would never consent, except if they were forced to, to the surrender of part of their country to an immigrant race. And if a Jewish state were established, the Arabs would only await the day when they could attack that state and drive the Jews out.'[6]

The Mufti and the extremists 'seem so powerful that they virtually dictate Arab policy,' MacDonald noted sadly. He nevertheless added that Tannous was 'the one faint ray of hope'. He was on his way to Palestine and might even visit the Mufti. Useful contacts like this might succeed in driving a wedge between the 'moderate members' and the 'extremist front'.

And so MacDonald did what he could, lobbying friendly Arab governments – Egypt, Iraq and Saudi Arabia – using his armies to fight the rebellion, stamping hard on Jewish extremism, trying to quieten Arab fears over immigration and even sending feelers to the rebel headquarters in Damascus. His problem was an old one. He wanted to defuse the rebellion by making concessions politically, while keeping up the pressure militarily. He was ready to make these concessions, even though he knew that they would anger his Zionist friends, but how could he do this without losing face and appearing to yield before rebellion and murder?

Arab Palestine was not a recognized country with diplomats or representatives. Their moderates were supposed to exist, but, as Tannous had shown, their language in public or in Whitehall was indistinguishable from that of the Mufti. Either they were terrorized or else they were, deep down, loyal to the extremist leader they pretended to oppose. So what could he do that would break the Mufti's hold and allow the moderates to emerge?

A gesture of friendship to the Mufti would be taken as a sign of surrender. Requests to France to curb the Mufti had not been answered. Tougher action in Palestine would alienate the Arab population as a whole. And meanwhile the rebellion was tying down British forces, the Mufti's propaganda was blackening Britain's name throughout the Moslem world. Hitler was making aggressive noises and the Jews were begging Britain to help relieve their sufferings. Both sides were reminding Britain of past promises and demanding their fulfilment.

For years MacDonald had supported Zionism, but after a few weeks as colonial secretary he was being converted to the view that Britain's interest lay elsewhere. He still remembers those hectic and painful weeks of 1938 quite vividly. He decided that Britain had made inconsistent promises to Jews and Arabs during the war. Now both sides were justifiably accusing Britain of breach of faith. It was all very unsatisfactory and distressing. But he was a British minister and in the final analysis it was his duty to devise a policy that was in his own country's interest.

Today he says: 'I was advised that unless we reduced Jewish immigration there was a real risk of the Arabs joining Germany and Italy. In 1938 it looked as if there was going to be another war and it was vital that we won it. If war came, we knew that the Jews would be on our side anyway. They had no alternative. But the Arabs were doubtful. If they turned against us, we could lose our position in the Middle East, including the Suez Canal, and a large part of our war potential. Britain was my main consideration, but I also thought that our winning the war was equally vital for the Jews, because if we lost there probably wouldn't be a national home at all. I put this to them and begged them to make a temporary sacrifice, on the ground that Britain's interest was also the interest of the national home.'

But in 1938 of all years it was difficult for the Jews to make any such sacrifice. MacDonald found himself assailed not only by Weizmann and Ben Gurion, but also by members of the British Parliament: 'One of my problems was that there were about 30 Jews in the House of Commons, almost all of them Zionist, and there were other non-Jewish members who were influenced by having a big Jewish vote in their constituencies. But there wasn't a single Arab member or any significant number of Arab voters in Britain, just a handful of members who supported the Arab cause.' He remembers, for instance, having 'one hell of an argument' in the lobby of the House of Commons with Winston Churchill: 'He told me I was crazy to help the Arabs, because they were a backward people who ate nothing but camel dung.'

This was the pressure in Parliament. But it was balanced by the pro-Arab pressure of the Foreign Office, which had many missions in the Arab world and therefore a professional interest in good British-Arab relations. By contrast, except through the Washington embassy, they had little contact with the Jews. A rain of memoranda, drafted both in Whitehall and overseas, descended daily on MacDonald's ministerial desk, urging the Arab side of the case. For instance, there was the remarkable document of advice sent on August 30th by Charles Bateman, British minister in Egypt, who later became ambassador in Mexico and Poland. He began with the familiar theme that 'the balloon in Europe may go up this autumn' and that if Arab hostility closed the Mediterranean and Red Sea to Britain, 'we shall be in queer street'. The only way out was by 'placating the Arabs' until the crisis passed.

'The Jews? Let us be practical. They are anybody's game these days,' ran Bateman's bizarre paper. There were six million of them homeless in Europe. In no way would Palestine ever be able to take them all. There would have to be a halt to immigration sometime. So why not now? They had waited two thousand years for their home and they would just have to wait a little longer before getting 'their last pound of flesh'. And as for Parliament, the government would have 'to bring the pro-Jew element into line by pleading what is practicable as opposed to what is desirable'.

'Please don't think from all this that I am pro-Arab or anti-Jew,' the minister went on: 'I think them each as loathsome as the other.' But he saw no point in British involvement in a quarrel that brought nothing but abuse from both sides. Palestine was like an incurable disease. The only possible treatment for it was opium to reduce the pain. To be specific, he wanted Britain to invite the Mufti to London and promise him a complete stoppage of Jewish immigration in return for his calling off the revolt. After all, his crimes were not much worse than those of other nationalists like Michael Collins and de Valera of Ireland or Gandhi of India, and 'we'll have to meet him some day – unless he's bumped off'.

It is fair to say that the offensive tone of this paper is not reflected in other official British documents on the subject. But Bateman's political views, as opposed to his prejudices, *were* those of the Foreign Office, who were generally agreed on the advisability of ending Jewish immigration. His colleagues in London differed from him only on the question of inviting the Mufti. The general feeling was that the Mufti stood for all that was worst in Arab methods, that there *were* Arab moderates in Palestine with whom Britain might agree a policy and that therefore the Mufti was not essential to the pro-Arab agreement they sought. With this exception, noted Lacy Baggallay of the Foreign Office: 'Tell Mr Bateman that we sympathize with all he says.'

It was thus under the influence of much conflicting advice that MacDonald paid a flying visit to Jerusalem on August 17th, 1938, to confer with MacMichael and his army chief Major-General Robert Haining. Because of the security situation he travelled in secret and saw hardly any Arabs or Jews. He told MacMichael and Haining that he was on the brink of accepting the advice of his officials, especially since it seemed that the Woodhead Commission were about to declare partition impossible. He would then be faced with a new set of tasks. He would have to explain to the Jews why they would not have their state, to the Arabs why they should end the revolt in the face of continuing British rule and Jewish immigration, and to the world why Britain's ability to keep her word or make decisions should ever again be trusted.

It was the next month – September – that finally tipped MacDonald over the edge. On September 12th Hitler delivered a furious speech at a rally in Nuremberg, attacking Czechoslovak President Eduard Beneš for illtreating the Sudeten Germans. For a few days it seemed certain that Nazi Germany would invade Czechoslovakia. MacDonald was in regular contact with Weizmann, Ben Gurion, Elliot, Baffy Dugdale and other Zionists. On September 15th he told them that he still favoured partition. That same day, quite suddenly, Prime Minister Chamberlain flew to Berlin to see Hitler. It seemed that war might be avoided after all, but only by abandoning all British and French pledges to Czechoslovakia. On September 19th MacDonald spent the evening with Weizmann,

Ben Gurion and Baffy Dugdale. After dinner, while Baffy played bezique with Vera Weizmann, MacDonald spoke earnestly to the other two. Baffy had to wait until MacDonald left at midnight before finding out what had been said: 'They are going to sell the Jews also, give up partition, for fear of the Arabs and the Germans and the Italians. . . . We are all stunned. Ben Gurion's first reaction and mine was that the Jews will fight, physically, rather than go back to the Mandate as it will be. Chaim said nothing much.'

This decision, this revelation, took place of course against a background of continual violence in Palestine. That same night in Palestine a gang of three hundred Arab rebels invaded the town of Hebron, burnt Barclays Bank and the post office, killed six police horses, shot an Arab police driver, stole six rifles and destroyed an armoured car.[7] A few days later rebels visited Beersheba, stole arms and burnt government buildings. Then the same happened in Bethlehem. In the Christian town of Ramallah rebels took control and terrorized the population for three weeks, before troops came from Jerusalem on October 2nd and threw them out. Between fifty and a hundred people, mainly Arabs, were killed that week in Palestine.[8]

It was almost as if the rebels knew what was happening in Europe and were exploiting it. Because of the Czechoslovak crisis one army brigade had been ordered out of Palestine and was on its way home. If war broke out, more troops would have to be withdrawn and the way would be clear for the rebels. But on October 1st Hitler, Chamberlain, Mussolini and French Premier Daladier signed an agreement in Munich, without reference to the Czechoslovaks, authorizing Hitler to take the Sudetenland. The crisis was over, but it left Britain badly frightened and all the more anxious to end the Arab revolt at any cost. After Munich the Palestine problem was to be treated primarily from the short-term standpoint of Britain's national survival.

Britain was in the mood to take drastic action. Four days after the Munich agreement was signed MacMichael flew to London. After consulting High Commissioner MacMichael, Foreign Secretary Lord Halifax and Iraqi Foreign Minister Tawfiq as-Suwaydi, MacDonald outlined the new 'stick and carrot' approach to the rebellion. They would increase the armed forces to a level of 18,500 men, impose martial law in the towns and move the army into the streets. The native population would have to carry identity cards and would need permits to travel from one city to another.[9] At the same time moderate Arab opinion inside and outside Palestine would be wooed by a decision to abandon partition and impose far-reaching restrictions on Jewish immigration. It was the only plan Britain could devise to isolate the Mufti by driving a wedge between the rebels and the rest.

On October 17th an outbreak of rioting in the Old City of Jerusalem met with a quick army response. Soldiers broke through the rebel barricades and fought their way through the narrow streets. For a few days and nights bullets flew about the Arab quarter, but within a week the rebels had withdrawn and order was restored. British troops captured quantities of arms, though they believed that the main arsenal was in the *haram esh-sharif*, which they could not enter. Soon there were troops stationed in most of the other large towns. An attempted boycott of the travel permit system, ordered by the Mufti, was defeated by the economic need to transport and sell the Arab-owned citrus crop.[10] The administration announced that only 4500 Jews would be allowed to enter Palestine during the six-month period that was to end in March 1939.

Two days after the outbreak (October 19th) MacDonald explained his plan to the British Cabinet. The security situation was deplorable, he said, and he must take some responsibility for failing to appreciate what was happening, but strong measures were now in hand. There remained the general question of policy, which was still officially partition, as recommended by Lord Peel: 'The Secretary of State said that in the past he had been a firm adherent of this view, but that further personal inquiries had led him some time ago to the conclusion that partition was not the right policy.'[11]

The Woodhead Commission was about to confirm MacDonald's new conviction that the two proposed states would be too small for economic viability and would involve large-scale movements of population. He would therefore convene a conference in London, with the Jewish Agency on one side and on the other side the Arab representatives of Palestine, Transjordan, Iraq, Saudi Arabia and Egypt. The Cabinet, chaired by Chamberlain in the full flush of his achievement at Munich, agreed to set up an eight-man committee to consider the matter. MacDonald emphasized that they would have to work out how to 'stage' the change of policy, so as not to make it seem that Britain was yielding to the success of the rebellion.

This new approach to Palestine was publicly supported in *The Times* by Roy Spicer, now home in London intact from his hazardous duties as police chief. It was his expert opinion that the rebellion had the tacit approval of most of the Arab population and could be crushed only by ruthless force. To do this Britain would have 'to bring them to their knees, as indeed the Turks would have done, and once this had been done to deal with any recrudescence with inexorable severity'. In this case the Jews would be able to build up their National Home into a flourishing state. The alternative was to tell the Jews that Arab objections made it impossible to fulfil their idea of the Balfour Declaration: 'You must abandon any further expansion of your Zionist dreams. What you have you may hold, but it must stop there, both in regard to immigration and to land. The problem of persecuted Jewry must be dealt with outside Palestine.'

But for the Jews it was a crisis rather than a problem. On November 7th, 1938, a month after Spicer's letter appeared, a German diplomat in Paris was murdered by a seventeen-year-old Jewish refugee. Nazi German organizations immediately arranged for mobs of violent men to attack Jews all over the country and destroy their property. During the night of November 9th thousands of Jewish shops and hundreds of synagogues were burnt. Jews were beaten up, raped and murdered, then subjected to a communal fine of one billion marks ($250 million). About twenty thousand were arrested and sent to concentration camps. The whole episode was celebrated in Nazi folklore as 'crystal night' or 'the night of broken glass'.

The United States, Britain and a few other countries were taking in some refugees from Germany and Austria, but not nearly as many as sought asylum from the persecution. Also the Jewish leaders did not believe that their nation's agony would be diminished by a further diaspora. The Western world was not inclined to receive Jews in large numbers. In some democratic countries public opinion was sympathetic to Jewish sufferings, but not to the extent of wanting to open the door to large-scale Jewish immigration. Nor could these countries be relied upon to remain for ever free of anti-semitism. The Jewish leaders decided that their only long-term and short-term salvation lay in Palestine, which they proposed to make their own country, where they would not be a minority to be used every few years as a scapegoat for the nation's ills.

During these terrible weeks they made their first plans to resist Britain. Their friend Walter Elliot, a member of the Cabinet Committee, told them about the secret meetings and advised them that the Cabinet was inclined to accept MacDonald's new line. So they prepared for conflict. 'Everything is kosher now,' wrote Baffy. They would not rebel physically against Britain, for the idea was still repugnant to most of them. Anyway they did not have the means to do so. But if they were forbidden to buy land in

Palestine, they would acquire it by some other means, if they were forbidden to carry arms in self-defence, they would arm and train their Haganah (defence force) on an unofficial basis, and if immigration was halted or reduced to a trickle, they would bring the people in illegally. The Jewish Agency was to maintain these three policies of defiance until the end of British rule.

At the same time Britain was intensifying her pressure on the rebels, pressure which inevitably caused distress to many innocent Arabs. During October the small village of Miar, north of Haifa, became known as a centre of rebel activity. Troops who ventured near it were fired upon, roads were dug up with pneumatic drills, landmines were laid and electricity cables skilfully cut. On October 26th two British battalions launched a punitive raid against Miar and started blowing up the main houses of the village with dynamite. The village chief (*mukhtar*) was then told that if the rebels' rifles were handed over the dynamiting would stop and no questions would be asked. But no rifles appeared and the punishment continued.[12] A *New York Times* correspondent on the spot wrote: 'When the troops left, there was little else remaining of the once busy village except a pile of mangled masonry.'[13]

The Cabinet Committee continued deliberating in London. MacDonald told them that he thought a conference in London might reach agreement on short-term policy, especially as friendly Arab countries would be represented and would urge their Palestine brothers to go some way to meet the Jews. He believed that once the Arabs were satisfied that there would be no Jewish majority in Palestine, they would agree to Jewish immigration 'on a reasonable scale'. He also believed that the Jewish leaders could be persuaded to make such immigration dependent on Arab consent. Such was the over-hopeful basis of his new policy, which he believed had a genuine chance of being accepted by both Jew and Arab.[14] Today he says: 'In my Cabinet paper I did write that the omens were not good, but I would agree that one of my faults is that of wishful thinking.'

The Committee was told by Lord Zetland, Secretary of State for India, that Moslem public opinion in India was aroused by the plight of the Palestinian Arabs. There had also been a protest from Afghanistan, which had up to then shown little interest in Palestine. Everyone except Walter Elliot agreed that partition was no longer possible. If the British Empire was to survive, defences must be shored up and alliances protected.

On November 2nd MacDonald told the full Cabinet: 'There was much to be said for allowing the Mufti to represent the Palestine Arabs. Those who took this view urged that he was the only man who could deliver the goods.' His deputy Lord Dufferin believed quite simply that if the Mufti came to the conference it might succeed, but if he did not it was bound to fail. MacMichael, on the other hand, had made it clear that if the Mufti were invited, Britain would have to find another High Commissioner. MacDonald said that so long as the government stuck to its guns on this point, the Mufti's prestige would suffer and he would probably soon cease to be a big figure. Chamberlain agreed: 'The question of prestige was of the greatest importance in dealing with oriental people. If the Mufti was invited to the discussions, his prestige would be enormously enhanced.'[15] The new plan was approved and announced publicly on November 9th, 1938.

At first it seemed that the plan might work. Six days after the announcement Fakhri Bey Nashashibi published a letter expressing 'unlimited satisfaction' at the abandonment of partition, accusing the Mufti of using his official position and funds to exterminate his opponents. He looked forward to the success of the conference.[16] But within a few days the Arab press was full of protestations of loyalty to the Mufti, two members of the National Defence party were murdered in Lydda and the party leader Ragheb Bey Nashashibi renounced his kinsman's letter.[17] It was clear that Britain would need a broader base of Palestinian Arab support. The Nashashibis and their supporters would not be enough. Britain would draw the line at the Mufti himself, but everyone else would have to be included – members of the Higher Committee, exiles from the Seychelles, even perhaps a few who had taken part in the rebellion.

MacDonald's hopes of being able to fulfil Zionist requests were being eroded more and more by what he saw as the practicalities of Britain's position in 1938. He had already retreated from partition. On July 5th he had told Weizmann that if this happened he might propose 450,000 Jewish immigrants over a ten-year period, followed by a re-examination of the problem. Now at the end of the year he was being told by senior officials that even this fall-back proposal, which Weizmann had rejected, was too pro-Zionist. He was being advised that the only way of keeping Arab friendship and Britain's Middle East interests was by stopping immigration completely.

The most pro-Arab diplomat of them all was Miles Lampson, Britain's ambassador in Egypt, for whom it was an axiom of life that Jewish immigration must end at once, otherwise the Arabs would get together 'to turn the Jews and ourselves out of Palestine'. Unless immigration ceased, he wrote, Britain might soon have to take on the Arabs as well as the Italians and Germans: 'What would our position then be in the Middle East? I shudder to think. . . . Can't the Jews themselves realize that it is suicidal for Jewry to weaken Great Britain so perilously in the face of the obvious dangers that threaten? One would have thought that a man of Weizmann's intelligence would have seen that quick enough. It's such an obvious truth.'[18]

'So far as I am concerned Sir Miles Lampson is preaching to the converted, if not to one born of the faith,' noted Lancelot Oliphant, a senior man in the Foreign Office, but MacDonald wrote angrily to the Foreign Secretary, accusing Lampson of 'out-Arabing the Arabs' and 'throwing more sand into the machine'.[19] MacDonald's position was now quite precarious. He agreed with Halifax about 'the imperative need of going as far as possible to meet the Arabs' views'. But at the same time he was opposed to 'completely breaking our promises to the Jews'. Was it possible to meet the Arabs' wishes without breaking those promises? Did it make sense for MacDonald to continue trying to reconcile the irreconcilable? On November 22nd Halifax told US Ambassador Joseph Kennedy à propos of Palestine that 'nothing short of the Archangel can bring order out of this chaos'.

MacDonald therefore placed his main hopes on the forthcoming conference. At the Egyptian prime minister's request he tried unsuccessfully to stop the army from dynamiting houses in suspect Arab villages. (The Cabinet preferred the army's view that dynamiting was a good deterrent.[20]) In his speech in the House of Commons on November 23rd he tried to choose words that would encourage both sides. In one passage he paid generous tribute to Jewish achievement in Palestine. In another he said: 'If I was an Arab, I should be alarmed at the increasing rate of Jewish immigration.'

He learned that the Palestinian Arab leader Musa el-Alami was in London. 'I was in a café near the National Gallery, when a messenger came up to me and asked me to come to the Colonial Office,' says Musa el-Alami. Their two meetings on November 25th and 28th were calculated to convince Musa el-Alami that Britain was moving even more towards the Arab position. MacDonald's own record contains the sentences: 'All sorts of things might happen in Palestine and an Arab state would not be ruled out by what I had said. . . . I had never said anything which closed the door completely to an entire stoppage of immigration.'[21] Musa el-Alami took the notes of his meetings with MacDonald to the Mufti in Syria and he believes that it was largely because of them that the Mufti agreed to have his supporters attend the conference. He feels, though, that he was misled by MacDonald into believing that immigration would end and that Palestine was to become an Arab state.

The Jewish Agency, because of the 'night of broken glass' in Germany, asked for special immigration certificates for ten thousand German Jewish children. For the British Cabinet it was a particularly cruel dilemma. Their decision could well be one of life or death for the children. It could also, they believed, ruin any chance of success in the forthcoming conference, a meeting which would perhaps discover a solution for the Palestine problem as a whole. They therefore decided on November 22nd, 1938, in spite of what had happened in Germany a few days earlier, not to admit the children.[22] It was a moment that marked the end of the Weizmann-MacDonald friendship. On December 12th Weizmann told the Colonial Secretary: 'They [the Jews] were not Czechoslovaks who would give way under pressure. Their people would take up the battle all over the world and fight for their rights in Palestine as they had never fought before. They had got the courage of desperation.'

Anxious to reassure Weizmann, just as he had reassured Musa el-Alami, MacDonald suggested that the London talks 'would be worth more from the Jewish point of view than any temporary advantage'. But Weizmann seemed to sense that Britain was again involving herself in conflicting promises. The Jews were being led up the garden, he said, and they would not take part in the conference unless the question of the children was reconsidered. MacDonald says: 'I remember at the time that Weizmann's attitude shocked me. He insisted on the children going to Palestine. As far as he was concerned it was Palestine or nowhere.'

MacDonald conveyed this message to the Cabinet meeting two days later. The ten thousand children all had Jewish homes waiting for them in Palestine and could be received there without injuring anyone, he suggested. But the other ministers were unanimous in their view that such a massive exodus, even of children, would end all hope of agreement with the Arabs. Chamberlain said that in his view the Jews were in no position to carry out their threat and would not in fact do so. And it turned out that he was right. A few days later the Jewish Agency agreed to attend the conference. The children were excluded from Palestine, though they were subsequently admitted to Britain.

The Arab side kept up its pressure too. The British forces were gaining the upper hand, but only gradually. During November there were eleven British soldiers killed, as well as thirteen Jews and several dozen Arab rebels. The assassination of Arab by Arab continued unabated – on

December 2nd three Arab *mukhtars* and on December 15th Sheikh Mahmud el-Ansari, curator of the *haram esh-sharif* and an old enemy of the Mufti.[23]

The British gradually realized that the most violent aspect of the revolt was not the rebels' attacks against themselves, or even their attacks against Jews, but their treatment of fellow Palestinian Arabs who defied them or were lukewarm in supporting them. This inter-Arab strife received little publicity, because the Arabs kept it to themselves, especially the surviving victims. Only occasionally would they talk to an outsider, and then only if they were sure that he would not reveal their names or any details that could identify them.

But gradually the truth emerged about what was happening. Large numbers of Arabs were being spirited away into the hills. Sometimes they were simply abducted at gunpoint. Sometimes they were lured into a trap on some pretext – a call from a relative or the promise of a job. Arab policemen in uniform were bundled into cars and used to get past British roadblocks.

The kidnapped victim would be forced to march blindfolded to a rebel hideout, either a commandeered house in a remote village or a cave in the hills. He would then be robbed, handcuffed and taken before a 'general' to be told what 'crime' he had committed. This would range from the ultimate offence of disloyalty to such minor matters as holding an identity card, buying in a Jewish shop or failing to give enough to rebel funds.

In the prisoner's crime was serious, if he had given information to the British or sold land to Jews, he might be executed on the spot. Otherwise, if for instance he had refused to wear the traditional Palestinian *hatta* and *agal* head cover, he would be severely flogged and then thrown into a makeshift prison – a ruined house, a cave or even a well. Here he would find fellow-Arabs of every rank and occupation – beggars and sheikhs, peasants and landowners, street cleaners and rich merchants. Then, as the weeks passed, they would be moved from place to place, handcuffed in pairs, usually at night, to keep one step ahead of the army search teams and the spotter aircraft.

Eventually, if he was lucky, he would be released to return home, semi-starved and ill-treated, and to make the rest of the community aware of the fate that awaited all those who dared oppose the rebels' will. It was thus hardly surprising that, as Roy Spicer pointed out, the rebellion was tacitly supported by almost all the Arab population.[24] Many, it is true, were its out-and-out devotees. Others sympathized with its aims, if not with its violent methods. The vast majority of the rest, one can be sure, were intimidated by the Mufti's men and would never have dared oppose it publicly.

This was the sort of rebellion that Britain was trying to crush. But at the same time as she pursued the diplomatic method, hoping that pro-Arab policies would remove the rebels' basis of operations, she intensified the military method, and naturally it was innocent Arab villagers who suffered the most. For instance, if rebels operated from a village, it was with or without the villagers' consent. They did not ask for the villagers' permission. But when their base was discovered, they would withdraw, leaving the villagers to bear the brunt of the soldiers' anger. Sometimes, inevitably, though how often it is hard to say, the soldiers would punish the village illegally, looting property and misusing the people. But even staying strictly within the law, which they did most often, they were allowed to take certain measures against the village as a whole. These were the 1930s, and the idea of collective punishment did not carry the cruel Nazi-German undertones that it does now. The idea was not rejected by British public opinion on principle.

District officers could submit a village to a collective fine. Then, if the villagers would not or could not pay, they could round up the entire village's flocks of sheep and goats, confiscating them as security for the fine. They were also empowered to impose punitive police posts, to enforce a village's good behaviour at the villagers' expense. A typical post might involve fifteen policemen at £6 a month for three months. Either method could cripple a village financially.

But the most effective and most controversial method was the blowing up of houses, an example of which was the October 26th, 1938, Miar incident. Under Emergency Regulation 19b a district commissioner could appropriate any house for demolition, if he was satisfied that a firearm had been discharged from it or a bomb thrown from it. But he also had a wider power to order the destruction of a house in no way connected with any violent incident, so long as he was satisfied that a violent act had been committed or connived at by unknown men from the same village.

'The provision is drastic, but the situation has demanded drastic powers,' noted MacMichael in justification of this practice. It made the rebels unpopular and encouraged villagers to give information to the British army and police. It was indeed effective, but it was also unfair. It punished many Arabs who had done nothing to help the rebels and it placed them in an impossible position. No villager with any emotional desire for an independent Arab Palestine would ever refuse sanctuary to a rebel, especially a wounded rebel. No villager who valued his life would deny the rebels his house as an arms store or firing point. If he refused, he would be kidnapped, taken to the hills and killed or ill-treated. If he agreed, sooner or later British troops would arrive and blow up his house. To this extent, British suppression of the revolt involved punishing the innocent as well as the guilty.

An example of police illegality emerged when four British constables were tried in Jaffa in January 1939 on charges of murdering an Arab prisoner. All four were convicted of manslaughter and awarded light sentences, three of which were quashed on appeal. By contrast, Arabs convicted of violent acts were often sentenced to death. In the two years following November 1937 there were 112 death sentences passed, almost all of them executed. Several hundred more were sentenced to long terms of imprisonment or whipping.[25]

It was Britain's case that, given the extent of the revolt and the brutality of the rebels, such measures were not excessive. During the above-mentioned period searches of villages produced about 2500 rifles, 1000 pistols and more than 100,000 rounds of ammunition. In answer to allegations of British brutality, MacMichael wrote: 'In the hundreds of operations carried out by some 1500 troops and police it is obvious that incidents must occur, which can provide a substratum of truth capable of being made the basis of grossly exaggerated accusations.'[26] But in general, he insisted, his troops and police behaved with discipline and restraint in the face of severe provocation.

This was not the view of Izzat Tannous's Arab Centre in London, which published several colourful booklets on the subject of British brutality, details of which were eagerly picked up by the Nazi German press. They alleged, for instance, that soldiers had occupied the Arab village of Attil, murdered five civilians after gouging out their eyes and burned three others to death in a shed. The German reader was fed the simple idea that the Arab rebels were fighting for freedom against the combined forces of world Jewry and British imperialism.

Adolf Hitler himself made use of the situation. In a speech on October 9th, 1938, he said that Germany would no longer tolerate 'being lectured to by governesses' about how she treated her own citizens within her own borders. Britain would do far better, he said, to concern itself with its own excesses in Palestine. With deep foreboding British officials observed the effect of Nazi German support for the rebels and the Mufti, wondering how successful Hitler's men would be at discrediting Britain in Arab eyes.

The problem was, the Colonial Office advised MacDonald, 'to assess the relative inconvenience of the Arab frying-pan and the Jewish fire'. But British officials had weighed the balance and made their choice. They agreed that the new pro-Arab policy might damage Britain's relations with the United States, where Jewish influence was strong. But in their view American dissatisfaction would be short-lived, while Arab hostility was likely to be permanent. The suggestion that the Jews of Palestine too were capable of rebellion provoked Charles Baxter of the Foreign Office to remark: 'I do not think that the Jews would be so unwise.'[27]

So it was with this in his mind, full of a hundred conflicting arguments and several thousand years of historical background, that MacDonald wrote the January 1939 Cabinet paper that was to become the basis of British policy for the remaining nine years of the Mandate. Like Lord Peel's report, it devoted some pages to an analysis of the past, before proceeding to proposals for the future. The basis of these was to make Palestine neither a Jewish state nor an exclusively Arab state, not to partition it, but to build up its self-governing institutions and move the country steadily towards independence with an Arab majority. In the meantime land sales from Arabs to Jews would be greatly reduced by being restricted by law to certain parts of the country.

The crux of the paper lay in the proposals on immigration. Here Mac-Donald developed the theory he had put to Weizmann in July, that the Jews should be set a ceiling, a proportion of the population which they would not exceed. At the end of 1938 the Jews were twenty-nine per cent of the people of Palestine. MacDonald proposed two ceiling figures which the Jews might reach over a ten-year period – forty per cent and thirty-five per cent. By judicious soundings before and during the conference Britain was to work out which figure to suggest.

On the forty per cent basis, it was calculated, the Jews would be able to bring in 29,840 immigrants a year for ten years. On the thirty-five per cent basis the annual intake would be 15,300. Both figures were well below the 450,000 that MacDonald had suggested in July, but they were still considerable and would do much to help the plight of European Jewry.

MacDonald also proposed a second and more fundamental retreat from what he had said to Weizmann in July. He had then suggested that the whole question of immigration be considered at the end of the ten-year period. Now, six months later, he was suggesting that it be suspended at the end of ten years and continued only if the Arabs of Palestine gave their consent. 'This would give the Arabs an actual veto for any further extension of the Jewish National Home after ten years,'[28] he wrote. He said that he would prefer not to tie Britain's hands on such a matter, but the veto would do much to soothe Arab fears and would be accepted by many moderate Arab leaders.

If the Arab veto was imposed, MacDonald argued, it would in his view be unfair and unwise to set the Jewish proportion at much below forty per cent. But he felt it necessary to record that his colleague Lord Halifax and the Foreign Office took a different view. They thought that the prospect of 300,000 more Jewish immigrants would be alarming to the Arabs and damaging to Britain. MacDonald argued that this was not necessarily the case. But, he added: 'I agree that, if any widespread hostility to us in the Moslem world is really involved, we cannot afford that, and must yield to the degree that may be necessary to avoid it.'[29]

But even these proposals would not satisfy the Foreign Office. Charles Baxter wrote that the Arab delegates would consider the higher immigration figure so unreasonable and unjust that they would regret having come to London. His objections to 'sending more and more Jews into Palestine against the wishes of the Arab inhabitants' were even stronger than MacDonald's. He preferred instead to insist on 'the moral right of the Arabs to have some say in the question of admission of aliens into their country'. MacDonald had told him privately that, contrary to what was in his Paper, he was ready to agree a final figure of 153,000 Jews over ten years. Baxter thought that he must be ready to come down much lower than that.

Baxter's thinking, especially his reference to 'aliens', was in line with that of George Antonius, one of the few Western-educated Arabs in the Palestine political world. His excellent book *The Arab Awakening*, published in English at the end of 1938, was perhaps the first serious presentation of the Palestine Arab case to the Western world. The treatment meted out to Jews by the Hitler regime, he wrote, was a disgrace to its authors and to modern civilization,[30] but the duty of relieving this suffering belonged to the world as a whole: 'To place the brunt of the burden on Arab Palestine is a miserable evasion of the duty that lies upon the whole of the civilized world. It is also morally outrageous. No code of morals can justify the persecution of one people in an attempt to relieve the persecution of another.'

Baxter too believed that Palestine had already done more than her share to relieve the problem of the Jews in Europe. Any more large-scale immigration would rouse anti-Jewish feeling throughout the Middle East and cause damage to Britain, the Jews' only friend. The possibility of a Jewish rebellion, mentioned by MacDonald at some length, could be dismissed. Baxter held the strange belief that 'most moderate Jews' were ready to abandon their hope of a Jewish state and come to terms with the Arabs. Lancelot Oliphant noted: 'Mr Baxter in his Minute has expressed admirably the view of the Department . . .'[31]

The new policy conceived in Whitehall was being adopted with enthusiasm by all in the Cabinet except Walter Elliot. This was because the new policy seemed to be working. The security situation in Palestine continued to improve. Palestinian Arabs, now convinced that there was something to be gained by cooperation with Britain, were beginning to speak out against the revolt and even against the Mufti. On November 30th MacDonald was able to report another improvement. The Jewish Agency had agreed to attend the conference and so had the governments of Iraq, Saudi Arabia and Egypt.

After all, what had Britain to lose by abandoning the Zionists? They had nowhere to run. They were tied to Britain with an unbreakable chain. After a few weeks the Cabinet had even convinced themselves that the Jews might be persuaded to recognize this simple fact of life and accept it. Surely Weizmann must realize that the only hope of stability in the Middle East was to agree to the principle of a final intake of Jewish immigrants and a cut-off date, after which no Jews would enter without Arab consent? In all seriousness, MacDonald was invited to try to persuade Weizmann to make a unilateral declaration to this effect.[32]

It was a weird request, in view of the angry Jewish reaction to the rumours of Britain's plans. The Jewish-Agency-controlled *Palestine Post* wrote, on hearing of the release of the Seychelles deportees: 'The present British Cabinet is committed to a policy of appeasement, in Europe and elsewhere. It is anxious for peace and is not prepared to examine too closely the price.'[33] A few days later a long editorial referred to the December 8th House of Lords debate: 'The devaluation of the British undertaking to the Jewish people struck a new low level . . . The British government is launched on a course which aims at reducing Zionism to paltry and ludicrous proportions . . .'[34] Dr I. Hertzog, chief rabbi of Palestine, said: 'There is no room for concessions in the sphere of immigration.'

But the general feeling of optimism continued to grow. George Wadsworth, US consul-general in Jerusalem, reported that MacDonald, ably supported by Miles Lampson in Cairo, was being 'eminently successful'[35] in preparing the ground for the conference. A Palestinian delegation was being formed and was likely to include two Nashashibis as well as the

Arab Higher Committee members. Paul Knabenshue, US minister in Baghdad, wrote to Washington that Palestine must become an Arab state with a Jewish minority under British protection: 'There will never be lasting peace in Palestine until this solution is adopted.'[36]

The American State Department was of one mind with the Foreign Office on the overriding importance of Arab and Moslem opinion. President Roosevelt, more tuned to domestic pressures, was inclined to take the opposite view. His mid-October private statement to Senator Robert Wagner that he would do all he could to dissuade Britain from restricting Jewish immigration was widely publicized in the American and Arab press, provoking anti-American demonstrations in Arab cities, but relief among the Jewish community of the United States.

In the first days of 1939 a great gathering of the Arabs took place in Cairo: Egyptian Prime Minister Mohammed Mahmoud and King Farouk's chief political adviser Ali Maher Pasha, four Arab Higher Committee members from the Seychelles, Saudi Arabian Foreign Minister Emir Faisal and his deputy Fuad Hamza, Iraqi Prime Minister Nuri es-Said, Emir Abdullah of Transjordan's personal minister Fuad Pasha al-Khatib and many others. On January 11th the Palestinians flew to Beirut to confer with the Mufti, their French visas provided only after heavy British and Egyptian intercession.

At a plenary meeting on January 15th the Arab Higher Committee issued a document accepting the invitation to London and proclaiming a covenant which demanded the end of the Jewish national home, Jewish immigration and land transfer to Jews, the end of the Mandate and an independent Arab Palestine linked to Britain by treaty. The Mufti's cousin Jamal al-Husseini would lead the delegation, which would include two Nashashibis and George Antonius, who acted as secretary of all the Arab delegations.

On January 31st the elected Assembly of the Yishuv issued *their* proclamation. Their essential demand was the fulfilment of their understanding of the Balfour Declaration 'which was endorsed by the states of the civilized world' and which 'has redeemed the soil of Palestine from age-long desolation'.[37] They were entitled, they said, to enlarge and extend the Jewish national home, to buy land freely and to bring in as many immigrants as the country's economy could absorb. They objected strongly to Britain's decision to discuss their fate with supporters of the Mufti, who were no better than murderers, and with other Arab countries, who legally had no standing in the matter and who, not being part of the 'civilized world', had not approved the Balfour Declaration.

The difference between the two sides was fundamental. The Arabs believed that Palestine was theirs by virtue of occupation over many centuries. The Zionists believed that Eretz Israel had always belonged to the Jewish nation, even though it had been stolen by foreign invaders in the early years of the Christian era. A Jewish immigrant was seen by the Arabs (and by Charles Baxter of the Foreign Office) as an alien, by the Zionists as a citizen returning to his own country after centuries of forced separation.

Arab passions were aroused by fears that they were being swamped by new arrivals, whose aim was to supplant them, expel them and rebuild the Temple on the *haram esh-sherif.* Jewish passions were aroused by the woeful plight of their Austrian and German brothers, by their fears of what might (and did) shortly happen to them and the other Jews of Europe. It is hard to imagine a more intense and irreconcilable conflict of interest. Nevertheless, the British government believed that the conference was worth holding and that it might achieve a negotiated solution.

The moral and legal merits of the Arab-Jewish dispute played, of course, only a secondary role in forming Britain's policy. The over-riding aim in the minds of the British decision-makers was to protect Britain's Middle East position in preparation for a likely war against Nazi Germany. And on this point the advice of the chiefs of staff – the heads of Britain's navy, army and air force – was in full agreement with that of the Foreign Office.

On January 14th they summarized the strategic importance of the Arab and Moslem world. They pointed out that Egypt gave Britain control of sea and air communications with India and the Far East, as well as Alexandria, the only large harbour in the Eastern Mediterranean, that there were crucial British oil interests in Iraq and Iran, protected by British air bases at Habbaniya and Basra on Iraqi soil, that Saudi Arabia could with ease cut Britain's land and oil communications, especially with German or Italian support, then go on to threaten British-protected sheikhdoms in Kuwait and the Gulf, and that the Yemen could likewise threaten the British port of Aden, which was vital to the Royal Navy as part of the sea route to India.[38]

Palestine itself provided added depth for the protection of the Suez Canal and was a stage on the air route to India. Its small port of Haifa was the outlet of the pipeline from Iraq, a potential base for light naval vessels and the starting point of land communication with Habbaniya. These were the main reasons, the chiefs of staff concluded, 'which made the goodwill of Egypt and the Arab countries in the Near East of great importance to our Imperial strategy'.

If British policy on Palestine became unacceptable to the Arab states, they might well 'become alienated, if not actively hostile', with consequent grave dangers to British security. This was the basis on which the matter was decided in London. The promises given to both sides in the past, the intrinsic rights and wrongs of the issue between Jew and Arab, the plight of Jews in German-occupied Europe – all these were considered and taken into account, but on a secondary level. In the final analysis they all had to yield before one main consideration – the need to decide which course of action best suited the vital national interest of Great Britain, threatened as it was with war and destruction by Nazi Germany.

And so the conference opened at St James's Palace in London on February 7th, 1939. Chamberlain spoke first and in reply Weizmann expressed the Jewish nation's 'unshaken confidence in British good faith', a confidence he and his colleagues in fact no longer felt. Two days later Jamal Husseini, leader of the Palestinian delegation and the Mufti's cousin, put forward the Arab demands decided three weeks earlier in Beirut. It was Husseini, Weizmann wrote, not the British government, who was really running the conference: 'Whatever he gives his consent to goes through. The moment he puts in a *caveat*, the thing is dropped.'[39]

MacDonald says: 'We had terrible trouble, because for days neither side would sit round the same table in the same room. We had to talk to the Arabs in the morning, the Jews in the afternoon.' It did not take long for him to come to the unsurprising conclusion that neither side was ready to make any substantial compromise and that any idea of a negotiated agreement would have to disappear from British minds. In that case, Britain would have to work out her own proposals and impose them on Palestine unilaterally, in her capacity as Mandatory power. The talks could still be useful. They could be a sounding board for the British team and a guide to the Cabinet on which policy they would be best advised to impose. But their original aim would have to be abandoned.

In the first week of the conference MacDonald met several non-Palestinian Arab leaders in private and submitted his 'Plan A' for 300,000 Jewish immigrants over ten years. The reaction, as Baxter had predicted, was an angry one and the normally pro-British Nuri es-Said immediately began arguing for the full Palestinian claim. MacDonald realized that, as usual, immigration was the key to the problem and that, if he wanted to keep the 'moderating influence' of the Arab states, he would, as the Foreign Office had advised him, have to come down much lower than that.

So what figure should he insist upon the Arab leaders accepting? Should he bargain with them like a buyer in an oriental bazaar, or should he as a last resort be ready to stop immigration completely?[40]

On February 10th Weizmann made a formal reply to MacDonald's outline of the Arab case, particularly to the argument that the Jews had entered Palestine without Arab consent. The time had come to decide, he told MacDonald. Was the Balfour Declaration an act of restitution or was it not? If it was not, then Britain could tell the Jews that they had no business in Palestine. If it was, then Britain should tell the Arabs that the Jews entered by right. Baffy noted that the Jewish delegates were winning many of the arguments, but that it was a barren triumph, given the decisions Britain had already made, details of which were regularly communicated to her and the Jewish delegates by Walter Elliot.[41]

The Zionists, by now reaching the point of desperation, decided to approach the United States. On February 25th two American Jewish delegates at the conference, Stephen Wise and Louis Lipsky, saw Ambassador Kennedy and spoke of a Jewish appeal to President Roosevelt. The situation needed careful watching, noted Wallace Murray, head of the Near East Division of the State Department.

A protest by some of the nine thousand American Jews resident in Palestine was printed the same week. Their community, they said, had in the past twenty years invested no less than $80 million in Palestine 'only because we had and still have unlimited confidence in our United States Government'.[42] They had come to build the National Home, not to be a minority in an Arab state. They referred to the 1924 American-British Mandate Convention which, they believed, did not allow Britain to change its policy in the way proposed, at least not without American consent.[43]

Wallace Murray's reaction to this was a note to Secretary of State Cordell Hull rejecting these arguments as 'wholly untenable'. The United States had no responsibility for administering the Mandate, it said, and as for the National Home, 'the British Government may now deem that objective has been achieved'. Americans in Jerusalem insisted to Consul Wadsworth that their government was committed to supporting Zionism 'at least morally',[44] the latter phrase being added, if at all, only grudgingly. On March 9th a statement to this effect was issued by seventeen US senators, but the State Department was not convinced and would not interfere.

And so on March 1st the Zionist delegation, having from the beginning declined to accept British hospitality, announced that the British proposals did not provide a basis for discussion and withdrew from the formal conference. They still took part informally, however, and the high point of the proceedings was reached on March 7th, 1939, when the British, Jewish and non-Palestinian Arab delegates actually met in the same room and around the same table.

Ali Maher Pasha, in what MacDonald described the next day as 'an excellent statement', told the meeting that the Jews had made great progress in Palestine, but that they must now allow a period of consolidation, after which more immigration might perhaps be allowed, but only with Arab consent. According to MacDonald, Weizmann did not dissent from this, but David Ben Gurion, who with Moshe Shertok is described in the Cabinet minute as the 'extreme Zionists' of the delegation, took the line 'that Jewish immigration should continue at an ever-increasing rate'. MacDonald recalls the situation thus: 'Now and then Weizmann seemed to be moving towards some sort of concession, but he was always stopped by Ben Gurion, who was tough and rigid. Weizmann was the boss, but Ben Gurion could stop the boss in situations where he could rally the Zionist rank and file.'

Therefore on March 8th Halifax and MacDonald reported that their tripartite meeting had achieved nothing and that the only way of keeping Arab friendship was to decide a final figure of Jewish immigrants. MacDonald's original July figure of 450,000 had been reduced by him to 300,000. The 300,000 had been totally rejected by the Arabs, as had the 150,000 envisaged by 'Plan B'. The most that he could possibly propose was something between 50,000 and 100,000, over a period of five years, not ten years, and on the basis of its being a final figure, not a temporary figure that would be re-examined at the end of the period.

Walter Elliot was the only one to object. He pointed out that these figures were a far cry from what had been originally proposed and that the prospect of an Arab veto over Jewish immigration might lead to serious trouble in the United States and Palestine: 'The Jews might adopt a policy of despair, which would lead their extremists into violent action, such as had occurred in Palestine a week ago.' But Prime Minister Chamberlain said that he had 'with some reluctance' come to believe that MacDonald's plan was inevitable: 'He would have liked, if possible, to have done rather more for the Jews, who might be considered to have been rather roughly treated, if the various expectations held out to them in recent years were taken into account. He was satisfied, however, that it was impossible to obtain a better bargain for them.'

MacDonald said that the Jews had made no attempt to cooperate with the Arabs in the past twenty years, but they would now have to do so. Chamberlain said that such cooperation would mean that immigration could continue. The difference between 80,000 and 100,000 was not very material to the Jewish refugee problem as a whole, but he hoped that MacDonald would be able to negotiate a figure as close to 100,000 as possible. And as for the damage the new policy would cause in America, it was better for it to happen now than at a time of crisis.

MacDonald then returned to the bargaining table with Fuad Hamza, Ali Maher and Tawfiq as-Suwaydi – the 'moderate' delegates from Saudi Arabia, Egypt and Iraq – and after some discussion the Arabs agreed to urge their Palestinian colleagues to accept a final batch of 75,000 Jews during the next five years.[45] Arab and Foreign Office pressure had thus persuaded MacDonald to approve a figure one-sixth of what he had proposed to Weizmann nine months earlier. Even this figure the Foreign Office felt was too many, although Charles Baxter had to admit that the independent Arab states were not greatly perturbed by it. The Palestinian Husseini delegates of course rejected the figure, although the National Defence party approved it, but since it had been accepted by the other Arab leaders there was little they could do. At least they now had a promise that Jewish immigration would end in March 1944.

MacDonald feels today that, given the strength of feeling in Cabinet and in Whitehall, he did as well as he could by his former Zionist friends in getting them this final batch of 75,000: 'Our impression was that this would offend the Arabs grossly, but we would get by with it. So we fixed the quota of Jewish immigration and the spread of years at the maximum we thought the Arabs would swallow.' The figure of 75,000 was to be codified into law, rigorously enforced to prevent evasion and to be the lynchpin of Britain's new policy statement, the 1939 White Paper on Palestine.

Walter Elliot went from the March 8th Cabinet meeting to lunch at the Carlton Grill and, quite improperly, told Baffy Dugdale and the Weizmanns what had been decided. It was a filthy trick, Baffy noted in her diary, to place future immigration into Palestine, which was a matter of survival for the Jews of Europe, as a bargaining counter against an independent Palestine state, which was only a matter of politics. And the supposed agreement with the Arab countries was 'Dead Sea fruit'.[46] Weizmann went immediately to Paris, where he told US Ambassador William Bullitt that zero hour had arrived for the Jews of Palestine and once again begged the United States to intercede. All he asked for was a little delay. In six months' time the international situation might change completely, making Britain's new pro-Arab policy unnecessary. Bullitt sent a personal telegram to Roosevelt: 'He [Weizmann] felt that nothing could save the Jews of Palestine or keep open the door for Jewish refugees except a quiet word from you to the British authorities.'[47]

But Roosevelt was receiving conflicting advice. While his many pro-Zionist political allies were advising him to intervene, the State Department were advising him not to, implying indeed that British policy was the right one. He personally felt 'a good deal of dismay' about the British plan, but he did nothing to prevent it, and the British-American quarrel which Walter Elliot and others had predicted did not materialize, doubtless to Chamberlain's great relief, because in his reference to it at the March 8th Cabinet meeting he had not anticipated that the next great crisis was only a week away. On March 15th, 1939, Hitler's armies entered Prague, annexing Bohemia and Moravia to Germany and finally convincing the British prime minister that he had been deluded by Hitler all along.

March 15th was also the day when MacDonald gave the two delegations Britain's final Palestine proposals: a final immigration quota of 75,000 spread over five years, after which no Jews could enter Palestine without Arab consent, prohibitions or restrictions on land sales to Jews in all but a small Tel Aviv-Haifa coastal strip, the build-up of self-governing institutions with the eventual aim after ten years, with the consent of the Jewish community, of an independent Palestine with an Arab majority: thus independence would be subject to Jewish consent and future Jewish immigration to Arab consent. In this way, it was hoped, the two communities would be induced to cooperate.

The Arabs complained mainly about the length of the transition period and asked for time to discuss it. Musa el-Alami says: 'The conference wound up unexpectedly. MacDonald read the proposals to us at top speed and would not even give us copies to take away. We asked him whether it was a matter of take it or leave it. MacDonald said, "Yes." We said, "In that case we leave it." ' The other Arab delegates, most of whom were privately in favour of the British proposals, felt bound to follow the lead of Haj Amin al-Husseini's party and reject them publicly. They then returned home. The British press noted ominously that two of the Palestinians passed through Berlin on the way.

But MacDonald was able to tell the Cabinet on March 22nd that some of the Arab delegates 'had told us that they regarded our proposals as wise and reasonable'. The two Nashashibis, Ragheb Bey and Fakhri Bey, said that the proposals 'would eventually produce peace' and that the unanimous formal rejection 'was no index of their real opinions'.[48]

The weak point in the plan, from the Arab point of view, was that independence could be delayed indefinitely by Jewish refusal to take part in government. Halifax was tempted to make yet another concession on this point, in the hope of getting the Arabs to agree publicly, but other ministers saw merit in the 'double veto' plan. They believed that it would force Jews to work with Arabs to obtain more immigration and Arabs to work with Jews to obtain independence.

This was the basis of a strangely optimistic note sent by the Foreign Office on March 17th to the State Department in Washington: 'It would seem that the elements of a compromise are present. His Majesty's Government feel that most important consideration regarding Palestine is that Arab and Jews should learn to work together and they think the present scheme offers the best prospect of favouring the growth of such cooperation.'[49]

During the next two months the Zionists continued to hope that world pressure, especially from British and American Jewry, would delay the announcement of the new policy and eventually kill it. At a meeting at the Hotel Roosevelt in London on March 16th Rabbi Stephen Wise spoke warmly of Britain as 'the defender of all that is democratic in the world',[50] and promising full Jewish support in her struggle against fascism.

But he spoke with great emotion about the prospect of Britain abandoning a solemn pledge in order to appease Hitler, Mussolini and the Mufti: 'Do you know what a permanent minority status means? It means that for 1900 years we have prayed and dreamed, and for sixty years we have worked and toiled and our best have put their most into the upbuilding of Eretz Israel, and after all that, and the promise of the Mandate and the [Balfour] Declaration, Palestine would become nothing more than another Jewish ghetto.'[51]

Weizmann spoke in the same way on May 2nd to US Consul Wadsworth in Jerusalem: 'His policy, one for which he had been all too often censured by many leaders of the Zionist Movement, had been consistently for 25 years one of full cooperation with the British Government. That cooperation was the keystone on which his life had been built, his Rock of Gibraltar. But no cooperation was possible under the new policy. He must, with its publication, declare himself irrevocably in opposition and commit the Zionist Movement to a policy of non-cooperation with Great Britain.'[52]

Weizmann returned to England and used the full force of his eloquence to put across his anger and despair to British ministers. On May 11th he told Chamberlain that the British government were 'entirely ignorant' of the situation they would soon face in Palestine: 'There was more moral and intellectual strength to the square kilometre in the Jewish part of Palestine than in any other country in the world. What the Arabs were after was their very blood. They wanted their lives, their houses, their gardens, and they would set about getting them as soon as they were given the chance. They had been promised by Hitler the £90 million which Jews had invested in Palestine. The tragedy of it was that the laws would be on their side and British bayonets would be there to help them to achieve their purpose.'[53] According to a record of the meeting made by Moshe Shertok, Chamberlain replied in startled fashion that surely Weizmann must be overstating the case. Weizmann replied that he was stating the exact position and that his mother was already preparing his trousseau for the Seychelles.

But the boiling point of Weizmann's fury was reserved for MacDonald, now seen as the great traitor to Zionism, at a meeting on May 13th at his country house at Great Waltham in Essex. MacDonald recalled: 'Baffy Dugdale and the others told him not to come, because I was such a beastly chap, but he wanted to make one last attempt to get me to change the White Paper.' It was a distressing interview, in which MacDonald tried to reassure and pacify, while Weizmann tried to explain to his former friend the enormity of what he was doing.

MacDonald said that the Jews had made mistakes in the past, to which Weizmann replied: 'Oh yes, we have made mistakes, our chief mistake is that we exist at all.' He added that at least in Hitler one found the virtue of absolutely frank brutality, while MacDonald was betraying the Jews and handing them over to their assassins under a semblance of legality. MacDonald said that he knew well that the Jews were calling him a hypocrite and a coward. Weizmann answered icily: 'I have never called you a coward.'[54] He then drove back to London, remarking that he was now returning to Palestine to help the Yishuv to bear the shock.

MacDonald says: 'It was eighteen months after my father [Ramsay MacDonald] died and he knew my deep affection for him, but he said, "Malcolm, your father must be turning in his grave at what you're doing." Now, I'd sympathized with every other argument he had put, but this was a bit much. I realized then that he had come to hate and despise me. What had been a close friendship on both sides had become, on his side, enmity. I absolutely respected him for hating me and never lost my admiration for him. But it was very sad.'

Four days later (May 17th, 1939) the White Paper appeared. The Irgun blew up the Palestine broadcasting station at the moment when the announcement of the new policy was timed to begin. During the days that followed they also killed a Jewish policeman, fired shots in Arab areas, and put bombs in telephone boxes, Arab houses and the Department of Migration. A copy of the White Paper was torn up by the chief rabbi in the main synagogue of Jerusalem. At meetings throughout the country Jews took an oath not to tolerate the treacherous new policy, to 'spare no sacrifice to frustrate and defeat it'.[55]

On May 19th MacDonald endured yet another painful experience. Baffy Dugdale called on him in the Colonial Office to tell him that he had broken the love and loyalty of the Jews, which she had thought unbreakable, and ruined the fair name of Britain. Like Weizmann, she referred him to his father's record of support for Zionism and to his own role in amending the Passfield White Paper. At this point, according to her diary entry, MacDonald leant his arm on the table, hid his face, gave out sounds like groans and said: 'I have thought of all that.'

In Palestine the army was finishing off the revolt. During April and May they searched nine Arab villages, finding arms caches in all of them. These searches were without doubt most unpleasant for the villagers. Before beginning their work, the troops put all the village's men into wire openair enclosures, the women and children into houses. Jamal Husseini complained to the League of Nations that it was torture under the guise of investigation. The men were kept under the burning sun for hours or days without food or water, he alleged. MacMichael replied that Jamal Husseini – 'the leading henchman of the Mufti' – was hardly the right man to complain about torture and brutality. The caging of the villagers was a 'temporary inconvenience', which was not a severe punishment in view of the quantities of rifles and ammunition found in most of the villages.

It was true, he said, that in the village of Halhoul, searched on May 6th, eight Arabs had died of heat exhaustion. But this was due to 'a combination of unfortunate circumstances' – the abnormally hot weather and the low resistance of the older men – and could not be classed as an atrocity. Because of the 'unfortunate circumstances',[56] the dependents of the eight dead men would receive compensation totalling £2065.

But when the Palestine question came before the House of Commons on May 22nd the rights and wrongs of Britain's military measures were not part of the discussion. A year earlier the Arab Centre's allegations were dismissed by Colonial Secretary Ormsby-Gore as lies.[57] There was no British member anxious to insist that Arabs were being ill-treated. The most eloquent speeches of the debate consisted in strongly worded attacks on the government's new pro-Arab policy. Philip Noel-Baker predicted that, if Jews were excluded from Palestine legally, they would enter illegally and that the only way to stop them would be 'to tell those kindly British soldiers to shoot them down'. For this, if for no other reason the policy would fail and the Jews would not be denied their Promised Land.

Winston Churchill was one of the several members to suggest, in a speech that would be quoted back at him many times, that the land restrictions and the proposed Arab veto on Jewish immigration were contrary to Article Six of the Mandate, which bound Britain to 'facilitate Jewish immigration under suitable conditions' and to encourage 'close settlement by Jews on the land'. The Jewish nation had made the desert bloom, started a score of thriving industries and founded a great city on the barren shore. Far from being persecuted, the Arabs had thrived under Jewish colonization. And now the House of Commons was to decree that it should all come to an end. 'What is that but the destruction of the Balfour Declaration? What is that but a breach of faith?' asked Churchill. But the House of Commons approved MacDonald's plan by 268 votes to 179.

The British government could not treat lightly the suggestion that it was breaking its promises. It had a majority of 248 over other parties in the House of Commons. For this to have sunk to eighty-nine on such an important issue was a measure of parliamentary concern. And international opinion was equally important. Palestine was not part of the Empire. Its ultimate authority was not the Crown, but the Council of the League of Nations, which had entrusted it to Britain under certain conditions. If this Council now decided that Britain was in violation of the terms of the Mandate, the White Paper policy would become invalid under international law.

President Roosevelt, for instance, did not agree with the State Department's view that the new policy was legal. 'Frankly, I do not see how the British government reads into the original Mandate or into the White Paper of 1922 any policy that would limit Jewish immigration,' he wrote on May 17th, 1939. His first thought was that the White Paper was 'something that we cannot give approval to by the United States'.[58]

Roosevelt did not share the British view that it would be illegal to convert Palestine into a Jewish state against Arab wishes. In his view, the reference to maintaining 'the civil and religious rights of the existing non-Jewish communities' meant only that the Arabs could not be deprived of citizenship or of the right to take part in government. It did not mean that they could not be deprived of their majority status. The impression given to the whole world at the time of the Mandate, he wrote, was that Palestine would be converted into a Jewish Home 'which might very possibly become predominantly Jewish within a comparatively short time'.

Britain therefore had to face the indignity of having its policy and behaviour examined by a group of foreigners, the members of the Permanent Mandates Commission, a League of Nations advisory body. MacDonald had to spend most of June making tedious journeys to Geneva, answering the questions of the seven French, Portuguese, Belgian, Dutch, Norwegian, Swiss and British commissioners, whom he found 'very inquisitive and difficult'.

'For seventeen years they have been the prey of carefully directed Zionist propaganda,' MacDonald reported. Weizmann had visited all of them except Lord Hankey, the British commissioner, and persuaded them that British policy was contrary to the Mandate: 'They take a narrow legalistic view of these matters, and, though I think that I have shaken them a good deal, they are still not persuaded that we are right. At the moment my impression is that three of the members are for us, and four against, and decisions are by a majority.'

Sure enough, when the Mandate Commission's report appeared in mid-August, it emerged that only the French and Portuguese commissioners supported Lord Hankey. The other four were of the opinion that the new immigration and land purchase proposals violated Article Six and that the plan for an eventual handover to Arab majority rule was inconsistent with Britain's duty to establish the Jewish National Home.[59]

Britain continued to argue that she was not bound to carry on Jewish immigration indefinitely, that she could not prejudice Arab rights by allowing indiscriminate Jewish land purchases and that Arab constitutional rights were just as important as Jewish. British spokesmen let it be known that they expected the Council of the League, which was to consider the matter on September 8th, to take a broader and less legalistic view. Meanwhile the Commission's verdict was an opinion, nothing more. But they could not disguise the fact, as *The Economist* of London put it on August 19th, that the Commission's report was 'anything but a severe rebuke to Great Britain'.

In the event, of course, the Council of the League did not meet on

September 8th. Hitler's plan to invade Poland was already mature and, when on August 23rd he signed a non-aggression pact with the Soviet Union, it was put into effect. The next day Weizmann made a deeply emotional speech to the delegates of the 21st Zionist Congress in Geneva, many of whom were about to return to their deaths in Eastern Europe: 'It is with a heavy heart that I take my leave . . . There is darkness all around us and we cannot see through the clouds . . .'[60] On September 1st Germany invaded Poland. Two days later Britain and France declared war on Germany.

At this disastrous moment in British history the White Paper was seen in London as an important British achievement, one of the few bright spots on the international scene. Although publicly the Arabs rejected it, in private they spoke of it with growing approval. It succeeded in its main purpose, which was to drive a wedge between the Mufti and the rebels on one side, the 'moderate' Palestinians and the Arab states on the other. George Antonius, while emphasizing his disappointment that Britain still recognized the validity of the Balfour Declaration and the Mandate, although the Arabs had been consulted about neither, and in the continuing denial that Palestine was promised to the Arabs by the MacMahon letter, called the White Paper 'a substantial advance towards the recognition of Arab rights'.[61]

Auni Bey Abdul Hadi, another delegate at the London conference, explained to a senior policeman why the rebellion was being called off. He told Kingsley Heath that, while principles were worth fighting for, details were not, and since the White Paper had to a great extent accepted Arab demands, there was no point in fighting for points of detail.[62]

Major-General Bernard Montgomery ('Monty') was able to report while on leave from Palestine on July 21st: 'This rebellion is now definitely and finally smashed. And we have such a strong hold on the country that it is not possible for the rebellion to raise its head again on the scale we previously experienced.'[63]

The new American consul, Christian T. Steger, reported from Jerusalem that, while a few murders were still being committed by Arabs who preferred banditry to hard work, the revolt 'may be considered to be at an end'. MacMichael wrote in October: 'Arabs as a whole are giving no trouble and are cooperating well with the government.'[64] This was, from Britain's point of view, the dividend of the White Paper policy.

The calculation that the Jews would support Britain in all circumstances, cynical though it was, also seemed to be turning out well. Weizmann and the Jewish leaders were in no position to carry out their threats of non-cooperation and resistance. The Jewish Agency existed, under Article Four of the Mandate, 'for the purpose of advising and cooperating with the Administration'. If its declared policy was the opposite of this, it could be delegalized and excluded from all consultation. Britain could, in such circumstances, have brought economic pressure to bear on the Yishuv, refused contracts to the Histadrut construction agency (Solel Boneh), closed Tel Aviv port, disbanded Jewish police units and put Arabs in place of Jews in administrative posts. Quite simply, Britain was at this stage in a position to make more trouble for the Yishuv than vice versa.

Likewise on the international scene the Jewish leaders felt obliged to support Britain publicly, however much they seethed with resentment. Weizmann wrote to Chamberlain on August 29th: 'The Jews stand by Great Britain and will fight on the side of the democracies.'[65] Past differences with Britain, he said, must give way before greater and more pressing necessities. Britain accepted the offer with gratitude, but said little about it in public, not wishing to provide British opponents of the conflict with Germany – Oswald Mosley and others – with grounds for their cry that Britain was being led into the war by the Jews.

Anyway, no Jewish volunteers could be accepted for the moment, because there was not the equipment to arm the manpower of Britain, let alone anyone else. Almost everyone in Whitehall agreed that Jewish cooperation was something to be taken for granted and should not influence policy. The plain and simple fact was that for the first time in years Britain was receiving support from Jew and Arab alike. In fact, the Palestine situation had improved enormously. Therefore the White Paper policy must be right.

It was, as with most British decisions on Palestine, a judgement limited to the short term, an opiate to reduce the pain, as Charles Bateman put it. 'I'm not saying that the White Paper was right. All I'm saying is that this was the reason for it and I'm damned if I see what else could have been done,' is MacDonald's verdict on what he did forty years ago. 'From the Zionists' point of view they were right to oppose me, but I was not a Jew or a Zionist and my first thoughts had to be for Britain and the cause of democracy in general.' He sympathized very much with the Jews, but they were only part of the world political scene, a small part.

He does not share the view that at that time Arab and Moslem power were negligible and that Britain would have been better advised to ally herself with Zionism: 'My opponents might be right, we might have been able to get away with provoking the Arabs, but after taking the best possible advice, especially from the Foreign Office and the Chiefs of Staff, I had to come to the conclusion that they were wrong, that we simply could not take the risk. After all, *they* were the experts. And who was I, a young man of 37, to tell them all that they were wrong, even if I *was* colonial secretary?

'The only point over which I criticize myself is that perhaps I should have held out for a higher figure of Jewish immigration. I have sometimes felt conscience-stricken. But, honestly, I did my darnedest. I had very few allies, either in Whitehall or in the Cabinet, and in the end I was persuaded that the new policy was inevitable, not only from the British point of view, from the Zionist point of view too. It was vital for the Jewish national home that Britain should win the war. If Britain lost and Hitler won, there would be no national home. The Jews would be killed or expelled from Palestine, just as they had been 2000 years earlier.

'And at the back of my mind was the idea that, if we won the war and I stayed in office, I would then be able to give the Zionists a better deal. It would have meant abandoning the White Paper, yes, another change of policy, but that's nothing new, is it? Policies change as circumstances change. We were obliged under the Mandate to facilitate Jewish immigration under suitable conditions. Once those conditions improved, we might have been able to allow in more Jewish immigrants. But in 1939 the conditions were very *un*suitable.'

The Yishuv's friendly attitude to Britain suffered a blow from which it never recovered. The views of Weizmann's followers were weakened, those of Jabotinsky and the Irgun strengthened. MacMichael reported on July 27th: 'The general attitude of the Jews locally is one of calculated resentment and opposition plus periodic acts of violence by criminally minded individuals.'[66] On August 26th the Irgun committed their first serious act of anti-British violence, laying a trap mine which killed two police inspectors, Ralph Cairns and R. E. Barker.

On August 31st several members of the Irgun high command, including Abraham Stern, were arrested by Frank Rawlings in Tel Aviv. But this seemed no more than a ripple amid the European tempest and was not detected in London. On September 1st a ship carrying illegal immigrants was waylaid by the Royal Navy off the coast of Palestine. When it refused to stop, shots were fired and three Jews were killed. The incident, which many Jews still remember with bitterness, happened on the day Hitler invaded Poland and was hardly even noticed outside Palestine. Ben

Gurion calmed his people down with the news that war had broken out, which meant that the incident was not to be discussed.

The rebuff that Britain had received from the League of Nations was also submerged by the war and forgotten by most. But it remained on the record, even though the Council did not confirm it, and provided an arguable basis for Zionist claims that the White Paper was illegal under international law. 'We shall fight the war as if there were no White Paper, and the White Paper as if there were no war,' said Ben Gurion – a statement that reflected political reality within the Yishuv more closely than did Weizmann's unreserved promise of support. The Zionists faced a cruel political dilemma. How could they oppose the White Paper without at the same time damaging Britain's war effort, which they genuinely wanted to help? They were resolved to fight Britain in certain areas, for instance over illegal arms and illegal immigration. But if they did this too much, or spread the fight against Britain into other areas, they ran the risk of helping their nation's mortal enemy.

Montgomery summed up the situation in his usual terse style: 'Jew versus Arab – this is what is going on in Palestine now. And it will go on for the next 50 years in all probability. The Jew murders the Arab and the Arabs murder the Jews.' But this was now an oversimplification. By the end of 1939 both the Arabs and the Jews of Palestine nursed strong resentments against the British authorities. The Arabs thought that the British had betrayed them, that they were pro-Jewish. The Jews thought that the British had broken a sacred promise made in 1917 to their people, that they were pro-Arab. Many Arabs hated Britain for the strong measures she had taken against the rebels as well as against ordinary villagers. Many Jews hated Britain for slamming shut the gates of Palestine at the time of European Jewry's direst need.

Since taking over the government of Palestine, Britain had been able to justify her position as one of arbiter between two warring nations. She had tried to reconcile them, in her own interest. Constant civil strife was transforming Palestine from a useful asset into a military and political liability. The solution seemed obvious. Jew and Arab must learn to work together under British guidance until they could achieve independence. MacDonald says: 'This was another important part of the White Paper, to make each community dependent on the other. For instance, we thought that the Jews might agree to make Palestine an Arab state, if the Arabs agreed to more Jewish immigration. We wanted to give both sides a weapon.' But it was like trying to mix oil and water. Both Arab and Jew wanted to rule Palestine, not to share it.

So Britain failed, resorting instead to a series of temporary expedients, opiates to reduce the pain, each one designed to quieten the side which made more trouble and to soothe any dangerous situation that arose. The White Paper quietened the Arabs, but did not satisfy them, and it earned the hatred of the Jews, albeit a hatred subdued by events in Europe. The question was, how painful would it be for Britain when the effect of the opium wore off and both sides gave violent expression to their resentments?

3

The Little Death-Ships

THE Poles fought very bravely, but they were no
match for the enemy. Their British and French
allies did nothing to protect them against the German forces, who
reached the outskirts of Warsaw after a week of fighting and by September
16th, 1939, had overrun the entire western half of Poland. The next
day the Red Army administered the *coup de grâce*. Under the pretext of
a desire to protect the Ukrainian and Byelorussian population of eastern
Poland, but in fact as a result of a Soviet-German agreement signed in
Moscow at the end of August, Stalin's soldiers swept across the eastern
Polish plains, meeting little or no resistance from the crushed and
dispirited people.

By the end of September Warsaw had surrendered, the fighting was
over and the Polish lands were shared out between her two rapacious
neighbours. A few Polish Jews – Menachem Begin and Nathan Yalin-Mor
were two of them – made their way across to the Soviet side or to Wilna
in Lithuania, but the majority of the Jewish community of nearly
3,500,000 stayed on the Nazi-German side of the line.

Weizmann wrote to Shertok that half of the world's Jews were now
under the control of Hitler or Stalin. He was trying to find out what was
happening to the Jews of Poland, but the country was sealed and the few
who escaped told conflicting stories. 'They did not know what fate had in
store for the Jews in Germany during this war or at its end, but they were
certainly justified in expecting the worst,'[1] Shertok told MacDonald on
October 23rd. Weizmann wrote: 'One stands appalled before the dimen-
sions of the disaster, which is unfortunately in inverse proportion to our
power of sending any assistance.'[2]

As soon as the Polish campaign was over, Hitler applied himself to the

Jewish question. On September 27th he signed a decree creating a Reich Security Office (RSHA) under Reinhard Heydrich, with a special section for Jewish affairs under Adolf Eichmann. The first stage in the plan was to be the settlement of Jews in a marshy area of south-east Poland, near Lublin, between the rivers Vistula and Bug. Eichmann visited the area with German, Austrian and Czech Jewish leaders to discuss a mass transfer of the population.[3]

Polish Jews were immediately deprived of their commercial enterprises, excluded from business life, forbidden to use public transport, ordered to wear a Star of David distinguishing badge and made liable to forced labour. Many were arrested, loaded into trains with just a few belongings and dumped in the Lublin 'reserve' to survive as best they could. The number of Polish Jews who died in these first months of Nazi occupation is not known, but it was certainly more than 100,000. Heydrich explained to his men on September 21st that these were only the first steps towards 'the final aim, whose attainment will take some time'.[4]

The outside world knew little of all this. Even the Zionist leaders in their worst nightmares, despite expecting the worst, hardly imagined that Hitler planned to exterminate every Jew in his empire. But they were sure, now that war had broken out, that the sufferings of the Jews would increase. It was with this thought in their minds that they visited MacDonald and other ministers again and again to beg for more life-giving immigration certificates.

'Every Jew brought into Palestine in time was to them one more Jew saved,' Shertok told MacDonald. There were, for instance, the thirty thousand Polish Jews who had escaped to Romania, Hungary, and the Baltic states. And there were the Jews of those countries themselves. Within a few months they too might be at risk. In an interview on September 6th Vladimir Jabotinsky told MacDonald that 'shipload after shipload of Jewish refugees would soon be arriving off the Palestine coast'[5] and asked him deliberately to wink at illegal immigration.

The Zionists explained that they had declared their loyalty to Britain in full knowledge of the White Paper: 'They had made no stipulations, asked for no *quid pro quo*.' But they did expect the unexecuted parts of it, especially the proposed land restrictions, to be shelved for the time being. They offered their services in the fight against Hitler. With their help, Palestine could be made the main base of British influence in the Middle East.

They had invited volunteers to register for military service in the British forces and 130,000 Jews had responded.[6] The information provided by Jewish refugees from Hitlerism, some of them people of influence and scientific achievement, was at Britain's disposal. They would do their best to involve the United States more closely in the war. In fact, they could be a most valuable ally. Because of the war, said Shertok, 'they had again begun to breathe the air of Anglo-Jewish cooperation.'

In these new circumstances, was Britain really going to continue to enforce the White Paper? The policy was not only dishonest and inhuman, in the light of Britain's past promises and the Jews' present sufferings, but also absurd. Until a few months ago the Arabs had been in full-scale revolt in Palestine. The Jews had been loyal to Britain then and, now that war had broken out, were doubly loyal. But the White Paper was a threat to this loyalty. If Britain persisted with the immigration and land purchase restrictions, Shertok told MacDonald, 'they could hardly expect the Jews to take it lying down'. Jewish public opinion would react 'and this might make things in Palestine very unpleasant'.[7]

But these arguments made very little impression on the British government. Lacy Baggallay wrote: 'The Middle East is at present quiet and pro-Allied, remarkably and rather unexpectedly so. For this the White Paper is largely responsible.' In his view Jewish support for the war effort could never be decisive. It could even, in certain circumstances, be counterproductive. It could encourage fringe groups in Britain and America to believe Hitler's line that the war was only being fought to please the Jews. And as for Shertok's veiled threats of rebellion, Baggallay noted: 'Since HMG are the sole hope of salvation for millions of their fellow-Jews in Europe, the plain fact is that they cannot turn against us, however much they resent our Palestine policy.'[8]

MacDonald noted at the end of September: 'It is self-evident that there is no reason to change the policy because of Jewish support in the war, since we are also receiving Arab support.'[9] He told Shertok that he knew the Jews were trying to undo the White Paper. Over the decades, he said, they had always managed to undo every anti-Jewish decision or policy over Palestine. This was perfectly honourable, from their point of view. But the British government was determined that the White Paper would not be undone.[10]

This was the precise basis, noted Baggallay, of any remaining Arab hostility to Britain. Auni Bey Abdel Hadi was one of many leading Palestinians who had made this point. He and his colleagues had nothing serious against the White Paper. He told Walter Smart, Oriental Secretary in Cairo and George Antonius's brother-in-law, that if it was implemented 'Arab cooperation would come almost naturally'.[11] It promised an eventual stoppage of Jewish immigration, which was 'the essential Arab requirement'. 'The real Arab difficulty,' he said, 'was due to the fear that HMG under Jewish influence would eventually go back on it.'[12]

The Zionist leaders wanted their men to join the British army and carry arms against Germany. The British authorities viewed this offer with grave suspicion. Firstly, there was not enough equipment for them. Secondly, they would infuriate and provoke the Arabs. Thirdly, they might eventually be used by the Zionist leaders as a lever to prise Britain away from the White Paper. There was no guarantee that Jewish units would always obey British orders. No doubt they genuinely wished to fight the Nazis, but if circumstances changed they might turn these arms against the Arabs, or even against the British.

For years the British in Palestine had suffered from Arab rebel bands. To fight them they had armed a number of Jews, thus conceiving the Jewish Supernumerary Police. This legal body soon became a foundation stone of the illegal Haganah, the armed force of the Yishuv, which took its orders from the Jewish Agency, not Britain. This was a situation that Britain found hard to stomach. Now that the rebellion was over, now that the threat to Jewish settlements was removed, or at least greatly reduced, Britain wanted to eliminate all armies not under her own control. Arabs were still being convicted and hanged for carrying arms. In the mood of those days it seemed wise for Britain 'to show her impartiality,' to punish Jews who carried arms as well as Arabs.

One of the earliest victims of this policy was the future Israeli general Moshe Dayan, who had fought with Orde Wingate against Arab rebels. In mid-August he joined an illegal Haganah platoon commanders' course in Lower Galilee. On October 5th he and forty-two other Haganah men were seen by a British patrol, armed and in uniform, marching in military formation. They were arrested and taken to a police station. Dayan writes that he was threatened with the death penalty for carrying arms and that his colleague Zvi Brenner was beaten up for refusing to answer questions.

At their trial on October 27th they all put forward the same defence: 'We were a group of young men training to prepare ourselves for the fight against our common enemy, Nazi Germany, and should receive the understanding and indulgence of the court.'[13] Shertok explained to MacDonald in London: 'They had no doubt thought that they might be called upon to perform certain duties by way of assistance to British troops and were anxious to get ready for the job.'

But this was not the view of MacMichael or his army commander

Lieutenant-General Michael Barker. Neither they nor MacDonald saw the Haganah as Britain's faithful ally. MacDonald noted that it was 'in no way an outcome of the present war'. Its aims, they thought, were to establish a Jewish army and to secure 'eventual Jewish military supremacy in Palestine'.[14] It was designed for use against the Arabs, but it might in certain circumstances be used against the British.

MacDonald told his men in Palestine to take 'the firmest possible measures' to 'suppress this illegal Jewish organization'. He told Ben Gurion that Arabs were still being hanged for the possession of arms. To tolerate the Haganah would be to provoke serious trouble in the Arab and Moslem world. And so on October 30th the Haganah prisoners were sentenced to long terms of imprisonment. Moshe Dayan and his friends were taken to Acre fortress, where they slept between a rag mattress and two thin blankets each on a concrete floor. Weizmann wrote to Halifax: 'Men who have done distinguished service with the British forces in Palestine are now lying in prison on rags, half-starved, and treated as criminals.'

General Barker took a firm line with Ben Gurion on November 1st: 'This was a most serious thing. Their aim was clear. They were preparing for rebellion against Great Britain . . . In Great Britain the build up of a private army would be considered high treason and he was not going to tolerate such things in Palestine.'[15]

Two weeks later MacDonald put the same arguments to Ben Gurion in London. Ben Gurion replied that the Haganah was Britain's creation, a thoroughly necessary body for defending Jews against Arab bandits. Even with the revolt at an end, could British forces guarantee to defend all Jewish settlements? Of course they could not. The Jews had the right to arm themselves in self-defence and they were ready to bear these arms against Nazi Germany.[16] The sentences on the forty-three were cruelly harsh. He left the interview, he told his colleagues back at the Dorchester Hotel, feeling as if he had swallowed a frog. Lewis Namier gave him a cake of Palestine soap to wash the hand that MacDonald had shaken.[17]

The incident of the forty-three was an early example of Britain's confused attitude to the Haganah. In the war against Arab rebels Britain had armed a number of Jews, created a Jewish police force. These men and the arms they held were legal. But over the years the Zionist leaders had illegally added more men and more arms. Some British administrators saw this as a good thing and winked at it. The Haganah, partly legal and partly illegal, behaved generally with restraint and defended Jewish settlements efficiently.

To compare the Haganah with the Mufti's rebels, who had murdered large numbers of Jews and Arabs quite brutally, was quite unfair. But in political terms, given an overriding need to show impartiality between Arab and Jew, the two could be equated and categorized by Britain as private armies. And while the Haganah were loyal to Britain in 1939, they might not always be so in the future. This was how MacDonald justified to Ben Gurion the severe sentences on Moshe Dayan and the other forty-two: 'We believe that there must be absolute fairness between Jews and Arabs in this matter of arms.'

Weizmann too complained to MacDonald (December 2nd) about Barker's suggestion that the Haganah might one day turn against Britain: 'That idea was fantastic. No doubt there were a few extremists who toyed with the idea, but it was repulsive to the Jewish community as a whole.'[18] Weizmann added, with a touch of cynicism, that if there really was a Jewish secret army Britain must extinguish it and he would cooperate in this task. The number of Jews who advocated violence was so small as to be insignificant. MacDonald replied that, although these men of violence might be few in number, they posed a real danger.

Britain had just watched Poland, her ally, collapse within a few days. She knew that she had done nothing to prevent it, that she had suffered a humiliation. In the Arab world her position had improved, but it was the view of the Foreign Office that this improvement needed consolidation. On October 26th MacMichael noted that 'Arabs are essentially fickle and unreliable' and that 'Jews are determined to sabotage White Paper somehow'. British reports were full of fears that the Arab world might be 'set ablaze' by any gesture in favour of the Zionists. Britain was deeply anxious not to risk such a disaster.

Ambassador Basil Newton reported from Baghdad that 'the Palestine question remains a major political issue in Iraq'. Nuri es-Said, a friend of Britain, had made spirited public defences of the White Paper, but his position was undermined by Britain's failure to impose the promised restrictions on Jewish land purchase: 'If there is continued delay, doubts as to our good faith are bound to increase and be exploited by our enemies.'

Lacy Baggallay noted that the land regulations would emphasize 'that the White Paper is being continued without qualification'. Archie Wavell, commander-in-chief in the Middle East, reported that military security would be 'gravely affected' if Britain hesitated in implementing the White Paper, that this 'would give enemy propaganda a very powerful weapon'.[19]

Halifax and MacDonald discussed briefly the possibility of avoiding another anti-Zionist act by making a gentleman's agreement on land purchase with the Jewish Agency. But they concluded that this was not possible. On December 20th Weizmann left London for New York with a letter from Halifax[20] that was, in Baffy Dugdale's words, 'a cold, stiff restatement of the White Paper position'.

The British minister in Saudi Arabia, Hugh Stonehewer Bird, reported King Ibn Saud's 'grave doubts'[21] about Britain's policy. Months had elapsed and nothing had been done, the king complained on February 12th, 1940. No high administrative post had been offered an Arab; sales of land continued. And the Jews could boast, as Shertok did at a Zionist Federation meeting in London three months earlier, that immigration figures for the past year were 35,000 already – nearly half the full five-year allowance.[22]

The decision to go ahead with the land regulations was not taken without vigorous protests from Winston Churchill, the new arrival in the War Cabinet, whose pro-Zionist views were well known. On December 25th, 1939, he sent a paper to his Cabinet colleagues asking for 'softer and smoother processes' in public references to Palestine. The White Paper policy, he suggested, could lose Britain the powerful factor of American Jewry. It had caused vigorous controversy in the House of Commons the previous day. The Labour party had opposed it and so had many Conservatives. If the war sharpened and a Coalition government had to be formed, he prophesied, the White Paper would have to be shelved.

But Churchill was only First Lord of the Admiralty, a force to be reckoned with and a possible challenger for the premiership, but not yet a serious decision-maker. When the land regulations were discussed on February 12th, he told his colleagues that he 'regretted greatly' the 'short-sighted policy' of denying land to the Jews, a nation whom Britain had promised to protect, and of 'bringing this great agricultural experiment to an end'. He argued powerfully, but no one supported him. Chamberlain even referred to a 'consensus of opinion' in favour of MacDonald's policy. Churchill summed up the difference between the two sides: 'The political argument, in a word, was that we should not be able to win the war without the help of the Arabs. He did not in the least admit the validity of that argument.'[23] But his colleagues disagreed.

And so on February 26th MacDonald invited Shertok and Berl Locker to his office to give them the bad news that the land regulations would be published in Palestine the next day. The Jewish leaders told him that they had nothing to say. MacDonald explained that the regulations were necessary. It was sad that they would complicate relations between Britain and the Jews, but they would have to be. They were the only way of avoiding overpopulation and a large number of landless Arabs: 'Land-lessness on a large scale would inevitably result in a rebellion and the government must heed the warnings it had repeatedly received.'[24] Shertok and Locker said that they had nothing to add and left. The interview lasted ten minutes.

The new laws were announced and on February 29th there was dancing in the streets of Arab Jaffa. In Tel Aviv and Jewish Jerusalem there were strikes and violent demonstrations. The demonstrations, which lasted several days, were met by strong police action. In Jerusalem a seventeen-year-old boy, Menachem Prives, died of head wounds after a police baton charge. The result was a stream of official Jewish protests. Mayor S. Stamper of Petah Tiqva described police behaviour as 'a veritable pogrom' and claimed that police 'beat up peaceful passers-by in a most terrible manner' after 'a quiet demonstration'[25] against the land regulations. A number of such complaints were sent by Bernard Joseph, a member of the Jewish Agency Executive, to Chief Secretary John Macpherson.

A different emphasis appears in the British record of these incidents, which gives details of large crowds rioting and stoning police in Tel Aviv and Haifa. In Hadar Hacarmel rioters tried to burn down the lawcourts and injured four policemen. In Petah Tiqva crowds carried banners com-paring MacDonald with Hitler and referring to the new regulations as 'Nuremberg laws'.[26] (Under these Nazi laws Jews were forbidden to own land.) Two police inspectors were injured in Petah Tiqva, one seriously. Many hundreds of Jews were arrested.

Meanwhile, as soon as war broke out, the Mufti of Jerusalem contacted Nuri es-Said and offered Britain his support – an offer that was dismissed as nothing more than a ruse to get back into Palestine and recover power.[27] In October 1939 British Consul-General Godfrey Havard wired from Beirut: 'A car containing veiled women, one of whom is supposed to be the Mufti in disguise, left his house and did not return.'[28] A few days later he appeared in Baghdad and resumed his anti-British outbursts.

Even the land regulations failed to please him. 'The sale of land should be prohibited in all regions, not only a few,' he wired the London *News Chronicle* on March 3rd. He saw the Jewish riots in Palestine as a clear demonstration of their plan to expel all Arabs and take over their land. And the British were, as usual, helping the Jews: 'The continuance of executions of Arabs on a large scale, and the presence of thousands of them in prison without reason, prove that the authorities have not actually altered their tyrannical policy towards the Arabs. This is due to the Jewish influence.'[29]

It was telegrams like this that filled British official minds with foreboding and strengthened their resolve to implement the White Paper. In theory the rebellion was crushed and the Mufti was finished. MacDonald had told Shertok on October 10th that Britain 'did not care a straw' about the Mufti. But the real British view was not so complacent. By a deft piece of political artistry, they felt, they had eased the Mufti off the stage and into the wings. They now had to keep him there. And the key to this achievement remained the White Paper.

The Foreign Office noted with satisfaction Ali Maher Pasha's speech on April 22nd to the Egyptian parliament, in which he described the White Paper as 'a satisfactory basis for the final solution of the Palestine problem',[30] hinting that Britain would soon be promoting Arabs to high positions, preparing the way for independence with an Arab majority.

Such statements caused the Zionist leaders great distress, but they delighted the Foreign Office, because they showed that the wedge was holding, that the Mufti was still being isolated. However, his charisma remained, he still counted for something, even hundreds of miles from Jerusalem. The Foreign Office knew, for instance, that he received regular gifts of money from Mohamed Jinnah, the Moslem leader of India.[31] This was why it was vital for men like Ali Maher Pasha to continue to make friendly speeches. Without them, the Mufti might re-emerge as the embodiment of Arab aspirations in Palestine. The White Paper had scotched the snake, but not killed it. The stick had still to be held steady.

In Baghdad the Mufti had an operational base and a safe haven. Paul Knabenshue advised Washington that the Mufti was 'the most respected and influential individual in Iraq today'. Nuri es-Said hated him, but he had lost the premiership on March 31st and could not touch him. In Britain's view there was only one way of keeping him in political limbo. This was by starving him of political ammunition, by holding on to the White Paper as a drowning man clings to a lifeline. This was the Foreign Office reasoning behind notes such as that of Lacy Baggallay on May 3rd: 'The Arabs have to be thought of as well as the Jews. Morality points in one direction, the implementation of the White Paper.'

These words were written at a time when Hitler was making steady progress towards one of his cardinal aims, the total physical destruction of Europe's Jews. In February the US State Department was told that the whole Jewish population of Stettin had been sent to the Lublin reserve for forced labour, even eighty-year-old women. Assistant Secretary of State Adolf A. Berle wrote to Secretary of State Cordell Hull suggesting a formal protest to Germany: 'I see no reason why we should not make our feelings known regarding a policy of seemingly calculated cruelty . . .'

But Breckinridge Long, another of Hull's deputies and the man responsible for refugee affairs, advised against taking any action 'which might tend to work the United States any closer to the state of war which exists in Europe'. Many observers believe that in early 1940 American opinion still counted for something in the minds of Nazi German officials and that a protest at that time might perhaps have slowed down the process of annihilation.

The ss district commander, Odilo Globocknik, carried on packing Jews into his Lublin reserve, which was eventually to hold five million Jews. These, Globocknik foresaw, would be 'decimated' by the natural course of events. The ghetto system was also put into operation. In February the Jews of Lodz were forced to live in a small walled area of the city on starvation rations and in conditions ripe for disease.

In October the Associated Press correspondent in Berlin, Alvin Steinkopf, was taken on a tour of the Warsaw ghetto. Half a million Jews were living behind an eight-foot wall in an area that had formerly housed less than 200,000. The American reporter's guide told him that the wall was only there to prevent the Jews from spreading typhus round the city.[32]

The United States did not protest for fear of bringing America closer to war. Britain was committed to a pro-Arab policy, which implied that any act or statement in favour of the Jews was liable to damage their war effort. But Jews in Israel and elsewhere are still hard pressed to understand how the two great democracies found it in their hearts to stand by in silence and watch the process of genocide gather momentum.

It remains a bitter sense of injury, one to which Weizmann referred in a letter to Halifax on November 30th, 1939: 'Just at a time when almost two million Polish Jews are completely crushed under the Nazi occupation regime, Great Britain [imposes] an absolute bar on the entry into Palestine even of those of them who have managed to escape.'

Their sense of injury is linked in particular with the person of Malcolm MacDonald, the architect of the White Paper who, Zionists believe, first espoused their cause and then betrayed it. An outburst by Weizmann in the Foreign Office on May 3rd of the following year shows the strength of this feeling: 'He had no intention of putting his views any more before the Colonial Secretary. It was useless for him to do so. He [MacDonald] had made his bed and he must lie on it. In due course nemesis would overtake him for what he had done to the Jewish people.'[33] These words were described as 'tiresome nonsense' by the official in question, who added:

'I wish I could see some hope of this ancient Greek myth overtaking Hitler, Himmler and Heydrich.'

It was during MacDonald's last months as colonial secretary that Britain decided to keep all Jewish escapees out of Palestine. Harold Downie of the Colonial Office told Shertok that there were already 21,000 unemployed Jewish workers in Palestine.[34] Additional immigrants would bring social problems and unrest. The White Paper quota also had to be observed. Most of the current quota had already been taken up by illegal immigration. An increase in the quota would give Nazi Germany and the Mufti valuable propaganda.

British officials believed that any significant rescue operation would damage the Allied cause and help Nazi Germany. It was now no longer a question of tens of thousands, but of hundreds of thousands, or even millions. Where would they all go? There was not the shipping to transport them or the room to house them. They would not only set the Arab world ablaze, they would also cause chaos in a country so small. The idea of a large-scale rescue plan was not even considered. It seemed so obviously impracticable and disadvantageous to the war effort.

But there was now a new reason for keeping the Jews out of Palestine. On January 15th, 1940, MacDonald explained to Selig Brodetsky and Aubrey Eban (the future Israeli foreign minister) that Palestine could now not even accept individual escapees: 'The Middle East was in a delicate situation. The German authorities were very anxious to get a few good agents back into that part of the world.' Specifically, he would have to cancel the certificates issued before the war to 161 adults. Now that they were under Nazi control, they might be sent to Palestine to work for Germany, their relatives remaining as hostages.

The Zionist leaders objected strongly. No Jew, they believed, would work for the Nazis, whatever the pressure, and even if one did, he would soon be unmasked and eliminated by his fellow-Jews. Brodetsky told MacDonald 'that his decision was virtually a condemnation of death upon these people'. MacDonald replied that he fully realized this, but in wartime the interest of the state had to prevail and such decisions had to be taken.

But it was the Jews who escaped by ship who put the greatest strain on Britain, forcing her to make a series of terrible choices between common humanity and the exigencies of war. Illegal immigration by ship, known in Hebrew as Aliya B, had increased in the last years of peace. The more Hitler tormented the Jews, the more restrictions Britain imposed on their immigration, the more urgent became the need to send Jews to Palestine illegally, to strengthen the Yishuv by taking them from Hitler.

On August 12th, 1939, for instance, about four hundred Polish Jews were landed near Herzlia from the Panamanian ship *Dora*, met by a guide and absorbed into the community.[35] During 1940 these expeditions became harder to mount, but of course, from the Jewish point of view, much more important, because they meant life or death for the passengers.

A few Jews were still able to buy themselves out of Nazi Germany, usually with funds provided by the American Jewish Joint Distribution Committee, which enjoyed the support of US Secretary of the Treasury Henry Morgenthau. Upon payment of this ransom, they were given German passports, exit visas and entry visas from a helpful Berlin embassy, usually Paraguay. They were given to understand that Britain, with her Jewish-dominated government, would welcome them in Palestine. They were then shipped down the Danube to the Black Sea ports of Constanza (Romania) or Varna (Bulgaria).

On December 27th, 1939, Reginald Hoare wrote from Bucharest: 'In spite of repeated representations, illicit traffic in Jews continues.' There were seven hundred of them waiting in the steamship *Sakaria* and three thousand on their way down the Danube in the *Ahms*. The *Sakaria* had no lighting or heating and there were cases of pneumonia. Two Jewish women from the ship had called at his legation and had gone away shocked at the unexpected news that Britain did not want them in Palestine and would give them no help.

Another party of one thousand Jews was iced up at Klavada, in the Yugoslav section of the Danube. The problem was, noted Downie, that American charities were raising money to help them through the winter, after which they would continue their journey. Downie proposed action 'to prevent the Committee from giving the suggested assistance', in which case 'they may be turned back by the governments of the territories in which they now are'.

On December 26th the *Rudnichar* left Varna with four hundred Jewish passengers, towing a motorboat to land them from outside territorial waters. News of the sailing reached Halifax, who sent an angry telegram to George Rendel, his man in Sofia, pointing out the seriousness of British objections: 'HMG and Government of Palestine are making every effort to check this traffic . . . Strongest efforts have in fact been made over the past six months to persuade Romanian government to prevent entry and transit of Jews in this manner . . . Such action strikes at the root of the whole visa system.'[36] Halifax told Rendel that every effort would be made to intercept the *Rudnichar* en route and to make it clear that Bulgaria would have to take the passengers back, at least those whose original journey was from Bulgaria.

Churchill was one of the few who questioned the policy. On learning that British ships had been ordered to stop the *Rudnichar*, he wrote to MacDonald: 'I should be glad to know how you propose to treat these wretched people, when they have been rounded up. Where are they to be sent and what will be their fate?'[37]

The Bulgarian ship managed to evade British patrols. On January 8th, 1940, a motorboat and five lifeboats landed at a beach near Haifa with 505 Jews, all transhipped from the *Rudnichar*, which was on its way back empty to Varna. MacMichael explained to MacDonald that, since the regular ships between Haifa and Varna only carried twenty-five passengers each, they would try 'to obtain accommodation for these immigrants on Romanian steamers' for the return journey.

But when later in January a Greek ship, the *Hilda*, was intercepted on its way from Constanza with some seven hundred refugees, the ship was confiscated and all on board were interned in Athlit detention camp. MacDonald wrote to Churchill that these arrests would have 'a most salutary effect' on the shipowners and might well prove 'an effective deterrent to the whole traffic'. Almost all the refugees carried German or Czechoslovak passports, MacDonald noted. The Nazi German authorites must have helped them to leave. And why should they do this, if not to embarrass Britain with the Arabs or to infiltrate their agents into the area?

Refugees from the Nazis had been impeded and arrested. Jewish citizens of Palestine were forbidden to buy land. Haganah men had been imprisoned, their offers to help the war effort spurned, their arms confiscated, and Jewish demonstrators had been roughly handled by the police. The Yishuv was understandably overjoyed when the British government responsible for these acts was forced to resign on May 10th. Their rejoicing increased when they learnt that MacDonald was no longer colonial secretary and that the new prime minister was their lifelong friend Winston Churchill.

Ben Gurion noted: 'Our best friends in the Conservative Party have become members of the government. And so have the leaders of the oppositions. Three of the five members of the War Cabinet are our friends, among them the Prime Minister himself. [Leo] Amery is in charge of the India Office. M.M. has left the Colonial Office – perhaps not without regard to the Palestine question. The new Colonial Secretary [Lord

Lloyd], though a known pro-Arab, is nevertheless an honest and sympathetic man.'[38]

But meanwhile Hitler's armies were conquering France and the Low Countries. Ben Gurion pointed out: 'The new government will from now on be wholly absorbed in the urgent and tremendous task of waging war and we can hardly expect them to spare much attention for our affairs.' Nor were they likely to change the White Paper, at least in the short term, even though many of them had opposed it in the House of Commons in May 1939: 'Such a reversal is rendered even more difficult and unlikely in the tremendous pressure of war.' There might be a few improvements – a new high commissioner, greater tolerance of the Haganah – but nothing much.

Ben Gurion's prediction was correct. In Cabinet on June 12th the three 'friends' he had mentioned – Churchill, Labour party leader Clement Attlee and his deputy Arthur Greenwood – made it clear that they opposed the White Paper. So did Archibald Sinclair,[39] the Liberal leader. But two weeks later at another meeting they all agreed 'that it was out of the question to revise that policy at the present time'.

In May 1939 Churchill had called the White Paper a gross breach of faith. In February 1940 he had called it a short-sighted policy. But in June 1940 he was prime minister. And so, as new prime ministers and presidents often do, he found himself compelled to carry on a policy which he had himself repeatedly and publicly denounced. He could only make it clear, as he did in private notes, that for him the White Paper was a temporary expedient, a moral burden that he would discard as soon as he was politically and strategically able to do so.

So while publicly Britain maintained her pro-Arab stance, reassuring in this sense an anxious Nuri es-Said, who was now only foreign minister, having been replaced on March 31st as premier by the anti-British Rashid Ali al-Kilani, in private Churchill spent time hatching various pro-Zionist plans, much to the consternation of the officials and generals who received his personal letters. He wanted, for instance, to bring home eight of the ten divisions then in Palestine and to replace them with Jews armed in their own defence. Officials in Palestine and the Colonial Office were outraged. Any such idea would undermine their campaign against the Haganah and the 'private armies'. It would also encourage the anti-British faction in Iraq, which was growing in strength.

Carefully argued objections poured into his office. Halifax sent a note suggesting that raising a Jewish army would set the Arab world ablaze. Lloyd sent a note referring to Britain's obligations under the White Paper.

Churchill scribbled at the end of the note: 'You know what I think about the White Paper.' He wrote to Lloyd: 'The cruel penalties imposed by your predecessor [MacDonald] upon the Jews in Palestine for arming have made it necessary to tie up needless forces for their protection.'

On June 28th he continued: 'This is the price we have to pay for the anti-Jewish policy persisted in for some years . . . I think it little less than a scandal that, at a time when we are fighting for our lives, these very large forces should be immobilized in support of a policy that only commends itself to a section of the Conservative Party.' And of the Palestinians he remarked dismissively: 'The Levantine Arabs are very poor representatives and are only a small part of the Arab world.'[40]

These were heady days for the Jews in Palestine. At last, it seemed, they would be allowed to fight against Hitler. The Yishuv must now gain greater armed might and greater political status. The collapse of France had restored good relations with Britain. The Irgun had called a truce and their leaders, including Abraham Stern, were released. There were even plans for Irgun-British cooperation. Their leader David Raziel was convinced that the Irgun must work with Britain against the greater enemy. Jabotinsky was preaching this same message in the United States when he died on August 4th. Only a few dissidents, led by Stern, were anxious to continue the struggle against Britain.

On July 15th the Zionist leaders were thrilled to learn that the War Cabinet had approved the formation of six Palestinian companies of soldiers. Baffy Dugdale noted: 'So the walls of Jericho fall at last.'[41] Leo Amery, Churchill's friend and fellow-Zionist, wrote to Halifax suggesting that, if the Arabs made trouble against Britain, the only policy would be 'to arm the Jews who are there as quickly as we can and invite as many more as are willing to come and occupy the country'.[42]

In September 1940 the plan to arm the Jews was taken a step further. Weizmann was told that the British army would recruit a Jewish fighting force. Jews, from Palestine and elsewhere, would fight in British uniform, but as national units, wearing their own insignia, just as the Poles and Czechs were doing. Weizmann told Baffy: 'It is almost as great a day as the Balfour Declaration.'[43] In a note written that summer Ben Gurion felt able to revive the dream of so many of the Zionist leaders – the transformation of Palestine into an independent Jewish state within the British Empire.

Britain's fortunes were at their lowest ebb. Her allies had collapsed. Her airfields were bombed, then her cities were bombed, including London. Thousands of civilians were being killed. U-boats were sending more and more of her food supplies to the bottom of the Atlantic. But in Palestine the Jews were elated, perhaps extravagantly so, by the thought of renewed cooperation with Britain, their former good friend, the country which had made it possible for them to return to their Promised Land.

But the situation of European Jewry was worsening steadily. More and more terrible stories were being told by the few refugees who made their way to Palestine in the 'little death-ships'. On November 14th George Hall, Lloyd's deputy, saw Weizmann and explained the latest situation. Two ships, the *Milos* and the *Pacific*, had been arrested and were in Haifa harbour. Their passengers, 1760 Jews, were in detention. Meanwhile another 1500 were expected aboard the *Atlantic*, an 800-ton paddle steamer presently in Cyprus. What was to be done with them? And how was the situation to be avoided in the future?

The governor of Cyprus reported that conditions aboard the *Atlantic* were shocking: gross overcrowding, no washing or laundry facilities, no proper cooking facilities and very bad sanitary arrangements. The weather was cold. The passengers were suffering from exposure and were emaciated. Many had influenza and there was one case of typhoid. They were being fed at a cost to the Cyprus government of £75 a day.

George Hall had a plan for keeping the ships away from Palestine altogether. The captain could be invited to select a port outside Palestine. He could then be escorted by British ships most of the way to his selected port and left there with enough fuel to reach that port, but with not enough fuel to get back to Palestine. 'The Colonial Office are showing guts at last' was the Foreign Office reaction to this idea.

But in the end Lloyd decided that the best course would be to ship the refugees to the colony of Mauritius. He wrote to Churchill: 'All these immigrants came from enemy or enemy-occupied countries. We have no check whatever over them. There are indications that the axis powers are encouraging the movement not only because it is exceedingly embarrassing to us, in view of the inflammatory effect upon Arab sentiment, but also because it affords the opportunity of introducing enemy agents into Palestine and the Middle East. In times like these we cannot afford to take risks or allow our authority to be openly flouted.' He hoped that the Prime Minister would support him in his decision: 'They will be shipped by the S.S. *Patria*, recently confiscated from the French.'[44]

Weizmann told Hall he admitted the force of British arguments and would do his best to damp down Jewish agitation. He even offered to cable Shertok in Jerusalem, summarizing what Hall had said and appealing for calm. He also told Lloyd that, although he did not assent to the Mauritius plan, 'in substance he could not dissent from it'.[45] It was only two months after Lloyd and Eden had promised him a Jewish fighting force. Discussions were proceeding about its constitution. It may be that Weizmann wanted to be particularly helpful to Britain at this time, even at the expense of the 3600 Jewish refugees.

After all, there *was* force in the arguments, even from the Jewish point of view. German and Italian radio stations were telling the Arabs that the shiploads of Jews came at Britain's invitation, that they were part of Britain's plan to bring in Jews by the million and drive the Arabs out. They also on October 3rd had broadcast an official proclamation in support of Arab independence: 'In their efforts to achieve this goal the Arab countries can count on Germany's and Italy's full sympathy.'

British officials believed that this propaganda was very dangerous – a threat to her Middle East position and even her war effort. Weizmann clearly shared some of these fears, though he thought them exaggerated. Of course, they would never have justified in his mind the sacrifice of Jewish life. But deportation to Mauritius was not death. It was discomfort and inconvenience. And therefore, he may have thought, it would have to be endured. The rewards that might be gained from the new British government were too great to be ignored.

But this was not the end of the matter. The Mauritius plan would remove the immediate problem, the 3600 Jews, but not the long-term problem. The Foreign Office pointed out the difficulty: 'Once belief is engendered that illegal immigrants will be maintained at the expense of HMG in the British colony until the end of the war, with the prospect of them being allowed to enter Palestine as legal immigrants, every persecuted Jew in Europe will wish to take advantage of so attractive a programme.'[46]

Britain therefore decided to take another step, one which Weizmann did not approve. On November 20th MacMichael declared publicly that none of the deported refugees would ever be allowed to enter Palestine. They would be kept in Mauritius until the end of the war and then repatriated to their country of origin. Thomas Snow of the Foreign Office wrote: 'The certainty that one and all of these will for ever be debarred from Palestine is perhaps the only effective weapon left to prevent them starting.'

The captains and crew members of illegal immigrant ships were now liable to a maximum of eight years imprisonment. The Foreign Office hoped that they would now decide that the game was not worth the candle, that they would give up 'this lucrative traffic' and that the Jewish refugees would be deterred by the permanent ban on entry into Palestine from ever starting. It was a vain hope. Perhaps they did not yet know the full extent of the Nazi persecutions, which had now spread to Romania. In fact, of course, nothing that Britain could devise would ever have deterred Jews from trying to escape from Europe.

Constantly on the move between Britain and the United States, elated by his talks with the new British government, Weizmann did not realize the anger that Britain's policies were arousing within the Yishuv. It was left to Shertok to tell MacMichael the effect of his permanent ban on the Mauritius deportees: 'It was difficult to exaggerate the provocative effect that this sentence had upon masses of Jews. It had made the blood of tens of thousands boil.' And on this occasion anger was transformed into action.

On November 24th the *Atlantic* reached Haifa. The British went to work transferring her 1800 passengers and 1800 others from Athlit camp to the *Patria*. But the Haganah – the military arm of Ben Gurion, Shertok and the other members of the Jewish Agency – had decided that the *Patria* would not take the refugees away from Palestine. They would explode a bomb against her hull. This was no single act of violence, it was Haganah policy. Any ship used to carry Jews away from the national home or to prevent their entry there was liable to Haganah attack.

Bobby Lustig, like most Jewish policemen an undercover Haganah member, was interrogating refugees in the *Patria* saloon when the bomb exploded: 'We didn't know what it was. We thought that maybe the Italians were bombing Haifa. But then the ship lurched over and there was a mad rush to get on deck. I climbed on to the side as she turned over and I was rescued. Others jumped into the sea and swam ashore. But 200 of the immigrants were trapped below and they were drowned.'

The Haganah had made a mess of it. Senior Haganah commander Israel Galili says: 'No one imagined that the sinking would end as it did. Either there was an error in the calculation of the quantity of explosives, or perhaps the steel plates near the spot where the explosives were placed were particularly decayed and could not stand the shock of the explosion . . . The error was made by the professionals.' The aim of the explosion had been to cripple the ship, to prevent it from taking the refugees away, but in fact it tore the bottom out of the ship and cost the lives of two hundred people.

In 1940 the Haganah's part in the affair was not known. In British memoranda all sorts of groups were blamed – Arab extremists, Jewish extremists, Nazi agents. For many years it was widely believed among Zionists, and repeated in such books as Arthur Koestler's *Promise and Fulfilment*, that the refugees, in despair at the prospect of being taken from the Land of Israel, had themselves made the explosion. A booklet recently published in Israel by Betar, a Revisionist publishing house, claims that Lord Moyne was responsible for the order to deport the *Patria* refugees and for their deaths.[47] In fact, Lord Moyne spent the whole of 1940 at the Ministry of Agriculture.

On November 27th Shertok spoke to MacMichael after attending the funeral of the *Patria* victims and visiting the injured: 'They were human wrecks, completely broken by the experience. You felt that you were in the presence of people who had looked death in the face.'[48] MacMichael replied that it was indeed a tragedy and that 'the fellow who had done it deserved to be hanged sky-high'.[49] But, he added, this did not change the situation of the survivors. The decision had been taken and they would have to leave Palestine.

Shertok probably knew that it was his own military men who had exploded the bomb. But this in no way lessened his readiness to blame Britain for the disaster. It was, he said, 'the result of most acute provocation'. The whole of Haifa had seen the wretched ships in the harbour, witnessed the plight of the refugees and been infuriated by the cold tone of the British announcements. MacMichael protested strongly against Shertok's language: 'One might think that the British government was going to do something inhuman. It is going to do nothing of the sort. These people are refugees and the British government is going to take care of them, but not in Palestine.'

It seemed to MacMichael that Shertok and his colleagues were concerned less with the fate of the refugees themselves, more with building up the numerical strength of the Yishuv, presumably in preparation for some future struggle against the British or the Arabs. 'To you all this is something purely political,' he told Shertok. The Zionist leaders believed that every Jew in the world had a natural right to enter Palestine. The British view was entirely different. Of course the Zionist leaders were genuinely concerned about the refugees. But, MacMichael implied, they were also using them to establish the political objective of unlimited Jewish immigration and eventual Jewish sovereignty.

That same day the matter was being reconsidered by the Cabinet in London. Lloyd pointed out that about 35,000 Jews had entered Palestine in the past eighteen months, almost half the White Paper quota of 75,000.[50]

He might have added that twenty-three different ships had brought illegal immigrants to Palestine during the two years 1939–40, that four of these ships had made repeated voyages and that they had landed in all around thirteen thousand immigrants. A decision to let the *Patria* survivors remain in Palestine, said Lloyd, would weaken government policy and encourage further acts of sabotage. But the Cabinet, probably at Churchill's instigation, decided to let the survivors stay in Palestine as an exceptional act of mercy.

All through November the decision-makers in London were also being bombed. In the two years 1940–41 about 43,000 British civilians, half of them Londoners, were killed in German air raids. During the night of November 14/15, at the height of the discussions about the Jewish refugee ships, the city of Coventry was bombed for ten consecutive hours, one third of its houses were made uninhabitable and 554 of its people were killed.

These facts and Britain's general catastrophic state at the end of 1940 go some way towards explaining British officials' lack of sympathy for the *Patria* victims and the Mauritius deportees. Colville Barclay wrote: 'It will be hell for Mauritius. The Jews should be glad that they are to be sent to such a lovely place.' He also suggested sending their ships to Paraguay, since many of them had visas from the Paraguayan legation in Berlin. Charles Baxter noted that 'the prospect of eternal exclusion from Palestine' was the proper deterrent to illegal immigration, rather than 'a year or two in a British colony at the expense of the British taxpayer'. Harry Eyres wrote: 'Presumably any ship carrying illegal immigrants in future will be furnished with bombs, with which she can be sunk on being brought into Haifa harbour.'

General Archie Wavell, about to lead a large army through Egypt against the Italian forces of Marshal Rodolfo Graziani, protested against the decision to keep the *Patria* survivors: 'From military point of view it is disastrous. It will be spread all over Arab world that Jews have again successfully challenged decision of British government and the policy of the White Paper is being reversed . . . It will again be spread abroad that only violence pays in dealing with British . . . Please exert all your influence. This is serious.'[51]

The Cabinet maintained its decision and Churchill sent Wavell a letter of explanation: 'Personally I hold it would be an act of inhumanity unworthy of the British name to force them to re-embark . . . I wonder whether the effect on the Arab world will be as bad as you suggest. If their attachment to our cause is so slender as to be deterred by a mere act of charity of this kind, it is clear that our policy of conciliating them has not borne much fruit so far. What I think would influence them much more would be any kind of British military success.' Wavell wired back agreeing with Churchill that British victory would remove any Arab desire 'pro patria mori' – to die for their country, or for the *Patria.*

This 'exceptional act of mercy' did not apply to the other immigrants in Athlit camp. Within a few days arrangements were made to embark them for Mauritius. The Zionist leaders had warned Britain what this would mean. The immigrants would refuse to move. Two policemen would be necessary to carry every person. The operation was therefore taken in hand by the Inspector-General of Police himself, Alan Saunders. He had all Jewish guards and employees at the camp relieved of their duties during the evening of December 8th. In their place he put 150 British police. It would be their job to supervise the loading.

There are various versions of what happened during the morning of December 9th. What is certain is that the Jewish women started shouting and protesting in their huts at 5 o'clock. The police were then told that the refugees would not leave their huts, that they had scattered all their belongings over the floors and that they were lying on their beds, semi-naked or naked. At 6 o'clock the refugees were told that breakfast was ready, but they made no movement.

They were then warned that loading would commence at 7.30 a.m. and that, if they refused to move, they would be carried to the trucks. Superintendent F. M. Scott wrote in his diary: 'Took the party into the men's compound and cleared the huts out one at a time. These men were all naked, most of them lying on their beds and refusing to get up. They were tipped off their beds and pushed outside and given a blanket apiece.'

Saunders writes: 'As soon as the British police squads entered the first huts and took the blankets off the occupants, with very few exceptions the men walked to the lorries without any need of coercion whatsoever . . . I personally witnessed the embussing of the entire company. There were a few carried in blankets to the lorries who refused to walk and two on stretchers who had worked themselves into a state of hysteria and whom the doctor saw. The demeanour of the males was, with the few exceptions referred to, one of sullen resignation.'[52]

Meanwhile another ship, the *Salvador*, had left Varna on December 3rd with 380 Czechoslovak and Bulgarian Jews. The Bulgarian police had confiscated all their passports, presumably to try to prevent their being sent back. On December 7th the ship reached Istanbul, where she was delayed for four days by strong westerly winds, and it was during this

colm MacDonald, British
onial Secretary 1938–40, author
he 1939 White Paper.

Chaim Weizmann, chief architect
of the Balfour Declaration, first
President of Israel.

Abd ul-Aziz ibn Saud, King of Saudi Arabia.

Haj Amin al-Husseini, Mufti of Jerusalem and leader of
the Palestine Arabs, seen talking to Heinrich Himmler in 1943.

An Underground poster blames High
Commissioner MacMichael for the drowning of
eight hundred Jewish refugees, February 1942.

Lord ⸻
British Colonial Secretary ⸺
later Minister Resident ⸺
Middle East, assassinated ⸻
Stern group in November ⸺

רצח!
סיר האַרוֹלד מק מייכל,
הידוע כנציב העליון לפלשתינה (א"י),

מבוקש עבור רצח

80 פליטים יהודים במימי הים השחור באניה "סטרומ

MURDER!
SIR HAROLD MAC MICHAEL
Known as High Commissioner for Palestine

WANTED for MURDER
OF 800 REFUGEES DROWNED IN THE
BLACK SEA ON THE BOAT "STRUMA"

A Jewish immigrant ship alongside the quay in Haifa harbour.

Stern group advertisement in New York monthly *Jewish Forum*, March 1946.

A British sailor, with helmet and truncheon, stands guard over a small boatload of young Jewish imm

period that British officials made strong efforts to persuade the Turkish authorities not to allow the *Salvador* to proceed.[53]

One official pointed out that under Article Three of the Montreux Convention, which governed traffic through the Dardanelles, the Turkish authorities were entitled to submit ships to sanitary inspection. This examination, he wrote, could prove 'an excellent pretext' for delaying the ship, or even stopping it completely, if any one of the diseases mentioned in the Convention were discovered on board. Colville Barclay had another suggestion, that the Turks 'might be prepared to stop the ship or send it back' because the Bulgarians had violated the Convention for the Safety of Life at Sea in allowing the ship to sail.

The *Salvador* did not reach the Dardanelles. She left Istanbul on December 11th in calm weather, but late that night a south-westerly gale blew up. Heavy seas drove the ship on to rocks near Silivri, thirty miles west of Istanbul, her hull was smashed and she sank almost immediately. Two hundred of the Jewish passengers were drowned, including seventy children.

British ambassador Hugh Knatchbull-Hugessen received a message from London on December 18th: 'In interests of Middle East stability please press Turkish government to do everything possible to prevent survivors from attempting to reach Palestine by overland or other route.' The ambassador replied two days later: 'I am informed by Turkish government that survivors are in pitiable state at Istanbul. Turkish government are going to inform Bulgarian government that these Jews will be sent back to Bulgaria.'[54] The word 'good' is scribbled in the margin of this note.

For the Zionists it was a cruel dilemma. They opposed Britain's policy in Palestine. But how could they do this effectively, while at the same time longing and working for her victory over Nazi Germany? To make matters worse, on the British side there was no such dilemma. Churchill spoke for his country when he said: 'I have only one purpose, the defeat of Hitler, and my life is much simplified thereby.' His sympathies with Zionism were secondary to this basic determining urge.

Britain looked at the Middle East problem logically, from the point of view of the war effort. And she expected the Jews of all people to support her without reserve, not to complicate the great conflict with outside elements, to subordinate to it their desire for Palestine and even their human concern for their fellow-Jews in Europe. It seemed to the British, even under Churchill, that some Jewish leaders were not doing this.

Instead of concentrating on winning the war, they were harping on about their own political aspirations and their own personal concerns. And this was absurd, even from their own point of view.

In the cool hands of the London decision-makers it made no sense to encourage or permit the flight from the Black Sea ports. Did the Jews not realize the likely military consequences of this traffic, cunningly engineered as it was by the Nazi authorities? How many Jews did they expect to save in this way? A few thousand, perhaps? A few dozen thousand at the most. And what would be the result, if not another Arab rebellion and an Arab alliance with Nazi Germany, followed inevitably by the expulsion of the British from Palestine and a massacre of the Yishuv. Was it worth risking such a calamity for the sake of ten thousand or twenty thousand pitiable individuals?

Such careful, emotionless calculation made little impression on the Zionist leaders and even less on their constituents, the Jews of Palestine and the United States. It seemed to them that their brothers were being callously sacrificed by men who had already broken their promises to build the Jewish national home. If the lives in question had been British, they surmised, London would have moved heaven and earth to save them. They did not believe in the Arab threat. The Arabs would not make trouble, because they were negligible militarily and tied to Britain politically.

Even if there were a few very broad-minded and politically conscious Jewish leaders who shared Britain's fears of Arab rebellion, who saw the problem involved in absorbing very large numbers of immigrants in wartime, there was still no way for them to fall in with Britain's wishes. They were politicians and their electors, the Yishuv, were in a state of despair and anger over the issue. Nor, one presumes, did they have the emotional power to keep silent at the sight of these few poor creatures who had managed to buy themselves out of Nazi Germany being man-handled by police and treated as criminals.

So it was that on January 24th, 1941, Weizmann wrote to Lloyd with very serious allegations against the police who had removed the *Atlantic* refugees from Athlit on December 9th and embarked them for Mauritius. According to three Jewish eye-witnesses, whose statements Weizmann attached, the police had acted with sadistic brutality: 'It was a fearful sight to see the women, half-naked, screaming, rolling in the dust and tearing their hair . . . British policemen who saw that scene laughed at them . . . After one company of police had entered one barrack, the terrible shrieks of beaten animals were heard coming from within . . . With each stroke that fell on naked flesh there went up the cry of a wounded animal . . . To every cry from those who were beaten, to every cry of despair, the reply was an outburst of laughter and jeering.'[55]

Shertok enclosed an emotional letter in which he claimed that the Athlit events were worse than anything that had ever happened in the history of the Yishuv, even under the Turks. The idea of a Jew being deported 'after it has been vouchsafed to him to set foot in the Promised Land' was likely to provoke 'masses of people from the Yishuv streaming to the scene of action, barricading roads and railways, and entering into a bloody struggle with the authorities'. 'Our blood boils when we listen to the baseness meted out to us,' he continued. Lloyd was advised that there was a chance of the Zionists spreading stories of British brutality over the United States. He asked MacMichael for an inquiry.

Saunders and his men were never confronted with the three unnamed Jewish eye-witnesses and in long point-by-point statements they denied all the allegations. 'You try to move a group of people who don't want to be moved. You have to use *some* force,' says one of the policemen involved. MacMichael reported that, once the refugees refused to move from their huts, once they started using 'the weapon of nudism' and 'dukhobor* tactics',[56] the police were entitled and obliged to use a certain degree of force in carrying out their orders.

The conflict of evidence, the anonymity of the Jewish witnesses and the demands of war did not allow for the sort of inquiry that would have established the whole truth, in particular whether or not excessive force was used by the police, so the Athlit scandal was never fully resolved. Weizmann told Lloyd that in his opinion the allegations were correct. This infuriated MacMichael, who retorted that Wiezmann's opinion was based on third-hand evidence, that Shertok's 'ululation' was based on second-hand evidence and that 'the Jewish picture of the Inspector-General of Police presiding with malicious enjoyment over a sadistic orgy of British brutality' was 'merely ridiculous'.

MacMichael took this opportunity of expressing some of the irritation that British officials were beginning to feel against the Jewish leaders: 'Here is the principle at stake. Has every Jew the right to come to Palestine? Has every Jew who can reach Palestine the right to remain there?' He advised Lord Moyne, who had now succeeded Lloyd as colonial secretary, that on this point the views of the government and the Jewish

---

* The dukhobors are a Russian religious sect, now resident mainly in Canada, well known for their resistance to all temporal authority and for demonstrating nude during their civil disobedience.

Agency were irreconcilable. But the Agency were entitled under the Mandate to a say in the administration of Palestine. They were, so to speak, 'imperium in imperio', an empire within an empire. For how long, MacMichael wondered, would Britain be prepared to stomach this situation 'and collaborate with a body which is openly determined to defy us, our policy and our laws'?

4
Nazi Invasion

MOYNE'S accession to the Colonial Office on February 4th, 1941, brought the Zionists two welcome changes. The first was the release on February 27th of Moshe Dayan and his forty-two Haganah colleagues.[1] Their talents would soon be required for important matters, it was assumed. The second was the departure of Malcolm MacDonald to Canada as high commissioner. MacDonald says: 'Churchill may have meant it as a demotion, but that wasn't the way he put it to me. He said that Prime Minister Mackenzie King had specially asked for me.' He was later to hold many senior administrative posts in the Empire and Commonwealth, but he never returned to political life.

Great was the Zionists' rejoicing at MacDonald's departure across the Atlantic. 'Sing the Song of Deborah,' said Walter Elliot to Baffy Dugdale. He was referring to the poem in Chapter Five of the Book of Judges which commemorates the defeat of the Canaanites and the driving of a tent peg by Jael through the skull of their leader Sisera: 'Praise ye the Lord for the avenging of Israel . . .'

This was also the period that marked the beginning of small-scale Jewish participation in the war. Churchill had always wanted the Jews to play this part and to defend their own settlements. The Foreign Office and War Office advised him of the great dangers of any such plan. He therefore decided to concentrate less on the idea of a formal Jewish army, which seemed fraught with political difficulties, and instead to make informal arrangements with the Haganah to train them for active service. All this would have to be done in secret through MI4, a branch of military intelligence, and through the well-known espionage body known as Special Operations Executive (SOE). The Palestine authorities could know nothing of these activities, since they were strongly opposed to the Haganah. Only a year earlier they had denounced it as a private army and imprisoned some of its members.

And so at the end of 1940 a strange threesome – Churchill's friend Arnold Lawrence (a professor of archaeology and brother of T. E. Lawrence), Nicholas Hammond (a university lecturer) and Henry Barnes (a cockney adventurer) – came to Palestine to launch the modern Jewish army from a small hotel, the Pension Wolstein, on Mount Carmel. They had a contact in the Jerusalem Secretariat, Colonel Shelley, who helped them communicate with SOE headquarters in Cairo, and another contact in Haifa docks, who helped them to bring in their equipment – Sten guns, hand-grenades and plastic explosives.

Hammond recalls: 'I knew nothing about soldiering in the beginning. I was a classics don. But Barnes taught me a lot and soon I was able to pass it on. We had a lot of new devices to teach them – plastic explosives, for instance. It had a very high detonating rate and you could direct the explosion by enclosing it with a thin plate around one side and thick plates around the rest. You could make a limpet mine no bigger than a bowler hat that would blow in the side of a ship. You needed the explosive, a container, a detonator and a timing device.'

Lawrence soon left the team. His sympathies, like his brother's, were with the Arabs and he was worried by the thought that the training he was providing might one day be used for purely Zionist objectives, against the Arabs and the British. But others came out from Britain and their three-week courses in kibbutzim (farm settlements) were soon a feature of the 1941 Palestine countryside. They were joined by a small team of Gaullists, who set up a radio station on Mount Carmel, sending propaganda into Vichy-controlled Syria, They were given three small ships, with which they planned to raid the Italian and Lebanese coast. 'We founded the Jewish navy,' says Hammond. They ran a training school, called 'ME 102', for Jewish secret agents whose native language was German to be dropped into Nazi Europe.

They also gained the trust of the Jewish Agency. Yigael Yadin, who became deputy prime minister of Israel in 1977, was then a member of the Supernumerary Police and the Haganah: 'These MI4 people were only interested in the war against Germany, not in any local problems. They didn't give a damn about British policy vis-à-vis the Jews. So both sides played a game. They knew that we were building up our arms reserves, that we were working for the Haganah as well as for them, and we knew that they knew it. But their objective was different from that of the main British authorities. And so they equipped literally thousands of people with money, knowledge, radios, weapons – all quite legally.'

The Haganah repaid these favours by providing SOE with valuable intelligence. For instance, they provided the linguistic expertise which the British conspicuously lacked. They could interrogate new arrivals from Poland, Romania and Germany not as foreigners but as fellow-Jews, and in their own language. Maps, documents, picture postcards and a mass of verbal testimony were collected in the Haganah's intelligence centre in Haifa, then delivered to SOE to help the war effort.

Aubrey Eban, because of his close contacts with both the Zionist leaders and the British establishment, became a link man between SOE and the Haganah: 'It was strange, because the basic policy was to disarm Jews, whereas here was a British organization trying to make them as armed and tough as possible. We were like an island, a watertight compartment. Jews would be picked up by the police for carrying arms and it would be my job to sort the imbroglio out. I would have to appear with my SOE identity card and explain that these were people allowed by SOE to carry arms. My SOE card could get them released.'

Another important go-between was David Hacohen. He recalls: 'The British knew that I was using my position to help the Haganah. They knew that I was helping illegal immigration.' They also connived at the Jewish recruits switching identities, in order to increase the numbers being trained. 'The numbers were constant, the people were not constant,' Eban remembers. And it was these same British officers who in May 1941 helped to found the Palmach – the 'crack forces' of the Haganah.

Yigal Allon was one of the early Palmach officers: 'I was a police sergeant, but I was also a company commander in the Haganah. So for the British I was a sergeant, for the Haganah I was an officer. The Palmach was recognized by the British to the extent that they gave me papers and permission to travel all over Palestine and even to Cairo. So I had the best of both worlds. I was independent of foreign authority, but at the same time I had the full backing of the British authorities.

'They also helped us to finance the Palmach, but if they gave us enough money for 500 people, we used it to pay about three times as many. We didn't pay proper wages, we just gave everybody their keep and a little pocket money. The British suspected that this was happening. Some of them were not so stupid. They kept seeing new faces arriving for training. But they were happy to cooperate with us. They trusted us and quite rightly so.'

The Palmach was soon in action. On April 6th, 1941, Germany invaded

Yugoslavia and Greece. The Greek army had fought bravely and successfully against Italy during the previous winter, but they could not with-
stand the German onslaught and, in spite of British reinforcements, they
surrendered on April 24th. British and Greek forces then fought a hard
and desperate battle for the possession of Crete, but at the end of May the
British were again forced to evacuate, again with heavy losses. By then
British intelligence had good reason to believe that the main body of the
German army was about to invade the Soviet Union. But Crete lies only
500 miles from the coast of Lebanon and Syria. British experts calculated
that a small German force might decide to occupy Syria with the consent
of the Vichy French authorities. They would then be poised to advance
through Iraq and Iran towards India. For Britain this would be a
catastrophe. She therefore decided to anticipate any such move on the
part of the German army by invading Syria and occupying its strategic
areas.

The Palmach was ready to help. Some members, often Jews from the
east who looked and spoke like Arabs, infiltrated Syria, carried out
sabotage and brought back information. On May 18th Major Anthony
Palmer set out in a small boat, the *Sea Lion*, with twenty-three young
Jews to destroy the oil refineries at Tripoli on the Lebanese coast. They
disappeared without trace, and to this day no one knows for sure what
happened to them. Other Palmach men, among them Moshe Dayan who
lost an eye in the fighting, acted as guides to the Allied forces – Australians,
British, Indians, Jews and Free French – who on June 8th began their
advance through the mountain passes to take Syria and Lebanon.

Yigal Allon led a small party of Jews across the Lebanese border,
captured a bridge over the River Litani and returned to Palestine with
four Vichy French prisoners. There Allon met a colonel in the 7th
Australian division: 'The colonel was very pleased with us and said he
would recommend us for decorations. We said that that was no good,
because we were not enlisted in the British forces, but could we share the
spoils of victory? He would take the prisoners and we would take their
arms. He agreed, gave us the arms and invited us to help ourselves from a
pile of other arms he had captured from the French. We loaded them into
a van, took them away, and used them against the British years later.'

Meanwhile Iraq was adding to Britain's anxiety about the Middle East.
Gone were the days of cosy pro-British rule under Prime Minister Nuri
es-Said and the Regent, Prince Abd ul-Illah. Doubts over Britain's
ability to continue the war and the restrictions of the British treaty had

led to the emergence of a discontented Iraqi army under four powerful colonels – the 'Golden Square'. Less and less were they inclined to fulfil British requests. At the end of January 1941, during a crisis which involved the resignation of Nuri from the foreign ministry and the Regent's temporary flight from Baghdad, the premiership passed from Rashid Ali el-Kilani to the weak Taha el-Hashimi.

That same month the Mufti of Jerusalem sent his secretary Osman Haddad to Berlin with a letter to Hitler, in which he repeated his sympathy with Nazi Germany and prophesied 'the well deserved defeat of the Anglo-Jewish coalition'.[2] He proposed a German-Arab alliance to achieve Arab independence, end the Jewish national home and solve 'the Jewish question' on a joint basis.

On February 28th Rashid Ali and a number of other prominent men met at the Mufti's house in Zahawi Street, Baghdad, to form a secret committee and break Iraq's close links with Britain.[3] Within a month they had obtained the support of most of the Iraqi army and were ready for a coup d'état, which on April 1st restored Rashid Ali to the premiership. Most of the pro-British faction escaped to Amman and the protection of Emir Abdullah of Transjordan.

The new Iraqi government took courage from the swift German conquests of Greece and Yugoslavia. Also, replying to the Mufti's letter, Germany recognized all Arab claims to independence and the common struggle against Britain and the Jews.[4] German tanks under Marshal Erwin Rommel advanced 400 miles from el-Agheila to the Egyptian frontier, taking Benghazi on the way and recovering all the territory that Wavell had won from Graziani in November. All this happened during April 1941.

Rashid Ali kept reassuring Britain that he meant her no harm, that his only aim was to preserve his country's independence and neutrality. But Britain knew about his dealings with Germany and Italy. She decided to strengthen her base at Basra in southern Iraq and, when Rashid Ali made difficulties, she went ahead with the reinforcement. Rashid Ali's reply was to send nine thousand men and fifty guns to attack the British air base at Habbaniya. On May 2nd fighting began, the Iraqis shelling the base and the British bombing the attackers.

For many of Britain's Arabists this was the nightmare that they had feared for years. By disregarding Arab feeling, especially over the Palestine issue, Britain had involved herself in conflict with an important Arab nation. Her only hope now was to negotiate her way out of the mess. Otherwise she would lose her whole Middle East position. Palestine officials reported that on the Prophet's birthday crowds had gathered to show their support for the Mufti, while those Arabs who had fought the Mufti were being threatened with the wrath to come as soon as he returned to Palestine at the head of the victorious Iraqi army.[5]

General Wavell, reporting to the War Cabinet, took the same pro-Arab line that he had over retaining the *Patria* survivors six months earlier: 'I feel it my duty to warn you in the gravest possible terms that I consider the prolongation of fighting in Iraq will seriously endanger the defence of Palestine and Egypt. The political repercussions will be incalculable and may result in what I have spent nearly two years trying to avoid, namely, serious internal trouble in our bases. I therefore urge again most strongly that a settlement should be negotiated as early as possible.'[6]

Churchill and his colleagues saw the situation differently. In their view, Rashid Ali had been hand-in-glove with Germany and Italy for months. His protestations of friendship were designed to buy time until help arrived from Germany and he was strong enough to act. Now that fighting had started, the dangers of hestitation were paramount. If Britain withdrew, Rashid Ali would ask for and receive immediate help from the enemy. Within a few days Syria and Iraq would be occupied. Britain's bases in Palestine and Egypt would be surrounded. They would never survive such a series of humiliating defeats.

Wavell was overruled and the British forces in Habbaniya were ordered to fight off the Iraqis, which they did with some success, raising the siege on May 7th. Churchill then ordered them to press forward. On May 11th Fritz Grobba, who had returned to Baghdad as German envoy, handed the Mufti a large sum of money and listened to his plans to launch 'a major action in Palestine very soon'.[7] The next day the Soviet Union, in one of the last and most bizarre acts of its pro-Nazi foreign policy, recognized Rashid Ali's government. A pogrom in Baghdad claimed the lives of some 150 Jews.

The Irgun appeared in the strange role of Britain's ally. Nicholas Hammond says: 'The Jews had a very good network in Iraq. We prepared explosive devices for them to plant in Rashid Ali's supply dumps.' Irgun commander David Raziel was invited by SOE to mount such an operation. He and his Tel Aviv commander Yaacov Meridor agreed to lead the party themselves, gather intelligence, destroy Baghdad's oil supplies and perhaps even kidnap the Mufti. In return, they hoped, Britain would give them arms, use them on operations and eventually grant some of their political wishes. On May 13th they flew to Habbaniya, but before they could proceed further towards Baghdad, Raziel was killed in his car by a bomb from a lone German aircraft. It was the end of the operation and of the Irgun's brief period of pro-British activity.

British forces converged on Baghdad from south and west. Minister Grobba pleaded for support and on May 23rd Hitler promised it, but his mind was concentrated on Russia, which he was due to invade a month later with no less than 164 army divisions – forces a dozen times stronger than those then in action in the Middle East. The British therefore took Baghdad by the end of May and restored their friends to power, the Mufti and Rashid Ali escaping to Mosul and then into Iran. Churchill writes: 'Hitler certainly cast away the opportunity of taking a great prize for little cost in the Middle East.'[8] 'German prestige will suffer for a long time,'[9] Grobba predicted. By her bold action in Iraq and Syria, Britain had recovered her dignity after the disasters of North Africa, Crete and the Balkans.

But it had been a near thing. Britain's puny forces had been stretched to the utmost. Against the advice of his commander-in-chief on the spot, Churchill had gambled that Hitler would not find it convenient to advance across Egypt or to reinforce the Iraqi and Vichy French armies during May or June. But what if the gamble had failed? The Mufti would have triumphed and the Arab world would have rallied to his side.

In Zionist eyes, Britain's victories had revealed the insignificance of Arab strength, the futility of her pro-Arab policy. But to most British officials the victories seemed little more than gambler's luck and an illustration of how precarious was Britain's position in that area. They merely strengthened the view that pro-British stability depended on the White Paper policy.

The fact that the Mufti had once again been defeated strengthened the general British view that the White Paper policy now stood a real chance of success. Three times the Mufti had escaped – from Jerusalem, Beirut and Baghdad – but now he was trapped in the Japanese embassy in Teheran, where he had taken refuge, and this time it really seemed that he would fall into British hands. Tom Dupree of the Foreign Office wrote of 'the fillip that our prestige would get if we caught the most elusive character of the age'.[10] Anthony Eden told the House of Commons that everything possible was being done to arrest the Mufti, who was regarded as the most dangerous anti-British agent in the East.

But then the question arose, if the Mufti was arrested, what was to be done with him? Should he be brought to Palestine and put on trial? If he was found guilty, should he be executed or merely exiled, say, to the Seychelles? Lord Moyne asked for MacMichael's advice on October 1st.

MacMichael's reply shows the extent of the nervous alarm which the name of Haj Amin al-Husseini aroused in official British minds, even at such a low point in his fortunes: 'In no circumstances whatever should the Mufti be brought to Palestine or its vicinity . . . It would be calamitous whether he was found guilty or not. In the former case he would be martyrized, even if not executed. In the latter case he would be triumphant. In either case the country would be rocked to its foundations . . .'[11] MacMichael suggested exile not to the Seychelles, because Arab notables had usually returned from the Seychelles, but to Mauritius, presumably to a part of the island far away from the Jewish refugee camp.

Britain never had to make this hard choice, because once again the Mufti showed himself master of the art of self-extrication. This time – the fourth time – he disguised himself as an Italian, left Teheran with the Italian community early in October, was taken to Rome, where he was promptly received by Mussolini,[12] and on November 6th arrived in Berlin, where three weeks later he was received by Hitler. Both men declared themselves in favour of Arab independence, against the British-Jewish coalition and their new Bolshevik allies.[13] (Hitler had invaded the Soviet Union on June 22nd.)

The Mufti told Hitler that he would recruit an Arab legion to fight for Germany. His word would produce 'a great number of volunteers eager for the fray' and would induce a widescale revolt against Britain. Hitler, perhaps realizing the limitations of the Mufti's influence after his defeat in Iraq, replied cautiously to requests for public German support. He assured him, though, that 'the hour of liberation had struck for the Arab world'. His armies were fighting in the Ukraine, had conquered huge areas of the Soviet Union and would soon reach the Caucasus, which was within striking distance of Iraq and Syria: 'The German aim would then be the entire annihilation of the Jews living in Arab territory under the protection of British power.'[14]

German broadcasts in Arabic highlighted the fact that Haj Amin had been received by the Führer. And the effect of the meeting was heightened by the murder in Baghdad a few days earlier (November 9th) of his old enemy Fakhri Bey Nashashibi, the moderate who had spoken out in favour of Britain's White Paper policy. The effect on the Palestine Arab community was electric. Again and again, it seemed, the British imperialists had come close to catching their leader, but always he had escaped them, and now, however far away he might be, the arm of his vengeance was long enough to destroy all those who betrayed the Arab cause by collaborating with Britain. One day he would return, if not with the Iraqi army, then with the German army, and that would be the day of reckoning for all Arab traitors, as well as for their British and Jewish friends. Few indeed was the number of Arabs who dared to show themselves publicly at the funeral of Fakhri Bey Nashashibi.

In fact, the 'British-Jewish coalition' was as tense as it had ever been since the proclamation of the White Paper. Military cooperation was still small-scale and unofficial. The promised Jewish contingent had been postponed for six months 'owing to lack of equipment'. On March 5th, 1941, Baffy Dugdale found Lewis Namier 'bitter beyond bearing'[15] after reading Weizmann's short letter from Moyne on the subject. The walls of Jericho had not fallen after all.

At recruiting centres for the British army Jewish stewards were refused permission to wear armbands in blue and white – their national colours. The armbands had to be red and white, the British ordered, or else they could not be worn at all. All mention of these activities, carried out by Jews for the British forces, was censored from the Palestine press. It was the same story as before. The Arabs would suspect that Britain was arming the Jews in order to turn Palestine into a Jewish state. At all costs Britain had to avoid giving this impression. But from the Jewish point of view it was a monstrous travesty of justice to deny them the right to take part in the war as a nation on the same basis as the Free French, Poles and Czechs.

British officials, on the other hand, were delighted to note that the dangerous idea of a Jewish army seemed to be dying a natural death. The decision to create it, one of them noted, had never been more than a sop to Weizmann from a Zionist prime minister. And after June 22nd, when Britain's efforts had suddenly to be diverted towards helping the Soviet Union, it became even more unrealistic. Britain was now relieved of the bombs and the fears of invasion, but she was now bound to devote every spare man and piece of equipment to the overriding needs of her new ally. 'Are the Jews so utterly unimportant as the treatment meted out to them suggests?'[16] Weizmann asked Churchill in September, by now almost in despair at the small attention that his great project was receiving.

The frank answer from most informed British officials and generals was that indeed the Jews were very unimportant – at least as far as winning the war was concerned. What really mattered to Britain and her allies in the last months of 1941 was the battle of Kiev, where 500,000 Red Army prisoners were taken, the siege of Leningrad, where in a few weeks more than a million civilians died of hunger, and the questions whether or not Moscow would fall, whether or not the American fleet would recover from the blow administered to it by Japan on December 6th, 1941, at Pearl Harbor.

The refugee question continued to sharpen the irritation. In April 1941 another boatload, about 750 from the *Darien*, had been detained in Haifa and interned in Athlit to await transport to Mauritius. 'They will be well treated and comfortably housed,'[17] noted Moyne in a Cabinet paper. But the Mauritius detainees, who saw their removal from Palestine as an injustice in itself, reported the opposite. The climate of Mauritius was dangerous for Europeans, husbands and wives were segregated, mail was delayed and people were dying of typhoid. Complaints poured in to the British embassy in Washington. Other complaints appeared in the American press.[18]

And therefore busy Foreign Office officials, who normally spend little time on complaints from unknown individuals, were ordered, because of the powerful political influence of American Jewry, to prepare full and detailed replies. Anthony Eden told Halifax in Washington that, in his opinion, the admission of the *Darien* passengers to Palestine 'would raise grave doubt in Arab minds' and 'would adversely affect our position in the Middle East'. Churchill happened to see the cable and scribbled in its margin: 'I think it all rubbish.'[19] But he did not press the matter further or make any attempt to reverse this cardinal Foreign Office belief. A proclaimed enemy of the 1939 White Paper, he nevertheless found it necessary to preside over the implementation of its detailed provisions.

Americans who inquired about the Mauritius detainees received re-assuring replies. The Jewish camp at Beau Bassin in Mauritius, they were told, was in one of the most pleasant spots in the island, surrounded by some sixty acres of gardens and parkland. There were sports fields, work-shops, schools, libraries, evening classes and swimming pools. A few refugees had died from disease, but only because of the wretched physical state in which they had arrived from Europe.

Whatever the truth about conditions in Beau Bassin, the fact is that American and Palestinian Jews believed that they were very bad and their relatives complained accordingly. One letter to Lord Halifax, which provoked much correspondence, accused the British authorities of 'sadism' and of 'running a refugee camp like a prison'. British officials reacted with growing anger to these allegations, which they considered rank ingratitude on the part of men and women who had found refuge from Nazi persecution on British territory and who were being maintained at British expense on a tropical island that was more like a luxury resort than a prison.

In short, British officials were beginning to find the Jews a serious diplomatic adversary. Again and again, it seemed, they spoke out in ways likely to damage the war effort. For instance, on March 28th, 1941, Weizmann told the New York press: 'Every Jew has the right to go to Palestine.' After the war, he said, 'we could absorb 2,000,000 to 2,500,000 in the course of 15 years.'[20] He rejected the idea of settling Jews in such 'exotic' places as the Dominican Republic, Madagascar or British Guiana, just as a year earlier he rejected Roosevelt's idea of settlement in countries 'such as Colombia'.[21]

These countries, the Zionist leaders believed, could provide only a temporary refuge for world Jewry, not a permanent solution. Indeed, as Ben Gurion wrote in his outline of Zionist policy of April 1941, Jewish settlement outside Palestine was a false solution. It was deceptive and harmful, because it merely perpetuated and aggravated the diaspora, where in the long term the Jews had no future. The only real solution was the settlement of Jews in Palestine 'on a vast scale' and 'as an independent nation'.

Ben Gurion pointed out that the Jews were a minority in every country where they lived. The Arabs, on the other hand, had many countries, large and underpopulated, which were entirely their own. The rapid growth of the Yishuv caused the Arabs no harm. On the contrary, it improved their position. Common justice therefore demanded 'the right of the Hebrew nation, like every other nation, to its own independent state'. This aim would therefore be pursued by all political means and would be helped by the Haganah, which was 'the backbone of the Yishuv, the instrument of the Zionist struggle and a force for achieving settlement'.

All this was anathema to Britain. Weizmann's statements, Ben Gurion's confidential memoranda – it all seemed calculated to inflame the Arabs and damage the war effort. The Zionists seemed to have got their priorities wrong. Why could they not forget, at least for a year or two, their dreams of massive Jewish immigration to Palestine? Did they not realize how dangerous such remarks were, the use that was made of them in Nazi radio broadcasts to the Arabs? And when they clamoured for Britain and the United States to save the persecuted Jews of Europe, what was their primary aim? Was it humanitarian – to protect those threatened with extermination? Or was it political – to build up a Jewish majority in Palestine?

On this question there was no doubt in the mind of High Commissioner

MacMichael. The main aim of all the Zionist campaigns, he wrote, was political. No doubt they genuinely wished to fight Nazi Germany and to save their European brethren, but their priority was 'to ensure that they will be sufficiently strong and united in will to dictate to His Majesty's Government'. If they could get enough men under arms, they might eventually secure a seat at the peace conference table after the war 'and nothing short of Palestine as a Jewish state will satisfy them'.[22]

The Jewish leaders also had to react, one must remember, to the pressure and anger of their constituents, and such was the situation of the Jewish people in Europe during 1941 that it would have been easier for Weizmann to steer a ship between Scylla and Charybdis than to satisfy the Yishuv as well as the British. The plan to herd millions of Jews into the Lublin reserve had withered away. After the fall of France, when the Nazi leaders expected Britain to make peace, they toyed with the idea of shipping four million Jews to the French colony of Madagascar, to live under SS control as hostages for the behaviour of their fellow Jews in the United States.

But Britain did not surrender. Germany did not gain control of the seas necessary for such a massive project. Instead, she turned her attention to the conquest of Russia, where the Jewish problem was to be solved by more simple means. On June 27th, five days after the invasion, several hundred Jews were burnt alive in the main synagogue at Bialystok. At the end of June seven thousand Jews were killed in Lvov. On October 29th the two thousand Jews of Taganrog were all taken to a ravine near the town and slaughtered. These are just a few haphazard acts of mass murder of Jews that happened during the early months of the Nazi occupation of the Soviet Union.

In Romania the situation of the Jews was no less wretched. In September 1940 King Carol had left his country to the rule of General Ion Antonescu, and in January 1941 the Iron Guards went on an anti-Jewish rampage. Frankling Gunther, the American minister in Bucharest, reported massive slaughters, with Jewish corpses exposed on butchers' hooks. It made him sick, he reported to Washington, to be accredited to a country where such things could be done by 'ignorant young savages'.[23] By February there were large numbers of German troops in the country and relations with Britain were broken. From then on Romanian Jews were treated by Britain as enemy aliens and as such were not eligible for entry to Palestine – this at a time when at home they were being murdered in large numbers, many of the atrocities being described in the Palestine press.[24]

It was under such circumstances that the *Struma* sailed from Constanza on December 12th, 1941, with a cargo of Romanian Jews. The voyage of the *Struma*, even though its details have never hitherto been fully recorded, is a well-known historical event in today's Israel, where it is remembered as one of the cruellest acts of the British authorities. It was mentioned by Menachem Begin in the first speech he made to the Knesset as prime minister in May 1977. It is depicted in Yad Vashem, Jerusalem's permanent memorial to the six million Jews exterminated during the Second World War, and thus officially labelled as a crime against the Jews comparable with those done by Nazi Germany.

The 769 *Struma* passengers, half of them women and children, spent 200,000 Romanian Lei (more than $1000) each for their places on a ship designed for no more than one hundred people. Just before she left Constanza, Romanian officials came on board and confiscated all the passengers' valuables and most of her provisions for the journey. The engines, which had been specially fitted, broke down shortly after departure and the ship had to crawl along the coastline, stopping several times for improvised repairs. Eventually she reached Kavak at the Black Sea entrance to the Bosphorus and was helped by a Turkish tugboat to the port of Istanbul, where she arrived during the morning of December 16th. She had taken four days to cover less than 250 miles.[25]

The *Struma* then became a problem for the Turkish government. She was obviously unseaworthy and the conditions on board were insanitary. As British legal experts had often pointed out, Turkey could therefore invoke the Montreux Convention and refuse her passage through the Dardanelles. But although her progress had been monitored in London, British ambassador Knatchbull-Hugessen was unaware of the political consequences of her arrival and he seems to have been ill-briefed when he came to discuss the problem at the Turkish Foreign Ministry on December 20th.

A Turkish official told Knatchbull-Hugessen that 'he himself was inclined to have her sent back to the Black Sea'. Otherwise, he said, she might sink in the Sea of Marmara and survivors would be left in Turkey, like the survivors of the *Salvador*. Would Britain therefore allow the Jews into Palestine? The ambassador replied that they could not go to Palestine, but 'that from the humanitarian point of view I did not like his proposal to send the ship back into the Black Sea'. He suggested that, if they reached Palestine, 'they might despite their illegality receive humane treatment'.[26]

The Colonial Office was incensed at Knatchbull-Hugessen's telegram.

This was the first time, noted Stephen Luke, that the Turkish government had shown any sign of being ready to help in frustrating illegal immigrant ships: 'And then the ambassador goes and spoils the whole effect on absurdly misjudged humanitarian grounds.' E. B. Boyd observed that Knatchbull-Hugessen had failed to make use of 'a heaven-sent opportunity of getting these people stopped at Istanbul and sent back to Constanza'.

Colonial Secretary Lord Moyne followed his officials' line in a powerful letter, in effect accusing the ambassador of condoning illegal traffic. Jewish immigration was already causing High Commissioner MacMichael great problems, he pointed out. The refugees from the *Darien* were still in Athlit, awaiting transport to Mauritius. The arrival of seven hundred more would add to these difficulties and 'will have a deplorable effect throughout the Balkans in encouraging further Jews to embark'. The traffic was encouraged by the Gestapo, said Moyne, and might be used to infiltrate Nazi agents.

Moyne was right in saying that Nazi Germany encouraged the refugee ships. As one American journalist had written, it was part of their strategy of refugee war 'to get rid of those they do not want to feed, squeeze as much as possible from them in the process and dump them where they will do the most harm'.[27] During 1940-41, before the decision to kill all Jews had been finally taken, advertisements could be seen in many Nazi-occupied countries, including Romania, offering immigration to Palestine, some claiming that Jews would be welcomed there by Britain, others admitting frankly that the immigration was illegal under Palestine law.

Where Moyne was wrong, though, was in insisting that this channel was being used to send Nazi agents. Richard Catling, a senior Palestine policeman specializing in Jewish affairs, confirms that not a single Nazi agent was ever discovered among the wartime refugees: 'An enemy agent would have been too conspicuous. He'd have been unmasked by the Jews themselves.' Early in 1941 the Colonial Office had been criticized by the Foreign Office over precisely this point, for misleading them into the belief that the shipments contained Nazi agents. Thomas Snow wrote: 'I cannot help feeling that we have been sailing a little close to the wind in several telegrams we have sent to the United States . . . Neither the authorities in Palestine or here know definitely that a single enemy agent has arrived in this way . . .'[28] Snow was concerned that, if Britain pursued this line, doubt would be cast on her good faith in America.

Moyne ignored these facts in his letter of complaint, which concluded: 'I find it difficult to write with moderation about this occurrence, which is in flat contradiction of established Government policy, and I shall be very glad if you could perhaps even now do something to retrieve the position and to urge that Turkish authorities should be asked to send the ship back to the Black Sea, as they originally proposed.'

The Foreign Office did not transmit Moyne's proposal to Ankara. Alec Randall scribbled on Moyne's letter: 'This illegal immigration business has many pitfalls for our American policy. We should risk serious repercussions if the Turks could say that we had formally requested them to send these unfortunate people back.' But by more careful handling of the situation, the same effect could be achieved. A cautious telegram was therefore sent to Knatchbull-Hugessen, asking him to make it clear to Turkey that the refugees could not enter Palestine, but not to suggest any particular course of action. The Turks had suggested sending the ship back and they would probably do this, so long as the ambassador did not interfere for or against the idea.

The *Struma* was an embarrassment to everyone. She had no cooking facilities and no fuel. The Jewish Relief Committee of Istanbul, the Turkish Red Cross and other bodies kept her supplied with food and water, but the passengers were cold, they were not allowed ashore and the conditions in which they lived were ripe for disease. Turkish officials explained to London that they were doing all they could. They had ordered the *Struma* to turn back, but her engines were now beyond repair, probably having been damaged by the passengers themselves. They had contacted various embassies in Ankara to find a country that would accept the refugees. No country was willing to do so. The Romanian embassy told Turkey, falsely, that the ship had left Romania illegally and would not be allowed to return.

Moyne made one concession. He persuaded MacMichael to accept the children from the *Struma*, those that were under sixteen, though not their parents. A few days later, on February 9th, 1942, Turkish Foreign Minister Sukru Saracoglu told the ambassador that 'as no alternative solution could be found, he would be forced to send the vessel and passengers back in the direction from which they came'. Knatchbull-Hugessen, under orders from London not to repeat his previous gaffe, replied: 'This was a matter in which it was quite impossible for His Majesty's Government to be of any assistance or to take any action. They had no means of doing so and the decision must rest with him.'[29]

A last desperate attempt to save the *Struma* passengers was then made by Anthony Eden's private secretary Oliver Harvey. It was very unusual, because secretaries do not as a rule take it upon themselves to initiate policy, especially policies that conflict with their superiors' known views. But Harvey was an unusual type of diplomat – left-of-centre politically, pro-Zionist, outspoken and emotional. On February 11th he drafted not a departmental minute, but a *cri de coeur*: 'Can nothing be done for these unfortunate refugees? Must HMG take such an inhuman decision? If they go back, they will all be killed.'[30]

The reactions to this outburst were, of course, coolly realistic. Alec Randall agreed that the refugees might be wrecked on the way back and that they were returning to 'very hard conditions'. But he then listed the problems of allowing the ship to proceed. If they went to Palestine, they would be an impossible burden for the High Commissioner and, 'what is perhaps worst of all, they will have succeeded in breaking through our policy'. The result would be many more ships and many more problems.

Interning the refugees in Athlit was expensive and risky. Transporting them to Mauritius was impossible. Ships were needed for the war effort, not for moving refugees. Room might be found for some of them in other parts of the Empire. Jamaica, for instance, had just taken two hundred Jews who had managed to escape from Poland to Portugal. British Guiana and Cyprus might take more, so long as the British government paid for their upkeep. But, Randall pointed out, it had to be remembered that the refugees were all enemy aliens, that their ship had set out under the enemy's auspices and that, if it was allowed through, it would be followed by many more.

Charles Baxter reacted even more strongly: 'If we were to accept these people, there would of course be more and more shiploads of unwanted Jews later!' But Harvey persisted, suggesting to Moyne's secretary, inaccurately, that Eden was deeply shocked by what was about to happen and suggesting to Eden, correctly, that 'the Prime Minister's heart had also been stirred by these latest telegrams'. He proposed diverting the *Struma* to Cyprus, even though the governor, after his experiences with the *Atlantic*, would want nothing to do with it.

'After all, these people are on our side,' continued Harvey on February 12th. Moyne's secretary replied that the children at least would be admitted to Palestine. Churchill's secretary had been so informed. 'This is at least something,' noted Harvey, apparently accepting that his efforts to save the whole shipload had failed and that their fate would be decided by Turkey. Britain, it seemed, would intervene only to accept the children.

But then doubts arose about the children too. Randall wrote: 'The process of selecting the children and taking them from their parents off the *Struma* would be an extremely distressing one. Who do you propose should undertake it?' And then on February 18th an even more serious difficulty arose. The British embassy in Ankara reported that Turkey would not allow the children to travel to Palestine overland. If a British ship was sent to Istanbul to collect them, they could be transferred to it. Otherwise they would have to stay on the *Struma*. There was no British ship available for this humanitarian task.

It has been suggested, incorrectly, that Britain's decision to admit the children reached Istanbul too late to be acted upon. In fact the decision was telephoned to the Jewish Agency on February 15th and raised with the Turkish authorities the next day. On February 20th Shertok wrote to Chief Secretary J. S. Macpherson thanking him for the decision over the children, but of course pleading for it to be extended to the rest of the *Struma* passengers, or at least some of them.[31] Several British officials noted that the Turkish decision to refuse transit facilities was unreasonable and they asked Knatchbull-Hugessen to try to have it reversed so that the children could travel overland to Palestine. But the Turks had by now lost patience with the *Struma* and her problems. On February 23rd they told the ambassador that she would be towed back into the Black Sea and cast adrift outside Turkish territorial waters.

No one knows exactly what happened to the *Struma* after this, whether she was torpedoed, whether she hit a mine or whether there was a bomb on board. All we know is that on February 24th, 1942, shortly after the Turkish tugboat left her and she was moving under her own steam about five miles from the entrance to the Bosphorus, there was an explosion and she sank very quickly. Lifeboats went out to her, but they recovered only one young man and one young woman – David Stoliar and Medea Salamovici. These two were admitted to Palestine 'as an act of clemency'.[32] The other 767 drowned in the Black Sea.

'We shall no doubt hear a good deal more about this most deplorable affair,' noted Randall as soon as he heard of the sinking. The news took two days to reach the Jews of Palestine. A few of them picked up a BBC radio broadcast about it, but because it was so sensitive and because it was unconfirmed, it was kept out of the press by the censors. For two days the Hebrew newspapers hinted at it by printing heavy black boxes with Biblical quotations about disasters at sea. Eventually, on February 26th, the news was confirmed and at once the Jewish elected body, the Vaad Leumi, declared a twelve-hour strike.

In the eyes of the Yishuv, Britain was responsible for the *Struma* deaths, just as she had been responsible for the *Patria* deaths. It was Britain who had slammed shut the gates of Palestine. If she had not, the refugees would have been saved. The Yishuv would have welcomed them as their own. They could have worked for Palestine and helped to fight the war. Instead, they had been turned back to the hell of Nazi Europe and had perished on the way. How could Britain do these things?

A token bomb was hung on the fence of Government House. Circulars in English and Hebrew proclaimed the barbarity of British rule. The most famous leaflet, a picture of MacMichael 'wanted for murder', is reproduced in this book. Other leaflets ordered Britain to hand the Mandate over to the United States. Dark hints of Jewish rebellion reached the ears of the Administration, arousing in British minds equally dark thoughts about the unreliable nature of Zionist loyalty to the war effort.

On March 1st a number of Jewish organizations held a meeting in New York's Capitol Hotel to mourn the dead and condemn British policy which, they said, violated every principle of justice and humanity. They resolved that Britain must share the guilt for the death of 'Jewish martyrs, seeking their rightful place in Palestine'. Britain had had the power to help and had refused to do so. High British officials in Palestine were using methods to be expected only from Hitler and his associates. The resolution was sent to Ambassador Halifax, who replied that he did not agree with it, but that he would forward it to London.[33]

The whole affair added to the conviction in most Jewish minds that it was only because they had no country of their own that their lives were being treated as something of little account. Only Eretz Israel had wanted to give sanctuary to the *Struma* refugees, and no other country, neither Britain nor the United States nor Turkey nor any of the countries that Turkey approached. Shertok wrote to Macpherson: 'Jews cannot possibly conceive that anything of the sort could have happened, if those fugitives had belonged to a nation which has a government, be it even one in exile, to stand up for them.'

In Britain the affair aroused not only apprehension at the damage it had done Britain's reputation in the United States, but genuine horror as well. It was reported widely in the press and discussed in Parliament. On March 5th the Cabinet decided that any Jews who reached Palestine 'should be treated with humanity', which meant keeping them in camps until they could be sent elsewhere. On March 11th Harold Macmillan, a deputy of Lord Cranborne, who had taken over the Colonial Office from Moyne on February 22nd, said in the House of Commons that Britain would do all she could to see that the *Struma* disaster did not recur.

But again it was Oliver Harvey who addressed himself most strongly to this crucial question. He heard that on March 17th another Romanian ship, the *Mihai*, had reached Istanbul with 1400 Jewish passengers. First of all he spoke to Cranborne's office and reported Cranborne's 'strong desire'[34] that Eden ask the Turks not to tow it back into the Black Sea. Eden noted his reluctant agreement. Then he cabled Knatchbull-Hugessen with instructions to tell the Turks, if they intended to turn the *Mihai* back, 'urgently to suspend such action'. Eden noted that this cable went beyond what he had reluctantly authorized. But the deed was done.

It turned out that the *Mihai* was a small yacht carrying fourteen Jews, not 1400, so it was allowed to sail on to Haifa. Its passengers and those from another small boat, the *Euxine*, joined the detainees in Athlit. MacMichael was told by London that illegal immigration would still be discouraged as far as possible, but that it was essential to avoid another *Struma* disaster. The atmosphere was very tense, he reported: 'I take the view that there is quite a likelihood of Jewish insurrection in Palestine unless some concession is made to them.'

But what concession was there that would not lead to a landslide? What was to be done with the refugees? For how much longer could they be kept in Athlit? Cranborne proposed establishing a temporary Jewish sanctuary in Eritrea, but his idea was quickly rejected. There were too many political problems and there were not enough ships. And so the torment of the Jews in Europe continued. The concern of the Jews of the United States was turning to anger, the anger of the Jews of Palestine to civil disobedience and violence. And Britain was held responsible.

The Arabs continued to feel that they were being treated like pawns in the great game. They knew only that they were physically weak, that powerful nations were at war, that if they interfered they would be brushed aside or crushed like insects. The White Paper was a reassurance, but great forces were at work that might turn it into yet another broken British promise. In their eyes, the Jewish refugees came not to seek sanctuary but to rob them of their entitlement. Every new arrival was another nail in the coffin of an independent Arab Palestine. And Britain was responsible.

For most British ministers and officials, preoccupied with aid to Russia, shocked at the sinking by Japanese aircraft of the two great ships *Repulse* and *Prince of Wales*, dismayed by the capture of Hong Kong, Malaya and Singapore, the Jewish refugees were simply an irritant. Randall noted: 'We may shortly have to face the choice between raising world Jewish opinion against us and trouble with the Arabs.'

It seemed so unfair. Britain was engaged in mortal combat against Nazi

Germany and Imperial Japan. Why should she be lumbered with other responsibilities, why should she divert valuable manpower and shipping from the war effort? Why should she be embarrassed and abused for refusing to give in to the blackmail of Nazi Germany's 'war by refugee'? She was fighting for her life. Why should she be expected to feed Romanian refugees and build camps for them in Eritrea? In what way would the expenditure of such efforts and funds help towards winning the war? And why was it automatically assumed that every humanitarian task was a British responsibility?

This irritation shows itself in many official British comments on the *Struma* disaster. On March 28th, 1942, for instance, when Oliver Harvey asked his foreign secretary to support the plan to house Jewish refugees in Eritrea, the latter replied coldly: 'No! I think that Lord Cranborne is going to land us with a big problem and that it would be more merciful in the end to turn these ships back.'[35]

It is to the Foreign Office's credit that this proposal by Anthony Eden, which ran along the same lines as his approach to the problem of Russian refugees in 1944–5, received little support at any level. The lesson had been learnt from the *Struma* horror, and no Jewish refugee ship was ever turned back again to Nazi Europe.

Confronted by Nazi Germany's ruthless exploitation of Jewish refugees for political and military gain, Britain had adopted, as is fitting in wartime, a policy of similar ruthlessness, of refusal to surrender to blackmail. But she now discovered, as a result of the *Struma* catastrophe, that she was unable to carry this ruthless policy through to its logical conclusion, that in a civilized country ruthlessness has its proper limit, even in wartime, and that this limit was passed when a boatload of Jewish refugees was sent back to a country under Nazi rule.

5
Partition and Terror

THE *Struma* affair brought Jewish anger against Britain to fever pitch. But simultaneously the British were becoming furious at what they saw as the destructive policies of the Jewish leaders and the criminal activity of a large part of the Yishuv. MacMichael's letters to London in 1941–2 show a growing irritation that reached its peak around the time of the *Struma* crisis. And this feeling was mirrored by those in the Foreign Office and Colonial Office who read his letters.

Britain was at war, a war to which she could see no clear victorious end. She was weak militarily, but strong internationally. She ruled an Empire, she led and largely answered for a group of Dominions, and her links with the United States were close. In other areas, the Middle East for instance, her influence was powerful, often dominant. In fact, she was a star on the international stage. And, such is the temperament that stardom induces, she resented the challenges of minor actors, particularly when those minor actors assumed airs that did not correspond with their modest station in life.

To British officials, brought up in such beliefs, the continual complaints and bickerings of the Jewish leaders, supported apparently by their American and Palestinian constituents, seemed grossly pretentious and offensive. In the many territories they governed they expected a certain deference from the local inhabitants. In most territories they received it. They therefore came to assume that they were entitled to it. But, whether relations were good or bad, they certainly never received it from the Jews of Palestine.

The relationship between the Yishuv and their supposed British masters is amusingly summed up by David Hacohen: 'I had a lot to do with the top British officials as director of Solel Boneh. Undoubtedly they were decent people, with very few exceptions. But there was one psychological problem that affected them. They came from different places – India, Gold Coast, Nigeria, Ceylon, Malaya – and they had never met natives of our sort. The best doctors in the country were Jews. The best architects were Jews. I remember sometimes I'd get a government building project and I'd send it straight back and I'd say, "Look, your plan is no bloody good!" And the next day I'd send him the corrections, worked out by *our* architects.

'We paid taxes, but we never went to the government schools. We went to our own schools, paid for with the money we collected from Jewry. The Weizmann Institute and the University belonged to us. The place belonged to us. There were more English books in our houses than in their houses. Most of the local British administrators didn't read serious books. They read detective stories.

'There was a very select British club in Haifa. I remember the chief engineer of the Palestine railways, Scrivener by name, saying to me, "Now look here, Hacohen, we want to get a few Jews and Arabs into the club and people are suggesting you." I said, "What the hell do I want to join your club for?" He said, "We meet for a club lunch every Wednesday." I said, "What's wrong with my wife's cooking on Wednesday?" I simply had no interest in joining his club.

'All this was pressure on them. They couldn't come to terms with us. I don't say that there were not such people in India, but in Palestine it was the whole mass of the Jewish *halutzim*, the young pioneers, who had come to the country from good European schools and universities, having made a conscious decision to become hewers of wood and drawers of water.'

Robert Scott, a senior political officer with the Secretariat, listed a series of British complaints in an eloquent document in October 1941. His main point was that the Yishuv were meant to be subject to British rule. Instead, they behaved as if they were an independent nation. The Jewish Agency was meant to be a purely advisory body: 'The Agency is bound by the terms of the Mandate and indeed by any canons applicable to government to cooperate with the local government. In fact they oppose it.'[1]

Scott recalls, for instance, Ben Gurion's statement to the press of May 12th, 1939: 'We obey a higher moral law, which overrides the authority of Britain when she acts contrary thereto.' Scott's report may be summarized as follows. The Jewish leaders admit that the Haganah is illegal, that the arms they hold are illegal. They dispute the illegality of unauthorized Jewish immigration. Under their interpretation of the Mandate, every Jew is entitled to enter Palestine and the illegality is in the British immigration laws. But in the final analysis these questions are no more than technicalities. They appeal to a higher law. The right to self-defence and the right to give persecuted Jews shelter in the Land of Israel are not, in their opinion, matters on which Britain is entitled to legislate.

In fact, the Yishuv is governed not by Britain, but by a network of Jewish organizations, some open and established, others secret and illegal. The Histadrut has, 'by an adroit policy of strikes, to bend employers to its will, and violence against the labourers of other organizations', achieved a virtual monopoly of the labour market. Its welfare benefits include a sick fund as well as housing, bank and insurance schemes. The admirable features of this work 'need not obscure the fact that they make the worker utterly dependent on the Histadrut for his well-being'.

Jewish discipline is equally tight in imposing unofficial taxation. Contributions to the two main Jewish treasuries, Kofer Hayishuv and Mas Cherum, were once voluntary, but now every Jew is assessed on his means by a local committee and required to pay regular sums. Sometimes the Haganah have acted as tax gatherers and have taken stern measures against 'refusers', beginning with economic boycott and social ostracism, ending with destruction of property and death threats. A Jewish business organization complains: 'During November and December, 1940, five Jews of means in Haifa were visited by persons representing themselves to be collectors from Mas Cherum . . . None of the five men paid the sum demanded and on January 11th a bomb was exploded on the doorstep of each.'

Scott describes how the Haganah, numbering about 100,000 men and women, have not in general stooped to 'mean and murderous terrorism' but 'they remain a secret army whose leaders are in a position to sway public policy and private arguments by the threat of force'. Nor can they always control their extremist elements. In February 1940, for instance, thirty-eight Arabs were killed by the Hatkouma, one of their offshoots, and although the responsible Jewish leaders disapproved of such reprisal action they did not condemn it publicly. In short, although there is a credit side to the Haganah, their general conduct 'affords not the slightest justification for their existence'.

Scott explains that the unofficial groups, of course, are a different story. The Irgun Zvai Leumi has never been reticent about its aims and actions.

They take their inspiration from the passage in the Book of Exodus, where Moses slew the Egyptian and hid him in the sand. Their martyrs are such men as Yaacov Raz, who was killed trying to plant 'a particularly loathsome timebomb' in an Arab market, and Ben-Yosef, hanged for firing on an Arab bus. Their own pamphlets boast of the indiscriminate killing of Arabs, listed day by day, and go on to claim that the murderers are 'those who saved the honour of Israel', that their acts 'were fighting acts of persons who believe that the Jewish kingdom will be created by force, after having overpowered the Arab enemy in the battle'.

The Irgun cannot be dismissed as mere criminals. They feel that they are heirs to a great tradition, predestined to create the Kingdom of God in Israel: 'They remember that Joshua hanged the five kings on five trees, that Absolom murdered Amnon after two full years because he forced his sister Tamar. They remember Judith who murdered Holofernes and Esther who had Haman, the Jews' enemy, hanged.' It is this meretricious claim to represent the Jewish past that appeals most to the Irgun's five to eight thousand members, attracting the loyalty of a minority of the Yishuv, especially young people, bored by the laboured political science of orthodox Zionism, and winning the unwilling respect of many others, who nevertheless reject it because of its brutal methods.

It was Scott's report, summarized above, that MacMichael submitted to Moyne in support of his view that Britain faced 'as grave a danger in Palestine from Jewish violence as it has ever faced from Arab violence'. And any such rebellion, he warned, could not be put down by the 'methods of repression' used against the Arabs in the late 1930s. In the first place, unlike the Arabs, the Jews of Palestine enjoyed great moral and political support in Britain and the United States. Their political ability would help them to blur the issue and keep this support, even if they took up arms against Britain. Secondly, the Jewish rebels would be a more formidable enemy than the Arabs had been. Large numbers were armed and had received military training. They were disciplined and highly motivated. And they believed that their cause was just.

Jewish discipline, MacMichael went on, had turned the community into a 'closed oligarchy'. And, however admirable such a strong civil loyalty might appear from a certain point of view, there was a point beyond which national discipline left the democratic world and joined that of the totalitarian enemy: 'Those who direct Zionist policy ignore everything that is not consistent with their own ideals and plans. And to realize these ideals and plans they adopt dangerous means and measures. As matters now stand it seems to me inevitable that the Zionist juggernaut, which has been created with such intensity of zeal for a Jewish national state, will be the cause of very serious trouble in the Near East.'

The Jews would never revolt. This had been an axiom of British policy since 1938. Britain was their main ally, since mid-1940 their only ally, in the life-and-death struggle against Hitler. Of course they hated Britain's Palestine policy. They might complain to the authorities in Whitehall and the Jerusalem Secretariat. They might make extravagant speeches in their various assemblies and fill their newspapers with emotional diatribes. They might strike, but only for a day or two. They might protest in the street, but with a minimum of violence. They might – and it was only this that Britain really feared – agitate among the American Jews.

But the idea of their using violence against the British authorities was absurd. Weizmann had declared that it was repugnant to the Yishuv and Britain did not even take it into consideration when forming her policies. But now, at the end of 1941, High Commissioner MacMichael was advising London that the prospect of Jewish violence was a 'grave danger'.

True, the Haganah and Palmach were helping the British war effort in various ways, but by Britain's choice this help was unofficial, almost secret. And the Haganah too was playing a double game. As well as helping Britain, it was disobeying Britain by training more men and women than was permissible and, more importantly, by acquiring illegal arms, sometimes with the connivance of SOE and the 'unofficial' British military, sometimes simply by stealing them from British arms dumps or 'buying' them from British soldiers. In short, the Haganah was friendly vis-à-vis the war, but an irritant vis-à-vis Middle East policy and a potential threat.

The Irgun was quiescent. Its members still obeyed the decision taken by David Raziel to be helpful to Britain. They continued their propaganda. They used violence against Arabs as part of their policy of counter-terror and occasionally against Jews, in order to extort money, but not against the British. But there was one group, a small breakaway faction of the Irgun, ready even at this crucial stage in the war to use methods of terror against the British authorities. Known as Lohamei Herut Israel or 'Lehi' (the Fighters for the Freedom of Israel), they were led by a man by whose name they were usually known – Abraham Stern.

A hundred or two young men and women, mainly from Eastern Europe, students of Russian history, Lehi accepted personal terror and assassination as an effective and morally justifiable means of achieving a political aim, admiring particularly such groups as the Russian 'People's

Will' movement, which assassinated Alexander II in 1881, and the Irish Republican Army.

Nathan Yalin-Mor, who reached Palestine from Lithuania in January 1941 and was soon among the Lehi leadership, explains why at that time they hated Britain even more than they hated Nazi Germany: 'We had to distinguish between an enemy and an arch-enemy. In the Book of Esther there was Haman, who wanted to kill all the Jews of Persia. He is an enemy, because he killed our people. But the arch-enemy is the Roman emperor Titus, because he destroyed Jewish sovereignty. We considered that Britain was playing the role of Titus in our age. Also we saw that Britain was in difficulties and, like the Irish Republicans, we believed that this was our opportunity. It made it all the more important to fight Britain and make her give in to our demands.'

Stern therefore conceived the bizarre idea of working with the enemy, Germany and Italy, against the arch-enemy. He sent his representative Naftali Lubentchik to Beirut and presented German agents there with a plan to send shiploads of Jews from Italy to Palestine. Itzhak Shamir recalls: 'I was against making approaches to Italy. I didn't think it would do any good. But Stern had good memories of his work in Poland before the war. He had got many Jews to Palestine by exploiting the anti-semitism of Polish officials. He thought it might work in Italy. At least he felt he had to try.' Stern thought that the idea might appeal to the Nazis. It would rid them of their 'Jewish problem' and at the same time embarrass Britain.

Stern's ambitious plan disgusted almost the whole of the Yishuv. Lubentchik was arrested, probably through a tipoff from Israel Pritzkier, an Irgun double agent. Richard Catling confirms that during 1941–2 several Irgun men gave him information about Lehi. Yalin-Mor says: 'After our split with the Irgun hard feelings grew up. And hard feelings between comrades-in-arms can be worse than between enemies.' In January 1942 he too was arrested by the British military mission in Syria, while on his way to discuss Stern's plan with 'various contacts in the Balkans'.

The moral level of Lehi, Robert Scott wrote, was that 'on which guys are merely bumped off, rubbed out or put on the spot'. In fact, in spite of their tortuous plots and the sheer brutality of their operations, they were not gangsters, but a highly motivated ideological group. They dealt in bullets, but they also dealt in ideas, and these ideas they distributed in leaflet or newspaper form to a largely sceptical and hostile Yishuv. Geula Cohen, now a well-known member of the Knesset, was then a teenager:

'I usually went about with a young man as a cover, so we looked like a boy and his girl friend. Our job was to stick up posters and hand out leaflets.' The posters urged Jews to fight the arch-enemy and to refrain from taking part in the 'imperialist war'. Their propaganda was close to that of the Communist party before the June 1941 German invasion of Russia.

On January 9th, 1942, two Lehi men, Yehoshua Becker and Nissim Reuven, were arrested after robbing a bank and shooting dead two Jewish cashiers. On January 20th a Lehi bomb at 8 Yael Street in Tel Aviv killed two Jewish policemen, Solomon Schiff and Nahum Goldman. Bobby Lustig says: 'After that there was a lot of ill-feeling against the Stern group among Jewish policemen and there were probably some who gave information to the British about them.' After one such tipoff Geoffrey Morton, the British policeman in charge of the case, led a party to 30 Dizengoff Street and discovered four Lehi leaders. Avraham Amper and Zelig Jacques were shot dead. Moshe Svorai and the Lehi technical expert Yaakov Levstein were arrested, Svorai after being shot by Morton trying to escape through a lavatory window down a drainpipe.

On January 21st the German offensive in Libya began. On January 28th German forces retook Benghazi. Morton says: 'It was a very critical time in the war. We were fighting with our backs to the wall, not only to protect ourselves and Britain's strategic position, but also to protect the lives of the Jews of Palestine. Lehi terrorism and constant Haganah arms thieving meant that thousands of British soldiers were tied down in Palestine, when they could have been better employed fighting the Germans in the Western Desert.'

The Yishuv as a whole would not have agreed with Morton's indictment of Haganah arms acquisition. They saw this as essential to their self-defence. But in early 1942 they rejected Lehi as strongly as the British did. On January 30th the pro-Jewish Agency *Palestine Post* called on 'the whole population to put a stop to such unprecedented crimes'. A reward of £1000 was put on Stern's head. His photograph was displayed on walls and in the press. No one would shelter him. Eventually, in spite of the obvious risk, he hid out in an attic belonging to Moshe and Tova Svorai at 8 Mizrachi B Street, Tel Aviv.

The British record reads: 'Information leading to the tracking down of Stern was cleverly obtained by police through secret censorship of notes smuggled out of Jaffa hospital by two wounded members of the gang.'[2] Lustig says that Svorai persuaded a British policeman, Sergeant Stow, to take his wife a letter, which indicated that there was someone else in the apartment. Morton writes that the actual address where Tova Svorai and Stern were staying was whispered by Moshe Svorai to Levstein's mother during a hospital visit and overheard by the guard on the door.

What happened next has been the subject of much controversy and several lawsuits. Everyone agrees that a party of British and Jewish policemen – including Geoffrey Morton, Tom Wilkin, Bobby Lustig, Bernard Stamp and Alec Ternent – descended on the apartment and arrested Tova Svorai, and that they then searched the apartment and found Stern hiding in a cupboard. Lustig was sent out to find a wardress. Wilkin went to see a Jewish friend, Itzhak Berman. Four men stayed in the room: Stern, Morton, Ternent and Stamp.

Morton writes: 'He [Stern] was taken out and, while he was bending down to tie his shoelaces prior to being taken to headquarters, he suddenly dived under the gun of the policeman who was covering him and made a mad rush towards the open window leading on to the flat roof . . . Stern could not possibly have got away, for the house was surrounded and he knew it. What, then, was his object? I could only conclude that he had some infernal machine rigged up and that he was making a desperate attempt to reach it. None of the police in the room could get to the window before him. So, in order to prevent another shambles, I shot him dead.'[3]

Inquests returned verdicts of justifiable homicide in the cases of Stern and the two men shot at 30 Dizengoff Street. The British record states that Stern was 'shot dead whilst attempting to escape'.[4] Morton says: 'I dislike the term "shot trying to escape" both because of its inaccuracy in relation to the death of Stern and because of its emotive and Nazi-like connotations.' He maintains that Stern had in the past threatened, if ever he was faced with capture, to blow up himself and the police: 'So when he dived for the window, I shot him. Full stop.' He has won three libel actions in England against publishers of books that have suggested otherwise.

But the fact that Stern was shot while in police custody aroused sympathy for him among many Jews who had previously condemned him and gave fuel to already widespread rumours about high-handed police behaviour. It helped to build a myth around Stern, to project him as a hero killed fighting for his country.

Not every Israeli today accepts this glamorized view of the Lehi leader. Bernard Joseph says: 'Stern's ideas were totally crazy. It's true that he was an idealist, but an idealist with a kink. If he'd been tried for murder and executed according to law, he wouldn't be commemorated now as a martyr. His reputation depends a lot on the way in which he met his end.'

Efraim Dekel, then head of Haganah intelligence ('Shai'), says: 'It was not a very good way for a leader of a guerrilla group to die, being dragged out of a cupboard. He could at least have shot his way out, taken one of the policemen with him, died like a hero. He was more of a poet than a fighter.'

But former Irgun and Lehi members, many of whom joined the Israeli government in 1977, see Stern as an inspiring force in the fighting underground that eventually drove Britain out of Palestine, a martyr who perished in the struggle for Jewish nationhood.

Lehi vowed to avenge their leader's death. Morton had to go about with three police bodyguards, all crack shots. On May 1st, 1942, he and his wife were driving from his house in Sarona to Jaffa when a landmine, triggered some distance away, exploded near the car. Morton says: 'They must have set it off a second or two early. My wife and I were not badly hurt. They were so sure that they were going to kill us that they had two more landmines buried at the cemetery on Mount Zion, ready for our funeral, which I expect would have been quite a posh affair, with a lot of senior British officials.'

On February 17th MacMichael reported that most of the main members of the gang, about eighty people in all, were under arrest. But what was to be done with them? Steven Luke of the Secretariat noted that ordinary court machinery could not be used. There was not enough evidence to convict them of complicity in murder and there would be no Jewish witnesses to help such prosecutions. The only alternative was to keep them in Masra and Latrun camps, where they were always liable to break out and become once again a menace to security.

Yehoshua Becker and Nissim Reuven were convicted of murder. But then they were reprieved, much to the disgust of the British police, who could not understand why Jewish criminals always seemed to gain the sympathy of the Yishuv as soon as they were condemned to death. Morton says: 'In those days possessing firearms was punishable by death, even if you didn't kill anybody. But this was murder in the course of a major felony. If they'd been Arabs, of course they'd have been hanged. More than a hundred Arabs were hanged during the revolt. But the Jewish community applied political pressure. It made us in the police very angry.'

Lehi had surfaced with a flurry of violence, succeeding, it seemed, only in discrediting themselves and getting themselves arrested or shot. But they believe that these events, especially the death of Stern, strengthened their ideological resolve. Yalin-Mor says: 'Morton helped us in a way. He destroyed our illusions. He brought us to the Rubicon, made us realize, as Julius Caesar said, that the die was cast.' The incidents had also for the first time shown the Jewish community the effectiveness of urban guerrilla warfare.

It was a taste of what might be in store for Britain if MacMichael's predictions of revolt materialized. On February 23rd Steven Luke noted: 'The underlying spirit of the Jewish community in Palestine has changed profoundly in recent years as the result of the disturbances of 1936–39 and the publication of the White Paper. There is undoubtedly even among the most pacific and liberal Jews in Palestine a tendency to feel that they cannot hope to achieve the ends of Zionist policy by evolutionary constitutional means. They argue (however falsely it does not matter) that the Arabs' resort to arms in 1936–39 drove the British government to concede their demands and that some such resort to direct action by the Jews may ultimately become necessary.'[5]

As Rommel's armies advanced across the desert, Britain now faced yet another crisis, this time in Egypt. As had happened in Iraq a year earlier, the pro-British political leaders were being undermined by German military success and by the natural resentments that arise whenever a country's affairs are largely under foreign control. Ambassador Miles Lampson, the 'high priest' of Britain's pro-Arabists, was on bad terms with the twenty-two-year-old King Farouk, who, he claimed, had surrounded himself with a group of 'palace Italians', all enemies of the Anglo-Egyptian Treaty of 1936 – another of the unequal agreements on which British power in the Middle East was based.

Matters came to a head on January 26th, 1942, when Lampson discovered that Farouk was proposing to dismiss Salib Samy, the pro-British minister of foreign affairs. It seemed to Britain that Farouk was preparing for the enemy's arrival. Anti-British student riots, which the King did nothing to stop, occurred regularly. Britain decided that her prestige and position in Egypt would not allow the sacrifice of such an important friend as Salib Samy, that his removal would be inconsistent with Article Five of the Treaty of Alliance, which forbade association with either country's enemies. Unless she acted, her position would slip away and her base of operations against Rommel would be weakened.

She therefore decided to dispose of the problem by sharp military action, just as she had disposed of the less-than-friendly governments of Syria, Iraq and Iran the previous summer. Lampson believed that in this case Britain would not have to use actual force, only a show of it. He quickly prepared a masterpiece of intimidatory diplomacy.

On February 4th Lampson sent Farouk an ultimatum, requiring him to replace Prime Minister Hussein Sirri with Nahas Pasha, who had signed the 1936 Treaty in London. He resolved that, unless he received a satisfactory reply from Farouk by 6 o'clock that evening, he would insist on an audience at 8 o'clock, at which he would be accompanied by his commander-in-chief Lieutenant-General Robert Stone and that 'necessary military dispositions would have been made meantime'. Farouk received the ultimatum, consulted his advisers and sent Lampson a reply rejecting it as 'a great infringement of the Anglo-Egyptian Treaty and of the independence of the country'.

Lampson's audience with the King took place, as he records, in most dramatic circumstances: 'At 9 p.m. I arrived at the palace accompanied by General Stone and an impressive array of specially picked stalwart military officers armed to the teeth. On the way we passed through lines of military transport looming up through the darkened streets on their way to take up their positions round the palace. I could see by the startled expression of the Court Chamberlain who received me at the palace entrance that this imposing arrival registered an immediate preliminary effect. Whilst we waited upstairs I could hear the rumble of tanks and armoured cars taking up their positions around the palace.'

Lampson entered the King's presence, with General Stone, and went straight to business, reading aloud what must be one of the most amazing documents ever presented by an ambassador to a ruling monarch: 'It has for long past been evident that Your Majesty has been influenced by advisers who were not only unfaithful to the Alliance with Great Britain but were actually working against it and thereby assisting the enemy . . . Your Majesty has moreover wantonly and unnecessarily provoked a crisis . . . Finally, having failed to secure a coalition government, Your Majesty has refused to entrust government to the leading political party . . . Such recklessness and irresponsibility on the part of the sovereign endanger the security of Egypt and of the Allied forces. They make it clear that Your Majesty is no longer fit to occupy the throne.'

Lampson thereupon handed Farouk an instrument of abdication, telling him that, unless he signed it, he would have 'something else and more unpleasant with which to confront him'. Completely cowed, Farouk asked Lampson to give him one more chance. He would summon Nahas Pasha immediately and invite him to form a government of his own choosing. As this was the original British demand, Lampson knew that he was bound to agree, but he paused, feigning reluctance and, by his own account, enjoying the King's humiliation. Eventually he assented and made a triumphant withdrawal 'through passages filled with British officers and court chamberlains, the latter a crowd of scared hens'.

Back at his embassy, Lampson was quickly telephoned by a chamberlain with the tragi-comic complaint that British tanks were blocking Nahas's way to the palace. The ambassador graciously arranged for a way to be cleared and a few minutes later, at the King's request, Nahas visited him as prime minister, promising to get rid of 'the evil elements both in the palace and outside'[6] and to form a pro-British government, after which they would have a serious business talk.

The ambassador's triumph and the King's surrender were thus complete. Britain, hard pressed in mortal combat, had by resolute action restored yet another crumbling corner of her Middle East bastion. But the way in which she did it was, as in Iran, bitterly resented not only by the King and his pro-Axis entourage, but also large numbers of ordinary people who felt their country humiliated.

The Zionist leaders were delighted to note the ease with which Lampson disposed of King Farouk. It seemed to confirm what they had said all along, that Britain had nothing to fear from Arab hostility, that Arab rebellion was a mirage, Arab military might a mere façade. What would have happened, Golda Meir asks, if Britain had made it clear to the Arabs that the White Paper was suspended until after the war? Arab leaders would have made threatening speeches, there might have been protest marches, but nothing much else. Samuel Katz, one of Menachem Begin's senior advisers, regards British fears of Arab violence in 1942 as 'plain poppycock' and 'a good story for kindergartens'.[7]

Churchill's view was much the same, but although he expressed it from time to time in his personal memoranda, he was still not ready to reverse the main stream of British policy, born of the Arab revolt in Palestine and encapsulated in the White Paper. The view of the majority was still that Britain's armed forces alone could not maintain her position. She also needed a measure of political support from 'moderate' Arab leaders. And time and again these leaders had made it clear that without the White Paper they would be swept away. Anti-British resentment would turn to hatred and, whatever the British army did, violence in the streets and hills would become a constant threat to her bases.

The mass murder of Jews in Europe was gathering momentum. At the time of his invasion of Russia (June 1941) Hitler coupled Jews with communists as the two categories of the Soviet population due for instant destruction. The regular German army, advancing across Russia, was followed by *Einsatzgruppen*, whose task it was to root out the two groups and kill them. Modern Jewish studies of the period emphasize the terrible fact that these murder squads usually found members of the local population who, in return for reward, helped them to find Jews and distinguish them from others. Exact figures are not available – the Soviet government avoids discussion of the special wartime sufferings of the Jews – but some sources suggest that as many as ninety per cent of the Jews from occupied Soviet cities were dead by the winter of 1941–2.[8]

The most famous of these incidents, now something of a legend in Russia, was at Babi Yar, a cliff-edge near Kiev, where 34,000 Jews were murdered by *Einsatzgruppen* at the end of September 1941. But this quasi-military method of destruction was not efficient. Substantial forces were needed to surround a ghetto and massacre its inhabitants, to round up several thousand Jews of all ages and both sexes, herd them out of town to some convenient field or gully, shoot them and bury their bodies in pits, as happened in Smolensk, Vinnitsa, Vitebsk, Poltava and countless other towns.

By the end of 1941, at a camp near Chelmno, a method was introduced of locking Jews in the back of vans and gassing them with carbon monoxide exhaust fumes. But the troops complained because of the disgusting nature of the work in clearing up the bodies and their dirt. The conventional method of shooting the victims also aroused resentment, because it involved *Einsatzgruppen* being attached to regular army units, and the latter viewed the former with distaste and fear.

On January 20th, 1942, in the Berlin suburb of Wannsee, Reinhard Heydrich explained to a group of senior ss-men that the time had come to begin the Final Solution of the Jewish problem. Of the 250,000 Jews living in the Germany of 1939, he said, about half had been killed, but there remained no less than eleven million in Europe – five million in Russia, three million in the Ukraine, two and a quarter million in Poland, three quarters of a million in France and a third of a million in Britain.

In due course all of these would have to be brought to camps in the East and put to hard labour 'in which task undoubtedly a great part will fall through natural diminution'. The survivors would be the toughest. Therefore these 'must be treated accordingly' to prevent their becoming 'the germ cell of a new Jewish development'.[9] In short, it would be necessary eventually to kill all eleven million of them. For this great task quicker and more efficient methods would have to be devised than were presently available.

Therefore in 1942, for the first time, camps were built with the aim not of confining Jews and exploiting their labour, but of exterminating them. In March the first camp equipped with lethal gas chambers was brought into operation at Belzec, eighty miles south-east of Lublin. By the following spring more than half a million Polish Jews had met their deaths in this camp alone. Other camps at Sobibor, Treblinka and Majdanek were 'converted' to the business of extermination, as was part of the huge Auschwitz complex, which began as a labour camp for non-Jewish political prisoners and was eventually capable of killing tens of thousands daily.[10]

Other authors have described this diabolical operation in great detail. It is enough to record, for the purposes of this account, that while the three main Allies were preoccupied with the great military events of 1942 – Rommel's offensive across Libya in May, the main Germany army's advance across the Ukraine to Rostov in June and July, the Japanese conquest of Burma – the Jews of Palestine were concerned more by the news of the destruction of European Jewry. It was with these thoughts uppermost in their minds that on April 11th a Zionist conference at the Biltmore Hotel in New York passed a resolution demanding the establishment of a Jewish state in the whole of Palestine. British officials, on the other hand, thought it most dangerous and inappropriate for Jewish bodies to make extravagant claims for sovereignty at such a time.

On June 30th Rommel reached el-Alamein, only 150 miles from Cairo and 60 miles from Alexandria. He was also, incidentally, only 500 miles by road from Tel Aviv. At this point, with German forces converging on Palestine from the Sahara and the Ukraine in a huge pincer movement, Abba Eban's work as liaison officer between the Haganah and the 'unofficial' British assumed a new and terrible significance, forcing both teams to plan for the eventuality of the fall of Egypt and occupation of Palestine. The British position was weak, the Jewish position on the brink of disaster. For a brief historical moment the two sides needed each other again.

Hammond says: 'We thought that, if Palestine fell, the Arabs would probably help Germany actively. They didn't like us very much and of course they shared the Germans' anti-Jewishness. And there was a lot of anti-British feeling in Syria. When we invaded Syria the previous spring, they thought that we had come to liberate them from the French, but all we did was to install another French administration under General Catroux, a Gaullist.'

Well-informed Britons felt that, after the experience of recent months, they could expect similar reactions from the peoples of Egypt and Iraq. The prospect was truly appalling – the dominance of the Middle East by

the enemy's armed forces, who would be supported, at least in the beginning, by the Arab population, even though in theory they too were condemned by Nazi ideology to the category of subhuman. These forces
would cut Britain's communications with the Far East and would be ready
to invade Russia from the south.

More and more Haganah men were therefore trained by Hammond and
his colourful soe colleagues. Eban recalls: 'There was an expert sniper
called Grant Taylor. He used to sit in a chair in his room in Talbiya and
shoot a lamp off the chandelier to illustrate his skill. He would offer to
shoot a cigarette out of your mouth, but there were no takers.' The British
were training the Jews for desperate measures. If Palestine fell, they
would withdraw to the north and fight a rearguard action in the moun-
tainous 'Lebanon box'. As for the Yishuv, with luck some of them would
be assembled in the valley around Mount Carmel and evacuated from
Haifa, while others would stay and fight as their ancestors had at Masada
1839 years earlier.

Outside the 'Lebanon box' the British-Jewish allies would carry on
guerrilla warfare. Yigal Allon was chosen by both Haganah and soe to
command an Arabic-speaking undercover unit in Syria: 'We were disguised as Arabs, boys and girls. We lived as families and we got jobs as
shopkeepers, clerks or craftsmen. But we were trained snipers, saboteurs,
intelligence operators and wireless operators.' If Syria were to come under
German control, they would go to work.

Abba Eban was closely involved in the Palestine scheme: 'If disaster
had occurred in Alamein, we would have gone into various caves and
hide-outs near the Dead Sea and near Haifa. A scheme was prepared by
Professor Ratner of the Techneion. Those who spoke Arabic would have
mingled with the population. The idea would have been to make the
occupation as expensive and unprofitable as possible. As for what the
Germans would have done with the Jewish population, we could only
believe the worst, although the news of the Wannsee Conference had not
yet percolated. We would live as the guerrillas did in Yugoslavia, but we
assumed that our existence would not be very long prolonged.'

The terrible news was, however, beginning to percolate. On July 1st,
1942, a document was published by the Polish government in London
listing the number of Jews killed in various Polish cities, estimating the
total number at 700,000. On August 1st the representative of the World
Jewish Congress in Switzerland, Gerhart Riegner, received from a German contact an amazingly accurate summary of what had been decided at

Wannsee in January. All Jews, he wrote in a draft cable, 'should after deportation and concentration in East be exterminated at one blow to resolve once and for all the Jewish question in Europe stop action reported planned for autumn methods under discussion including prussic acid...'[11]

Arthur Morse describes in his book *While Six Million Died* how, during the second half of 1942, Riegner's initial revelation was confirmed beyond doubt by numerous American and British sources. The American minister in Bern, Leland Harrison, reported that 'ghettos of larger cities such as Warsaw are being cleared and that the Jews evacuated therefrom have been sent eastwards to an unknown fate'. Ernest Frischer, a leading Czechoslovak exile, wrote in a document forwarded to the White House: 'There is no precedent for such organized wholesale dying in all Jewish history . . .'

On December 7th the matter was made public by *The Times* of London, using the now hackneyed phrase 'the final solution of the Jewish problem'. Ten days later, in reply to a question by Sydney Silverman in the House of Commons, Anthony Eden confirmed that his government now had 'reliable reports' of the Nazi plan to deport all Jews to the East and kill them. At this point the House rose and observed two minutes' silence.

The question therefore was, what should the United States and Britain do? After some hesitation their governments had established what was happening in Europe and proclaimed it publicly. For years Hitler's threats had not been fully believed. His regime was anti-Jewish. So much was plain. Everybody knew that he had treated the Jews harshly, dispossessing them and confining them in camps, and that there were many incidents of Jews being killed. But now, at the end of 1942, it was finally certain that he planned to exterminate the whole race, several million people. The Allied governments knew it. The Jews in the United States and Palestine knew it.

On March 1st, 1943, Chaim Weizmann told a mass rally in New York's Madison Square Garden: 'The democracies have a clear duty before them. Let them negotiate with Germany through the neutral countries concerning the possible release of the Jews . . . Let the gates of Palestine be opened . . .' Pressure mounted for the Allies to appeal to Germany through neutral countries and the Red Cross, to propose a rescue operation, to extract the Jews from Nazi Europe for settlement elsewhere or, if this failed, to send food and medical supplies to them in the concentration camps.

Britain and the United States had spoken out against the massacres of Jews. They had also set up a War Crimes Commission, making it plain that individuals who committed atrocities of any sort would be brought to justice after Allied victory.[12] But would they do more? The matter was soon put to the test. In February the Romanian Nazi-satellite government offered to 'sell' seventy thousand Jews. The Allies must bank $170,000 for them in a blocked Swiss bank account. The Jews would then be released.

This idea was quickly smothered by numerous State Department and Foreign Office objections. Every plan to rescue or help persecuted Jews seemed to involve aiding the enemy or hindering the Allied war effort. According to Richard Law, the chief British delegate at the refugee conference in Bermuda that April, there was only one solution to the refugee problem – victory. The Jews and other persecuted peoples should not be led into a fool's paradise: 'In fact we are unable to give them immediate succour.'[13]

The Romanian suggestion was described by several British officials as a 'flagrant piece of blackmail'.[14] Alec Randall thought that Britain and her Allies should do everything possible to help refugees, but that these efforts must be subject to the overriding need of the war effort. Giving in to 'blackmail and slave purchase' would damage this effort: 'The blunt truth is that the whole complex of human problems raised by the present German domination of Europe, of which the Jewish question is an important but by no means the only aspect, can only be dealt with completely by an Allied victory . . .'[15]

Mrs K. M. Crump of the Ministry of Economic Warfare noted: 'It is impossible to countenance a scheme that would enable Germany and her satellites to unload their unwanted nationals on the Allies in return for payment.'[16] Where would they go? There was no country that wanted them or where they could be housed except Palestine, which Britain would not allow. American Secretary of State Cordell Hull said: 'The unknown cost of moving an undetermined number of persons from an undisclosed place to an unknown destination, a scheme advocated by certain pressure groups, is, of course, out of the question.'

Breckinridge Long of the State Department feared that any special efforts made on the Jews' behalf 'may lend colour to the charges of Hitler that we are fighting this war on account of and at the instigation and direction of our Jewish citizens'.[17] This impression was already widespread in Spain, Turkey and the whole Moslem world, he noted, and it was extremely damaging. Other American officials pointed out the undesirability of such dealings on principle, the problems involved in picking any race out for special assistance. H. S. Gregory, a British official whose job it was to prevent trading with the enemy, noted that the idea of buying seventy thousand Jews for $170,000 – 'say twelve shillings a head' – was incredible. He was amazed that anyone was even considering it.

At the same time the Mufti of Jerusalem was sending stern letters from his office in Berlin to Foreign Minister Ribbentrop. It pained him, he wrote on June 10th, to see Germany's allies, Romania and Bulgaria, facilitating Jewish-British schemes by allowing their Jews to leave for Palestine. It was true, he went on, that their departure 'would relieve the Balkans of their evils', but their presence in Palestine would cause Nazi Germany even more evil. They should therefore 'be placed under strict surveillance in Europe itself'.[18] He asked Ribbentrop to do everything necessary to prevent the departure of Bulgarian and Romanian Jews.

The proposal thus ground to a halt. Randall pointed out that the Romanian Jews' claims on Allied humanity were probably less than those of the Polish Jews: 'Once we open the door to adult male Jews to be out of enemy territory, a quite unmanageable flood may emerge. Hitler may facilitate this.'[19] Ian Henderson saw the problem as purely one of balance. Which was more important to the British national interest, to help the American government to meet Jewish pressure in an election year, or to satisfy the anti-Zionist demands of the Arab rulers, on whom Britain's Middle East position was believed to depend?

The humanitarian need of the Jews in Europe did not enter the argument, except in as much as it aroused public, mainly Jewish pressure. The simple fact was that the doomed Jews, while they had powerful friends and brothers in Britain and America, were themselves of no political or strategic significance. The British and American governments saw no military advantage in trying to rescue the Jews or send them food, rather the contrary. They therefore abandoned them.

World Jewry could not but draw conclusions from all this. The Jews were not the only persecuted group in Nazi Europe. Poles and Russians too were being slaughtered by the million. But more and more Jews were coming to the conclusion that they suffered from a particular disability. They had no country, no place of their own, no government, no embassies, no armed forces. There was no one to protect them or care about them.

A Russian living under Nazi rule might, if he was lucky, escape across the lines into Soviet territory, his own country. (The NKVD usually arrested those who did, but that is another story.) A Pole might contrive to escape to a neutral country. If he did, he would find an embassy representing his government-in-exile in London. This embassy would give him documents and help him to join an émigré Polish community. But who was there to represent the Jews of Romania or Germany? What if the seventy thousand refugees had been British or American? Perhaps a little more energy would have been spared for their salvation?

And so, as the war continued, as awareness of European Jewry's torment deepened, more and more Jews were converted to the Zionist idea that their nation's fate could not be solved by assimilation, that anti-semitism always lurked in the shadows even of the most tolerant societies, that the only answer to their situation, the only guarantee of their survival, was separation, self-government and self-defence, and that in the final analysis the only way of achieving all this was by setting up a Jewish state in the Land of Israel.

After Montgomery's forces won the battle of el-Alamein in October 1942, Britain could forget the physical threat to Palestine and her contingency plans for underground warfare there against the German occupying forces. During 1943 her attitude towards the Haganah hardened. For more than a year her forces had taken a tolerant attitude towards the illegal Jewish units. If Rommel had broken through Egypt, the Jews would have been used as allies, whatever the Arabs might say. But once the danger passed, Jewish armies reverted to their earlier illegal and undesirable status, becoming once again no more than a thorn in the flesh of the White Paper policy and the core of a possible rebellion.

Britain therefore withdrew her SOE 'irregulars', abandoned the Palmach and once again looked sternly on the Haganah. They were, after all, in spite of the help they provided against Nazi Germany, the military arm of a political organization irrevocably opposed to an important section of British foreign policy. They would have to be tamed and, if not actually destroyed, at least brought more closely under British law and administration.

The Haganah reacted accordingly. If they could not arm and train themselves with British help, they would do so without it, whatever the law. The Palmach refused to give up the weapons they had been 'lent'. Yigal Allon remembers how, on the break-up of the partnership, British forces removed Palmach arms to a camp on Mount Carmel: 'This was a thing which we could not tolerate. Two or three nights later we raided the camp, took back the weapons and warned them, "Never touch Haganah arms again." ' Arms acquisition, even arms theft, was seen as a matter of survival and hence morally justifiable.

In May 1943 Major-General Douglas McConnel, Britain's army chief in Palestine, reported to British intelligence (MI2) the existence of a 'highly organized racket', involving at least one important member of the Jewish Agency, that was systematically stealing arms for the Haganah. Jewish guards from the Palestine Regiment had connived at thefts from British arms dumps. So had a small number of British soliders: 'One method adopted is to contact, befriend and finally bribe deserters to work for racket. All necessary forged documents and even military vehicles are then provided by Jews and orders given for a particular theft. Deserter on completion of a successful job may receive as much as £400.'[20]

A report compiled by the Office of Strategic Services in Washington told of widescale thefts from Allied arms dumps in Palestine and Egypt: 'Ordinary thieves, many of them Arabs, worked hand in glove with corrupt guards in stealing various quantities of small arms and cartridges, which were later sold on the Jewish market for fabulous profits.'[21] According to a reliable American source, one haul alone comprised six hundred rifles, twenty-two machineguns, two tons of high explosive and eight thousand detonators.

Jewish settlements also acquired arms illegally after the fall of Syria, as Yigal Allon describes. In February ten thousand rounds of French rifle ammunition had been found in a Jewish truck. Armoured car bodies, capable of being fitted over a truck in forty-five minutes, were being produced at a rate of twenty a month. In all, the report estimated with some exaggeration, the Haganah possessed more than 35,000 arms of various types: rifles, machineguns and revolvers; British, German, Italian, French and Polish.

It was, the Foreign Office noted, 'a most disquieting state of affairs', but there was a chance of turning the situation to the benefit of British policy. Police investigations were at an advanced state. They might well lead to the arrest of 'some big noise in the Jewish Agency', after which British forces would find it easier to bring the Haganah under control. Robin Hankey wrote: 'It might also give us a plank on which to mobilize public opinion against Jewish activities harmful to the war effort, if publicity were handled just right.' Deputy Superintendent Tom Wilkin, perhaps the most skilful policeman in Palestine, one of the few who spoke good Hebrew, was ordered to redouble his efforts to unmask the gunrunners.

The Arabs, true, were also acquiring arms illegally. They too had looted arms from the Vichy French and stolen from the numerous camps of the British Ninth Army. By 1943 nearly a third of the eight thousand Arabs in British uniform, seven thousand Palestinian and one thousand others, had deserted with their rifles, mostly during Rommel's advance the previous summer. There were probably twice as many arms in Arab hands as in Jewish. The oss reported that 'about 40,000 Palestine Arabs with small-arms for all could be mobilized for a future revolt'.

But the British authorities did not take this Arab activity so seriously. The illegally held Arab arms that they discovered from time to time – in mosque areas, orange or olive groves, caves, cornbins or oil jars – were as often as not faulty or rusty. Sometimes they were kept not for any political purpose, but for self-protection or show. Many were collected either by individuals for their own use or by professional thieves, who made large sums out of every country Arab's inborn desire to own a firearm.

The Arabs of Palestine were politically quiescent. Their rebellion had failed. Their main leader, the Mufti, had miscalculated, fled ignominiously from country to country and was now in Berlin, isolated and discredited. But while he could no longer guide Palestinian aspirations towards an Arab state, neither could his opponents of the Nashashibi clan and the Defence party. Latent loyalty to the Mufti and Husseini-controlled assassination squads were still strong enough to prevent a takeover by the moderates. The White Paper policy likewise confused Arab minds. Did it mean that they would eventually gain independence with Britain's help? In that case they should do nothing. Or would the White Paper be revised as circumstances changed? Would British policy be reversed yet again? In that case they should fight. It all meant that in 1943 there was no coherent Arab political organization pressing the Arab case before the Palestine authorities.

The Jews were a different story. When the British unearthed a cache of Jewish arms, they found them well oiled and carefully stored. And usually they had been stolen not haphazardly, as had Arab-held arms, but efficiently and cleverly by organized military groups, acting on orders of the Haganah and the Jewish Agency, partly for reasons of self-defence (a legitimate aim) but also with an eye to the eventual struggle towards the (in Britain's opinion) improper and unjustifiable political objectives outlined in the Biltmore Resolution.

The British decided to mount a show trial, in the words of the oss report, 'to give the whole subject of Zionist participation in the illegal arms traffic a public airing'. They did this to demonstrate their good faith to the Arabs, to undermine the Jewish Agency's prestige in the United States and to discourage future arms theft. By the summer of 1943 police investigations were complete. Two British private soldiers, Stoner and Harris, and two Palestine Jews, Leib Sirkin and Abraham Rachlin, were tried by a military court in Jerusalem before a large number of invited journalists.

The four accused were convicted and, although the Jewish press cast doubt on the verdicts, were doubtless guilty, but the main feature of the trial was prosecuting officer Major J. L. Baxter's efforts to expose the Haganah as thieves and the Jewish Agency, or at least the supporters of Ben Gurion, as accomplices in theft. Sirkin and Rachlin, he said on September 25th, were members of 'a powerful and sinister organization', 'a cancer in the Middle East war effort' which had 'apparently Nazi power'[22] over its members. He linked the Haganah with the followers of Stern by reading Lehi leaflets to the court and referring to the murder on September 3rd of Israel Pritzkier, the Irgun intelligence officer who gave much information on Lehi to the British police. It showed, he said, 'the existence in this country of gangsters of the worst sort, terrorists who prevented witnesses from coming forward'.

He also cross-examined Goldie Meyerson (Golda Meir), a senior Histadrut official, and poured scorn on her when she protested: 'We are interested in this war and in the victory of British forces and stealing from the army is a crime in our eyes.'[23] The British view was that Golda Meir was being less than frank. Someone of her seniority must have known about the Haganah and its methods of acquiring arms. Her reply was that, without Jewish self-defence, the Yishuv would be destroyed by Arab violence. Ben Gurion told the Jewish Elected Assembly on October 4th, comparing the trial to the classic anti-semitic forgery *Protocols of the Elders of Zion*: 'Helpless Jews were slaughtered under the eyes of the British authorities in Hebron and Safed in 1929 because they had not got a Haganah.'[24]

In British official circles the trial seemed to reveal yet another example of Jewish Agency hypocrisy and narrow-mindedness. Everyone knew that the Haganah were stealing arms from British dumps. How could the official Jewish bodies and well-known figures like Ben Gurion and Golda Meir condone such illegality, at the same time denying that it was happening? It could only be because they were ready to put their aspirations for a Jewish state before the war effort as a whole. And why should they react with anti-British tirades, shrill allegations of anti-semitism, when obvious thieves were convicted and sentenced to prison?

In Jewish eyes the trials were no better than a witch-hunt, a crude political display. Their aim was not to establish the facts about the accused, but to vilify the Jewish Agency and to deny the Yishuv the right of self-preservation. Could not the British understand what it meant to a

Jewish community to find itself unarmed and surrounded by hostile forces? An unarmed Jewish settlement was a hostage to fortune. British forces had neither the means nor, apparently, the will to protect them. Therefore the Jewish community must protect its own. The right to self-defence overrode all other laws.

Again, the extravagant Jewish reaction to the arms trials must be seen against a background of what was happening in Europe. Five months earlier (April 19th, 1943) the Warsaw ghetto, containing sixty thousand survivors of an original 400,000-strong community, was attacked by two thousand men from the German army and Waffen SS under Major-General Jurgen Stroop. Starved and armed with only a few dozen smuggled weapons, Jewish men and women fought the soldiers back, bombarding their armoured cars with petrol-filled bottles and home-made grenades. Eventually the invaders blasted the small area, 1000 by 300 yards, with gunfire and razed it with flamethrowers, forcing the Jews out of their defensive positions, the cellars and sewers of the ghetto. A few dozen Jews escaped through underground tunnels.[25] The rest were killed in the battle, shot on capture, or else shipped to the extermination camp at Treblinka.

Chaim Weizmann, the architect of the Balfour Declaration and for decades the main impetus behind Zionist aspirations, was going through a series of personal crises. In February 1942 his much-loved son Michael was killed over the North Sea, flying for the Royal Air Force. He approved the Biltmore programme in May, but without enthusiasm, and he was constantly being criticized, especially by Ben Gurion, for his insufficiently militant approach. His health was declining. He was tormented by the thought that the Yishuv was discarding his ideas and moving towards extremism. His policy of close cooperation with Britain was under question. Since 1917, what had Britain done for Zionism? Why should their leader continue so singlemindedly in Britain's support?

Weizmann needed to reassert himself and prove to his followers in Palestine and elsewhere that there was sense in his policies. So early in 1943, in the wake of the el-Alamein and Stalingrad victories, with the war turning decisively in the Allies' favour, he made several new approaches towards his goal of a post-war Jewish state in Palestine. On January 19th, with the Zionist leader Nahun Goldmann, who moved to the United States in 1941, he put his ideas before the Near Eastern Division of the State Department – Wallace Murray, Paul Alling, Gordon Merriam and others – most of whom were as anti-Zionist as their British colleagues.

Weizmann told the Americans that it would be 'a misconstruction of democracy in the real sense' to have 'a dynamic group', about one third of the Palestine population, subjected to 'a backward majority'.[26] He did not believe that the legitimate rights of the Arabs would be affected by the Zionist programme. All that was needed was for the Western Allies to tell the Arabs this. They would then most probably fall into line. He then mentioned the plan, which he had discussed in March 1941 with Winston Churchill, of engaging the help of King Abd ul-Aziz Ibn Saud of Saudi Arabia to persuade the Arabs to accept Zionist aims. The Prime Minister had said to him: 'I am thinking of a settlement between you and the Arabs after the war. The man with whom you should make the agreement is Ibn Saud. He will be the lord of the Arab countries.'[27]

The originator of this bizarre plan was the famous Arabist and explorer Harold St John Philby (father of the traitor Kim Philby), a convert to Islam well acquainted with Ibn Saud and his entourage. In late 1939 he told Sumner Welles, a Zionist sympathizer, that Ibn Saud would approve a Jewish state west of the River Jordan on condition that all other Arab lands received independence and that he personally received 'compensation' of £20,000,000. Around the same time, October 6th, Philby repeated the idea at lunch with Weizmann, Shertok and Namier. The following January, according to his account, he discussed the plan with Ibn Saud, who said that 'some such arrangment might be possible in appropriate future circumstances', that 'he would keep the matter in mind'.[28]

The Foreign Office reacted with alarm three years later to the news that such ideas were flying around Washington and being lent respectability by the name of Churchill: 'I do not know how far Dr Weizmann has authority to speak in your name, but I am a little worried at the danger of confusion arising in Washington,' wrote Eden on March 3rd, 1943, in a respectful but gently chiding letter to his prime minister. Britain's policy towards Palestine had been approved by Parliament and had not been reversed, either there or in Cabinet. In Eden's view, Ibn Saud was very unlikely to receive Weizmann or even consider his plan.

Churchill replied six days later: 'Dr Weizmann has no authority to speak in my name. At the same time I expressed these views to him when we met some time ago and you have often heard them from me yourself...
As you know, I am irrevocably opposed to the White Paper which, as I have testified in the House, I regard as a breach of a solemn undertaking to which I was a party.' On April 18th he wrote to Eden and Cranborne, now working in the Foreign Office as Lord Privy Seal: 'I am sure the

majority of the present War Cabinet would never agree to any positive endorsement of the White Paper. It runs until it is superseded.'[29]

On April 27th he elaborated: 'The present Cabinet have never accepted the White Paper except as a modus vivendi pending a new declaration.' Likewise, David Lloyd George, prime minister at the time of the Balfour Declaration and still a Member of Parliament, wrote in a letter widely published in March: 'The revolting treatment of the Jews by the Nazis has made any other solution than a Jewish state in Palestine unthinkable.' Similar pro-Zionist statements were being made in the United States by former Under-Secretary of State Sumner Welles, Henry Stimson (Secretary of War), Wendell Willkie (the 1940 Republican presidential candidate) and many other leading Americans.

All this threw the Middle East experts into a flurry of alarm. Premier Nuri es-Said of Iraq complained to the British ambassador (Kinahan Cornwallis) that Lloyd George 'rightly enjoyed the prestige of an elder statesman' and that his letter 'would be hotly taken up by enemy wireless'.[30] From every Arab capital shouts of complaint made their way to London, moderate and pro-Allied Arab leaders explaining that the Zionists were undermining their support among the people, that the Biltmore programme violated the 1941 Churchill-Roosevelt Atlantic Charter, which guaranteed all countries the right to self-determination, that there was no point in supporting the Allies if they were planning to hand Palestine over to the Jews.

The State Department and the Foreign Office were confused. Both organizations were conditioned to operating in a pro-Arab fashion, but the political opposition to their traditional policy was growing. So what were they to do? How could British officials administer a policy which, in their prime minister's view, was a gross breach of faith? How could American officials administer a policy which cut right across the public statements of the most influential American political figures?

The American pro-Zionists were a particular irritation. Halifax's deputy, Ronald Campbell, reported from Washington: 'They are of course anxious to conciliate the Jewish vote, but not to the extent of advocating Jewish immigration into this country, which presents obvious difficulties. Hence their concentration on the Palestine solution.'[31]

Feeling was growing that the time had come yet again to face up to the Palestine problem, yet again to decide a policy and a solution. In late April 1943 Churchill and Eden, the leaders of the pro-Zionist and the pro-Arab factions of British politics, agreed that the matter would have to be thrashed out in Cabinet. On April 27th Churchill sent his colleagues a reprint of his famous May 1939 speech on the White Paper, making it clear that his opinion on the matter had not changed. The idea of an Arab veto on Jewish immigration, he said, was something that he could in no circumstances contemplate.

Churchill wrote that Britain had treated the Arabs very generously, especially by securing and maintaining the independence of Saudi Arabia, Iraq, Syria and Transjordan: 'With the exception of Ibn Saud and the Emir Abdullah, both of whom have been good and faithful followers, the Arabs have been virtually no use to us in the present war.'[32] Britain and the United States were therefore free to review the Palestine situation anew. It might be possible, for instance, to make Eritrea and Tripolitania into Jewish colonies, affiliated to the National Home.

This last idea, noted Cranborne in an unusually frank criticism of his superior, introduced an alarming new factor: 'I venture to suspect the Prime Minister of hankering once more after Palestine as a Jewish state.' 'Yes,' wrote Eden in the margin. Cranborne himself was in favour of a Jewish state in Africa, he wrote, but not for any love of the Jews: 'Only thus will we be able to silence the wealthy Jews in America who pay for this agitation without any intention of sacrificing their American citizenship. And only thus will we be able to get some of the Jews out of this country, in which there are now far too many.'[33]

But the Zionists were alert to these discussions and would not be diverted from Palestine to some other country, to be acquired through British conquest. Any such idea, said Shertok on March 17th, was like 'asking children to forget their mother, when they know she is alive and longing for them'. The Jews would not go cap-in-hand to the Arabs to ask permission to enter: 'The Jew feels that he has got to make good in Palestine or go under. He cannot blame anyone in the world for his being in Palestine. He can blame only the Jewish God . . . The choice of the country for the Jews was made by history once and for all. It cannot be undone.'[34]

Weizmann expressed the same opinion, less emotionally, in a melancholy talk with Isaiah Berlin in Washington on May 18th, recalling Baron Hirsch's failure to found a Jewish colony in the Argentine and the Soviet government's failure to do the same in Birobidzhan on the borders of Manchuria. He was sure that if only the British would make clear their commitment to the Jewish National Home in Palestine, the Arabs would acquiesce. He still hoped, he told Halifax, to achieve this agreement with the help of Ibn Saud and he agreed with him about the damage being done to the war effort and the Jewish cause by 'fanatics' like Ben Gurion.[35]

Various ministers and officials did their best to curb Churchill's enthusiasm for a Jewish state. On May 1st Cranborne again took issue with him. The question, he said, was not whether Britain owed the Arabs a debt of gratitude for their help in the war, but whether she had important interests in the Arab world. And her soldiers and diplomats all seemed to agree that she did. On June 10th the War Office reaffirmed the importance to Britain of the Iraq and Iran oilfields, their vulnerability to sabotage in the event of violent Arab discontent: 'However well disposed the Jews in Haifa may be, the value of these installations will be nullified if the Arabs are allowed to act against the pipelines leading to them.'

Oliver Lyttelton, minister of production, wrote of 'the permanent strategic importance of the Middle East to the British Empire', which meant that Britain must retain control of Palestine 'for an indefinite period'. Robin Hankey noted: 'We cannot put many more people into Palestine without permanently injuring our relations with the Arabs.' Charles Baxter suggested that a small Jewish state would be as dangerous as a large one. It would soon be overfilled with immigrants and would begin clamouring for *Lebensraum*, the right to expand 'into the rest of Palestine and probably Transjordan'.[36]

Clement Attlee, deputy prime minister, whose Labour party was officially pro-Zionist, wrote on June 23rd that the movement seemed to have fallen under the control of reckless fanatics: 'No one but a visionary imagines that Palestine can absorb all the Jews, even if they were willing to go. Millions will desire and be obliged to live in gentile lands, in Europe, America and other continents.' No fewer than ten ministers wrote papers for the July 2nd, 1943, Cabinet meeting, where Palestine was on the agenda.

The minutes of that meeting show Churchill only slightly restrained by the barrage of anti-Zionist memoranda. Of the six other ministers who took part in the discussion there were three – Attlee, Amery and Sinclair – who generally shared his Zionist views. Eden emphasized the 1940 decision not publicly to denounce the White Paper. Churchill emphasized the Balfour Declaration, on which he made his own position clear: 'At the proper time it would, in his view, be our duty to show that we were not prepared to be driven off solemn undertakings which we had agreed.'

They reached a compromise conclusion of short-term inaction and long-term decision. Until the end of the war, Britain would say and do as little as possible about Palestine, but they would set up a Cabinet Committee immediately to work out a once-and-for-all policy. Then, when the war was won, they would be ready with the decision and they would impose it on the area. The Prime Minister would nominate the members of the Cabinet Committee. They included Cranborne, Law, Moyne and the two veteran Zionists Archie Sinclair and Leo Amery.

The first act of Home Secretary Herbert Morrison, the chairman of the new Committee, was to order its existence kept secret. He was afraid that the Jewish organizations would redouble their pressure as soon as they heard that a new policy was being discussed. But secrecy was difficult to enforce. Chaim Weizmann, returning to London from Washington in June, was soon to extract a hint about the new initiative from his friend Amery. Then at the end of August he met Colonial Secretary Oliver Stanley, who 'talked about partition on a rather more generous scale than that proposed by the Peel Commission'. Weizmann noted that 'some sort of new policy was under consideration in Palestine', that 'something was brewing'.[73]

Weizmann also discussed with Stanley the Ibn Saud 'plan'. It had first been suggested to him by Churchill, he told the colonial secretary.[38] (In fact, he had earlier discussed it with Philby in October 1939.) Stanley tried to convince him that it would not work, but Weizmann persisted. He was more and more at odds with the more militant Zionist leaders and he was encouraged, both by the plan and by what he knew of the new British initiative, to believe that Zionist aims could be reached by negotiation, with Britain's help. If he could make progress on one or the other, he would be able to counter Ben Gurion's extreme demands.

Britain could not understand Weizmann's faith in Philby's idea. On May 3rd the Foreign Office received a report from Thomas Wikeley, their representative in Saudi Arabia, stating clearly that in no way would Ibn Saud act in the way suggested. The King, said Wikeley, was actuated in life by three main motives – his Islamic beliefs, his Arabism and his friendship with Britain, in that order. But of these his religion was by far the most important. 'I am therefore convinced that he would not tolerate, let alone assist, a solution of the Palestine problem along Zionist lines. Palestine is a holy land for him and he would never acquiesce in the Moslem holy places being placed, even indirectly, in the hands of the Jews . . . The proposal, which is being so gaily bandied about, that Weizmann should visit the King fills me with alarm. I am sure Ibn Saud would refuse to meet him . . .'[39]

This turned out to be the case. Lieutenant-Colonel Harold Hoskins, an OSS Middle East expert, visited Ibn Saud with a message from Roosevelt and put the plan directly before the King, who immediately reacted angrily. In a verbal reply, summarized in writing on August 20th, Ibn

Saud assured President Roosevelt that it was his custom to welcome all who visited him, no matter what their religion: 'But the Jews are on a special footing. The noble President is well aware of the enmity that exists and has existed between us and them from of old. It is an enmity well known and treated of in the books that we possess and from first to last has always been deep rooted in us. Hence it will appear that we do not feel ourselves safe from Jewish treachery and can neither hold discussions with them or trust their promises . . .

'As for the person mentioned, Dr Chaim Weizmann, he in particular is my enemy, for it was he who had the outrageous impudence to single me out among all the Arabs and Moslems to address to me the base demand that I should turn traitor to my religion and my country. By that act he has increased my hatred for him and all who follow him.' Ibn Saud recalled that in 1940 Weizmann had sent 'a certain European' (Philby) with an offer of £20 million for his help over Palestine: 'Could there be impudence or baseness greater than this? Could there be a crime greater than the crime this man has dared to commit in making this request to me and in making the noble President the guarantor of so dishonourable an act?'[40]

Amazingly, even after this colourful rejection, the gist of which he was told, Weizmann continued to press his plan, relying on a dubious reassurance by Philby that Ibn Saud had only reacted angrily for tactical reasons, that he would be more receptive as soon as the plan was put to him delicately by Roosevelt or Churchill, rather than by a messenger. On December 13th he wrote to Sumner Welles: 'I therefore feel in spite of Colonel Hoskins's adverse report that, properly managed, Mr Philby's scheme offers an approach which should not be abandoned without further exploration.' The Foreign Office's reaction to this letter was expressed by Robin Hankey: 'Anyone who thinks Ibn Saud will look at this hare-brained scheme, after what he has said about it, must be quite cracked. This correspondence does Dr Weizmann no credit.'[41]

Weizmann was clutching at straws. After decades of effort he was no nearer persuading the Arabs to acquiesce in any Zionist solution. He wrote to Sumner Welles: 'Our heritage in Palestine was cut down to the bone when Transjordan was separated in 1922.' But even Ibn Saud, the most moderate and pro-British of the Arab rulers, would not admit the existence of this heritage: 'All that we desire is that the clear rights of the Arabs, which are as obvious as the sun, should not be smothered by a falsification of history and the social and economic theorizations of the Zionist Jews, for God has invested these with no authority.' The objections of the other Arab rulers, especially the Palestinians, were of course even stronger.

But if he could not persuade the Arabs, Weizmann seemed to be having better luck in persuading the British. After a lunch with Churchill and Attlee on October 25th, he was able to report that both Conservative and Labour party leaders remained staunch Zionists, that Churchill had promised shortly to plunge into the pie and hand the Zionists a real plum.[42] A few days later Amery told him that the Committee had reached its decision.[43] He did not actually tell Weizmann what it was, but his observation that the Jews would be wise to accept it, otherwise by obstinacy they might lose the whole loaf, made it clear that Britain was about to produce another partition scheme. At the end of 1943 Weizmann wrote to Meyer Weisgal: 'There are all sorts of rumours flying about concerning partition.'[44]

The Foreign Office were furious. Hankey wrote: 'A good many remarks made by the PM and Colonel Stanley in confidence to Dr Weizmann are being bandied about as gossip in Washington . . . I am quite sure that the public use of the PM's encouragement of Dr Weizmann is directly contrary to Great Britain's war interest.' Freya Stark, the famous writer on the Middle East, heard the rumours and complained that such ministerial leaks were 'a sabotaging of one's own side'. She tried to console Harold Hoskins by telling him: 'It is usually the Civil Service that wins versus the Cabinet in the long run.'[45]

Various Committee members offered their individual views. Richard Law was the only one to reject a Jewish state entirely, proposing instead Jewish semi-autonomous areas within a Greater Syria. Amery, Stanley and even Moyne, hated by many Jews for his anti-Zionist speeches and his part in the *Struma* tragedy, proposed Jewish states of different sizes, Amery's state being the largest and including the Negev Desert. Moyne proposed giving the Negev to Transjordan, but allowing the Jewish state to develop parts of it under the aegis of a chartered company.[46]

In their November 20th report the chiefs of staff finally accepted that Britain was committed to establishing a Jewish national home. Their advice, of course, was based on the strategic interests of the British Empire, which they believed would continue as the main Middle East power for the foreseeable future. 'We shall always have to maintain a strong garrison in the Middle East, which is the hub of our Imperial sea and air communications,' they wrote, emphasizing again the importance of Iraqi and Iranian oil. But, in the light of Britain's past promises, there was no other way out: 'Wherever we establish the Jews, there we shall have a military commitment.' This commitment might as well be in Palestine, therefore, as anywhere else, especially as a garrison there would help Imperial communications. On December 20th the Committee recommended the partition of Palestine on the basis of the 1937 Peel Report, for the moment leaving open the question of ownership of the Negev.

On January 9th, 1944, a very ill-timed plea arrived from Halifax, complaining again about Zionist pressure in Washington and recommending a paper by Freya Stark, in which she described the White Paper as 'an embodiment of the principle of government by consent'.[47] Churchill, fortified by the Committee's report, reacted angrily against the pro-Arab line he had tolerated for so long: 'Surely we are not going to make trouble for ourselves in America and hamper the President's chances of re-election for the sake of this low-grade gasp of a defeatist hour?' He told Eden that he would personally denounce any such line as Freya Stark's: 'You should warn Halifax, who is as usual on the wobble.' At last he was able to state his own position clearly: 'Some form of partition is the only solution.'[48]

So here was a concrete achievement, one to which Weizmann himself had contributed and in which he could take pride. 'Mr Churchill does not like to see me, because he has nothing to tell me,' he once remarked. But in spite of this lack of personal contact since 1940 his ideas still counted for much with the Prime Minister and now seemed to be gaining the acceptance of the Cabinet. The idea that Britain's interest would not permit the emergence of a Jewish state had prevailed since 1938, but was now dying.

In November 1943 Ben Gurion resigned his chairmanship of the Zionist Executive. He had known nothing of the Ibn Saud plan and, when he discovered about it, he was furious with Weizmann for discussing such ideas behind his back. He objected to Weizmann running the Zionist movement from London rather than from Palestine. And, of course, he thought Weizmann far too conciliatory towards Britain.[49] Weizmann was confident, though, that his moderate line had been the right one and the Committee's decision in December seemed to justify him. In London and Washington moderation was overcoming extremism.

In Palestine the mood was different. Mutual suspicion between Jews and British had been increased by the September arms trials. On November 16th it was aggravated by a large-scale search of the settlement of Ramat Hakovesh. A mêlée ensued, a settler was killed and several others, Jews and British, were injured. The Jewish Agency claimed that the police and soldiers had behaved with Nazi-like brutality. MacMichael replied that, on the contrary, the security forces acted 'with commendable restraint under great provocation'.[50]

Another Palestine development at about this time, as important as Ben Gurion's resignation, was Yaacov Meridor's withdrawal from the leadership of the Irgun Zvai Leumi. The truce with Britain, which had lasted since the outbreak of war, no longer seemed to the Irgun to be serving a useful purpose. German and Italian forces had been beaten out of Africa. There was no longer the fear that a fight against Britain would threaten the security of Palestine.

The Irgun was weary of inactivity and inflamed by Britain's continuing pro-Arab policy. Since mid-1942 its ranks had been swelled by Jews from Poland, evacuated from the Soviet Union with General Anders's forces, many of them former members of Jabotinsky's Betar movement, desperate in the knowledge of what was happening to their families and friends in Auschwitz and Treblinka. They were hardened by years of underground activity or by imprisonment in Stalin's camps and they wanted action immediately.

The unthinkable was about to happen, something that Weizmann had always described as repugnant to the Yishuv. The Irgun was planning armed action against Britain under its new commander, a recent arrival from Poland, Menachem Begin.

6

The Rise of the Irgun

THE man who was to become prime minister of Israel in 1977 was born on August 16th, 1913, in Brest-Litovsk, on the present Polish-Soviet border, of a family of timber merchants. From the age of fourteen he attended a Polish government school and there, according to his biographer Eitan Haber, 'acquired the patina of Polish aristocratic etiquette'. But at an early age he decided that his main identification was with his Jewish origins, rather than with Poland, and was convinced that the Jewish communities scattered about the world must return to Jerusalem and the Land of Israel, which was theirs by historic title.

Begin reacted strongly against the anti-semitic outbursts of sections of the Polish population: 'When I was a student, we were forced to sit on the left side of the room during lectures. Anti-semitic students often used to beat us up. But we were not frightened Jews who succumb to persecution. We used to retaliate. I remember pitched battles with these students. We were proud Jews, proud of our heritage. But when we finished university, we had no future. We couldn't get jobs as lawyers, we couldn't do anything.'

When war broke out, Begin and his wife Aliza made their way to Lvov, in the Soviet-occupied area of Poland, and from there to Wilna in Lithuania. In September 1940, soon after Lithuania's incorporation into the Soviet Union, he was arrested and interrogated by NKVD officers, who unsuccessfully tried to convince him that Zionism was an offshoot of British imperialism. He was convicted in his absence of being a 'dangerous element in society' and sentenced to eight years' imprisonment. He spent some months in Wilna's Lukishki prison and in a labour camp by the Pechora River in north Russia. After Germany invaded Russia in June

1941 he was released and joined Wladyslaw Anders's army on Soviet soil. Anders soon quarrelled with Stalin and arranged to take his army to serve under British command in the West. Begin was one of many thousand Polish soldiers, Jewish and non-Jewish, who were taken across the Caspian Sea to Iran and then overland to Palestine, which he reached in May 1942.

Still a Polish soldier, Begin spent the next year in torment and fury at the thought of what was happening to those he had left behind in Poland. Both his parents, several members of his family and countless friends were murdered by the Nazis. And, according to Eitan Haber, the guilt of Great Britain seemed to him on a par with that of Nazi Germany. 'You must understand what happened,' says Begin. 'Our people were promised a national home in this country. I don't want to go into the details of interpretation or misinterpretation, but in the 1930s our people faced the prospect of extermination and we needed this country. My master and teacher Jabotinsky told the Peel Commission in 1937, "A Jewish state is now necessary to save us. Our people are living on a volcano." '

The Irgun's anti-Arab retaliation (or counterterrorism), frequent during the Arab rebellion of the late 1930s, continued during the war and increased during 1943. Pamphlets were pasted on walls and passed around in Palestine cities, emphasizing the Revisionist belief that Palestine was the Land of Israel and that a Jewish state must be established, by force if necessary. 'The Arabs must be forced to be conquered . . . They must be removed as a political factor,'[1] said one Irgun pamphlet quoted in an oss bulletin that August.

Begin himself wrote a broadsheet in his underground headquarters in Tel Aviv's Savoy Hotel: 'On the way to achieving Jewish rule in the Land of Israel, we must beware of compromise . . . Rule means real rule – a Jewish government and not some religious, cultural and municipal autonomy, with a Jewish community under a foreign ruler. The Land of Israel means the territory not only within the historic frontiers, but also within the natural and strategic frontiers of this region . . .' The Irgun emblem showed a map of the whole of Palestine and Transjordan, superimposed on which was a hand holding a rifle and a slogan: 'Only thus!'[2]

At the end of 1943 he had been in Palestine only eighteen months. It nevertheless seemed to him natural to consider Palestine as his own country. This was the Land of Israel, which belonged to all the Jews of the world, wherever they might have been born. And it was the Jews, rather than the then Arab majority, who had the right to rule that country. The function of the Irgun was therefore to fight for that right against the Arabs and British who opposed it. The first aim, Begin writes, was achieved in the early days of the revolt: 'We succeeded in nullifying the local Arab factor.'[3]

It was therefore against Britain that Begin was resolved to concentrate the conflict. He saw Britain not as the Jews' ally against Hitler, but as the enemy who had denied the Jews refuge in their own country. A few weeks earlier (December 15th, 1943) US Ambassador John Winant had been told in London: 'The Foreign Office are concerned with the difficulties of disposing of any considerable number of Jews, should they be rescued.' This sentence is heavily underlined in the copy of Arthur Morse's book which Begin showed the author in support of his view that Britain and the United States were accomplices in Hitler's extermination of European Jewry: 'During the 1940s Britain could have saved several hundred thousand Jews. It was a horribly decadent act not even to try to save them.'[4]

In Begin's eyes, Britain's anti-Zionist policy was based on nothing more than cold, calculated selfishness. And Arab objections to Zionism were no more than a British invention. In his book *The Revolt* he writes: 'The Arabs were encouraged, sometimes quite openly, to organize attacks on the Jews.'[5] He puts forward the bizarre idea that the 1936 Arab rebellion was deliberately instigated by Britain in order to provide an excuse for limiting Jewish immigration. His friend Samuel Katz, the political specialist in the Irgun high command, also writes that the Mufti and his followers were encouraged to rebel, in order to stem growing Jewish influence in Palestine and perpetuate British rule.[6]

But it is the British and American reaction, or lack of action, in the face of Hitler's holocaust that arouses Begin's most bitter feelings: 'First he imprisoned the Jews and noted the world's indifference. Then he starved them and still the world did not move. He dug his claws in, bared his teeth. The world did not even raise an eyebrow.'

Those who formed Britain's policy towards Jewish refugees were motivated not by lack of will, indifference or the overriding priorities of the war effort, but by something much more sinister and wicked: 'One cannot say that those who shaped British Middle East policy at that time did not want to save the Jews. It would be more correct to say that they very eagerly wanted the Jews not to be saved . . . They were highly interested in achieving the maximum reduction in the number of Jews liable to seek to enter the Land of Israel.' He believes that what Nazi Germany did helped to fulfil 'the fundamental British plan for Eretz Israel'.[7]

On February 1st, 1944, Begin issued his declaration of war against

Britain. After outlining his view of the progress of the war – the Jews' support of the Allies, the Arabs' hostility – he announced that the war had now reached its last stages and that the fate of future generations was about to be decided. The time had come to strike against Britain: 'She herself has written the bloody chapters in the history of Jewish re-patriation – Patria, Mauritius and Struma . . . Her agents murdered in the towns and in the country. Her judges slandered evilly and went out of their way to dishonour the Jews of the world . . . There is no longer an armistice between Jewish youth and the British administration in the Land of Israel, which hands our brothers over to Hitler.'

Begin decided that the Irgun would fight Britain selectively. So long as Britain was at war with Nazi Germany, they would not attack the British military. They would only attack the British police and certain government offices. Begin says: 'We decided that we would not tolerate an office which kept Jews out of Palestine at a time when our brothers were being dragged to death in Europe. And we would not pay taxes to a government that did these things.' On February 12th they blew up the immigration offices in Jerusalem, Haifa and Tel Aviv. On February 27th they blew up the tax offices in the same cities. There were no casualties.

It was not until March 23rd that the Irgun's activity assumed a really new dimension with a series of bomb attacks on the police stations of Jerusalem, Jaffa and Haifa. In this simultaneous operation, the first Irgun assault on the British police since the assassination of Cairns and Barker in August 1939, six British policemen were killed. Three of them died in their beds on the third floor of CID headquarters in Haifa, where a powerful explosive device planted in the basement brought down one whole corner of the four-storey building.[8]

That same night in Jerusalem, in the Russian Compound, Irgun raiders in police uniform were spotted climbing a ladder into the main CID building by Assistant Superintendent John Scott. When he opened fire, the raiders fired back and killed him. A Jewish suspect was grabbed and taken to the office of Arthur Giles, assistant Inspector-General of Police. Richard Catling says: 'John Scott was a good friend of mine. When he was murdered, I was beside myself with grief and anger. We had this un-fortunate suspect in Giles's office and I was knocking him about like hell. I freely admit it. Then the bomb went off. We were thrown across the room and covered in plaster.'

The use of the word 'murder' in this context irritates Begin strongly: 'There was no murder. John Scott fell in battle, a fair battle. One of our men was also killed, a young man called Asher Benjamin. They fell in battle.' He sees the Irgun's campaign against Britain as a thoroughly justifiable war of liberation. At the same time he sees a clear distinction between the Irgun's methods and those of Lehi: 'We never attacked individuals, not even policemen or soldiers. To see a man in the street, a policeman, and to shoot at him – this was never done by the men of the Irgun. That was the method of the Stern group and it was taken from the Russian socialist revolutionaries who believed in killing individuals to frighten the regime. Our opinion was that if you kill an individual, there will be another individual. So we did not use this method.'

MacMichael immediately imposed a nine-day curfew on Jerusalem, Haifa and Tel Aviv. The Palestine Arab press accused the Jewish community of 'raising a white flag with the left hand and shooting with the right',[9] asking the obvious question: 'Is it an expression of the war effort that we should stab Britain in the back?'[10] But the main Jewish press was just as severe, referring to the Irgun as 'criminal lunatics' who were 'deeply despised by every member of the Jewish community'.

The Haganah leader Eliahu Golomb and the Vaad Leumi (National Council) called on the Yishuv to isolate the Irgun. The Jewish Agency declared: 'The deadly hand which directed these crimes is unwittingly or maliciously helping the enemies of the Jewish people.' But at this stage, in spite of their protestations of shock and disgust, the official Jewish bodies did not invite the Yishuv to cooperate with the British police in finding those responsible for the explosions.

From then on, until they left Palestine four years later, this was to become the main theme of British complaints against the Jewish Agency and its offshoots. Were they sincerely opposed to Jewish terrorism? They replied that they were, that they had frequently declared their opposition publicly. Did they sincerely want to see terrorism destroyed? They replied that they did. In that case, why would they not take the obviously most effective course of action – invite their people to denounce the terrorists to the police? Over the years Jewish officials gave a number of reasons for refusing this request, all of which the British found quite unconvincing.

Bernard Joseph says: 'The Jews have a daily prayer called The Eighteen Blessings. One of them contains the sentence, "There shall be no hope for the informer." This is ingrained in the nature of the Jew. Over the centuries the Jews have been victims of persecution by governments. A Jewish informer was in these circumstances a great danger to the whole community. So it became part of our ethical make-up that informing on a Jew to the government was a great evil.'

On March 9th, 1944, Bernard Joseph argued this question for ninety minutes with Inspector-General John Rymer-Jones and on March 27th with Chief Secretary John Shaw. Joseph explained that the Administration's behaviour was unfriendly to the Jewish cause. Rymer-Jones replied that as a policeman he was concerned with stamping out terrorism, not with the rights and wrongs of policy, and he expected the Jewish public to cooperate in apprehending murderers. Joseph's answer was that terrorism could not be considered in a vacuum.

Rymer-Jones then asked him a specific question – would the Jewish Agency find out and let him know where the Sternist leader Friedmann-Yellin (Yalin-Mor) was hiding? (He and twenty other top Lehi men had tunnelled their way out of Latrun four months earlier.) Joseph was unable to give the police chief any such assurance. He explained to Shaw that the British police in Palestine did not enjoy the confidence of the public as they did in Britain. Shaw told him firmly that statements of condemnation were all to the good, but they were not enough: 'If the public would not help the government in apprehending these criminals, the government would have to find other ways of doing so, as a result of which the public might possibly suffer.'[11]

The March 23rd explosions nevertheless gave the police their best chance to behead the Irgun. Yaakov Chylewicz, a Revisionist party fundraiser with many Irgun connections, contacted Catling and asked to talk to him. Catling remembers picking him up in Jerusalem in his car some time during the nine-day curfew: 'We drove around and talked it over. He was adamant that what happened on March 23rd was the wrong thing to do, that it damaged the Jewish cause. He said he would tell us all he knew about the Irgun, if we could guarantee to get him out and give him enough money to get started in the United States.'

Catling immediately contacted US Consul General Lowell Pinkerton. On March 28th Pinkerton cabled Washington: 'Chilevicius [sic] willing to give names and whereabouts of leaders of terrorist groups, but if he does so, he must leave Palestine immediately to avoid revenge.'[12] The State Department quickly gave Chylewicz, a Pole from Wilna, a priority place on the April quota for Lithuanian nationals and advised their consulate in Cairo to issue him an American visa. Catling arranged to provide him with a sum of money, about £2000.

In Begin's book Chylewicz appears in a different light and under a different name: 'Tsorros was a gambler and liked to dress well. He was short of money and, it seems, he was also a coward. Once he had begun to slip, he continued going downhill.' Begin has vivid memories of Chylewicz visiting him in Jerusalem: 'I remember him standing by the

cradle of our one-year-old son and giving him a present. He had asked
to see me specially, in order to find out my address and give it to Mr
Catling. So he was, if I may say so, a very base man, not only because he
betrayed us, but also because he visited a father with a present for his
child, then went away and took steps to deprive that child of his father.
I suppose that if the British police in those days had captured me, there
wouldn't have been a trial at all. They would have opened fire. I assume
so.'[13]

Begin and his intelligence chief Eli Tavin say that they had long suspected Chylewicz of being an informer, that an agent of theirs in the police
gave them a copy of his list, which included almost the whole Irgun high
command. Begin says: 'My friends came to see me and put it very simply.
This is the law of the underground, we must kill him, because he betrayed
us and may betray us again. I did not agree, because it would have been
against the ethics of the Irgun.' All Begin did, he says, was to send
Chylewicz a message inviting him to appear before an Irgun court. He
refused to come. Then, says Tavin, 'I went to interview him, to ask him
to explain himself and eventually perhaps to see that he was put on trial.
But he had left his apartment a few minutes earlier.'

Catling gives a different version of these events. He dismisses as absurd
Begin's idea that the police would have shot him out of hand. There was
no case in which his men in Jerusalem opened fire without good reason,
he says, whatever may have happened in Tel Aviv. He also rejects
the theory that the Irgun knew about Chylewicz's plan in advance: 'I
didn't get the list myself until the last minute. I remember Chylewicz
dictating about 30 or 40 names and addresses to me down in Beersheba on
his way out of the country. He was taken on to Cairo in someone else's
car. I returned to Jerusalem and the operation went ahead that night. I
dare say that Tavin and his friends wanted to "interview" Chylewicz,
but on that occasion they were a bit slow off the mark. It's nonsense to
suggest that Chylewicz's list got to the Irgun before we moved in, because
practically the only name on it that we didn't lift that night was Begin.'

Begin only escaped because, quite by chance, he left his Jerusalem flat
a few hours after Chylewicz's visit: 'My wife said to me, "Stay for the
Sabbath." But I said that I had things to do in Tel Aviv. I left early Friday
morning [March 31st] and later that day the police were in our flat. My
wife told them the truth, that she didn't know where I was. She had a
difficult time, because the police came back every day looking for me. But
I had been warned not to go back there. I stayed on at the Savoy Hotel in
Tel Aviv.'

MacMichael was thus able to report: 'Acting partly on information collected by the police previously and partly on information communicated on March 31st by member of Irgun who turned informer, intensive police drive in the principal towns was carried out on March 31st and April 1st.'[14] By April 2nd fifty arrests had been made, including that of Irgun high command member Arieh Ben Eliezer. It was the nearest Catling ever got to a decisive blow against the Irgun.

Chylewicz reached America safely. The Irgun soon tracked him down and Begin believes that he is still alive in the United States: 'But we don't care about him now. We've forgotten about him.' Tavin says that the Irgun decided not to kill him because he was in contact with the FBI and his violent death would have put at risk their political activities in the United States. Their agent Peter Bergson (Hillel Cook) had recruited several prominent Americans – Congressmen Will Rogers and Andrew Somers, Bishop Edward Demby of Ohio, the writer Ben Hecht – to an Irgun 'front' organization called the American League for a Free Palestine.[15]

The League was outlawed by the main American Zionist bodies. On May 21st Senator Robert Wagner told Will Rogers that it 'served no useful purpose'. When questioned about it, Assistant Secretary of State Edward Stettinius confirmed that from the official viewpoint it was unrepresentative of Jewish opinion. But it gained some support among American Jews who felt that the line taken towards Britain by the official bodies was too soft. Its proclaimed aims were the opening of Palestine to free Jewish immigration, the formation of a Jewish army to fight with the Allies and the rescue of European Jewry. It also raised money for the Irgun, helping it to acquire arms and supplies.

Lehi too were back in action after their leaders' escape from Latrun. The followers of Abraham Stern led an extraordinary life, only a few hundred strong, hiding in the few houses that would give them sanctuary or living as old-fashioned outlaws in the caves and sand dunes of Holon, near Tel Aviv. 'Our headquarters was always on the move. Where we met once, we didn't meet twice,' recalls Itzhak Shamir. Yalin-Mor says that he could have taken fifty more Lehi men through the Latrun tunnel with him, but there would have been nowhere to hide them: 'We were really a hunted group. We were hunted by everybody – by the British, by the Haganah and even by the Irgun. The prisons were the only place where we were a majority.'

Yalin-Mor did not share Begin's ideas about the ethics of underground struggle: 'The Irgun were only attacking buildings. And we were laughing at them. We said that the British would simply reconstruct the buildings with our money. We thought it more effective to aim at the *lives* of the British.' Shamir believes that Lehi's personal-terror tactic was more humane than the semi-military style of the Irgun. He points out that a frontal attack on an army camp or bomb in a police station kills men at random, while Lehi were selective in their targets, killing on an individual basis, each time for a specific political or tactical reason.

Unlike the Irgun, Lehi men always carried guns and always resisted arrest. Yalin-Mor says: 'Our slogan was, "Kill or be killed, but don't be arrested." Prison could have destroyed our movement. Conditions in the detention camps were not bad and many people inside were broken. They became neutral. And I admit that in 1944 most Jews were quite satisfied with British rule in Palestine. They did business, they were quite well off. If you had taken a vote, perhaps eighty or ninety per cent would have given a good opinion of the British. But this was not the point. They were the alien power and we had to fight them to gain our freedom, whether they were liberal or inhuman.'

Therefore, when on February 14th two Lehi men were surprised sticking up posters by two British policemen they reacted at once, drew their guns and shot the policemen dead. On February 24th Lehi again blew up the car of Geoffrey Morton, their prime target, again failing to kill him. On March 23rd, while the Irgun blew up three police stations, Lehi gunmen shot down three British policemen in the streets of Tel Aviv, killing one. The Tel Aviv municipal council and Mayor Israel Rokach at once denounced the terrorists as 'lacking even a spark of humanity and Jewish conscience'.[16]

Yalin-Mor had several meetings with Haganah leader Eliahu Golomb, during which he explained why Lehi used such harsh methods: 'The political result of a terrorist action is a multiple of two factors, the numerical strength of the terrorist body and the intensity of its deeds.' The Haganah were numerous, so they could afford to be restrained, he told Golomb. The Haganah leader tried without success to persuade Yalin-Mor to call off his gunmen. They were violating the discipline of the Jewish community. What did Yalin-Mor know of the politics of the matter, the international status enjoyed by the Jewish Agency, the assurances recently given to Weizmann by Roosevelt and Churchill that there would be a Jewish state after the war? Lehi's flamboyant behaviour was putting it all in jeopardy.

Yalin-Mor told him that there would be no British change of policy. Britain would never allow a Zionist solution: 'I told him that sooner or later he would have to start fighting the British too, otherwise the Jewish Agency would lose control over the people here. So even if he was only considering the possibility of one day having to fight the British, he ought to come to terms with the Irgun and ourselves.'

To the Zionists in London in 1944 this sounded like the voice of madness. At last, after years of negotiation and struggle, the British Cabinet had been brought back to partition – a policy acceptable to Weizmann and every moderate among them. Abba Eban says: 'In 1944 there seemed every likelihood that the partition plan would go through. It was approved not only by the pro-Zionists, but also by Stanley, MacMichael, Moyne and others. These were very powerful auspices.'

Arthur Koestler met Weizmann frequently and discussed his hopes: 'He believed in maximum pressure for minimum demands. He believed that the British would partition Palestine. And if the frontiers imposed were impossible, there would be rectifications later, either by force or by negotiation.' The followers of Jabotinsky, the Irgun and Lehi included, believed exactly the opposite, that Zionists should make maximum demands – an immediate Jewish state on both sides of the Jordan – perhaps intending to reduce these demands later. Weizmann saw this approach as likely to isolate Zionism and antagonize its powerful friends, especially Roosevelt and Churchill.

Harold MacMichael, the man held responsible by Zionists for the *Struma* tragedy and countless other crimes, was now transformed into a secret ally of the moderate Zionists. On January 30th he congratulated Stanley on the result of the Cabinet Committee: 'Final success seems to be in sight, provided that HMG are completely firm and final, both in the taking of their decision and in carrying it out . . . The air is too full of 'partition' for the issue to be smothered much longer.'[17] Six months later, in his farewell dispatch from Palestine, he was to confirm his conversion to the desirability of a Jewish state.[18]

MacMichael was concerned about the effect of any announcement on ths Arab troops that Britain commanded. He believed that the Sarafand-stationed companies of the Arab Legion would riot in Jaffa. But other Arab units would stay calm, especially if they could be temporarily removed from the Middle East beforehand. As for the neighbouring Arab countries, they would denounce the plan, but cause little serious trouble, turning their attention instead to the 'advantages to be secured by themselves from the *fait accompli*'.

Another encouraging aspect, reported MacMichael, was the attitude of

Taufiq Abu el-Huda, prime minister of Transjordan. Taufiq told Alec Kirkbride, MacMichael's deputy in Amman, that 'he did not in fact see any alternative to partition'. Much depended on what sort of partition it was. Of course no Arab, himself included, would agree to partition publicly, but if Britain imposed it the Arabs would acquiesce in the end.

Would it then be a good idea, Kirkbride inquired diplomatically, for Transjordan to absorb the section of Palestine to be allocated to the Arabs? Taufiq replied: 'They would not be enthusiastic, but if they were simply told they would be placed under the Emir [Abdullah], they would have to accept the position. It would, however, be a great mistake to consult them first.'

MacMichael believed that keeping Jerusalem under Mandatory rule would meet the religious objections of Jews and Moslems, as well as satisfying many of Britain's strategic requirements. It would dilute the classic Jewish anti-partitionist objection – 'What is Zionism without Zion?' – which had been raised in answer to the 1937 Peel Commission proposals. American Zionists in particular might find it an acceptable second-best for a Christian power to hold Zion in trust for humanity against every possible aggressor, at the same time guaranteeing Jewish access to the holy places.

Amid this almost unanimous acceptance of partition, the only serious British opposition came from the diplomatists, especially from such well-known Arabophiles as Lampson and Cornwallis in Cairo and Baghdad. Douglas Harris, one of Palestine's chief irrigation and economic experts, recalls a meeting in Cairo under Moyne's chairmanship on April 6th when the two ambassadors clung to the White Paper tooth and claw: 'When at last it was hammered into them that there was not the slightest hope of its being implemented, they fell back on drawing gruesome pictures of the situation that would arise on the announcement of partition.'

Their gloomy forecasts reminded Harris of the fat boy in *Pickwick Papers*: 'I wants to make your flesh creep.' The Egyptians would stop cooperating and start sabotaging British ships in Alexandria. In Iraq wild tribes would rebel. The whole Arab world would have to be held down indefinitely by force. The meeting struck him as a contest between 'ambassadorial clichés' and the 'reasoned arguments' of Moyne and MacMichael in favour of partition.

At this point – early 1944 – a fourth participant entered the conflict between Jews, Arabs and British. The United States could now no longer avoid direct intervention. Halifax reported from Washington: 'There is now in progress a gigantic campaign by means of speeches, meetings, articles, paid advertisements and political pressure to influence American opinion in favour of Zionism.' In early February the Foreign Affairs Committee of the House of Representatives discussed a resolution in favour of a Jewish state. Several of Churchill's pre-war Zionist speeches and statements were read to the Committee, much to the British embassy's embarrassment.

The Committee heard from the War Department, however, that any such declaration would damage the war effort and lead to a commitment of American troops after the end of the war against Germany and Japan. These were the weeks when preparations for the Allied invasion of Europe were at their height. Hundreds of thousands of British and American troops were about to go into action. The idea of committing troops to more conflict overseas after the war was won did not appeal to American public opinion.

The Foreign Office took a serious view of such 'irresponsible and un-balanced clamour' which 'has already created despondency and alarm enough in Arab countries'. Any pro-Zionist Congressional resolution would be lumped together in Arab minds with the British declaration for partition, which they believed to be imminent. It would become, reported Halifax, 'a new Magna Carta for Zionism'. The result would be in-flammatory.

At the end of February Syria, Iraq and Egypt protested officially to the United States about the proposed resolution. But in the atmosphere of 1944 Arab complaints, while they were taken seriously by the Near East Division of the State Department, made little or no impression on Congress. Representative Emanuel Celler of New York declared that Arab protests were purely the result of British machinations. Few Americans believed the Arabs to be a force of any sort, whether militarily or politically.

On March 9th, 1944, an all-day Zionist conference in Washington was addressed by Vice-President Henry Wallace, Senator Robert Taft, Senator Robert Wagner, Wendell Wilkie and various Church and Labour representatives, most of whom spoke enthusiastically in favour of the official Zionist programme. Before the conference began, Stephen Wise and Abba Hillel Silver visited the White House to seek the President's support. Roosevelt had to bear in mind that eight months later there would be a presidential election and that several million Jewish votes would be influenced by his attitude.

But on this occasion the President was also influenced by the State and

War departments, the British government and perhaps even the Arab protests, all of which suggested to him that Jewish pressure was damaging the war effort. His March 9th statement confirmed that the United States had never approved the 1939 White Paper, promised justice to 'those who seek a Jewish national home' and referred to 'hundreds of thousands of homeless Jewish refugees'. But it did not demand a Jewish state in Palestine or unrestricted immigration. Halifax noted that the pendulum seemed to be swinging away from the Zionists.

In June Isaiah Berlin, still in Washington, advised the Foreign Office that much could be done to reduce the damage being done to Britain by American Zionism: 'The quarrel is between the majority of American Jews and HMG, not between the American public and Britain.' The State Department and War Department were against Zionism, but both the President and Congress were influenced by it, partly for electoral reasons, also because they were regularly advised by 'a number of influential Jews of varying degrees of quasi-Zionism'. It was among these individuals, Berlin believed, that careful work might improve Britain's position.

A minority of America's Jews, for instance the recurrent presidential adviser Bernard Baruch, saw Zionism purely as an obstacle to assimilation and were opposed to it on principle. Many more were enthusiastic supporters of the Biltmore programme or even, like Ben Hecht, advocates of Irgun's plan to restore the Land of Israel on both sides of the Jordan. But another large number, including many of the country's most powerful Jewish citizens, fell between these categories.

Henry Morgenthau, the banker Eugene Meyer, the former governor of New York Herbert H. Lehman and Roosevelt's friend Felix Frankfurter were some of those Berlin mentioned as possible converts to Britain's short-lived 'quasi-Zionist' policy of 1944. The partition policy recommended by the Cabinet in January had already broken the unity of Arab opposition. It might also, if skilfully explained, neutralize American Jewry, the other rock of the Scylla-and-Charybdis threat to Britain's position as a leading Middle East power.

But in mid-1944 the two Allies' main concern was with landing their armed forces in Normandy, not with Palestine. On Anthony Eden's initiative, the Cabinet had authorized a period of consultation on the partition plan. Representatives overseas were asked for their advice and ordered to prepare for the announcement. It was a laborious process that took many months. So long as the American and British public was obsessed with D-day and the fighting in France, the two Whitehall departments were not pressed by the Cabinet to reach a speedy conclusion and had every chance to delay the implementation of a decision they deeply deplored.

Churchill, his attention consumed by more vital matters, decided not to bring matters to a head by publicizing the Cabinet Committee's existence. As Eden noted on June 10th, the one point on which the Cabinet was unanimous was that the White Paper would not continue after the war. By a majority, the Cabinet was in favour of partitioning Palestine. But in spite of this and apart from a small amendment to allow unused immigration certificates – about a third of the 75,000 total – to be taken up after the official March 31st cut-off date, the White Paper remained as Britain's policy during 1944. There was not yet any basis for discussion or negotiation with 'semi-Zionist' American Jews, although Churchill confidently expected that that day would soon come.

But whatever Britain did or did not decide, D-day or no D-day, the American people had to elect their president and the two main parties had to make their position clear on the electoral issues, Palestine included. On June 27th the Republican party declared that free Jewish immigration into Palestine was guaranteed by the Balfour Declaration and the Mandate. It demanded the restoration of this right and condemned Roosevelt's failure to insist on Britain enforcing it. A month later the Democratic party demanded that same immigration policy, adding for good measure its hope that the result would be 'a free and democratic Jewish commonwealth'. Each party was trying to outdo the other.

These pressures finally forced Roosevelt to abandon the neutral position he had taken in March. On October 15th, three weeks before the election, he announced in a letter to Senator Wagner his approval of the Palestine plank in the Democratic platform: 'I know how long and ardently the Jewish people have worked and prayed for the establishment of Palestine as a free and democratic Jewish commonwealth. I am convinced that the American people give their support to this aim, and if reelected I shall help to bring about its realization.'

And so it happened that, at a particularly close moment in British-American military cooperation, a serious political rift opened between the two allies over Palestine. The essential aim of Palestine policy, Anthony Eden noted in June, was to keep the issue from harming the war effort or the British Empire, its interest in oil and communications. Eden expressed the fear that Britain might lose her place in the Middle East. There was no doubt in his mind, he wrote, that the Americans had thoughts of 'usurping' it.[19]

The United States, of course, shared Britain's war aims entirely. But most American leaders did not share Eden's concern to preserve British control over Middle East oil and communications, still less Eden's assumption that Britain was more entitled than the United States to hold such a position. By and large, they saw little merit in the British Empire and little reason for committing American resources towards perpetuating it. On the other hand, they *did* care about the rights of the Jews in Palestine. The Jewish vote was big enough and Jewish influence strong enough to make this an important political issue in America.

But Roosevelt's unequivocal pro-Zionist statement of October 15th seemed more than a political manoeuvre to many in Britain, Eden included. To them it looked suspiciously like the first step in an American bid for Middle East supremacy. It seemed a total surrender to the Zionist credo, a gesture that went far beyond the President's electoral requirements. Already suggestions were being made that Britain, having violated the Mandate by restricting Jewish immigration, ought to be forced to surrender it. And if that happened, who but the United States would have the resources or the inclination to take it up? In any case, she would continue to use her Jewish citizens to build a bridge to the Yishuv, to establish an American base in Palestine that would serve American interests rather than British.

Meanwhile the two Allies were faced with another terrible dilemma, highlighting the conflict between common humanity on the one hand and the demands of politics and military strategy on the other. At the end of May 1944 a Hungarian Zionist representative, Joel Brand, and a Gestapo agent, Bandi Grosz, reached Istanbul with an amazing proposal which, they said, had been made by Adolf Eichmann, the architect of the mass extermination programme. Eichmann had promised, said Brand, to close Auschwitz camp and release one million Jews from Europe in return for two million cakes of soap, two hundred tons of cocoa, eight hundred tons of coffee, two hundred tons of tea and ten thousand trucks. He had told Brand: 'Blood for money, money for blood,'[20] promising that the trucks would be used only on the Russian front.

The British refugee committee, under Oliver Stanley's chairmanship, discussed the matter on May 31st. From the outset their attitude was negative, as it had been over the Romanian Jews in 1943. Alec Randall said that there were 'substantial reasons for having nothing to do with the proposals as they stood'. His concern was that the idea 'might secure sympathy beyond its merits in Washington'. The US War Refugee Board had, he observed, committed itself to rescuing Jews 'partly for electoral reasons'.[21]

The committee agreed that the evacuation of any large numbers of people to Turkey presented military risks and that the political risks would be especially acute because those people were Jews. The general view was that 'the necessary operations could not be undertaken without altering the course of the war'. It was also unthinkable to bargain with the Gestapo and to consider supplying them with stores, let alone war material.

A further problem was foreseen in Eichmann's cunning assurance that the ransom trucks would be used only against the Red Army, not against the Western Allies. In those early days of June the West had good reason to be grateful to Stalin. He had loyally mounted a powerful offensive on the eastern front to coincide with the June 6th American and British D-day landings. The invasion had been successful and it was obvious that Hitler's days were numbered.

The one thing that could possibly ruin the great Allied endeavour was internal dissent or suspicion. The Brand proposal was therefore at once communicated to the Soviet government. And within a few days (June 19th) Deputy Foreign Minister Andrey Vishinsky explained to US Ambassador Averell Harriman that, in his government's view, no conversations with Germany whatever were permissible.[22]

But the Jewish Agency, in their agony, could not simply let the matter drop. Their information was that 1,500,000 Jews had been murdered in Nazi Europe during 1943. Thousands every day were being gassed in Birkenau and Auschwitz. There were still 300,000 Jews in Budapest, awaiting their doom, expected to be taken to Poland within a few days.[23] Something had to be done. It was unthinkable just to ignore the offer. The Agency therefore suggested sending British and American officials to Istanbul to discuss a rescue operation with Nazi agents, while Brand and Grosz returned to Budapest. They invited the Allies and neutral countries to open all their territories to Jewish refugees. They wanted the British and American air forces to bomb the death camps and the railway lines leading to them.

Discussing the matter with Eden on July 6th. Weizmann and Shertok did not press for the supply of trucks to Nazi Germany. They knew that the Allies would never provide Germany with war material and would never risk a rupture with the Soviet Union. They suggested instead a cautious but positive response to the Nazi offer: 'It might be a trap. He [Shertok] was prepared to take the risk. On the other hand, all it might boil down to might be a question of money. They believed that, if that was so, the ransom should be paid.'

Eden was not enthusiastic: 'They could not possibly agree to anything that looked like negotiating with the enemy.' But he promised to speak to Churchill about issuing a warning to the exterminators' Hungarian accomplices and to raise the idea of bombing the railway. Weizmann pointed out that such bombing 'would have a far-reaching moral effect'[24] and would give the lie to the suggestion often made by Nazis (and others) that the Allies were not really displeased about the massacres of Jews.

Brand was arrested as an enemy alien as soon as he reached Aleppo in Syria. He was interviewed by Moshe Shertok, who came away much impressed by his courage and spirit, then taken to Cairo, where he was seen by Ira Hirschmann of the US War Refugee Board, who came to Moyne with a letter from Roosevelt. Hirschmann too considered the Hungarian a truthful man, obviously genuine in his desire to help his fellow-Jews. He recommended sending Brand back to Budapest to see what he could achieve.[25]

At this point Brand had his famous meeting with a British official in the garden of a British-Egyptian club in Cairo. He mentioned Eichmann's offer, whereupon the official replied: 'What on earth are you thinking of, Mr Brand? What should we do with a million Jews? Where should we put them?'[26] The speaker may have been Moyne, Brand writes, but he is not sure.

In a note to Eden on July 11th Churchill described the massacres of Jews as 'probably the greatest and most horrible crime ever committed in the whole history of the world', promising that all who took part in it and fell into British hands would be put to death. But in another note around the same date he ordered 'that no negotiations of any kind should be entered into'.[27] Brand's mission was therefore doomed and he remained in comfortable custody in Cairo.

Many books have been written about this tragic story, none of them explaining fully why in July 1944 Churchill and Roosevelt dropped all plans to rescue the remnants of European Jewry. One may guess, though, that Soviet unwillingness was an important factor, expressed as it was in support of the usual objections of the two Western foreign ministries. The Foreign Office, apparently, had secret information that the main aim of Eichmann's offer was to drag the United States and Britain into tortuous discussions, thus driving a wedge between them and the Soviet Union.

This information, together with Andrey Vishinsky's blunt June 19th rejection, may well have persuaded Roosevelt not to follow Hirschmann's advice and proceed with the rescue attempt, with or without Britain's help. On the one hand, as Eden pointed out, Roosevelt thought that failure to act might cost him New York State in the election. He was also, to be fair, deeply concerned to save lives.[28] So was Churchill, though the Foreign Office saw nothing but the political difficulties involved. On the other hand, both men were advised that, if the offer was a Gestapo trap and they fell into it, the whole war might be at risk.

The proposal to bomb the machinery of extermination also fizzled out, perhaps for the same reason. On July 4th Assistant Secretary of War John McCloy wrote that it would involve diverting air support from vital operations, that it was unlikely to be effective and that it was impracticable anyway. On September 1st Richard Law wrote to Weizmann on the Foreign Office's behalf to tell him that 'in view of the very great technical difficulties involved' there would be no bombing. Weizmann complained to the Prime Minister and on October 30th his secretary John Martin replied tersely: 'We have discussed this matter with the Soviets and that's it.'

The former Irgun leader Samuel Katz, like his friend Menachem Begin, believes that something far more sinister lay behind Britain's motives: 'Mine is a very brutal conclusion, because the facts are brutal. I do not suggest that anybody in the British government would have lifted a finger to kill one single Jew. But they were not prepared to lift a finger either to stop the process of killing in Nazi Europe, because they knew that at the end of it all there would be fewer Jews worrying about Palestine. Eden was getting ready to make a pact with the Arabs. He was, after all, the founder of the Arab League. I see a correlation between his refusal to help save the Jews in Europe and his plan to do a deal with the Arabs, to get them to accept the 1939 White Paper, which was to become the coffin of Zionism.'

Katz believes that the British (and presumably the American) decision to abandon all rescue attempts was one of cold calculation, based on their plan for an Arab Palestine and the preservation of Britain's position in the area after the war. British documents for 1944 do, it is true, reveal a certain indifference to the sufferings of European Jewry. Agonized Jewish appeals, explaining what was happening in its full enormity, did not arouse the shocked sympathy and helpful understanding that one would justly expect from any normally humane person. Instead they produced irritation and resentment against a powerful pressure group, persistently and eloquently pleading its own narrow interest with complete disregard for the wider demands of the war effort.

This feeling is illustrated by a note written in the Foreign Office by

Armine Dew on September 1st, 1944: 'In my opinion a disproportionate amount of the time of this office is wasted on dealing with these wailing Jews.'[29] The documents show no other outburst quite so offensive, but it is nevertheless illuminating that a British official could write such words at such a time in the context of what was happening to Jews in Europe, which he and his Foreign Office colleagues well understood. But although the tone of this note was exceptional, the content was effectively in line with the rest of the properly expressed advice that ministers were receiving. It reflected the general lack of sympathy among British officials to all Zionist aims and Jewish requests. They believed that these were fundamentally unjust, dangerous to the war effort and to Britain's post-war interest. They therefore averted their eyes from the most pressing humanitarian considerations imaginable.

This general attitude, this indifference to the Holocaust, this refusal to recognize what seemed to most Jews the obvious *justice* of the Zionist cause – all this crept into the souls of the Yishuv and increased their resentment against the British, for befriending them and then betraying them. The attitude seemed typified by the remark attributed to Moyne, probably wrongly – 'What would I do with a million Jews?'[30] – which spread through the Yishuv by word of mouth during the autumn of 1944 and helped to inspire another series of Lehi assassinations.

'We made several attempts on the life of High Commissioner Mac-Michael,' says Yalin-Mor. 'Unfortunately we did not succeed. The closest we came was in our attack on his car on August 8th, 1944. It was ordered by the Lehi central committee of three, of whom I was one.' MacMichael reported: 'This afternoon my wife and I were motoring to a farewell function when my car under police escort was ambushed, presumably by members of Irgun or Stern group at kilometre four from Jerusalem on the Jerusalem–Jaffa road. My ADC Nicholl was shot through the lung and is seriously wounded in the neck. I was only very slightly wounded in the hand and thigh. My wife is unhurt.' His driver too was hit in the neck and lost control of the car, but his bodyguard Micky Hills was able to get the driver's foot off the accelerator, then steer the car behind cover off the road.

Yalin-Mor says: 'Please tell Mr Hills that I admire very much his bravery, his ability to judge the situation and choose the best solution.' The driver and aide-de-camp were seriously wounded, but Hills fired back at the Lehi men until they retreated, then called for reinforcements, who arrived soon with police dogs and trailed the attackers to the village of Givat Shaul. But, as usual, no one in the village would help them to trace them further. No one would admit to seeing or hearing anything suspicious. The authorities therefore punished Givat Shaul with a collective fine of £500.

This act was at once criticized in the House of Commons by Reginald Sorensen, who pointed out that it would cause hardship to innocent people and smacked of the methods used by Britain's enemies. Oliver Stanley replied: 'Here is a case where in a small settlement the perpetrators of potential murder must have been known. Not one inhabitant assisted the law in bringing these criminals to justice.' More and more often this was to become the basis of Britain's complaints against the Jewish community.

The feeling among the Arabs in Palestine was that the £500 fine was absurdly lenient. A British policeman, E. P. Horne, explains: 'During the Arab revolt you only had to suspect that someone had harboured or helped a rebel and his house was blown up, razed to the ground. This was the traditional way of doing it. You had it in India and you had it in Africa. It was done by administrative order. There was another order, a food control ordinance, under which anyone caught hoarding more than a ton of sugar was fined £500. The Arabs made a joke about this in August 1944. They used to ask us, which is more valuable, a ton of sugar or the life of the High Commissioner?'

The British in Palestine generally shared this view, that their army and police forces were being held back by politicians, that if they were given the freedom to take stern measures of reprisal, as they had been during the Arab revolt, they would easily be able to destroy Jewish terrorism. In this, they probably underestimated the skill and motivation of their enemy. Many Irgun and Lehi members were highly educated and trained in the use of arms. A few were experienced in underground work during the early Nazi occupation of Poland. These qualities, combined with the driving force induced by despair and fervent belief in Zionism, generated a guerrilla movement more powerful than that of the Arabs in the late 1930s, one which has hardly been surpassed.

The British police were not similarly skilled or motivated. They had come to Palestine either from Britain or from various parts of the Empire to find themselves deeply involved in a conflict that was not theirs. Nor were they trained to fight guerrilla tactics. Some of them, true, were veterans of the Royal Irish Constabulary, disbanded after the creation of the Irish Free State in 1919. They had fought the enemies of British rule and, known to the Irish as 'Black and Tans', were known for their tough methods and the summary justice they meted out to rebels. But they had no knowledge of conspiracy and rebellion in the cities, which was an East European phenomenon and had hardly been known before under British rule. They did not study Jewish history, Zionist politics or the Hebrew language. They did not understand their enemy.

Tom Wilkin was an exception. Begin writes: 'Wilkin was as cunning as a fox and one of the few really capable members of the British detective force. He had risen from the ranks, knew Hebrew well and was a good psychologist.'[31] He lived with Shoshannah Borokhov, an attractive young member of the Jewish community, the daughter of Ber Borokhov, famous for his ideological writings linking Zionism with socialism. Yalin-Mor says: 'Wilkin was a very dangerous man for us. He was involved in Jewish society, and he had friends in the Irgun. He sat in cafés, talking to people in Hebrew and picking up gossip. He collected a mass of information, most of which he kept to himself. So we decided to get rid of him.'

Yalin-Mor believes that it was personal ambition that made Wilkin keep what he knew out of the files. In fact there was good reason for this. Another policeman, C. A. Wade, explains: 'We had to have Jewish policemen and we had to try and infiltrate the Jewish community, but this meant giving them the opportunity of infiltrating us. Wilkin had a Jewish inspector working with him who was one-hundred-per-cent Haganah. A lot of Wilkin's information it would have been dangerous to put in the files. It would all have gone straight to the Haganah and goodness knows who else.'

Early in the morning of September 29th Wilkin was walking towards his office at Jerusalem Police Headquarters, when Yaakov Banai and 'Eli' Sobol came towards him, drew their pistols and put eleven bullets into his body. Horne says: 'It demonstrated how deep was this compulsion and hatred in the Stern group. The pathologist worked out that he was killed instantly either by the first or the second bullet. But they fired nine bullets after he was killed. They must have stood over him and pumped the bullets in.'

Catling says: 'It shows, I think, that we did not take the terrorist threat seriously enough in 1944. Wilkin was worth his weight in gold. We ought to have guarded him night and day. As it was, when we lost him, it was like losing a good part of our filing system.' This is confirmed by many Lehi veterans, who even after thirty-five years remember Wilkin with a mixture of fear and hatred, tinged with admiration.

Geula Cohen says: 'Wilkin had Jewish eyes and a Jewish mind. We relied on the average British policeman being professional and uninvolved but Wilkin put his emotions into the fight against us. His Jewish friends liked him and often gave him information unintentionally. This could mean Lehi men being arrested or killed in an ambush. So that's why we had to get rid of him. We knew that so long as he was alive, many of us would be dead. I'll never forget the sigh of relief we all breathed, when we heard that our boys had killed him.'

The Irgun too were at work. Two days before Wilkin's death (September 27th, 1944) was Yom Kippur, the Jewish Day of Atonement, when by tradition a ram's horn (shofar) is blown by the Wailing Wall, the last vestige of the Jewish Temple, with the symbolic purpose of blasting a way through the Heavens for the prayers offered by Jews on this holiest of days. For years the British authorities, remembering how the Arab community had rioted in 1928 because of alleged Jewish encroachment on the *haram esh-sharif*, had forbidden the blowing of the shofar. Begin decided that the time had come to challenge this ruling. He had Irgun posters pasted all over Jerusalem announcing that anyone who interfered with the ceremony would be treated as a criminal and punished.

In fact the British police did not interfere, nor did the Irgun take action against the individual officers who guarded the Wall from a distance, having first taken the precaution of removing their identifying numbers. Instead they attacked four police stations, causing considerable damage, killing four Arab policemen and acquiring quantities of British arms. 'We did our duty. We defended the nation's dignity and sanctity,' wrote Begin in explanation. The Jewish Agency issued their usual denunciations, but many Jews noted that the British police had backed down when challenged over the shofar. Furthermore they had not reacted, as many in the Jewish establishment had feared they might, by taking drastic reprisal against the Yishuv as a whole.

On the British side this very point was becoming a bone of contention. What were the authorities doing to answer the terrorist outrages? All they seemed to do was mount searches and impose curfews, which lasted only a few days and merely irritated the population. Exceptionally, after the attempt on MacMichael's life, they imposed a collective fine, but it was only for £500 and, weeks later, it had not even been levied. Moyne reported that there was surprise in Cairo that Britain's reaction had been so weak. Arabs were recalling the 'prompt and stern' action taken after the murder of Yelland Andrews in 1937. In an obvious reference to the more militant figures of the Jewish Agency, Moyne suggested that Britain would be misunderstood if she failed to take action against various individuals who were inciting the Yishuv.[32]

'I feel bound to call the attention of my colleagues to the deterioration of the situation in Palestine,' Oliver Stanley advised the War Cabinet on October 7th. He quoted John Shaw, who was acting as High Commissioner after MacMichael's departure, to the effect that the recent violent incidents revealed the existence of a 'formidable organization', rather than a small gang. The attacks on the police stations had involved 150 armed men. British estimates put the combined Irgun and Lehi strength at more than five thousand. And there were only three thousand British police to fight them.

So what could Britain do, short of punishing the whole Jewish community in Nazi or Soviet fashion? Some suggested suspending immigration, or at least the entry of male adults, so long as the violence continued. Others suggested exile. On September 29th John Shaw wrote: 'Latrun camp is a source of persistent anxiety. There is always the chance of a concerted attack being made on it, with the objective of releasing Jewish detainees.' There were, Stanley reported, 276 Jewish men and twenty-six Jewish women in Latrun, all terrorist suspects, as well as twelve 'particularly dangerous men' in Acre prison. He had reason to believe that a rescue raid was being prepared 'and the General Officer Commanding and the police cannot positively guarantee that it would fail'.

Stanley had therefore approved Shaw's proposal that the suspects 'should be removed from Palestine forthwith and detained in such country as HMG may select'. The operation would be difficult, but these difficulties were surmountable, 'though I think it may be found best not to deport the women'.[33] Accordingly 251 detainees were flow from Latrun camp and Acre prison on October 21st to a camp in British-occupied Eritrea. The Jewish bodies at once protested strongly. They had a deep revulsion to the idea of any Jew, even a terrorist, being forcibly removed from the National Home, just as they were opposed to the execution of any Jew, whatever he had done.

But well-informed British officials understood that curfews, searches and punishments would not be enough in themselves to destroy such clever and determined conspirators. In Palestine, as in every similar situation before or since, there was one key to the problem of security – good intelligence. And up to now, because of the Yishuv's opposition to British policies and its inbuilt reluctance to inform against fellow Jews, intelligence was what the authorities lacked.

On October 12th, 1944, John Shaw and Commander-in-Chief General Sir Bernard Paget spelled out their demand publicly in unambiguous terms: 'Verbal condemnation of the outrages on the platform and in the press may have its effect, but is not in itself enough. What is required is actual collaboration with the forces of law and order, especially the giving of information leading to the apprehension of the assassins and their accomplices.'[34]

'The authorities may rest assured that the Yishuv as a whole has its own accounts to settle with the terrorists,' wrote the *Palestine Post*. The Yishuv would therefore put up with the inconvenience of the searches and would give the police more help, 'knowing that they will thereby be helping to eradicate a dangerous cancer'. A joint Irgun-Lehi pamphlet, dated October 15th, promised that the struggle would continue and asked the Yishuv to ignore the British appeal. But clearly this time its seeds had fallen on fertile soil. Assistant Inspector-General of Police Arthur Giles noted in his report: 'Thinking Jews appear to have realized that the terror campaign has reached a stage where it is seriously damaging the Zionist cause abroad.'

Weizmann and his friends had a good enough idea of what was happening in Whitehall that October. The Foreign Office, mainly through Minister of State Richard Law, were still fighting the Cabinet Committee and the new detailed proposals for partition, which included a map. The Jewish state would be bound by long and complicated frontiers and would be smaller than the one proposed by Lord Peel. The main Galilee area, which Peel had awarded to the Jews, would be an Arab 'island', cut off from the rest of the proposed Arab state by a corridor linking the Jewish coastal strip with the Jewish settlements around Lake Huleh, Lake Tiberias and Metullah. The British-controlled Jerusalem state would include Bethlehem, Lydda airport and Ramallah radio station.

In Law's view the eastern part of the Jewish state was a 'needless excrescence' that would cause endless complications. The Negev, which would remain temporarily under the British Jerusalem state, would remain a bone of contention, an invitation to Jewish expansion. And as soon as Jews began to enter their state in large numbers, pressure for this expansion would mount. The plan seemed only to confirm the view which the Foreign Office had always held: 'It is not possible to devise any satisfactory or practicable partition scheme.'[35]

Nevertheless the Committee's revised report of October 16th was firm and unrepentant: 'Partition should be carried through whatever the opposition . . . When the time comes HMG should act with unhesitating decision.' They agreed that, while they would prefer to announce this decision at the end of the war, it might be necessary to act earlier if Britain's hand was forced. They did not believe in further negotiations

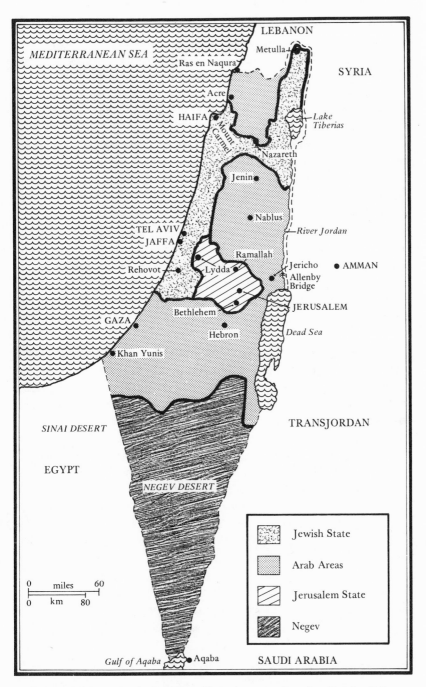

Legend:

- Jewish State
- Arab Areas
- Jerusalem State
- Negev

Proposed Scheme for the Partition of Palestine, 1944 (based on Foreign Office document FO 371 40133)

with Jews or Arabs. These would not produce agreement and would only muddy the waters. The only solution was a Judgement of Solomon, a swift and clean cut, after which there was at least a chance 'of each half of the baby surviving and leading a lusty life of its own'.

It is thus clear that in mid-October 1944 the British government was moving decisively towards the partition of Palestine. And it seems very likely that, had events followed a different course, Britain would have implemented the Committee's plan. Richard Law was the only Committee member to dissent. Churchill and Roosevelt both supported it.

These were some of the arguments that Moshe Sneh put to Begin on October 8th in a dramatic face-to-face meeting. The official institutions were elected. Begin and his High Command were self-appointed. The Jewish Agency enjoyed internationally recognized rights under the Mandate and had access to men in the highest positions. It negotiated, as was its right, on behalf of the Yishuv. It was on the verge of an important political breakthrough, of whose details Begin could know nothing. Who was Begin to decide what was right for the Jews of Palestine? How could he do it? He simply did not have the necessary information. And he had no democratic authority.

Begin told the Haganah chief, his old friend from Poland, that the Irgun must continue the fight against British rule. The rebellion had given the Jewish cause dignity and inspiration. Britain would now have to take account of the fighting Jew, a new phenomenon in recent history. With their White Paper they had tried to crush political Zionism and, for their own selfish and wicked reasons, they had helped Hitler in his exterminations. 'They deserve the whips that we now brandish over them.'

Sneh pointed out that Begin's actions could damage Haganah operations as well as Jewish Agency foreign policy. For instance, the Irgun might attack a factory, not knowing that it was a hiding-place for Haganah weapons. Also the Irgun's present 'mini-rebellion' was prejudicing the chances of success of a future full-scale rebellion of the Yishuv, which might become necessary if, as Begin predicted, the British were to revert to a clear anti-Zionist policy. Unless the Irgun desisted now, any such rebellion would lose its impact and political weight. And how could foreign governments be expected to recognize the elected Jewish bodies of Palestine if these were being defied and disobeyed by the Jews themselves?

The Palmach leader Yigal Allon says: 'We thought in the language of an underground government and we thought that it was not necessary to wait for the British Empire to recognize our government. In fact, when

I want to tease Mr Begin about the past – each of us is proud of his past for his own reasons – I say to him, "You see, I recognized the Jewish government years before the Americans and the Russians did. You recognized it only after the rest of the world had done so." ' On October 20th special courses began under Allon's command for the 170 Palmach members who were to take part in anti-dissident action.[36]

On October 18th the Haganah leader Eliahu Golomb, recently returned from London, criticized the terrorists at a press conference in Tel Aviv. On October 22nd the Jewish Agency Executive was advised by Moshe Shertok: 'The Yishuv, and primarily the Haganah, had to start now and cooperate with the authorities and the police.' But to many Jewish leaders this idea was still unthinkable. Executive member Rabbi Yehuda Leib Fishman said: 'If this proposal is accepted – and I hope it is not – we shall have voluntarily manoeuvred ourselves into the position of slanderers of our own people who, whether they are mad or merely foolish, are nevertheless our brothers . . . Have you so quickly forgotten the infamous Arms Trial and the insults that were heaped upon us then? Are we to lick the hands of those who kicked us?'[37]

There being no conscensus in the Agency Executive, the question was passed the next day to the National Council (Vaad Leumi), where a telling speech was made by Eliahu Golomb about the effect of terrorism on the London negotiations: 'If the Yishuv did not want to commit political suicide, it had to wake up to the fact that something was creating a stink right under its nose.' The discussions continued a whole day, after which the Vaad Leumi agreed to take action against the dissidents, but independently, without using the British.[38]

The summary of this discussion published in *Davar* on October 26th avoided any mention of the heated debates that had taken place, announcing only the 'unanimous decision' that 'the Yishuv and all its powers will do their best to stop' the terror. It did not explain, though, exactly what measures the Jewish bodies planned to take. Many Jewish leaders were still speaking angrily against the idea of working with the British, the perpetrators of the *Struma* sinking and the violence at Ramat Hakovesh, the authors of the notorious White Paper, the men who had just exiled 251 Jews from their homeland.

Sneh made another unsuccessful attempt to persuade Begin on October 31st, this time at a four-man meeting with Golomb and Begin's lieutenant Eliahu Lankin. But Begin was not interested in any British plan to create a Jewish state in part of Palestine For him there was no such thing as a 'good partition agreement.' He told Sneh: 'The Homeland is a unity and cannot be cut up.' There was no way of persuading him to call off his revolt for the sake of the British plan, which might have been acceptable to Weizmann, Shertok, Golomb and even Ben Gurion, but which would never have been acceptable to him. He did not believe that the British would create any Jewish state at all. Even if he had been persuaded to the contrary, he would still have refused to cooperate, because he was on principle opposed to the partition of the Land of Israel.

Golomb and Sneh did not realize how far the partition plan had progressed, but they knew about it in general terms. On November 4th Weizmann was given further information about it at a meeting with Churchill and his son Randolph. The Prime Minister told him that the matter had been investigated by a Cabinet committee, that a scheme existed, that he had not himself studied the details and was officially uncommitted. But he added that he was in favour of partition and believed that the Negev should go to the Jews.

John Martin's note of the talk says that it was made clear to Weizmann that any scheme approved by Churchill would be the maximum that the Zionists could hope to obtain, that to carry it through Churchill would have to overcome considerable opposition, especially from the Conservative party and the army. Zionism enjoyed more support in the Labour and Liberal parties. And nothing would be done to implement the scheme until the end of the war, probably until after the General Election.

Weizmann sent Abba Hillel Silver a less-than-full account of this meeting: 'There is some talk going on about partition, but no territorial project has yet been formulated.' He did not tell the American Jewish leader that a scheme already existed, or that Churchill favoured partition with Jewish control of the Negev. Instead, he emphasized Churchill's political difficulty over the issue and Churchill's worries about Jewish terrorism: 'I did my best to explain. But, as you will understand, it was none too easy.' He did, however, repeat Churchill's most reassuring comment, which many saw as the key to the approaching political conflict over the formation of a Jewish state: 'If Roosevelt and I come together to the conference table, we can carry through all we want.'[39]

Churchill had at last found it possible to authorize the formation of a Jewish Brigade. 'In view of the sufferings which Jewish people were at present enduring, there was a strong case for sympathetic consideration of projects in relation to them,' he told the War Cabinet on July 3rd. He had taken a personal interest in the Palestine Committee's deliberations and, although that autumn he had of course been concerned mainly with the progress of British and American forces in Europe, he had never forgotten his commitment to Zionism or his sympathy with the Zionists' aims.

Unlike the Foreign Office, he believed that Zionism ran parallel with Britain's interest, that a Jewish state in Palestine would be a more reliable and powerful ally to Britain than the Arabs, for whom he had little respect. There can be no doubt that he intended, with Roosevelt's and Weizmann's help, to establish this state in Palestine along the lines of the October 16th proposals, with Jewish control of the Negev, and that he would have succeeded in this aim in spite of the Foreign Office. But he and Weizmann as they lunched at Chequers that Saturday, could not take into account the shattering fact that a few days earlier the Lehi leaders had sent two men to Cairo to kill the Prime Minister's old and dear friend Walter Moyne.

Moyne had earned the particular dislike of Jewish militants. He had been colonial secretary when the ill-fated *Struma* reached Istanbul and, though they could not be sure of this, had urged the Turks to turn it back into the Black Sea. On June 9th, 1942, while briefly out of the government, he had said in the House of Lords: 'The Zionist claim has raised two main issues: firstly, the demand for large-scale immigration into an already overcrowded country; secondly, racial domination by these newcomers over the original inhabitants.' He had then observed that most Ashkenazi Jews were racially mixed and that large-scale Jewish immigration into Palestine was an impracticable dream. Zionists took great offence at his words. They also blamed him personally for Britain's failure to rescue European Jewry and for his apocryphal remark: 'What would I do with a million Jews?' In modern Israeli literature he is frequently described as a war criminal and an anti-semite.

Yalin-Mor explains, though, that the Zionists' personal quarrel with Moyne was not the main element in Lehi's decision to kill him: 'Really these acts by Lord Moyne were without meaning for us. They were useful only as propaganda, because they allowed us to explain to the people why we had killed him. What was important to us was that he symbolized the British Empire in Cairo. We weren't yet in a position to try to hit Churchill in London, so the logical second best was to hit Lord Moyne in Cairo.'

Shortly after 1 p.m. on November 6th a car containing Lord Moyne, his ADC Captain Andrew Hughes-Onslow, his secretary Dorothy Osmond and his driver Lance-Corporal Arthur Fuller came down the thirty-yard drive of the Minister Resident's house at 4 Galabiya Street in Ghezira, a pleasant suburb of Cairo. Hughes-Onslow got out of the car and walked up the steps to the front door, whereupon Eliahu Hakim and Eliahu Bet-Tsouri advanced down the drive towards the group, pistols drawn and at the ready.[40]

Bet-Tsouri pointed his gun at Hughes-Onslow and ordered him not to move. Moyne opened the rear door of the car and was making to get out when Hakim came towards him from behind and fired three shots into him through the open door. Simultaneously, according to Hughes-Onslow and the British police report, Bet-Tsouri turned his gun on Fuller, who was walking from the driver's seat round the back of the car to open Moyne's door. Like the others Fuller was unarmed, but Bet-Tsouri shot him through the chest, killing him immediately.

The two men ran back down the drive, mounted their two hired bicycles and pedalled furiously away, past the nearby residence of King George of Greece, where they were seen by the sentry at the gate, and on to the Zamalek Bridge, which leads to the Boulac district and the centre of Cairo. Meanwhile Hughes-Onslow ran to Ghezira police post and reported what had happened. They commandeered a car and gave chase, as did Police Constable El-Amin Mohammed Abdullah on his motorcycle.

It was this Egyptian who saw the two assailants on Boulac Bridge and caught them up threequarters of the way across. Bet-Tsouri turned and fired in his direction. (He was to say at his trial that he had orders not to harm any Egyptian and had therefore aimed wide.) Constable Abdullah fired back, wounding Bet-Tsouri in the chest. He then drove his motorcycle at Hakim and pinned him against a wall. An angry crowd gathered and seemed likely to attack the two gunmen, but police reinforcements arrived and took them away. At 8.40 that evening Moyne died.

In London that afternoon Churchill told his Cabinet colleagues of the attack and asked Oliver Stanley to have an appropriate talk with Weizmann. Stanley immediately sent a car to bring Weizmann to the Colonial Office from his hotel. The conversation between the two men was tense and angry. According to Abba Eban, Weizmann never forgave Stanley for the brutal way in which he gave the news. He nevertheless agreed with Stanley that special steps must now be taken to eradicate the Irgun and Lehi, that the Jewish Agency and its dependents must no longer approach this task halfheartedly.

The Jewish Agency and Vaad Leumi were already taking immediate action in this sense. The Haganah leader Israel Galili confirms that Moyne's death shocked them into drastic action. That same afternoon both bodies resolved to instruct the Yishuv to purge the Irgun and Lehi members from their midst, to deprive them of shelter and refuge, to defy their threats and, most importantly, to give the authorities all necessary help in destroying them. Full information of their whereabouts was to be given either to a responsible Jewish body or directly to the police.[41] These instructions were published in the Jewish press on November 8th.

In the House of Commons on November 17th Churchill mourned his friend's death with deep emotion. He also uttered a sombre warning: 'If our dreams for Zionism should be dissolved in the smoke of the revolvers of assassins and if our efforts for its future should provoke a new wave of banditry worthy of the Nazi Germans, many persons like myself will have to reconsider the position that we have maintained so firmly for such a long time.' His words had a profound effect on Weizmann, who had arrived in Palestine two days earlier. Did this mean that the encouraging words and reassurances he had heard from Churchill on November 4th were now withdrawn, that his decades of trust in Britain and painstaking negotiation were all wasted?

Most of the Zionist leaders reacted humbly to Churchill's words, seeing them not so much as rebuke, more as an appeal for help from an old friend. On November 19th Rabbi Fishman was the only member of the Jewish Agency Executive to oppose the anti-terrorist measures – the 'hunting season' or *saison*, as it came to be called. He was supported that same day by Peretz Bernstein in the Inner Zionist Council, who observed that terrorism was the result of gentile apathy to the Holocaust, that if the White Paper was annulled terrorism would be dead by midnight.[42]

But the pressure to take action overwhelmed such minority voices. Moshe Sneh said: 'It is not worth while to kick against the pricks on the eve of what we believe will be far-reaching concessions in our favour. In many ways it is much more convenient for us to hand over to the government the addresses of the terrorists. And they will not, in such cases, ask awkward questions as to how we got hold of them.' Several speakers pointed out that the Irgun and Lehi were just as much a threat to the Zionist institutions as to the British. They felt that they should kill the beast before it grew beyond their power to do so, and they voted accordingly.

The British authorities were now in a dilemma. Oliver Stanley wrote in a Cabinet paper: 'There is a widespread feeling in the Middle East that this shocking crime should not be allowed to pass without some striking reaction on the part of His Majesty's Government . . .' It might be desirable, for instance, to end Jewish immigration completely and simultaneously to mount a massive countrywide search for illegal Jewish arms. Others suggested imposing a heavy collective fine on the whole Yishuv and deporting their leaders, as the Arab Higher Committee had been in 1937. Arabists in London drafted numerous notes comparing Britain's failure to act with the draconian measures she had taken after the murder in Cairo in 1924 of Sir Lee Stack, governor-general of the Sudan.

On the other hand many Palestine officials, including the new high commissioner, Lord Gort, appreciated that terrorism would never be eradicated without the help of the Jewish organizations. And clearly this help would only be forthcoming if Britain showed forbearance. This point of view was strengthened by official Jewish announcements and various inspired leaks, all indicating that this time action really would be taken.

In a tough speech to the Histadrut Convention on November 21st Ben Gurion spelt out the measures to be taken against terrorists, not only the bombers and shooters, but also those who distributed their literature. Employers were to dismiss suspected terrorists from their place of work. If they were students, as many were, they should be expelled. 'Any landlord or flatowner must evict from his premises, despite any restriction to the contrary, anyone whom he knows to be a member or sympathizer of the terrorists, and not allow them to find haven in his property. All the long tradition of Jewish mercy must be forgotten, if we want our people to have mercy in the future.'

Ben Gurion devoted a special part of his speech to the last of his proposals, the one which he admitted had aroused more criticism than all the others put together, the proposal to cooperate with the British authorities: 'The tradition in the diaspora has always been to refuse the assistance of gentiles in our internal affairs. To a great extent, this same tradition holds good here in Palestine and we have established an almost autonomous regime of our own. But in those cases where our independence is just not enough and allows terrorist gangs to commit daylight robbery and murder, we must diverge from the tradition and ask the gentiles' help. I am sure that I do not exaggerate when I say that the terrorists constitute a far greater danger to us than they do to the authorities and the police . . . Without cooperating with them we shall fail to rid ourselves of this evil, and all who do not cooperate are helping the terrorists.'

The next day Churchill told the War Cabinet that the Jewish Agency were preparing to act: 'It was for the Zionists to satisfy us that they propose to take effective steps. If that were not the case, we might, however reluctantly, be driven to consider suspension of immigration despite the arguments against this course.' For the first time in his long career of support for the Zionist cause Churchill was contemplating a cessation of

Jewish immigration into Palestine. The pessimistic Zionists were the ones who were right. His enthusiasm for their cause had undoubtedly been weakened by his friend's murder.

Britain took none of the retaliatory measures suggested by Oliver Stanley – a fact which was noted with anger and disgust by the Arab leaders and their British supporters. Miles Lampson cabled from Cairo: 'It has taken the murder of one of our most distinguished public men to arouse us to our responsibilities and to indicate the direct results of our over-patience'. Eden replied on November 30th: 'I fully understand your desire for some dramatic action which would serve as a political gesture. But the really important thing is to round up the terrorists.' Britain had decided to accept the Jewish Agency's assurances. They would bury their differences and work against the common enemy on the basis of the assumption that, with American help, British policy was moving irrevocably towards the creation of a viable Jewish state.

At the end of October 1944 the Zionist leaders had good reason to believe that this was happening. Their talks with Roosevelt, Churchill and other Allied leaders confirmed them in the belief that they would soon have their own state. Weizmann knew – though he was careful to whom he passed on the information – that a partition scheme already existed, that it would have Churchill's and Roosevelt's support. When he came away from his November 4th meeting with Churchill, he must have believed that his plan of maximum pressure for minimum demands had worked after all.

But all this was changed by the assassination of Lord Moyne. Weizmann was welcomed to Palestine by the Yishuv with the panoply normally reserved for heads of state. But, as Begin writes, 'the shadow of civil war was in the air'. Begin had refused to retaliate, Yalin-Mor had been neutralized, but there was always the chance that some hothead would start attacking the moderate Jewish leaders. Weizmann's friend I. J. Linton recalls that they travelled round Palestine in a bulletproof car, until the heat made them open the thick glass windows. Weizmann knew that there were many in the Yishuv just as hostile to his 'good partition plan' as was the British Foreign Office.

But the historical significance of Moyne's death was its effect on Winston Churchill personally. Herbert Morrison, chairman of the Cabinet Committee on Palestine, records that Churchill had originally ordered the October 16th proposals to be raised in Cabinet. But then Moyne was assassinated and four months passed without any further action being taken. On February 26th Morrison reminded him: 'You felt that it was impossible to discuss future plans for Palestine while these outrages were going on and gave instructions that the discussion of the report should stand over.'[43] It was during these crucial months that the fire went out of Churchill's Zionism, that the partition scheme lost its momentum, allowing its opponents in the Foreign Office and the British army to gather their strength for a counterattack.

Former members of Irgun and Lehi reject this interpretation, insisting that the British were never willing or able to bring about a Jewish state. The only proper course of action, therefore, was to drive them out of the Land of Israel by force. And although the Irgun knew nothing in advance of the attack on Lord Moyne and for a time broke off relations with Lehi for keeping them in the dark, they soon came round to the view that the deed was one of heroism and patriotism.

'I am absolutely calm and my conscience is settled, because I have the feeling that I have done my duty,'[44] wrote Hakim to his parents from Cairo's central prison. At their trial in January 1945 they faced the prospect of the gallows with defiance, seizing every chance to turn the proceedings into an indictment of Britain's betrayal of the Zionist cause: 'Our deed stemmed from our motives and our motives stemmed from our ideals. And if we prove our ideals were right and just, then our deed was right and just.'

Such frank confessions, together with the eye-witness evidence of Hughes-Onslow and Dorothy Osmond, were more than enough to convict them of murder. On January 18th the papers on their case were transferred to the office of the Cairo Mufti, the only Egyptian authority permitted to impose a death sentence. Churchill had warned of the trouble that would ensue if the two men were not put to death 'with all proper despatch': 'I think you [Eden] ought to warn Killearn [Miles Lampson], so that he may not underrate the danger of which I speak. He is very astute.'[45]

Yalin-Mor remembers listening to the radio during the afternoon of November 6th. News bulletins were full of the re-election of President Roosevelt: 'Suddenly the BBC announced the attempt to kill Lord Moyne and from that moment everything about Roosevelt disappeared.' He believes that the deed did much to bring the Zionist cause to the attention of the world, to make it clear that the British were in Palestine as an alien occupying force, rather than as an impartial arbiter between two warring tribes. And if the assassination helped his cause, it was therefore justifiable and correct. As for the shooting of Arthur Fuller, Moyne's unarmed driver, Yalin-Mor believes that this too was necessary: 'Bet-Tsouri shot him because he was walking towards Hakim. He was putting the operation in danger.'

In fact, the killers gained more support in the United States than in Palestine. In New York particularly the view was widely expressed that Britain only had herself to blame for the murder of one of her leading political figures. *The Answer*, a pro-Irgun weekly published in New York, quoted Moyne's famous speech of June 19th, 1942, and concluded: 'The assassination of Lord Moyne can arouse in us no emotion stronger than regret.'[46] Andrew Somers, a New York congressman and co-chairman of Peter Bergson's committee, suggested on November 10th that Britain was just as responsible as Germany for the death of Jews and referred to the Colonial Office as 'the virtual partner of the bestial Nazis'.

This view found little or no support in Palestine, even from the Irgun, who were paying the price of Lehi's rashness and failure to coordinate operations. Begin writes that he was 'very angry'[47] with Lehi, that their deed provided the signal for launching the *saison*. On December 12th Weizmann wrote in a letter intercepted by British censorship: 'I warn you that I shall not be able to continue with my political work if terrorism is not suppressed. It must be, to prove to Mr Churchill that we earn what is given to us.'[48] On December 16th Rabbi Stephen Wise told a British official in Washington that 'it was better to destroy the assassins and have done with it'.

The Jewish leaders made no serious effort to have Hakim and Bet-Tsouri reprieved. For a few weeks it seemed that the two men might be saved by the indecision of Egyptian Prime Minister Ahmed Maher, but on February 24th he too was assassinated, a few minutes after declaring war on Germany, and very soon his successor Nokrashi Pasha signed the death warrant. On March 22nd Lord Moyne's killers were hanged, their deed and their methods rejected by the Yishuv almost without exception.

Attitudes in Israel changed over the years. The cold brutality of the double killing came to be seen as no more than a droplet, hardly significant when compared to the ocean of Jewish suffering. Admiration grew for the idealism and physical bravery of the two men. In June 1975 they were reburied with full military honours on Mount Herzl, in the presence of Israeli ministers. In April 1977 Itzhak Shamir, one of the three Lehi leaders who had ordered the killing, was appointed Speaker of the Knesset. But there are still many who believe that the two murders, especially that of the innocent and unarmed Arthur Fuller, discredited the Zionist cause morally, alienated Churchill and blocked the progress of the partition scheme.

This scheme, they believe, might well have gained the support of the Jewish Agency, in which case it could have been imposed by force of British arms as part of the rough-and-ready settlement of various similar disputes at the end of the war. In such circumstances the Arabs might well eventually have acquiesced, in which case Israel would now be smaller in size, but at peace with her neighbours.

A few weeks after Moyne's death Yalin-Mor had another meeting with Golomb to discuss the Haganah's new policy of cooperating with the British police. He accused him of the worst of all crimes – betrayal of the Jewish nation: 'I told him that I could understand a man who commits rape, but not a man who rapes his own sister.' He recalls Golomb's reply: 'You have the wrong impression. It is not we who are helping the British, but the British who are helping us. We have no accommodation for the people we arrest from the underground. We can keep them for a little while in a cellar or a kibbutz, interrogate them, get information from them, but then what do we do with them? The British have prisons and camps, which they pay for out of our taxes. Let them bother about these people.'

The upshot of the talk was that the Haganah did not operate the *saison* against Lehi. Yalin-Mor says that this is because he told Golomb: 'I will not say the same as Begin, that there will be no civil war, no fratricidal strife. If you fight us, we will not hand you over to the British because we have no relations with them. We have no facilities in kibbutzim to keep people and torture them. We shall rely on our guns. We shall kill you one by one.' However, most Israelis believe that Lehi obtained immunity from the *saison* not by threatening to retaliate but by promising to 'neutralize' themselves – to curtail their operations. Certainly for several months Lehi were inactive and their leaders were to be seen living freely in Haganah-controlled kibbutzim.

But life was harder for the men of the Irgun. Yigal Allon says: 'I was appointed commander of the main anti-dissident operation. Our duty was to get information about the people we were trying to catch, to capture them and not be captured ourselves, either by them or by the British. We operated as a sovereign armed force of a sovereign underground government. It was a very difficult task, a thankless task, and to do it under illegal conditions made it even more difficult.' His part in the *saison* was confined to the few weeks in which the Palmach fought the Irgun on its own, without British cooperation. After Ben Gurion's instruction 'to seek the gentiles' help', Allon and several other Palmach officers withdrew from the *saison*. 'I couldn't stomach it,' he says.

Teddy Kollek, now mayor of Jerusalem, acted for the Jewish Agency in liaison with the British. Reuven Shiloah acted for Haganah intelligence ('Shai'). Kollek says: 'My visits to the British were sporadic, not regular. We detained Jewish dissidents, interrogated them, then either released them or handed them over to the CID.' The Israeli historian Yaakov Shavit writes that there were almost daily contacts between the liaison officers and the CID, and that these Haganah officers often joined police in operations so as to identify suspects and prevent accidental arrest of Haganah men.[49] Shai provided the police with carefully selected extracts from their records. About 250 Palmach men, under the command of Allon's deputy Shimon Avidan, carried out the operations in squads of four or five men who lived together, made use of Shai information to trace suspects, then tracked down and arrested them.

Lord Gort was thus able to cable London on November 28th that the police had that month arrested 119 suspected terrorists. A single raid in Haifa, he said, had led to the discovery of thirteen Irgun men, a list of wealthy local Jews and their assets, a list of sums paid to the Irgun by such people, forged identity cards and illegal newspapers.[50] On December 22nd John Shaw reported that the Jewish Agency had supplied the CID with names of 561 suspects, 284 of whom were traced and arrested. They had also guided the police to a quantity of arms and a printing press.[51]

This was confirmed in a cable from Weizmann to Churchill on December 18th: 'Our cooperation with the authorities in stamping out terrorism is proceeding satisfactorily. 500 names of suspects have already been supplied to the police, as a result of which over 250 have been arrested . . . The assassination of Lord Moyne has caused abhorrence and violent resentment amongst all sections of the Jewish public, which is helping in tracing suspects, resisting extortions and morally isolating the terrorist group.'[52]

It is, from the Israeli point of view, an extremely sensitive issue even today. Galili says: 'We face great difficulties in explaining this matter, because people find it difficult to transfer themselves to the tragic circumstances of those days and also because of a traditional inherited revulsion against informing.' Young Israelis find it hard to understand that their leaders could ever have rejected a time-honoured law by cooperating with the British against the Irgun, an organization which, they are now brought up to believe, played a significant part in establishing their state and whose leader was later to become prime minister.

Begin himself does not hide his view that the *saison* was a shameful betrayal of the Jewish war of liberation. At the end of 1944 he used every shade of his colourful command of language to chastise the Haganah and the official Jewish bodies, likening them to Cain who slew his brother Abel in the Book of Genesis: 'You are raging mad, Cain. Thousands of your agents throng the streets of Jerusalem and Tel Aviv, the towns and the settlements, brought there to denounce, not to protect, to spy, not to work, for fratricidal war not for any war of liberation . . .

'You have chosen your ally, Cain. The oppressive government of the homeland and the Nazi-British secret police are your allies. You are serving them day and night, delivering men into hands which are stained with the blood of millions thrown back from the homeland's shore into the foundries of Majdanek, your own brothers . . . Sometimes by deceit, sometimes by stealth, but always brutally you drag suspects off to unknown destinations, subject them to Gestapo-like tortures in orange groves, then hand the victims over to the Nazi-British secret police, your ally, for further tortures and for deportation to Eritrea . . .'[53]

In his book *The Revolt*, first published in 1951, Begin writes more soberly but with equal feeling: 'The police were delighted. Lists of men they had long ached to get hold of were now coming in without cessation. Material worth its weight in gold – names, addresses, descriptions, types of duty, rank – all flowed into the files of Giles and Catling.'[54]

But the British were not in fact as delighted as Begin imagined. John Shaw wrote: 'On the whole the value of the information supplied has been poor and it may be that there has been a certain amount of working off of political scores.' Early in December the British protested to Haganah liaison officer Reuven Shiloah that they were only being given the un-important terrorists. He replied that the Jewish Agency did not know who the important ones were. The police then gave him a list of fifty-six men whom they regarded as the Irgun and Lehi 'cream'. But three weeks later, Shaw reported, only one of these fifty-six, Eliahu Lankin, had been handed over by the Haganah.

The British also complained that the Jewish Agency were feeding them the names of men they had quarrelled with, who had no connection with terrorism. Valuable time then had to be wasted sorting the sheep from the goats. And instead of handing over captured Irgun documents intact, the Haganah were digesting them and providing selected extracts. And they were giving the British no information at all about Lehi.

In other words, their 'cooperation' was half-hearted and based on their own political interest. The same principle applied to the capture of key Irgun officers. Instead of handing them all over to the CID, the Haganah were keeping the most interesting for themselves. Twelve cases of such kidnapping had come to police attention between December and February.

Gort wrote: 'Abducted persons have all returned safely, but more or less the worse for wear.'[55] Occasionally, the Haganah were using torture.

For instance, on February 17th Eli Tavin, head of Irgun intelligence, was spotted in the centre of Tel Aviv, bundled into a car, taken to a kibbutz at Ein Harod and chained to a bed. Haganah men interrogated him, charging him with extorting money and running Irgun 'military courts'. They asked him for the names of Irgun agents in their command: 'They accused me of trying to destroy their enterprise, of being a traitor.'

Tavin's treatment became harsher with every week that passed. At one point he was taken to an orange grove in Petah Tiava and put through a show of being sentenced to death and shot.[56] The Haganah then felt unable to release him. They were afraid that the Irgun would retaliate, once they heard what had happened to their intelligence officer. Nor did they feel able to hand him over to the British, for fear of the information he might divulge as an act of revenge. So they kept him month after month, releasing him only at the end of August, by which time he was very much the worse for wear.

On February 12th Irgun second-in-command Yaakov Meridor was arrested and nine days later deported to Eritrea. 'Collaboration has continued and in some respects has improved in quality,' noted Gort on March 1st.[57] By then the number of suspects denounced had risen to 850, of whom 357 were traced and 241 detained under emergency regulations. Golomb noted, 'The organized Yishuv has brought terrorist activity to a standstill.'[58]

Weizmann sent an envoy to reason with Begin, his friend Arthur Koestler, known for his contacts in the Revisionist movement. Koestler remembers Weizmann saying to him, 'Why don't you go to Palestine and talk some sense into those *meshuganeh* [madmen]?' He was duly provided with a place on the S.S. *Exeter*, reached Palestine at the end of 1944, had a meeting with Yalin-Mor and spent some weeks trying to arrange a similar meeting with Begin. The Irgun did not know – and Koestler was not authorized to tell them – that he came on Weizmann's instructions.

Eventually in the spring of 1945 Begin agreed to receive Koestler: 'My feelings about the Irgun were a mixture of admiration and anxiety. On the one hand there was a fanaticism about some of the members that I disapproved of. On the other hand I recognized them as the most combative element in Jewish society.' The meeting was 'a cops-and-robbers affair'. After changing from one car to another several times he was taken into a totally dark room and seated in a chair. When he tried to light a cigarette, the matches were snatched out of his hand. Begin, who apparently thought that Koestler only wanted to obtain colour for a book, writes that Koestler took specially long puffs on his cigarette in the hope of catching a glimpse of the Irgun leader's face.

Koestler says: 'I delivered my message, but I didn't get anywhere when I tried to argue with him in favour of partition. There was no rapport between us.' Begin told him that he did not believe in the existence of British circles 'friendly to Zionism'.[59] And this was true, from his point of view. Begin's plan for a Jewish state on both sides of the Jordan was a long way from even the most Zionist of plans then being discussed in London.

It all seemed to confirm the absurdity and destructiveness of the Irgun's crusade. Like Koestler, Weizmann had good friends in the British socialist movement, the electoral alternative to Churchill's Conservatives, and they seemed just as committed as Churchill, if not more so, to a Zionist solution of the Palestine problem. In December 1944 a Labour party document stated that the Jews must obviously be allowed to become a majority in Palestine – 'let the Arabs be encouraged to move out as the Jews move in' – and even proposed extending the country's frontiers. In April 1945 the party's executive committee reaffirmed its belief in Zionism. A Jewish state seemed certain to result, whoever won the British elections.

The supporters of partition – the British architects of the October 1944 proposals and their moderate Zionist friends – appreciated that the end of the war would provide a unique opportunity for imposing this solution. The United States was certain to agree, the Soviet Union likely to. The Palestine Arabs would be in no position to resist the British forces who implemented it. Their leader Haj Amin had broadcast German propaganda from Berlin and had helped Germany to recruit Moslems for her armed forces. Their cause had been thoroughly discredited by his association with Hitler. They had no alternative to him and so were politically helpless.

Nor would the Palestinians receive much help from their Arab neighbours. Transjordan was hardly independent, still officially forming part of the British Mandate. Iraq, Syria and Egypt were semi-independent, still suffering the indignity of British or French occupation. In fact, Britain held the field, and, especially if assisted by the Haganah, would be able to do all she wanted. For a brief moment she would be able to take advantage of post-war confusion and act, as the Cabinet Committee had proposed, with unhesitating decision and without further negotiations. True, she would have to develop the plan outlined to Weizmann on November 4th. It still needed to be refined into a document that would be presented to the peace conference and revealed to the world. But few doubted Britain's ability to achieve such an outcome. There was no one in a position to oppose it.

In such circumstances, with British forces proposing to act in harmony with the Haganah, there was no place in the political scheme of things for the Irgun or Lehi, whose operations merely damaged Zionism's unity as well as her relations with Britain. This was why the elected Jewish bodies, confident that British policy was moving in their direction, decided to eliminate the rival groups by methods which included denunciation and torture.

They would not have done this, one can be sure, had they known that as a result of Moyne's murder Churchill had frozen all discussion of the October 1944 scheme, that he was no longer using his personal influence on their behalf. The *saison* lasted several months, opened cruel wounds in the Yishuv and ended once it was clear that British policy was not responding. In fact, after a brief period of support for partition, British policy was about to revert to the line urged by the Foreign Office for many years, a line which on principle precluded the emergence of a Jewish state.

7

Churchill's Legacy to Bevin

MUSA EL-ALAMI was one of the few Palestinian Arabs with the intellectual equipment to make an impact upon Western opinion. He studied at the American school in Jerusalem and read law at Cambridge University. He was trained to discuss emotional issues with moderation, and to avoid the fervent tone of voice that Western officials find so off-putting in argument. Though connected with the Mufti through the marriage of his sister to Jamal al-Husseini, he never joined a Palestinian political party and clung firmly to his neutral position. As such he enjoyed great cultural and political advantages. He was related to the Mufti, the only real leader of the Palestinians, but he was not tainted by the odium of his many pre-war assassinations and his wartime collaboration with Hitler. He had no power base of his own, he was never a rival to the leaders of the various groups, so he could gain their trust. His cultural acceptability in European eyes made him doubly eligible as an occasional spokesman for the Palestinian cause. In November 1938 he was picked out by Malcolm MacDonald as the only possible envoy. In September 1944 he attended the Pan-Arab Conference in Alexandria, where he was recognized by King Farouk and other Arab leaders as his nation's representative.

In January 1945 he conferred with Ibn Saud in Mecca and on the way home put his views before an American official: 'Our solution is both broadminded and just. I can put it in a few words. We stand on the British White Paper.'[1] He explained how the Jewish population of Palestine had risen from 55,000 in 1919 to 400,000 in 1945. Those recent immigrants should be allowed to stay in Palestine, said Musa el-Alami, but only on the understanding that no more would come without Arab consent. In the future, perhaps, more Jewish immigrants might be admitted, but it would be up to them to prove this necessity. In the meantime they must play their part as nationals of the new Palestinian state, which would be ruled, as was only proper, by the elected Arab majority.

Musa el-Alami explained that the Zionists were trying to increase the Jewish population of Palestine, using the persecution of Jews as a pretext, until it passed the 1,200,000 Arab population. Their motives were not humanitarian but political. And they were the reason behind the basic Arab determination not to permit a Jewish numerical majority. Some months later Musa el-Alami asked US Senator Claude Pepper why of all places should Palestine be selected as a refuge for the Jews? Pepper mentioned the Jews' religious and historical connection with the area. Musa el-Alami then replied that, since Pepper had brought up the religious issue, he must tell him that every Arab saw every inch of Palestine soil as sacred, that they would never give their holy land to the Jews.[2]

Pepper mentioned that the Jews had brought great prosperity to Palestine. The Arab answered: 'While Senator Pepper, being a richer man than he, could undoubtedly embellish the house of el-Alami and clothe the el-Alami children in finer raiment, certainly the Senator would agree that this was no reason why el-Alami should be willing to relinquish his house and his children to the distinguished Senator.'

Nevertheless in November 1944 several moderate Arab leaders seemed almost resigned to the idea of partition. Taufiq Abu el-Huda of Transjordan told John Glubb, commander of the Arab Legion, that Arab leaders would reserve their opinion on that solution. If it was imposed, they would wash their hands of the business and wait to see how it turned out. Nuri es-Said of Iraq talked to Kirkbride of 'the cessation to the Jews of those areas where they constituted a majority' in order to confine Zionism within permanent boundaries. His main fear about partition, echoed by many Arab leaders and their British sympathizers, was that 'once the Jewish state had come into being and acquired international status, the Jews would use their powerful influence in Great Britain and the United States to secure a revision of the boundaries at the expense of its Arab neighbours'.[3]

But by December Nuri's attitude had hardened. He told Cornwallis that he was 'deeply despondent' about the rumours of the partition scheme. There could be no permanence in such a solution. If it was imposed, the Arab countries had decided what their policy would be: 'It will be one of complete boycott. There will be no recognition of or friendship with the Jewish partition state. There will be no commercial relations of any sort. No foreign Jews will be allowed into Arab land.'

High Commissioner Gort had come to similar conclusions after a visit to Baghdad in January 1945. He came home convinced that partition would lead to a permanent disorder and violence, that Nuri was right to favour a bi-national Palestine state, two-thirds Arab and one-third Jewish. This solution might allow Jewish immigration at the rate of 1500 or 2000 a month for a time, but would never allow a Jewish majority anywhere. Gort told US Consul-General Pinkerton why he rejected partition: 'He [Gort] likened this settlement to a bridgehead which must either be extended or wiped out. He said that any Jewish state which might be established in Palestine without agreement with the Arabs would have serious and continuous trouble in defending itself against Arab attack and Arab boycotts.'[4]

The erosion of Britain's partition plan continued as the three main Allied leaders – Stalin, Roosevelt and Churchill – met at the Yalta Conference in February. The Western armies had made few advances during the winter. They had just defeated the last great German offensive of the war, the 'Battle of the Bulge' in the Ardennes. The Red Army, on the other hand, had occupied Warsaw on January 19th and was advancing across the central European plain at high speed. The West felt itself in a position of weakness. It signed agreements surrendering Poland to communist rule and consigning several million Soviet citizens to a forced return home, followed by years in labour camps. Very important and complicated issues raised by the imminence of victory were decided at Yalta. Palestine did not have the same urgency as these and was hardly mentioned.

On this way home on February 14th Roosevelt met two Arab kings, Farouk and Ibn Saud, on an American ship in the Bitter Lake, south of the Suez Canal. He told Stephen Wise on March 16th: 'Every time I mentioned the Jews he [Ibn Saud] would shrink.' And when Roosevelt spoke of Jewish land reclamation, Ibn Saud replied: 'My people do not like trees. We are desert dwellers.'[5]

Three days later Churchill entertained Ibn Saud to lunch at the Auberge du Lac in the Fayoum oasis, fifty miles south of Cairo. His colourful account of the meeting makes it clear how deeply impressed he was by the legendary ruler. On the spur of the moment, embarrassed by the lavish silks and gems provided by the King for his party, he committed the British taxpayer to repaying him with a sumptuous automobile.[6] But, like Roosevelt, he found nothing but a stony hostility to Zionist aspirations, no trace of the conciliatory attitude which, on the basis of Weizmann's and Philby's information, he had reason to expect.

In the House of Commons ten days later Churchill thanked Ibn Saud glowingly for 'his steadfast, unswerving and unflinching loyalty to our country', concluding over-optimistically with the maxim: 'All legitimate interests are in harmony.' He wrote to the King, promising to put forward no Palestine solution 'which offends those rules of justice and equity which are the foundation of all true friendship'. It was a vague enough promise on the surface, but it was capable of being misunderstood. British representatives in Jidda reported: 'Ibn Saud assumes that HMG will abide by the proposals of their own White Paper of 1939. This belief is basic in his advocacy of the British cause.'[7]

It was presumably on a similar basis that Ibn Saud wrote to Roosevelt on March 10th suggesting that Palestine had already borne more than its fair share in solving the Jewish problem: 'The crux of the matter is that the formation of a Jewish state in Palestine will be a deadly blow to the Arabs and a constant threat to peace.' Roosevelt too had previously assured him that the United States would consult him before taking any decision, adding the vague promise that the decision would not be hostile to the Arab people. But at the same time, scarcely logically, he reassured Wise and Silver that he stood by the promise he had given Senator Wagner just before re-election to try to bring about a Jewish commonwealth.

It was becoming less and less likely that Britain would cooperate in this plan. Friendly Arab leaders were outspoken in condemning it and their voices were at last reaching the ears of senior Western statesmen. Churchill seemed to have withdrawn from the issue altogether, leaving a vacuum of influence eagerly filled by the memoranda of pro-Arab experts. On March 22nd the Arab countries made another political advance when seven of them signed in Cairo the Pact of the Arab League, which provided for the appointment of a Palestine Arab delegate to represent his people 'until that country enjoys effective independence'.

The nail in the scheme's coffin was the fact that the two latterday partitionists Moyne and MacMichael were now replaced by Edward Grigg and Lord Gort, and it had taken these two men only a few weeks in the area to convince themselves that any Jewish state whatever would be a disaster. 'I feel bound to state my conviction that partition offers no real solution,' wrote Grigg to the War Cabinet on April 4th. Privately he advised Anthony Eden that partition 'would very likely bring into existence a Jewish Nazi state of a bitterly dissatisfied and therefore aggressive character'.[8] He advised instead a continuation of the British Mandate, with future Jewish immigration decided by an international body with

British, French, Arab, Jewish, American, Soviet and French members, leading eventually to 'a peaceful bi-racial state'.

A few days later Eden gave the War Cabinet a further blast of expert advice. The end of the war would bring changes, he wrote, not all of them welcome to Great Britain, for twenty-five years the predominant power in the Arab world. Now both the United States and Russia were taking an interest in the area. The Americans had secured an oil concession at Dhahran in the Gulf and were 'pressing their lavish benefactions' on Ibn Saud, who had previously been dependent on Britain: 'If we lose Arab goodwill, the Americans and the Russians will be on hand to profit from our mistakes.'

Eden listed the familiar British interest in Middle East oil and communications. In Iraq alone Britain enjoyed the use of air bases at Shaiba and Habbaniya, controlled navigation on the Shatt el-Arab river and production in the Kirkuk oilfields. This had been vital to Britain during the war and would continue to be very important after it was over. If Britain incurred the Arabs' anger through a pro-Zionist policy in Palestine, all these facilities would become difficult to defend and costly to maintain. Large garrisons would be required to control riots and sustain pro-British governments.

Eden did not discuss any moral rights or wrongs. He dealt in the practicalities of politics. He did not try to prove that the Arabs were more entitled to rule Palestine than the Jews. Still less did he question Britain's right to control communications and extract raw materials in countries which belonged to others. He mentioned the promises made to both nations in the past, his hopes that they would prosper in the future, but only in passing. His overriding concern was to promote the power and wealth of the British Empire. And more and more influential Britons were coming to believe, like him, that this interest was incompatible with Zionism.

Roosevelt died on April 12th, 1945. It may have been this blow, which Churchill felt most painfully, that finally induced him to surrender to all the pressure and abandon his plan to implement a scheme of partition as soon as the German war ended. No longer could he count on Roosevelt's help to counter the growing strength of British objection to a Jewish state.

In early March, after four months of silence on the issue, Churchill agreed with Herbert Morrison to place his Committee's report on the Cabinet agenda. But on April 15th, three days after the President's death, he wrote: 'I am sure it is best to let it lie for the present.'[9] And by April

29th he had made up his mind in favour of postponement: 'It seems to me impossible for the present Parliament to deal with this matter or indeed with other mandated territories. The question will soon become one for the Peace Conference.'[10]

On May 8th the war in Europe ended. Three days later in a rousing speech calling for Jewish equality and statehood Moshe Shertok said: 'The present war was fought in rejection of false compromises and won because England was ready to fight alone . . . Blessed be the arms to which we owe our survival. Blessed be England who stood alone for a whole year when all seemed lost.'[11]

Early in March Weizmann returned to London full of hopes and arranged a meeting with Churchill, his first since November 4th. A few days later the meeting was postponed. The months of silence were becoming ominous. Finally on May 22nd he wrote to the Prime Minister to point out that the position of the Jews in Europe and Palestine was now desperate. So was his own personal position as leader: 'This is the hour to eliminate the White Paper, to open the doors of Palestine and to proclaim the Jewish state.'[12]

On November 4th the two men had seemed well on the way to agreement. But now the problem was in the hands of different and less exalted leaders. On May 25th Oliver Stanley told a group of them that 'the position in respect of partition had deteriorated'. The support for it was dying away. John Shaw, who had served many years in Palestine, put forward the view that, now that the war was over, there would be no more 'sentimental pressure' for the Jews to enter Palestine and he suggested abolishing the Jewish Agency: 'Administration was almost impossible with this parallel government in operation.'[13]

At this point Britain's position in the Middle East was briefly boosted by a conflict between France and Syria. Sporadic fighting had broken out between the two countries, Damascus was shelled and there were several thousand casualties. On May 31st Churchill cabled de Gaulle, insisting on a ceasefire 'in order to avoid collision between British and French forces'.[14] The result was humiliating for France but triumphant for Britain. Gort reported on June 3rd that he had made full use of the incident in talks with Shertok and Musa el-Alami: 'Our prestige is very high, indeed it has never been higher . . . It has been a wonderful opportunity to impress on all and sundry whose writ runs in the Middle East today.' He had only one complaint: 'I have been feeling for some time the lack of any settled policy towards which I should aim.'

But Britain was not inclined to use this euphoric moment, as the

Palestine Committee had envisaged, to impose a quick and final solution. Instead she took comfort in the welcome and unexpected respite from anti-British agitation and violence. In Europe, by contrast, the end of the war seemed to have multiplied her problems. Refugees by the million were using up British and American time and money. Guerrilla warfare continued in Greece, Poland and Yugoslavia. Doubts about the long-term intentions of the Soviet Union were growing. Churchill recalls: 'All the while I felt that much we had fought for in our long struggle in Europe was slipping away and that the hopes of a lasting peace were receding.'[15]

Oliver Stanley advised Gort that there would be no quick decisions. There was now a new scheme, Edward Grigg's, which would have to be considered as well as the Palestine Committee's. He himself was reluctant to abandon partition, but there seemed to be no urgency: 'The Government may be unwilling at this juncture to commit themselves to any new long-term policy.' Therefore, when Weizmann came to see him, much aged in appearance, scarcely recovered from glaucoma and temporary blindness, there was little that he could say by way of reassurance. Weizmann begged him not to allow the situation to drift: 'If that happened, the moderate Jews like himself would be thrown out and a very different type would come to talk to me or my successor.'[16]

But the really crushing blow came with Churchill's letter to Weizmann of June 9th: 'I have received your letter of May 22nd, enclosing a memorandum on behalf of the Jewish Agency for Palestine. There can, I fear, be no possibility of the question being effectively considered until the victorious Allies are definitely seated at the Peace Table.' This cold, brief note confirmed what the Jewish leaders had suspected, that Churchill had withdrawn from the issue after Moyne's murder and abandoned his decades-long support of Zionism.

Whatever reasons lay behind Churchill's change of heart, in Zionist eyes it seemed no more than another British betrayal of their cause. Abba Eban feels particularly strongly about the personal betrayal of Weizmann: 'And now he [Churchill] was winding up his historic ministry with the White Paper unabrogated, no commitment on the record and Weizmann left high and dry, standing before the Jewish people baffled, enraged, undermined and empty-handed.'[17]

On June 15th Weizmann wrote back to express his 'great shock'. He had always understood, he told Churchill, that Palestine would be discussed as soon as the German war was over, but now this seemed postponed to 'some indefinite date in the future'. This delay was having a tragic effect on the Jewish people: 'It bars the doors of Palestine against the surviving remnant of European Jewry. And many refugees have to wander or die, unable as they are to go to Palestine.'[18] Through the White Paper land regulations the Yishuv were still confined to a 'territorial ghetto' of five per cent of the country's land area. They had found this hard to put up with during the war. Now it was unbearable. He wanted Churchill to bear all this in mind.

But Churchill's mind was on other matters, the Potsdam Conference and the general election. He no longer seemed to feel any special involvement with Palestine or loyalty to Weizmann. His last ministerial note about the matter on July 6th, the day after the voting, bore the mark of a tired and disillusioned man, whose enthusiasm for the cause had turned into anguish at yet another insoluble postwar conflict. Why, he asked Stanley and the chiefs of staff, should Britain carry on being responsible for 'this very difficult place' while the United States sat back and criticized? Perhaps the Americans should take the problem over.

'I am not aware of the slightest advantage that has ever accrued to Great Britain from this painful and thankless task. Someone else should have their turn now,' continued Churchill in an uncharacteristic gesture of despair which ran counter to his three decades of Zionism. Perhaps it was not meant seriously, but it was taken seriously in Whitehall and, as is the custom, carefully analysed as a proposition.

Should Britain give Palestine to the United States? Within a few days a chorus of official voices were raised in protest at the idea. 'Palestine is the key to the security of the Middle East area,' noted General Ismay. The Foreign Office accepted Harold Beeley's view: 'Abdication in Palestine would be regarded in the Middle East as symptomatic of our abdication as a great power. It might set in motion a process which would result in the crumbling away of our influence throughout this region.'

Churchill would soon have received a note of Whitehall's negative reaction to his idea, but the day after putting it forward he left for a holiday near Bordeaux and on July 15th he flew to Berlin for the Potsdam Conference, which involved his first meeting with President Truman. On July 25th he returned for the counting of ballot papers. The next day, soundly defeated, he drove to Buckingham Palace to advise King George VI to appoint Clement Attlee in his place.

The King sent for Attlee, appointed him prime minister and then spoke to him in a way which, according to his July 26th diary entry, was to play an important part in Palestine's future: 'I told him he would have to appoint a foreign secretary and take him to Berlin. I asked him whom he would make foreign secretary and he suggested Dr Hugh Dalton, I disagreed with him and said that foreign affairs was a most important subject at the moment and I hoped he would make Mr Bevin take it. He said he would.'[19] Harold Beeley, who was later to work closely with Bevin on Palestine, recalls that in 1945 Dalton was the Labour party 'favourite' for the job: 'It was important because Dalton was very committed to the Zionists. Bevin had no thoughts on the matter at all at the time he was appointed, neither one way nor the other.'

In Berlin Bevin was handed the note from Truman, originally delivered to Churchill on July 24th, expressing the 'great interest' of Americans in the Palestine problem and their 'passionate protest' against the 'drastic restrictions' imposed on Jewish immigration by the White Paper. It asked for the removal of these restrictions so that Jews could enter the land 'which represents for so many of them their only hope of survival'.

This idea that Palestine represented the only hope of survival for the survivors of European Jewry was something the Foreign Office strongly rejected. It was one which 'the Zionists have been deplorably successful in selling', noted Beeley. But at this point Bevin made no judgement. In Berlin on his fifth day as foreign secretary he noted: 'I consider the Palestine question urgent and when I return to London I propose to examine the whole question, bearing in mind the repercussions on the Middle East and the USA.' On July 31st Attlee merely told Truman that his request would be carefully and quickly considered.

During August Bevin received a number of briefings from the Foreign Office on Palestine and it was not long before his own views fell closely into line with those that his department had held for many years. Beeley says: 'He at once had access to a lot of information that he had not seen before and a process took place which can be called the "absorption" of a minister by his department. He read our material and within the first few weeks he came to the conclusion, I think on purely intellectual grounds, that the traditional Labour Party policy was wrong. It's not true that Bevin was "got a grip of" by the Foreign Office. But it was only by becoming a minister in charge of a department that he could become fully informed of the issues.'

But meanwhile, unaware of what was happening, the Jewish leaders were in a state of euphoria at the Labour party's victory. Pinkerton reported from Jerusalem: 'Individual Jews are frankly exuberant, while Arab press is silent and Arabs are in a quandary.'[20] The Hebrew daily *Haboker* was one of several to remind readers that Labour was 'officially and un-reservedly committed to support Zionist aspirations'. Churchill's sullen refusal to fulfil his assurances of November 4th had lost all significance. The Labour party had always been more friendly to Zionism than its opponents. It could now be relied upon to do the right thing.

Bernard Joseph was similarly exuberant when he called to see John Shaw on August 27th on his return from a Zionist conference in London. (Gort was in London for medical treatment.) According to Shaw, Joseph said that a Jewish state would certainly be set up soon, probably in the whole of Palestine: 'Joseph airily brushed aside the contingency of Arab opposition with the remark that a few shots over their heads, or perhaps into the crowd, would be sufficient . . .'[21] He told Shaw how happy he was that the Yishuv would not now be compelled to fight against Britain.

The Jewish leaders did not realize the extent and depth of the Foreign Office 'absorption' process, the strength of the arguments then being put before Ernest Bevin. The gist of the latter was succinctly expressed in a message from Lebanese President Khalil el-Khoury: 'Zionism was not a British interest. On the other hand the Arab League, the sympathies of which were obviously incompatible with Zionism, was a vital British interest.'[22] Support for this view was coming to London from all over the world, for instance from Lord Wavell, now Viceroy of India, who reported that any solution damaging to Arab interests in Palestine 'would be likely to cause serious unrest in the Punjab,' perhaps followed by 'big hostile demonstrations in Peshawar'.[23]

On the crucial question of Jewish immigration, Bevin was reminded of the simple and unequivocal assurances given to the Arabs at the 1939 conference. Malcolm MacDonald had told Jamal Husseini: 'After five years, whatever the views of the British or the Jews, if the Arabs were not ready to acquiesce in it, further Jewish immigration could not take place.' Moderate Arab rulers, anxious to be helpful to Great Britain, still saw the White Paper as a pledge, a clear promise that Britain would not allow Jewish newcomers from Europe to 'swamp' the Arabs of Palestine.

This pledge had already been broken. The cut-off date for the 75,000 immigrants had been extended to beyond March 1944. Also the 1400 Jewish refugees shipped to Mauritius in 1940 were brought to Palestine in August 1945, in spite of MacMichael's previous assurance that they were excluded from Palestine for ever. Moderate Arabs might see these as minor departures from the White Paper, understandable in the circumstances. They might even agree to Palestine making 'a contribution' to the refugee problem by taking a further limited number of European Jews, provided that the United States and other countries did the same. But they would never agree to the massive immigration, beginning with the immediate entry of 100,000 refugees, that the Jewish Agency demanded, apparently with the support of the American president.

Nuri es-Said and Abdul-Ilah, the regent of Iraq, explained this to Bevin in London on August 27th. It was also made clear that Ibn Saud was observing the situation and expecting the new government to fulfil its predecessors' promises. Nuri repeated Shaw's inaccurate prediction that, now that Hitlerism was dead, there would be less Jewish eagerness to set sail for the Promised Land. Indeed some might want to return from Palestine to Europe.[24] Bevin's thinking too was moving in this direction. Beeley recalls his saying: 'What did we fight the war for, if not to make Europe safe for the Jews.' The war was over and Zionism seemed to him no longer necessary.

Bevin was convinced that much of the Zionist impetus came from British and American anti-semites, who simply wanted the Jews in their midst removed to the Middle East. His former colleague Cranborne had given his view that there were 'far too many' Jews in Britain, that somewhere else must be found for them. On December 19th, 1944, an article in the New York Post concluded: 'It would be better for the United States to have Palestine reopened to the Jews than to have millions of them coming over here after the war as unassimilated refugees.' Halifax reported: 'The average citizen does not want them [the Jews] in the United States and salves his conscience by advocating their admission to Palestine.'[25]

In her memoirs Golda Meir writes: 'I don't know (nor really does it matter any more) whether Bevin was a little insane, or just anti-semitic, or both.'[26] But those who worked with him feel that, on the contrary, he believed Zionism and anti-semitism to be two sides of the same coin. And this belief was the result not of any irrational prejudice, but of the expert advice which matured in his mind during his first weeks as foreign secretary, leading him (rightly or wrongly) to the firm conclusion that Zionist demands were fundamentally unjust as well as contrary to Britain's national interest.

The new Committee, of which Bevin was a member, therefore reported on September 8th: 'The Middle East is a region of vital consequence for Britain and the British Empire. It forms the nodal point in the system of communications by land, sea and air which links Great Britain with India, Australia and the Far East. It is also the Empire's main reservoir of mineral oil . . . To enforce any such [Zionist] policy, especially one which lays us open to a charge of breach of faith, is bound seriously to undermine our position . . .'[27]

But these were weeks when the truth about Hitlerism filled the news-papers and cinema screens of the Western world. American and British troops who had liberated concentration camps at Dachau or Belsen were returning home with excruciating eye-witness testimony. The Red Army invited observers to the extermination camps of southern Poland – Majdanek, Treblinka and Auschwitz (Oświęcim). The West could now know that wartime rumours of Nazi bestiality were no exaggeration. On the contrary, they had probably understated the truth.

And so, as they came to appreciate the full extent of the Holocaust, the Yishuv and the Jewish diaspora were aghast. Between a third and a half of their people were dead, murdered in cold blood by men in the grip of a brutish creed. The United States and Britain had known what was happening, at least since the end of 1942, and had made no special effort to save them. Ten million Jews were now safe, but for how long? Sooner or later other Hitlers would appear and, wherever they ruled, they would massacre the helpless Jewish minority. Surely the world must now realize that Jews were entitled to their own state, where they could build their own system of security and make themselves safe from the innate anti-semitism of gentiles, rather than relying on their occasional protection?

This feeling ran particularly high in the United States, which now housed half the world's surviving Jews. Halifax reported: 'There is a feeling in influential liberal quarters that, if HMG had admitted more Jews into Palestine before the war, more Jews would have escaped Nazi per-secution, that more might have been done to get Jews out of Europe into Palestine during the war, and that Palestine is the natural asylum for the many Jews who, it is believed, now wish to leave Europe.'[28]

In Berlin in July President Truman had advocated free Jewish immi-gration into Palestine. At a press conference on August 16th he spoke more carefully. The question of a Jewish state would have to be worked out with the British and Arabs, he said. He wanted as many Jews to enter Palestine as could be done without causing civil strife. But there was no question of sending an American armed force of, say, half a million troops there to maintain peace.[29]

Beeley at once noted the President's 'new and important'[30] qualify-ing reference to civil peace. But in the Arab world his remarks were condemned as a flagrant endorsement of Zionism. Syrian Prime Minister Saadullah Jabri announced that sixty million Arabs stood united in their resolve not to allow Palestine's 'amputation' from the Arab world and delivery into the hands of 'aliens'. The British embassy in Baghdad reported: 'Today five vernacular newspapers carried what seem to be officially inspired articles vigorously protesting against what they conceive to be the President's unqualified support of a Jewish state.'[31]

Such reports, which loomed large in Foreign Office memoranda, made little impact on President Truman. Apart from her new oil concession in Dhahran, involving a subsidy to Ibn Saud, the United States had little interest in the Arab world and no desire to preserve the British-dominated status quo. She was, on the other hand, directly caught up in the Zionist enterprise, not only through pressure from Jewish citizens, but also because of her new involvement in Europe as an occupying power. American soldiers and officials were busy trying to solve Europe's massive refugee problem. And to many Americans the Jewish element of this problem seemed by far the most tragic and deserving of their sympathy.

Truman therefore came to the conclusion, largely on the basis of a report on the problem by his representative Earl Harrison, that a large number of Jewish refugees in Europe had become 'non-repatriable' and 'stateless'. These Jews, numbering more than half a million, had lost their families and livelihoods. They did not want to return to their ruined towns and villages in Poland, Czechoslovakia or Romania. The same impression was gained by British Member of Parliament Richard Crossman, who had also toured the refugee camps: 'I realize now that in this sense Hitler has won. He has created in central and eastern Europe a Jewish nation without a home . . . This nation must emigrate.'[32]

On August 31st, 1945, Truman advised Attlee that the issue of 100,000 Palestine certificates 'would contribute greatly' to a solution of the refugee problem: 'I can concur [with Harrison] in the belief that no other single matter is so important for those who have known the horrors of con-centration camps for over a decade as is the future of immigration possibilities into Palestine.' The American people as a whole believed that 'a reasonable number' should be 'resettled' there as quickly as possible.[33]

Clearly there was now no chance of avoiding a British-American rift. Attlee and Bevin did not accept Truman's arguments. They were advised that Zionist officials were at work in camps, urging all Jewish refugees towards Palestine, discouraging them from the idea of asylum in the United States or other countries. They came to believe that, given a free choice, most Jews would want to return to their homes, that some would seek a new life in the Western democratic countries, but that very few would opt for the uncertainties of Jewish Palestine.

In May 1939 Herbert Morrison had referred to the White Paper as 'this breach of faith which we regret, this breach of British honour'. But by

September 1945, having spent a year chairing two government committees on Palestine, he had changed his mind completely. The document he signed on September 8th made it clear that the mass immigration demanded by the Zionists and approved by Truman was impossible, at least in the short term. The new committee agreed to set a quota, which was 'the most that could be contemplated without prejudicing long-term policy in advance'.[34] And this quota was to be 1500 Jewish immigrants a month.

A few days later (September 14th) US Secretary of State James Byrnes innocently told Bevin that Truman proposed making public his August 31st letter to Attlee, including the request to admit 100,000 refugees. Had Britain any objection? Bevin immediately replied that any such public statement 'could not fail to do harm to Anglo-US relations'. Byrnes agreed to ask the President not to do it. The same day Attlee confirmed in a cable to Truman that 'grievous harm' would result if the United States publicly endorsed the Zionist demand: 'The position in the Middle East is already one of great danger and difficulty and I fear that this action, had it been taken, would have precipitated a grave crisis . . .'[35]

Two days later Attlee wrote to Truman again. The Nazi concentration camps, he said, had contained people from every race in Europe and 'there appears to have been very little difference in the amount of torture and treatment they had to undergo'. He was therefore against placing Jewish refugees 'in a special racial category at the head of the queue'. Britain must also consider the feelings of the ninety million Moslems of India. He sympathized with Harrison's report, but there were other strong arguments which had to be balanced against its recommendations. Pledges had been made to the Arabs as well as to the Jews by Roosevelt as well as by British statesmen. 'It would be very unwise to break these solemn pledges and so set aflame the whole Middle East.' Truman replied the next day, promising to take no action before Byrnes's return to Washington: 'I am aware of the complications of the problem from your point of view. It also makes difficulties for us.'

It was around this time, mid-September 1945, that the Jewish leaders realized that their hopes in the new government had been misplaced. Since July 26th they had bombarded the new ministers with memoranda and requests for interviews, only to be told again and again that the matter was being urgently considered, that they would be informed as soon as any decision was reached. But the weeks passed and the silence seemed to them more and more ominous. Perhaps Weizmann and Shertok, who were in London, learnt what was in store from certain close friends with access to Cabinet decisions. Perhaps the gist of Attlee's two letters to Truman reached their ears from some American source. Anyway, it became clear at this point that their euphoria had been in vain, that they would have to fight Britain after all. Golda Meir says: 'We kept hearing the argument, "The Arabs can create so much trouble, therefore you have to give in." So in the end we decided, very well, *we'll* create trouble.'

The *saison* had scotched the Irgun, but not killed it. On May 14th, 1945, they resurfaced with a display of pamphlets in Jerusalem. Captain J. F. Whitefield noted: 'The pamphlets were well printed and the text was again in the three official languages.' They wanted the 'government of oppression' to evacuate everybody, both official and civilian, from all British-occupied buildings in Palestine: 'The civilian population – Hebrew, Arabs and others – are asked for their own sake to abstain from now on until this warning is recalled from visiting or nearing [*sic*] government offices. YOU HAVE BEEN WARNED!'

It was no idle threat. That same day three loaded mortars were found buried in the ground, primed on a time fuse and aimed at the Sarona police camp a few hundred yards away. On May 16th four forty-pound mortar bombs exploded near the same camp and two others near a Jaffa police station, causing some damage but no casualites. Also thirty-five telegraph poles were blown up and about two hundred others prepared for demolition. Whitefield noted that, although the damage caused had been slight, this had been through no lack of effort by the Irgun. Civilians could not evacuate every government-owned building. They had nowhere else to live. Several mortar bombs had fallen near the Sarona police married quarters.[36]

On May 22nd Acting Chief Secretary Robert Scott warned Shertok that 'very drastic measures' would be taken against any new outbreak of terrorism. Shertok replied that Britain was doing little or nothing to help the survivors of European Jewry.[37] The Irgun carried on planting their home-made three-inch mortars and there were regular explosions during the night. The British called them the 'V3', after the German 'V1' and 'V2' rockets that had blasted London the previous year. Arthur Koestler mentioned this to Begin at their secret meeting, much to the anger of the latter.

E. P. Horne recalls: 'Those mortars were very successful. The Irgun used to telephone a police station and say, "There's a mortar aimed at you and it's going to go off in the night." Sheer pride wouldn't let us leave the police station. We felt as if we were carrying the whole weight of the

Union Jack on our shoulders. So we used to sit there all night, sweating, playing cards, waiting for the mortar to go off.

'A few nights of this made us feel we were playing Russian roulette. It made us irritable, jarred on our nerves, which is very bad in a small police station. One day in a routine search we found two mortars aimed at a dais where Lord Gort was going to stand and present medals. There might have been others there that we'd missed. Of course we warned him, but he just said, "We're all expendable, gentlemen." The ceremony had to go on. Israeli literature has never made much of this mortar business, but I'd say that it was the one thing that had a serious demoralizing effect.'

On July 13th, 1945, the Irgun ambushed a lorry carrying explosives, killed Constable G. Wilde who was escorting it and drove it away, subsequently releasing the Jewish driver. On July 25th they blew up a bridge on the Haifa–Kantara railway. But then they paused, waiting to see what the new British government would do. It turned out that Begin's forecast was correct, the British were not going to be helpful, and to his delight he began to receive overtures of peace from the Haganah leaders, men who a few months earlier had tried to eliminate his organization. The suggestion now was for all three groups, including even Lehi, labelled a few months earlier by every responsible Jewish leader as a gang of murderers, to join in a united front of Jewish resistance.

By mid-September Weizmann knew that Britain proposed allowing only 1500 Jews a month to enter Palestine. Attlee had advised Truman that Nazi Germany had treated the Jews not much worse than they had their other prisoners. The Jews must therefore take their turn with the other refugees and wait to be resettled wherever space could be found. They could not expect special treatment as Jews. This would mean bringing a racial element into the refugee problem and would eventually bring about the opposite of what was intended – a revival of anti-semitism.

The Zionist leaders rejected these arguments. The idea that the Jews had suffered no worse than non-Jews in occupied Europe struck them as absurd and offensive. On September 21st Weizmann felt that it was time to send Attlee a letter of warning: 'It is apparent that discussions are in progress and decisions about to be taken which affect the future of Palestine. Reports which reach us are most disquieting.' In his view, if decisions indeed were imminent, it was only right for the Jewish Agency to be consulted: 'If what we hear is true, it would mean that nothing short of tragedy faces the Jewish people, that a very serious conflict might ensue, which we would all deplore.'[38]

In Palestine talks continued between the three armed organizations. On September 22nd the owner of the Yamiah Café in Tel Aviv was approached by Irgun men who complained that he was employing Arabs and demanded £300. He refused, so that evening a violent crowd led by four young men burst into the café and wrecked it. On September 28th another group, either Irgun or Lehi, waylaid a postmaster who was carrying £4760 from Barclays Bank to the Tel Aviv post office, shot dead Constable J. G. Barry who was escorting the money, and made off with it.[39]

The Haganah never carried out acts of this nature, but in late September they were preparing to ally themselves with the two groups who did, in order to prevent or frustrate Britain's return to an anti-Zionist policy. On September 23rd Haganah leader Moshe Sneh cabled the Jewish Agency's London office to suggest that they cause 'one serious incident', so as to warn Britain and raise the morale of the Yishuv. Sneh advised London: 'The Stern group [Lehi] have expressed their willingness to join us completely on the basis of our programme of activity . . . We assume that we can prevent independent action even by the IZL [Irgun].'[40]

What Sneh and his colleagues in the London office did not know was that British intelligence had already broken the Jewish Agency's code and that copies of all Jerusalem–London messages were available to the security authorities. So by September 23rd they knew about the proposed alliance. So, presumably, did Attlee and Bevin. This fact, together with the pushing and semi-threatening tone of Weizmann's letter, may have induced Attlee to send a particularly cold and discouraging reply: 'If we thought that further consultation were required at this stage or that it would serve any useful purpose, we would certainly arrange it. But at the present juncture that is not so.'[41]

One can therefore imagine Attlee's and Bevin's fury when, a few days later, a full summary of their correspondence with Truman appeared in the American press. The *New York Herald Tribune* of September 30th revealed the fact, which was supposed to be confidential, that Truman 'had appealed directly to the British government to open the doors of Palestine to Jewish refugees from Nazism who wish to settle there'. After more than a month, the report continued incorrectly, quoting the White House as its source, the President's appeal remained unanswered. Attlee at once felt bound to correct this, to make public the fact that he *had* replied. Then in a Senate debate on October 2nd Edwin Johnson revealed the content of the reply, that it was a rejection.

The *New York Times* reported the debate: 'Senators from both sides seemed to be completely informed of the nature of the President's proposal.' Robert Taft rose to express 'my strong approval and that I think of the majority of senators' to the idea of admitting the hundred thousand. He saw this as providing 'some atonement for what we have failed to do during the war'. Arab newspapers at once retorted that, if the United States and Britain wished to atone for their failure to save European Jewry, they could best do so by accepting the survivors in their own countries, rather than in an Arab country like Palestine.

The British leaders were very irritated. Attlee *had* replied to Truman's letter and he had been assured by him that nothing would be said publicly. He felt that he had been deceived and, as politely as possible, he made his feeling known to the President.[42] Nor was the situation improved when it emerged that the source of the leak was ex-Senator Guy Gillette, who had discussed the problem with Truman on September 14th.[43] Gillette was leader of the pro-Irgun American League for a Free Palestine.

On October 4th, therefore, Bevin decided that the United States could no longer remain on the sidelines. He did not revive Churchill's idea of handing her over the Mandate, but he was resolved to give her a formal status in the problem. Six days later Morrison's committee was ready with a proposal for an Anglo-American Committee to examine the problems of Palestine and European Jewry. Britain's long-term policy, wrote Morrison, would then be based largely on what the Commission recommended. The idea was not universally popular in Whitehall. American involvement was bound to be a step in the Zionist direction and, as such, to be resented in the Arab world. There were many who suspected the United States of wishing to usurp Britain's Middle East position. But these objections were conquered by the argument that in the Palestine question, as in others, British-American cooperation was quite essential.

The more the broad lines of this policy emerged, the more public security in Palestine deteriorated. On October 8th, 1945, the General Zionist Council passed a resolution: 'The Council encourages any attempt to increase Jewish immigration in defiance of the unlawful and immoral restrictions under the White Paper.' The British saw this statement not only as defiance but also as incitement to rebellion. Their lawyers had advised them that the White Paper was legal under international law, even though in 1939 the Permanent Mandates Commission had pronounced against it. The Commission was an advisory body, not a legislative body, so it could not override the law of Palestine. It seemed quite intolerable that responsible Jewish bodies were inciting clear breaches of this law.

Two days later, seemingly as a result of this incitement, a large number of Haganah men raided the camp for illegal immigrants at Athlit, cut an avenue in the wire and released 208 of the inmates. A police truck on its way there with reinforcements was ambushed, Constable B. Hill was shot dead and several other policemen injured.

Gort at once summoned Bernard Joseph and two other Agency leaders, Kaplan and Ben Zvi, to hear his list of complaints. The Hebrew press was irresponsible and inflammatory, he told them. British policemen were being murdered and armed bands were at large in the country carrying out raids and ambushes. It seemed to him that 'there must be some controlling hand behind these recent events'. He could think of nothing more likely to damage the cause of Zionism than for it to be believed that the Yishuv was trying to force the issue through violence. But though he delivered his rebuke in brave terms, his report of the meeting to the new colonial secretary, George Hall, was pessimistic. The Jewish leaders had listened to him carefully, he wrote, but he did not think that he had made much impression on them. It seemed to him that they had already made up their minds to go their own way, that the true leadership of the Yishuv had already passed out of Weizmann's hands to the 'implacable and unpredictable' Ben Gurion.[44]

On October 10th Bevin had his first short meeting with Weizmann, where he was told that the White Paper was born in sin and must be abrogated. Bevin was unwell and argued little, apart from making it clear that he was against allowing the hundred thousand to enter immediately. Instead they discussed the idea that was already forming in Bevin's mind as a long-term solution – a bi-racial Palestine with a cantonal system along the Swiss model.[45] It had been 'a very good talk', Attlee felt able to advise Truman, before continuing in a tone of studied irritation: 'We are giving deep thought to means of helping the Jews in Europe and to the question of Palestine. The two problems are not necessarily the same.'[46]

Attlee's curt note concealed his and Bevin's deep and growing resentment towards Truman's attitude on Palestine. Byrnes had explained in all frankness that the Democratic party badly needed to win the mayoral election in New York, which was to take place on October 30th. This was what lay behind the President's semi-public statements and the confusion in the White House. Truman simply could not afford to offend the Jewish voters of New York City, one third of the total electorate, the vast majority of whom were committed, to a greater or lesser extent, to Zionist aspirations.

By October 12th Bevin had recovered enough to let this resentment spill over in an angry telegram to Halifax: 'I feel that the US have been thoroughly dishonest in handling this problem. To play on racial feeling for the purpose of winning an election is to make a farce of their insistence on free elections in other countries.' He believed that Truman and others had 'exploited for their own purposes' the sufferings of Jews. Was it absolutely essential for all surviving Jews to leave Germany? Bevin thought not: 'They have gone through, it is true, the most terrible massacres and persecutions, but on the other hand they have got through it and a number have survived. Now succour and help should be brought to assist them to resettle in Germany and to help them to get over the fears and nerves that arise from such treatment.'[47]

Bevin was clearly misinformed about the desperate mood of the Jews in Europe. Beneath his bland conclusion that 'they have got through it and a number have survived' lay the stark facts that the majority of them had been slaughtered, that they had almost all lost their property and families and that anti-semitism, stoked up by years of Nazi indoctrination, still lurked in the minds of many of the population. Still, Bevin believed that most survivors would want to stay and participate in the reconstruction of their countries of origin. And he saw the urge to escape to Palestine, observed by Crossman and others, as no more than the result of Zionist intimidation. He believed what Nuri es-Said and the Iraqi regent had told him, that without this intimidation many Palestine Jews would be re-emigrating back to Europe.

Nor did Bevin believe that Palestine was capable of absorbing many new immigrants: 'Figures have been submitted to me that seem just fantastic.' Instead of reclaiming and developing desert areas, thought Bevin, the newcomers would inevitably be used to deprive Arab farmers of their land. He agreed that more information was needed about the Jews of Europe. This would be provided by the new commission, which would also fulfil Churchill's and Roosevelt's promises to consult both sides. Britain held a terrible legacy, concluded Bevin. At the moment he favoured a bi-national state: 'Obviously we must have a conference with Arabs and Jews in the same room somewhere.' This plan might fail, but Britain must continue to seek a just solution, undaunted by American pressure and 'the propaganda in New York'.

The same angry feeling emerged at Weizmann's meeting with George Hall on October 19th. Hall pointed out that such incidents as the Athlit raid showed 'widespread organization' among the Yishuv. He appreciated how strongly the Jews felt about immigration, but this could be no excuse for a revolt against the government. He then suggested to Weizmann something that British intelligence already knew to be a fact, that the Jewish Agency leaders, or some of them, were secretly conniving at and even organizing the violence.

Weizmann replied: 'He wished to give categorical assurance that neither he nor his colleagues of the Jewish Agency in London had any responsibility for the incidents mentioned by the Secretary of State. They did not know of them until they read them in the newspapers. He himself saw all the messages which went out, so that he was in a position to know.'[48] On the evidence of Sneh's September 23rd message to London this assurance was, of course, incorrect.

Weizmann went on to explain that bloodshed was unavoidable so long as there was no Palestine policy and no Jewish immigration: 'He was not defending it, but he did not think that he could prevent it. None the less he would do what he could.' Here Weizmann was being sincere. But the British knew that he was only telling them part of the truth. He was not telling them – something which they knew to be the case from the decoded cables – that the Haganah had, under the direction of Ben Gurion and other political leaders, carried out the Athlit raid, that they were negotiating with the Irgun and Lehi, and that they were planning a joint 'serious incident' as a warning to Britain.

It was true that Haganah violence was usually limited to the achievement of two aims: Jewish immigration and arms acquisition. The Haganah did not raid banks or launch attacks on police stations. They did not shoot British individuals simply to demonstrate their opposition to alien rule. When they hit an objective, always with a set political purpose, they envisaged the possibility of casualties on both sides, but they did not seek British casualties, as did Lehi. Indeed, unlike the Irgun, they went to complicated lengths to avoid them.

Nevertheless they were using violence for a political end and they were proposing to ally themselves with two less scrupulous organizations. The British found this an intolerable hypocrisy in a legal body established under the Mandate 'with the purpose of advising and cooperating with the Administration'.

This was the year 1945. In the Western world political terrorism enjoyed none of the legitimacy, respectability or glamour that it was later to acquire. And so, as the British leaders read the coded messages passing between London and Jerusalem, their blood boiled at the Agency's protestations of ignorance and innocence. And after the night of October 31st, when the promised serious incident occurred, their fury rose to a peak.

In coordinated action the Haganah exploded several hundred devices all over Palestine, causing 242 breaks in the railway network, the Palmach blew up two police launches in Haifa harbour and one off Jaffa, the Irgun raided Lydda station and goods yard, destroying a train and three locomotives, and Lehi unsuccessfully tried to blow up the Haifa oil refineries. One British soldier and two Palestinians were killed in the Irgun raid. Three Arabs died in the abortive Lehi raid. Intercepted cables told the British that the Haganah had approved the Irgun raid, that the attacks on the police boats and railway had been approved by the Jewish Agency Executive. Also, in spite of objections from some Agency leaders, 'a working arrangement' had been reached with Irgun and Lehi. The Lehi publication *Hamaas* revealed that henceforward a Jewish Resistance Movement (Tenuat Hameri Ha'ivri) would be 'guided by a single authority which would control the common fight'.

On November 2nd Bevin summoned Weizmann and Shertok. First he read them the cabled report that he had received from Palestine. Shertok writes: 'He spoke with great anger and tension, a muscle at the side of his mouth giving a warning signal and his eyes shooting lightning towards me.' Bevin emphasized the report's conclusion that the three armed organizations had acted together to cause the night of violence. He therefore considered that the Yishuv had declared war on Britain. If this was indeed their decision, they should make it clear publicly, in which case Britain would cease her efforts to find an overall solution. She would not negotiate under threat of violence.

Weizmann tried to explain what had happened. Formerly the supporters of violence had been very few in number. But now, as a result of British policy, they had multiplied. What then, asked Bevin, was the attitude of the Jewish Agency? Weizmann replied that only the previous evening they had issued a statement condemning the violence. They then looked through Bevin's newspapers and found it in the *Daily Telegraph*: 'The Agency repudiates recourse to violence, but finds its capacity to impose restraint severely strained by a policy which Jews regard as fatal to their future.'

Bevin read this out and observed: 'This is not a condemnation. It is a condonation.' He then emphasized the careful planning that had gone into the various acts of violence. Limpet mines had been attached to police launches. Some five hundred explosive charges had been prepared. The whole event had involved vast organization. And for this the Jewish Agency, as leaders of the Yishuv, must take responsibility.

Shertok reconstructs some of Bevin's other remarks: 'I cannot bear

English Tommies being killed. They are innocent.' Weizmann observed that millions of Jews had died too, that Jews were still dying in the refugee camps. Bevin went on: 'I do not want any Jews killed either, but I love the British soldiers. They belong to my class. They are working people ... I have never broken my word. The problem is intolerably difficult, maybe insoluble. It would have been difficult if the Balfour Declaration had been worded more clearly, if they had not tried to ride two horses at once. It is a very difficult business, but we are honestly trying to find a way out. In general we have terrible problems. The world is in ferment. The United States are pestering us.'[49] Shertok noted: 'His anger and fury against the United States are unimaginable.'

Bluntly, perhaps tactlessly, Bevin explained his resentment against the Americans' 'dishonest' approach to the problem: 'I thought it disastrous to the cause of Jewry that the US Government should, for electoral purposes, put up a claim for the immediate entry of 100,000 Jews into Palestine – a course which the President and everybody else who understood the problem knew was impossible today.' He struck Shertok as a man sincere, perturbed, distant from the matter and simply ignorant: 'He gets extremely angry, of course, but he is also shocked, shocked and stunned.'

Among Palestine Jewry the issue was being argued to and fro. What would be the effect of this clear challenge to the British Empire? Would it persuade Britain to listen to their case more carefully, or would it, as Weizmann feared, bring ruin on the Yishuv? They were, after all, a community of only a few hundred thousand, facing not only the forces of authority, but also a hostile population twice as numerous as themselves. Did they really have the military strength to oppose both Britain and the Arabs?

On November 1st the Jewish Agency cabled London in genuine fear of an all-out British attack on the Haganah.[50] How harsh would be the British reaction? It would not be, they could be sure, along the lines experienced by rebels against Nazi or Soviet rule. But it would be significant. The 6th Airborne Division of the British army, men who a year earlier had been invading France or fighting the German counteroffensive in the Ardennes, were pouring into Palestine to strengthen the garrison. They were crack troops, hardened by bitter fighting, who would not take kindly to becoming the targets of guerrilla fighters.

On the other hand, the operation had undoubtedly raised Jewish morale, convincing the Yishuv that their leaders were ready to fight both for them and for their brothers in Europe. And anyway, even if it came to a fight against the British forces, what could they do, how could they defeat the terrorists except by using counterterror against the Jewish population as a whole? Even Nazi Germany, using the most brutal methods of repression, had been unable to defeat the Polish resistance movement, supported as it was by almost the whole population. The Yishuv were similarly motived. And the British could be relied upon not to use Nazi methods.

British intelligence officer Martin Charteris noted in the early weeks of the revolt a severe but militarily accurate estimate of the two sides' possibilities: 'Actuated by a spirit of complete ruthlessness, which takes no account of human life, provided with an abundance of targets and the initiative, enabled to make their reconnaissance on the spot and, above all, protected by the local population who are at best too frightened to give them up and at worst entirely their supporters, they have an enormous advantage over the forces of law.'[51]

The majority view among Jewish Agency leaders was, therefore, that limited violence was a legitimate extension of the political battle. The personal view of Berl Locker was recorded in London: 'The operation of last week has had good results, but for the time being we must behave calmly. Nothing of this sort should repeat itself before the announcement is made. Ben Gurion probably holds a different view, but even he says that such things should not be done every day.'[52]

But one incident, even one as serious as that of October 31st, was not enough to divert Bevin from his view, now firmly embedded in his mind after three months of Foreign Office 'absorption'. He was already firmly convinced that Zionism in its late-1945 definition was fundamentally unjust and unnecessary, as well as contrary to Britain's national interest. He had won Truman's consent to his idea of an Anglo-American Commission and on November 13th he announced this to the House of Commons in a speech which exuded unjustifiable optimism: 'The Arabs are meeting me very well and I thank them for it. There is a great sense of response, except for one small section, among Jewry, and not all the Jews are Zionists.'

In fact, he had already antagonized most of world Jewry. And he antagonized them even more by the bluff comments, relaxed to the point of flippancy, which he made that evening to seventy British and Dominion journalists. Nothing would please him more, he told them, than for all the Jews to be gathered back into Abraham's bosom, but they should draw a distinction between Zionism and Jewry, they should not ride roughshod over Arab and Moslem opinion and they should read the Koran as well as the Bible. He then repeated Attlee's September 16th observation, still seen in Israel as an example of out-and-out anti-semitism, that the Jewish refugees in Europe must not try to get to the head of the queue. Britain had never promised to bring about a Jewish state. She had promised to create a Jewish home in Palestine. And this might still be achieved 'so long as it was recognized that the tragic task of saving the Jewish people was not one to be borne by Palestine alone'.[53]

That same day Bernard Joseph went with eleven other Jewish leaders to John Shaw's office in Jerusalem, where he read them a copy of the statement. Speaking for the delegation as a whole, Joseph made the briefest of previously rehearsed replies: 'We are deeply disappointed. The Yishuv will not submit to this.' He wrote to Shertok in London: 'It is difficult to convey to you the appalling impression created here by the statement.' He saw it as a 'determined attempt to liquidate Zionism and the Balfour Declaration'.[54] Similar reports reached London from British representatives in the United States. Particular anger had been caused by the reference to jumping the queue, which was interpreted as a racial slur, an allegation that Jews as a whole were prone to aggressive and unethical behaviour.

In Palestine the Vaad Leumi declared a general strike and the Chief Rabbinate a day of fasting. On November 14th thirty thousand people met in the outskirts of Tel Aviv and that evening part of the throng, reinforced by some hooligans and looters, attacked the post office, the income tax office and other government buildings. Troops from the newly arrived 6th Airborne Division came into town and were stoned by the crowd. Several orders to disperse were ignored. The stoning continued.

The officers in charge then faced a dilemma. It was the first time for many years that they had been called out in aid of the civil power to quell a large demonstration. According to their regulations they were armed only with soldiers' weapons, rifles and bayonets. They could not carry police weapons, sticks or truncheons, designed to facilitate arrest or execute summary justice. Their rules said that they could retaliate to aggression, for instance stoning, only by the use of firearms. And they were not allowed to fire into the air. Lieutenant-Colonel R. J. Kaulback recorded: 'If the strict letter of the law is complied with, fire must be directed at some particular individual and not over the heads of the crowds.'[55]

Major Dare Wilson writes that eventually that evening, after a dozen or two British soldiers had been injured by the stoning and several warnings had been issued, the troops opened fire. This was done according to standing orders, 'a small number of rounds being fired by a specified number of men under the direct supervision of an officer'.[56] By British practice, this meant that rounds were fired individually, each one specifically directed at one of the ringleaders. This method, it was appreciated, meant an inevitable civilian casualty, often a death, but experience in India and elsewhere had indicated that the collapse of a ringleader was a better and quicker deterrent to mob violence than a show of firepower into the air. In the latter case, it was said, the firing could be interpreted as bluff and an uninvolved person far away might be hit.

And so during the two days of Tel Aviv rioting six Jews were killed and sixty injured. Also forty-two British soldiers were hurt, twelve of them seriously, mainly by the stoning.[57] Many of the Jewish casualties were young and a few were children, which provoked *Davar* to print a cartoon showing a surgeon in a ward and the caption: 'Good marksmen, these English, not to miss such small targets.'[58] John Shaw suspended *Davar* and rebuked the Hebrew press as a whole for inciting public opinion. A fourteen-year-old boy, the British observed, can be a serious menace in a riot. Dare Wilson writes that the troops' 'firm handling' ensured that crowds never again demonstrated with such violence in Tel Aviv. His only criticism is that perhaps by opening fire earlier they might have nipped the rioting in the bud and reduced the number of casualties.

Bevin quickly selected a team of six for the British half of his Commission, including two Members of Parliament and two former members. He had considered inviting one or more women, he told Byrnes, but had been advised that this might 'give rise to undesirable reactions from Moslem opinion'.[59] He asked his American counterpart to make sure not to choose anyone who had publicly supported the Arab or Jewish side. The effect of this was to rule out Congressmen as a whole, since almost every member was on record on the issue, having spoken or voted either for or against a Zionist resolution. It was the general view of Congress, Byrnes reported, 'that one way to shelve an issue is to appoint an investigating committee',[60] but he expected to field a strong team, including a former presidential candidate.

But ten days later Byrnes was still without a team. Halifax wrote on November 30th, 1945: 'Although he had been spending nearly half his time in the last few days trying to persuade suitable persons to accept the task, they are to his extreme displeasure shilly-shallying about giving definite answers. Of course no one here wants to take it on.'[61] It was more than another week before Byrnes was ready with his six men, who included a Texas judge and a retired ambassador, but no political figures. The Commission was asked to report within 120 days.

The British government nevertheless felt pleased with the prospect of American involvement. Cooperation with the United States was seen as the key to Britain's survival as a world power in the face of postwar penury. Also, having agreed to take part in an impartial inquiry, Truman could no longer prejudge it by overtly supporting the Zionist case. As candidate for the vice-presidency in 1944 he had joined Roosevelt's letter to Senator Wagner supporting the idea of Palestine as a Jewish common-wealth. On November 30th, 1945, he withdrew his support from a simi-larly worded Senate resolution. Conditions had changed, he said, and American opinion would be represented in the Commission.[62] On December 5th he told David Stern, a member of Bergson's committee, that he was against a Jewish state, echoing Bevin's strictures on all racially and religiously established governments.

Attlee received a telegram from Mahomed Ali Jinnah castigating Truman for his interference: 'It is my duty to inform you that any sur-render to appease Jewry at the sacrifice of Arabs would be deeply resented and vehemently resisted by Moslem world and Moslem India.'[63] In New York the British consulate-general was bombarded with letters and con-tinual telephone calls from Bergson (pro-Irgun) supporters.

Bevin received the Bergson leaders at the Foreign Office, reminded them that Britain was the first country in the world to give Jews the full rights of citizenship and advised them that Jews now must be prepared to accept the nationality of the country in which they lived.[64] The six British members of his Commission crossed the Atlantic with their secretary Harold Beeley, a committed pro-Arab, for their first sessions in Washing-ton. The Arab League replied to his November 13th statement courteously, welcoming his opposition to a Jewish state and stressing the need to solve Jewish problems democratically. It would be undemocratic, they pointed out, to subject the Palestine majority to rule by Jewish new-comers.[65] He seemed at this stage to be succeeding in his plan to convert the United States and stem the Zionist tide.

But the Haganah and its new allies had no intention of permitting this process. On November 25th the Sidna Ali coastguard station, part of the lookout system for illegal immigrant ships, was attacked by fifty Haganah men and blown up. Police dogs tracked the attackers to Hogla and Givat Haim, two settlements near Nathanya, but the settlers refused to allow police to come in and identify the attackers. Troops were there-fore summoned to cordon off the settlements and prevent their escape.

These troops then came under fire from Jewish reinforcements. They returned the fire, killing six Jews, and were attacked in the Jewish press for the murder of unarmed civilians.

But Lieutenant-General Sir Alan Cunningham, the new high commissioner, protested vigorously to London: 'I should state that incitement by local press and leaders is directed to inducing in Jewish mobs a readiness to sacrifice their lives for the sole purpose of putting us in the wrong.'[66] One of his military subordinates put the situation more crudely: 'HMG's policy has caused more than a flutter in both Arab and Jewish dovecotes. As always the Jewish birds squawk louder.'[67] On the immigration and arms issues, he observed, the Yishuv was united in its opposition to Britain. British officers were finding that they were no longer welcome in Jewish homes where they had once received hospitality. During the night of December 27th the Irgun again attacked Jerusalem and Jaffa police headquarters, killing a total of ten soldiers and police. On both sides tempers were at breaking point.

The 75,000 White Paper certificates had now been used up and legal Jewish immigration ceased. The Arabs were still being consulted about an extension of the 1500-per-month quota. The Jewish answer was the obvious one, an intensification of illegal immigration. On Christmas Night 250 Jews were landed from the *Marie*, a small steamer that ran on to the beach near Naharia.[68] Its arrival demonstrated, said Shertok, 'the unshakeable right of every Jew to enter his Homeland unhindered'. At the same time a bill was being introduced into the Iraqi parliament in Baghdad. An obvious parody of the Balfour Declaration, it called for the establishment of a national home for the Arab people in California.

General Sir Frederick Morgan was dismissed from his post as a senior British relief officer with the United Nations in Germany. He had said that thousands of Polish Jews were entering his area with plenty of money, with rosy cheeks and 'a well-organized, positive plan to get out of Europe'. He feared a 'second Exodus' from Europe to Palestine.[69] His words showed a certain tactlessness and lack of sympathy, but Jewish leaders saw them as proof of brutal and pathological anti-semitism. Stephen Wise, president of the World Jewish Congress, said that the statement 'savours of Nazism at its worst'.[70] The New York daily *P.M.* decided that there was little to choose between Morgan and Heinrich Himmler.

Cunningham advised London that the defiant attitude of the Jewish Agency could no longer be ignored. He had summoned Ben Gurion and Shertok after the December 27th violence, only to be told that it would be 'futile'[71] for the Agency to intervene: 'Any appeals to Jews to obey the law would fall on deaf ears at a time when the Palestine Government itself consistently violated the fundamental law of the country.'[72] He therefore suggested occupying the Agency's buildings and placing the members of the Executive under police supervision. He had considered, but on balance was opposed to, a system of collective fines and a general search for arms. George Hall agreed that there were ample grounds for taking action against the Agency, but decided it could not be done for fear of ruining the chances of the Anglo-American Commission. The only possible British riposte was to 'eschew any undue official intimacy' with the Agency. so long as they 'secretly connive at and openly condone illegal activities'.[73]

The Commission's hearings began in Washington. Richard Crossman writes: 'They began with the presentation of the Jewish case, a monumental indictment of Great Britain. There were moments when I felt more like a prisoner in the dock than a member of a committee of inquiry.'[74] Zionism was clearly the dominant belief of American Jews – an opinion poll had shown 80.1 per cent in favour of a Jewish state, only 10.5 per cent against[75] – and its strength was reflected by a succession of witnesses all explaining that their claims were based on historical fact as well as on the clear intention of the Balfour Declaration, that the Arabs had benefited from Jewish immigration and stood to benefit even more under a Jewish state.

The witnesses made it clear that only British wickedness or stubbornness was preventing this desirable result: 'We were there to take punishment – and we took it . . . Each British member of the Committee was made to feel that he was held personally responsible for the death of six million Jews.'[76] By the end of January 1946 all twelve British and American members were on their way back in the _Queen Elizabeth_ to continue their work in London.

Britain announced her decision to grant independence to Transjordan. The Zionists were furious. Transjordan was for them part of the National Home, of the Mandate, and had been illegally separated from it by Britain. What was proposed was yet another violation of Balfour's promises. Martin Charteris reported: 'A subject dear to the hearts of the Yishuv, it gives them an opportunity to attack the Government, to sneer at the Arabs and to quote the Bible.' Transjordan would now be eligible to join the United Nations and it was a matter of concern and bitter resentment that membership was being granted to hostile, politically immature nations, who had done little to defeat Nazism, 'while we with our Einsteins and our Laskis will continue to be gypsies and to loiter in the lobbies'.[77]

Cunningham's next problem was a letter from Eritrea: 'On January 17th at 9 a.m. a terrible crime was committed in cold blood at the camp of Jewish detainees near Asmara. Concentrated machine-gun and rifle fire was opened on the camp by the guards without any reason or provocation. Two detainees murdered, twelve wounded, several seriously.'[78] He was told by a Jewish delegation that Sudanese guards had run amok and that news of the massacre was spreading across Palestine like wildfire.

The proposed 1500-a-month quota was as unacceptable to the Arab League as it was to the Jewish Agency. The White Paper, it seemed, was to become no more than another broken British promise. 'We do not know where we are with them. If we agree to this, would it be their last demand?' said Ibn Saud in Council on January 6th. What really alarmed him, he told British representative Laurence Grafftey-Smith, was not the rate but the absence of any certain end to Jewish immigration: 'Ibn Saud's advocacy of our cause during the war and his constant counsels to the Arabs of moderation and confidence in HMG's pledges now seem to him to have been betrayed.' Charles Baxter expressed the view of the Foreign Office as a whole: 'There is no hope of the two communities settling down together and cooperating so long as the Jewish national home is in a state of constant expansion.'[79]

But, in the face of pressure from the Americans and the Yishuv, this was no longer a position that could be maintained. Cunningham wrote: 'I hope that even if the Arab League refuses the recent proposals made to them for an interim quota, HMG will institute one.'[80] The League had declared a boycott of Zionist goods. The refugee camps in Europe were seething with discontent. For Jewish immigration to cease absolutely at such a time was unthinkable. An explosion could result. Arthur Creech-Jones, Hall's deputy, advised Bevin that the absence of a quota was dangerous and possibly illegal. On January 26th, in spite of vigorous British protests from various parts of the Arab world, Bevin agreed that there was 'no alternative' but to continue the 1500-a-month rate.[81]

Meanwhile the Commission was holding hearings in London. British Zionists argued their case with less aggression, but with the same conviction. Lord Samuel, the former high commissioner, spoke in favour of a cantonal system. Faris el-Khoury, the Syrian delegate, asked American co-chairman Judge Joseph Hutcheson: 'Why don't you give the Jews part of Texas?'[82] Other Arab witnesses spoke with apparent sympathy about Jewish suffering, observing however that it was Europeans, not they, who had inflicted these sufferings. Bevin gave the Commission lunch at the Dorchester Hotel. According to Crossman he told them that, provided that their report was unanimous, he would do all he could to implement it.[83]

The delegates dispersed to various parts of Europe to view the plight of the refugees. Crossman, arriving ten days later because of illness, found his colleagues deeply moved and changed: 'They had smelt the unique and unforgettable smell of huddled, homeless humanity. They had seen and heard for themselves what it means to be the isolated survivor of a family deported to a German concentration camp or slave labour. The abstract arguments about Zionism and the Jewish state seemed curiously remote after this experience of human degradation.'

The Jewish survivors were almost unanimous in their demands. Palestine was their first and only choice for resettlement. They explained that, while American Jews sent them money, the Jews of Palestine offered them a home and a country. Obliged to enter a second choice on their application forms, many of them simply wrote the word 'crematorium'. Palestine offered them hope, while Europe was only a graveyard.[84]

It all conflicted with Bevin's belief that, given a free choice, most Jews wanted to stay in Europe or cross the Atlantic. Some in London saw it purely as the result of Zionist pressure in the camps. Britain had secret information that Haganah and Palmach men were regimenting the refugees, coaching them in how to speak before the Commission. The Polish and Romanian governments were allowing all Jews to leave for British or American areas. The Joint Distribution Committee was said to be providing funds, sometimes as much as £350 a family.[85] But, in the eyes of the delegates, the universal urge to leave Europe for Palestine seemed genuine and inevitable.

In late February they flew from Vienna to Cairo to hear more of the Arab case. Its most eloquent presentation was by Arab League secretary Azzam Pasha, who spoke in words which mirrored the famous extract from *Thieves in the Night*, Arthur Koestler's novel about the Irgun: 'You must understand that this is our country. We want no foreign benefactors. We don't want to be patronized. We want to live in our own way, and we want no foreign teachers and no foreign money and no foreign habits and no smiles of condescension and no pats on the shoulder and no arrogance and none of your shameless women wriggling their buttocks in holy places. We don't want your honey and we don't want your sting. Get that straight – neither your honey nor your sting . . .'[86]

In Cairo Azzam used similar words to answer Zionist claims that the

alem Old City and the shattered south-west wing of the King David Hotel, August 1946.

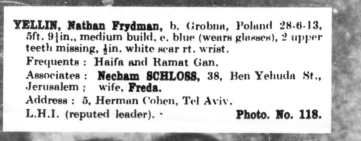

YELLIN, Nathan Frydman, b. Grobna, Poland 28-6-13, 5ft. 9½in., medium build, e. blue (wears glasses), 2 upper teeth missing, ½in. white scar rt. wrist.

Frequents : Haifa and Ramat Gan.

Associates : **Necham SCHLOSS**, 38, Ben Yehuda St., Jerusalem ; wife, **Freda**.

Address : 5, Herman Cohen, Tel Aviv.

L.H.I. (reputed leader). ' **Photo. No. 118.**

British CID [...] graph of Nat[...] Friedmann-Y[...] (now Yalin-M[...] with verbal description.

BEIGIN, Menachem, Polish, b. Poland 1906, 5ft. 9in., medium build, long hooked nose, bad teeth, wears horn-rimmed spectacles.

Frequents : Geula Qtr., Jerusalem ; Kafr Saba Colony and Tel Mont Colony.

Associates : Secretary of Kafr Saba Colony. I.Z.L. leader **Photo. No. 12.**

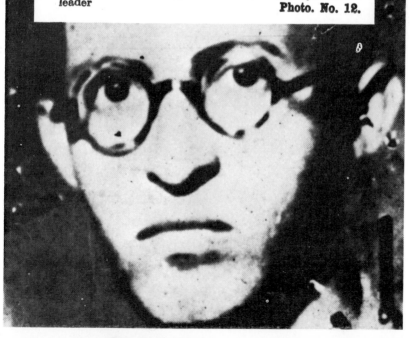

British CID p[...] graph and des[...] of Menachem [...] He says: 'Tha[...] photograph wa[...] expression of t[...] feelings of tho[...] printed it.'

A young Irgun member fastens a leaflet to a wall.

רק כך

אזהרה!

חייל עברי, שנפל בשבי האויב, "נידון" ע"י "בית-דין" ש
צבא הכבוש הבריטי למלקות.

אנו מזהירים את ממשלת הדכוי מפני הוצאה לפועל ש
עונש משפיל זה.

אם הוא יוצא אל הפועל, יוטל אותו עונש ע
קציני הצבא הבריטי. **כל אחד מהם יהיה על**

ללקות 18 מלקות.

הארגון הצבאי הלאומי
באר"ץ-ישראל   כסלו תש"ז

WARNING!

A Hebrew soldier, taken prisoner by the enemy, was
...tenced by an illegal British Military "Court" to the
...miliating punishment of flogging.

We warn the occupation Government not to carry out
...s punishment, wich is contrary to the laws of soldiers
...nour. If it is put into effect — every officer of the British
...cupation army in Eretz-Israel will be liable to be punished
...the same way: <u>to get 18 whips.</u>

HAIRGUN HAZVAI HALEUMI (N. M. O.)
b'Eretz-Israel

A warning against the flogging of Irgun men, drafted by Menachem Begin, December 1946.

A lance-corporal of the Irish Fusiliers searches an Orthodox Jew.

Orthodox Jews from the old Montefiore quarter of Jerusalem lined up for screening by police, June 1

Arabs would benefit from their movement: 'The Arabs simply stand and say "NO". We are not reactionary and we are not backward. Even if we are ignorant, the difference between ignorance and knowledge is ten years in school. We are a living, vitally strong nation, we are in our renaissance; we are producing as many children as any nation in the world. We still have our brains. We have a great heritage of civilization and of spiritual life. We are not going to allow ourselves to be controlled either by great nations or small nations or dispersed nations.'

But, in British and American eyes, the Palestine Arabs carried a heavy burden of responsibility in the clear collaboration with Nazi Germany of their leader, Haj Amin al-Husseini. Since 1941 he had been supervisor of Arabic programmes broadcast from Berlin, Athens and Rome. In 1942 he congratulated Mussolini on his victories in North Africa, calling on Egyptians to assist German and Italian troops, to punish the British oppressor. After Pearl Harbor he sent a message to Emperor Hirohito, assuring him that the Arabs were praying for the victory of Japanese arms. He protested against Bulgarian plans to release Jewish children to Palestine.[87] In 1944 he went to Yugoslavia to persuade Moslems to fight against Marshal Tito and was photographed in Bosnia inspecting Moslem troops in German uniform.[88] All this is certain.

There were other more serious charges – that he had incited Arabs to massacre the Yishuv and participated in the extermination of European Jewry. Rudolf Kasztner, a wartime Jewish relief official in Budapest, claimed to have been told by Dieter von Wisliczeny, a close colleague of Adolf Eichmann, that the Mufti took part in the Nazi decision to kill all Jews under their control: 'He [the Mufti] was one of Eichmann's best friends and has constantly incited him to accelerate the extermination measures. I heard say that, accompanied by Eichmann, he has visited incognito the gas chambers in Auschwitz.'[89]

Arab witnesses explained to the Commission that they did not view the Mufti simply as a war criminal or traitor. Anwar Nusseibeh, the former mayor of Arab Jerusalem, says: 'I do not believe that Haj Amin took part in the Holocaust or that he would ever have approved of it. His only aim was to prevent the conquest of Palestine by the Zionists. We did not approve of his going to Germany, but we could understand that he felt the he had no alternative.' This ambivalent attitude was understood in London at the time. George Hall wrote: 'The Mufti is still regarded with respect by Arab and Moslem peoples in many parts of the world and as a religious leader he retains a certain sanctity in their eyes.'[90] But it was not understood in the United States, whose links with the Arab world were looser, and it placed a definite stigma on the Palestine Arabs as a whole.

In May 1945 the Mufti fell into French hands and was held by them under house arrest near Paris. The British first tried to obtain his extradition, but soon decided, as they had more than once in the past, that they would prefer not to face the dilemma of what to do with him, that 'the balance of advantage was against putting these Palestine renegades on trial'.[91] In February 1946 the Jewish Agency formally asked Britain to bring him to trial as a war criminal and, when nothing was done, accused her of conniving at his escape.

On February 13th, 1946, Shertok stepped up the war of words in a fiery speech to the Vaad Leumi. Peaceful Jewish citizens were being shamelessly murdered by the British army, he said, and official communiqués were hushing up the bloody facts: 'Jews, abducted from their homeland by force and sent into detention abroad, are abandoned there to acts of murder by the human beasts who are put in charge of them.'[92] Cunningham then received the verdict of the Eritrea court of inquiry, which decided that the Sudanese guards only opened fire after a detainee threw a stone and twenty-five others tried to rush the gate. Far from being human beasts, it said, the guards were fully justified in what they did.[93]

Cunningham reported the speech to London as a good example of what he had to tolerate in Palestine. A senior Jewish Agency official, who had again and again proclaimed his rejection of terrorism, was in fact inciting terrorism: 'My legal advisers inform me that speech is undoubtedly seditious and, even if lack of evidence made prosecution inadvisable, it would anyway warrant detention under Regulations 142(1) of the Defence (Emergency) Regulations 1945.' But, as before, he concluded: 'After full consideration I have, with reluctance, decided to take no immediate action.'[94]

On February 6th Lehi pamphlets appeared in the streets, threatening further attacks and assassinations. That same day Lehi raided a bank, killing two Jews, and on February 15th they made another attempt on the life of Superintendent R. O. Cafferata, held responsible for the 1929 massacre of Jews in Hebron. Three days later eight Lehi men and one woman, Geula Cohen, were arrested during an illegal broadcast from the top floor of a house in Tel Aviv. Charteris records: 'While this transmitter was engaged in broadcasting its usual bi-weekly instalment of violent anti-Government abuse, police and military threw a cordon round the building and made a search.' Listeners actually heard the police entering the 'studio' and Geula Cohen saying: 'What's happening?'

On February 20th the Palmach damaged the radar station on Mount Carmel. 'This operation was well carried out and showed the marks of good planning and meticulous reconnaissance,' wrote Charteris. The next night they raided police stations at Shafa Amr, Kefar Vitkin and Sarona. The Sarona operation failed, because police were alerted and were lying in wait for the attackers. Four Palmach men were killed.[95]

It was the Jewish leaders' reaction to these deaths that caused the greatest shock of all. A crowd of about fifty thousand lined the route of their funeral procession on February 24th. The service was conducted by the Chief Rabbi of Jerusalem and attended by many leaders of the Yishuv, including David Remez, chairman of the Vaad Leumi. Jewish policemen and servicemen marched in procession. Kol Israel, the Haganah radio, proclaimed: 'Their blood was not shed in vain, not one drop of their sacred and innocent blood flowed in vain. It would not drop on the soil unless it had soaked through the walls of slavery and corroded the chains which for generations have fettered salvation and light.'

Cunningham reported: 'You will appreciate the implications of a situation in which, on the day of the arrival of Dr Weizmann in Palestine, Jewish terrorists of Palmach who had been shot *in flagrante delicto*, whilst attacking police camps with arms and explosives, were buried as national heroes.'[96] Martin Charteris noted in his fortnightly newsletter, 'It is as if the Speaker of the House of Commons and the Trades Union leaders attended the funeral, with deep respect, of four men who had been shot by the police during an unsuccessful attempt to blow up Scotland Yard.'[97]

The next day Irgun groups under the command of Amihai Paglin raided three RAF airfields – Qastina, Petah Tiqva and Lydda – placing bombs in or near a number of aircraft. There were no British casualties, but altogether twenty-two aircraft were extensively damaged or destroyed. In less than an hour the Irgun damaged British property to the value of nearly a million pounds. It was, one official noted, rather more than the Palestine government's entire estimate for education during the coming year.

On March 8th the Commission arrived in Palestine for the last series of hearings. Ben Gurion, Shertok and Golda Meir were interrogated about the Agency Executive's control of the Haganah. 'They all professed themselves ignorant of detail and innocent of control, yet there can be little if any doubt that they were avoiding the truth,' wrote Charteris. Ben Gurion repeated that it would be 'futile' for the Agency to try to suppress terrorism. Crossman commented: 'He seems to want to have it both ways, to remain within the letter of the law as Chairman of the Agency and to tolerate terror as a method of bringing pressure on the Administration. That's a doubtful policy.'[98] Cunningham recalls pointing out to Weizmann that, even though he rejected the terrorists, they were helping him to obtain power in Palestine. Weizmann replied sadly: 'I wish you hadn't said that, Your Excellency.'

Golda Meir told the Commission: 'I don't know, gentlemen, whether you who have the good fortune to belong to the two great democratic nations, the British and the American, can, with even the best of will to understand our problems, realize what it means to be a member of a people whose right to exist is constantly being questioned.'[99] She could in no way understand the turn that British policy had taken. Thirty years later she said, 'Here were the British who, we thought then and I think even now, were responsible more than anyone else for the destruction of Nazism and Hitler. We were full of admiration for the British. But then, having conquered the Nazis, it seemed that they had to conquer us, to send destroyers to stop Jews coming to these shores, the same destroyers that had fought the Nazi submarines. It seemed like an impossible world.'

On March 12th, no doubt adding to the confusion in the Commission's collective mind, Jamal Husseini told them frankly that his cousin Haj Amin was still the only man able to speak for the Arabs of Palestine. In Jamal's eyes, the Mufti had done nothing shameful during his years in Berlin. He had merely used whatever help he could find to oppose Zionist aggression. A few days later he told Crossman at one of Katie Antonius's (George Antonius's widow) famous soirées: 'I like English books and I read them in the internment camp. But I have spent most of my life fighting the British and from the look of things I shall be doing so again.'[100] Palestine was an Arab country, so he had every right to use force to prevent other people from stealing it.

The members then spent two weeks touring Palestine – Arab villages, kibbutzim, plantations, factories – immersing themselves in the problem. There was excitement during the night of March 26th, when the Haganah tried to bring in another immigrant ship, which they rechristened the *Orde Wingate*. They occupied a beach just north of Tel Aviv, mounted a number of diversionary attacks throughout the area and mined or blocked off all the roads with requisitioned trucks. Teams of civilians were there to help the immigrants ashore and a fleet of buses to mix them with the population.

But four miles from Tel Aviv the *Orde Wingate* was approached by a British destroyer, HMS *Chevron*, which ordered her to heave to and then, when she failed to obey, fired bursts of machinegun fire into her bows and rigging. She then surrendered and was escorted to Haifa, where 158 men and ninety women came ashore, to be interned and to await release against the quota. Intelligence officer David Barthall reported: 'This batch of illegals was an extremely tough-looking lot and there is obviously plenty of Irgun and Stern group material among the menfolk at least.'[101]

On March 28th the Commission flew off to Switzerland, to the Beau Rivage Hotel near Lausanne, where they had three weeks in which to condense their three months of concentrated exposure into a report, preferably unanimous. A few days later Charteris wrote: 'While the Anglo-American Committee sits in Lausanne trying to find a workable solution to the Palestine problem, fifteen Jewish leaders, specially chosen for their physical toughness, sit fasting in the Jewish Agency building making the problem more difficult to solve.'[102] It emerged that on April 4th the Italian authorities had stopped a convoy of thirty-seven British trucks near their north-west coastline and found that they were full of 1200 young Jews on their way to the port of La Spezia, where two schooners, the *Fede* and the *Fenice*, would take them to Palestine.

They were placed on the *Fede* under guard. Then, as the days passed, their mood became desperate. They threatened to commit suicide ten per day and to sink their ship in the harbour. Denis Hills, a Polish-speaking British major, was sent to interview them. He says: 'They pushed me around and called me an "English sadist".' The local Italian authorities saw no reason to take stern action against pitiful Jewish refugees. Workers in the port threatened to strike in sympathy. Eventually they were visited by the British Labour leader Harold Laski. British High Commissioner Noel Charles reported: 'The men were in an ugly mood and among other things accused the British of being responsible for the death of four million Jews. Mr Laski pointed out that if it had not been for the British none of them would probably have been alive today.'[103] But he agreed to put their case before Ernest Bevin.

Thomas Wikeley saw the incident as 'a particularly flagrant flouting' of British authority. He wrote to Bevin: 'The party originally entered Italy illegally. They were illegally convoyed to Spezia in 38 lorries belonging to the British army. Three Jewish NCOs illegally took charge of the convoy. And the party were illegally in possession of British army rations sufficient for the whole party for ten days. Now that they had been caught, they refuse to answer questions, they adopt a truculent attitude and they have even threatened to shoot the British officer who has been instructed to look after them.'[104] Major-General C. S. Sugden advised the Foreign

Office: 'I fully realize that there will be considerable political difficulties if they are returned to Poland, but the only alternative appears to be to release them in Italy, whereupon they will again take the first opportunity to emigrate illegally.'[105]

But this unsympathetic attitude was not that of the rest of the democratic world, where the refugees seemed not criminals but victims who deserved encouragement. On April 11th the Vaad Leumi held a special meeting. Three days later the whole Yishuv stopped work and its leaders began their protest, sustained only by unsweetened tea and cigarettes. Golda Meir warned Britain not to add another vessel to the tragic *Patria* and *Struma* fleet. George Hall wrote to Attlee: 'The hunger strike is a political move designed to force our hands.' The government had a difficult choice, either to give in to the moral pressure, which would encourage more illegal attempts, or to stand firm and risk the scandal that would ensue if harm befell any refugee or fasting Jewish leader.

On April 18th Laski interceded with Bevin, as he had promised, and sufficiently softened the Foreign Secretary's heart that he decided to admit the *Fede* refugees 'in driblets, say 100 at a time'[106] over and above the quota. By the end of May they were all in Palestine. It was a boost to the Jewish Agency, who badly needed a success to demonstrate that they were as efficient as the Irgun in challenging British policy.

In Lausanne the Commission had great difficulty achieving unanimity. After two weeks, a week before the text had to be ready, it seemed that there would be certainly two reports and probably three. Everyone agreed that Palestine must be neither a Jewish nor an Arab state, but on the other points there were conflicting views, especially over the hundred thousand refugees. Judge Hutcheson and three other Americans wanted them admitted unconditionally. Co-chairman John Singleton wanted their entry to be made dependent on the previous dissolution of Jewish armed forces. Crossman and two Americans, Bartley Crum and James McDonald, were in favour of partition.[107]

Truman's public statements and the pressure of Jewry bore heavily on the American members, while the British members were influenced by their pro-Arab advisers and the known anti-Zionist views of their foreign secretary. Singleton was particularly conscious of the views of the government that had appointed him. On the other hand, they had all been deeply moved by the plight of the Jewish refugees. They could not agree with Bevin that the Jews as a whole had 'come through' their wartime experiences. Nine tenths of the Jews of Poland, for instance, had not come through at all and the surviving one tenth were bitterly scarred.

A further weak spot in the official British position was that they desperately needed unanimity as a symbol of future Anglo-American co-operation in foreign affairs generally. Britain was no longer the equal partner of the wartime alliance. She was now the weary warrior, the poor relation, and she needed a massive American loan to rebuild her economy. Bartley Crum, who had by then become a firm supporter of the Zionist cause, sensed the attitude of the British side as that of an old actor coaching his understudy to take over from him the main part on the world stage.[108]

But, like most Americans, Crum saw no reason why his country's wealth should be used to prop up the dying British Empire, and he found his British colleagues, especially Beeley, most unreasonably afraid of the Soviet Union. In his view, while the British Empire and Soviet communism were in obvious conflict, there was no reason or necessity for such a conflict between Russia and the United States: 'If we travelled different roads, each still had much to learn from the other.'[109]

The British side thus needed unanimity, and they were in a correspondingly weak position when it came to a debate over the entry of the hundred thousand. Crossman writes: 'This was far the most ticklish point in the whole argument. We finally got unanimity by including in the factual report a full and objective statement of the facts about the illegal army and by drafting Recommendation Ten.'[110] Thus, instead of making the entry of the hundred thousand conditional on Jewish disarmament, as Singleton wished, they included in the report a description of the various Jewish forces, including the Haganah, and an appeal to the Jewish Agency to cooperate with Britain in suppressing terrorism.

Nevertheless the British government had some reason to be satisfied with the text that emerged from Lausanne on April 20th, 1946. The Commission achieved unanimity and rejected the Zionist arguments presented so eloquently in Washington, London, Palestine and the refugee camps. In certain important respects the document echoed the words of Ernest Bevin, that Palestine alone could not solve the Jewish refugee problem and that Palestine should not be either a Jewish or an Arab state. But it was soon clear that, in Bevin's and the Foreign Office's view, the recommendation of the hundred thousand cut right across British policy. The report as a whole was therefore an embarrassment.

Crossman's private report of April 22nd provoked scathing comment from Harold Beeley: 'In general it seems that Mr Crossman has become convinced that – quite apart from American reactions – the Jews represent a greater military danger than the Arabs. This is not the view of HMG's military advisers.' The text of the report, still unpublished, was at once submitted by Attlee to his chiefs of staff and to senior members of the Foreign Office, Colonial Office, India Office and Treasury. Crossman writes: 'In the Middle East we had sat in judgement, weighing all the conflicting views, including that of the British officials. Now, at the moment of decision, the officials gave judgement on our judgement.'[111]

On April 23rd the Irgun raided Ramat Gan police station. A Jewish telephonist gave the alarm and police reinforcements arrived from Petah Tiqva just as the attackers were withdrawing with the contents of the armoury. In the ensuing gun battle an Arab policeman and an Irgun member were killed. Another Irgun member, Dov Gruner, was seriously wounded and captured. Then on April 25th there took place the most ruthless Lehi operation of all, an event which inflamed British opinion, brought soldiers to the point of mutiny and, coming as it did five days after the Report's delivery, five days before it was made public, certainly strengthened Bevin's objection to future large-scale Jewish immigration.

Major-General James Cassels says: 'Two months after I took over as divisional commander, seven of my soldiers were deliberately murdered by the Stern gang in Tel Aviv. And there was no question about it, it wasn't a fight, it was a murder.' According to British war diaries, at about 8.30 that evening twenty-five or thirty Lehi men and women entered a house overlooking the guard tents of the 6th Airborne Division carpark on Samuel Esplanade, held up the occupants and established firing positions. These provided covering fire for the raiding party which, forty minutes later, rushed through the gate and shot a sentry dead. Four Lehi men then went to the guard tent that housed Sergeant Peat and two private soldiers.

Peat reported: 'I immediately put out the light and proceeded to the rifle rack to prepare them for action. I was in the middle of doing so when four armed men entered the tent. Myself, McKay and Gilliard were lying on the floor and the attackers shone torches on every one of us. They shone a torch on McKay, gave him a burst and then turned their attention to Gilliard doing the same thing. They used TSMGs ['Tommy' guns]. They turned their attention on me, fired at me, but missed. I feigned being wounded. They then took twelve rifles out of the tent.'[112]

Lehi men entered another tent and killed the two occupants, Privates Knight and Hope. The British report says: 'It is not known what happened in the third tent as both of the occupants were killed. They were however unarmed.' Two further unarmed soldiers, not members of the guard, were killed in the park before a bugle sounded and the Lehi team withdrew with the twelve rifles, the only arms in the park apart from two or three Sten guns carried by the sentries. The fifteen-man guard, commanded by a sergeant, was designed merely to prevent the theft of soldiers' cars.[113]

Geula Cohen says that the aim of the raid was to acquire arms: 'We simply wanted to steal the rifles and equipment without attracting attention.' But this hardly coincides with the eye-witness evidence of how the Lehi party carried out the operation, all of which supports MI6 officer Gyles Isham's conclusion that 'the object would appear to have been firstly to kill and secondly to seize all arms found in the vicinity'.[114]

Sergeant A. Bruce of the 5th Parachute Battalion recalls the devastating impact of this incident on the young British soldiers: 'The men I was with were close to mutiny. There was a secret meeting. Everyone who spoke was blacked out, so that they couldn't be identified and punished later. We were on the verge of going on the rampage and there was a general feeling that we ought to hit back. The only problem was, who could we hit back at?' In the end they did nothing. Officers discovered what was happening and took the steam out of the situation by locking up all the battalion's firearms.

Two or three dozen troops did retaliate in Nathanya, breaking windows and slightly injuring two Jewish civilians. In the settlement of Beer Tuvya, fifty miles south of Tel Aviv, about three hundred men from the 3rd Parachute Brigade at Qastina broke windows, wrecked a house and severely injured two settlers, before being broken up and removed by military police.[115] Cassels then went with his GOC, Lieutenant-General John D'Arcy, to see the High Commissioner: 'I told him that I was commanding a very high-spirited division of parachutists, that if I did nothing they could very easily mutiny. I wanted to take really strong action, but I got no support whatever. He said that if they mutinied he would find them a new divisional commander. So from then on he was not my favourite man.'

Cassels and D'Arcy asked Cunningham to impose a fine of £1,000,000 on the people of Tel Aviv, to requisition a block of buildings in the city for the use of troops, to give the Municipality a specified time to produce the killers, failing which a number of public buildings would be blown up, and to close all restaurants and places of entertainment from 8 p.m. onwards. Cunningham refused all these except the last.[116]

Cassels then made up for his frustration in the choice of words he used to the acting mayor of Tel Aviv: 'Mr Perelson, I have received your message of regret, but I have sent for you today to say how horrified and disgusted I am at the outrage committed by Jews on the night of April 25th . . . As a result I have decided to impose certain restrictions on the Jewish community as a whole . . . I am quite certain if you, as representative of the community in Tel Aviv, chose to do so, you could produce sufficient information to lead to the arrest of the criminals.'

Meanwhile Whitehall, far from exulting at the Commission's rejection of most Zionist claims, was reacting angrily to the proposals to admit a hundred thousand Jewish refugees and repeal the 1940 Land Regulations. The hundred thousand, they reported, would be seen by the Arabs as the first batch of half a million. The second proposal would at once create an embittered landless Arab peasantry. Bevin's committee of officials, under Norman Brook, took only a week to reach a number of alarming conclusions: 'The first reaction of the Arabs in Palestine will probably take the form of demonstrations and strikes, leading possibly to riots and attacks on isolated Jewish colonies.'

British forces on the spot could probably contain these initial outbreaks. But there would be real trouble once Britain began to put the report into effect: 'A general Arab rising in Palestine would probably follow . . . Two of His Majesty's representatives in the Middle East describe the report as a disaster for our interests and prestige . . . Implementation of the report would spell the beginning of a long period of unrest in the whole Arab world.'[117] In Iraq there would be serious riots, involving British residents, and perhaps a pogrom in Baghdad. Ibn Saud and other Arab leaders would see the report as a breach of faith and a perpetuation of an intolerable injustice.

Britain's chiefs of staff also predicted a general Arab rising, against which it would not be possible to use Indian or other local forces, who might themselves be in a state of mutiny. And there was no source of British reinforcements. There was, in fact, only one way in which it would be safe to admit the hundred thousand – by previously disarming and disbanding the illegal Jewish organizations, including the Haganah. If the Jewish Agency could be persuaded to help in this task, well and good. 'If, however, these peaceful methods failed, the Chiefs of Staff think it would be necessary to arrest the Jewish leaders and to suppress their illegal organizations by force.'

This was the message that Bevin gave Byrnes as early as April 26th at the peace conference in Paris, four days before the report was published: 'We were prepared to accept the figure of 100,000 Jewish refugees, but only on certain conditions. In the first place it must be clear that immigration must not start until disarmament of the Jews had taken place.'[118] Bevin then told his American colleague that many of the new arrivals in Palestine were not refugees at all. They were young men specially selected by the Jewish Agency for military purposes. The Jewish Agency were a real menace to peace. They were among the people in the world at present who had warlike and aggressive intentions. Byrnes must understand how distasteful Britain found it, having to keep four divisions in Palestine to carry out a thankless task. In fact, Britain was seriously thinking of throwing the whole matter up.

But Truman's statement welcoming the report's publication on April 30th, 1946, took no account whatever of the British foreign secretary's views. Once again he placed every emphasis on the need to admit the hundred thousand. This was the only one of the ten recommendations that he specifically mentioned: 'The transference of these unfortunate people should now be accomplished with the greatest dispatch,' he said. As for the other recommendations, he observed merely that they required careful study and that he would take them under advisement.

It was, from the British point of view, a most improper statement, even worse than the previous September's press leak on the same subject. The United States had agreed to cooperate with Britain over Palestine. How could her president then make public demands on Britain, without any discussion, which he knew that Britain was unwilling to fulfil? At once Bevin wrote angrily to Byrnes: 'I confess that the issue without consultation of the statement on Palestine of which you sent me the text last night seems likely to give rise to grave difficulties. I must remind you that in Palestine British soldiers have been foully murdered by the armed forces of the Jews . . .'[119]

It was a situation, Bevin continued, which the British people would no longer tolerate. The liquidation of private armies was essential, both to make possible the entry of the hundred thousand, 'to which the US statement attaches such importance', and to prevent a collapse of security in the Middle East. The United States must realize this necessity. On May 1st Attlee confirmed publicly in the House of Commons that the disarmament of Jewish forces and the surrender of Jewish arms were prior conditions to the entry of the refugees. And since the Yishuv were unlikely to permit the former, the British were unlikely to permit the latter. It seemed almost certain that Truman's demand would be refused.

Both Jews and Arab nevertheless believed at this stage that the hundred thousand would be allowed to enter. And this was a comfort to the Yishuv, a relief for their disappointment at the Commission's general rejection of Zionist arguments. Soon they would have a hundred thousand new citizens. And in due course, most of them assumed, they would be allowed to welcome more. What was at stake was, therefore, the first batch of a massive Aliya, the return of the Jews of the diaspora to the Land of Israel. It was a continuing process, a first step along the road which would lead inevitably to a Jewish majority and an independent Jewish state.

At this stage Attlee's statement that they would have to hand in their arms before immigration began made little impression. It seemed such an impossible idea. Jewish settlements *had* to be armed, to protect settlers' lives against Arab attack. Surely the British recognized the existence of this danger and the right of the Jews to defend themselves? It was true that the Haganah was now promoting 'Aliya B', unauthorized immigration, in defiance of British authority, but this conflict would cease as soon as the hundred thousand began coming in. The Jewish Agency would then have to cooperate with the Mandatory, to make sure that the newcomers were absorbed peacefully and economically. Anyway, one thing was sure, that Truman's original request for a hundred thousand certificates had been strengthened by the advice of twelve prominent and impartial men, British as well as American. The British government would now have to grant it.

The corresponding fury of the Arabs reflected these Jewish hopes. The Arabs would fight the report by all means in their power, Jamal Husseini[120] told the press on April 30th. *Ad-Difa'a* accused Britain and the United States of 'baring their heads before Jewish influence and money'.[121] Regent Abd ul-Ilah of Iraq sent a telegram of protest to Truman and the Iraqi consul in Jerusalem cancelled the May 2nd party for King Faisal's birthday. President Khalil el-Khoury of Lebanon advised Truman that the recommendations 'fulfil Zionist hopes to their fullest extent and give a death blow to the rights of the Arabs'.[122] On May 3rd the Palestine Arabs observed a general strike. King Ibn Saud once again urged Britain and the United States to fulfil their promises to the Arabs: 'I fear that we may have been under a great deception.'

Irgun and Lehi too were alarmed, because the Report seemed likely to gain the support of Jewish moderates, and once this happened, once the British rediscovered a basis for agreement with a substantial section of the Yishuv, however uneasy, it would mean the end of Irgun's and Lehi's usefulness. Yalin-Mor says: 'It was a very delicate moment for us, when the Commission made these recommendations. If Bevin had accepted them, we would have had to stop all operations for as long as immigration continued. The view of the masses of the Yishuv would have been, "Let's absorb the 100,000 immigrants and then we shall see." '

Most Israelis now agree that, if Britain had accepted the Report and for good measure offered to accept as British immigrants a good number of Jewish refugees from Europe, say twenty-five thousand, the steam would have been taken out of the maximalist demand for an immediate Jewish state. The moderate position would have been restored and terrorism crippled. It would also have concentrated American minds more closely on the problem. After all, if Britain had offered to accept twenty-five thousand Jews from Europe, the United States would be in honour bound to accept fifty thousand, if not more, and the Arabs would no longer be able to claim with some justice that the two democracies were unloading on to them a burden they were unwilling to bear themselves. It would invalidate Weizmann's statement that the world was divided into two areas, countries where Jews could not live and countries where Jews could not enter.

Yalin-Mor recalls in this context the saying of Mao Tse-tung: 'The guerrillas and the masses are like fish and water. If the water is clean, if the masses are sympathetic, the fish or the guerrillas can move freely. But if the water is dirty, if the masses are hostile, then the fishes or the guerrillas will die.' The Irgun and Lehi were a very small part of the Yishuv. They were able to survive and free to operate only because the Yishuv and its elected bodies gave them qualified and tacit approval. The constant danger they faced was that one day the British would find the right spot to drive a political wedge that would isolate them from the Yishuv. They would then find themselves being once again abducted by the Haganah and denounced to the British police.

But Britain was unable to drive this wedge. In Attlee's and Bevin's view the price of a hundred thousand immigrants was too high for them to pay. They were irrevocably convinced by their advisers that this part of the Report was unjust to the Arabs, that if it was implemented the Middle East would be set ablaze and Britain's interests in the area destroyed. And so seriously did they take this threat that they were prepared to face the alternative problems of an anti-Zionist policy – a serious disagreement with the American government, the bitter anger of world Jewry and growing terrorism in Palestine.

They underestimated the strength of the Yishuv's armed forces and the depth of its commitment to Zionist aims. They believed that the law-breakers, not only the Irgun and Lehi but also Ben Gurion and the Haganah militants, were an extreme and unrepresentative minority, that the Yishuv masses were being intimidated into supporting this minority, whereas in their hearts they were a moderate and law-abiding community, loyal to Chaim Weizmann and opposed to any form of violence. The problem could therefore best be solved in the short term by military means, by a single all-out effort by the army against the Haganah and the two other groups, after which the Yishuv would select less strident leaders and come to terms with British policy.

They were angry with the American government, perhaps not realizing that the United States felt itself severely provoked by Britain's behaviour. At Britain's urgent request the United States had agreed to cooperate over the problem and take part in a Commission. Bevin had promised that he would do all he could to implement a unanimous report. Then, when the Report turned out not exactly to the British government's liking, they had imposed on its implementation conditions which were not contained in the Report and which everyone knew were impossible to fulfil.

The American government knew what had happened in Lausanne. Only three members, all British – Singleton, Manningham-Buller and Crick – had advocated Jewish disarmament as a prior condition to the entry of the hundred thousand. The other nine, including all six Americans, had taken the view that the condition was impossible, that it would be, in Crossman's words, a virtual declaration of war against the Jews. In the end it had been specifically and unanimously rejected by the Commission. In spite of this, the British government had resurrected it, making it the keystone of Attlee's statement on May 1st.

Attlee's statement was thus seen in Washington as a slap in the face to the American members of the Commission and to the American administration. The British government had ostensibly accepted the Report. But in fact their intention was to wreck it, by imposing an impossible condition on its key point. The British government had given the world to understand that the Commission was a decision-forming body. In fact, they had turned it into a stalling device, a calculated waste of twelve busy men's time.

If the American government was angry, the Yishuv was beside itself with rage, when it emerged that the hundred thousand refugees might not be admitted to Palestine after all. 'Bevin helped us a lot. He was so rigid. He made everyone here so furious,' says Yalin-Mor. His men had just killed seven British soldiers in a Tel Aviv carpark. The Yishuv had been shocked. But this shock evaporated after Attlee's announcement a week later. The death of seven men seemed a mere pinprick compared to the open wounds of European Jewry, most of whom had been massacred by Hitler's followers, and hundreds of thousands of whom still languished in camps waiting for British certificates.

The Arabs felt just as strongly that, whatever the sufferings of the Jewish refugees, it was the height of cynicism and injustice for the Zionist leaders to use them as pawns in a political game whose clear aim was the conversion of an Arab country into a Jewish country. As decent men and women they felt sorry for the genuine refugees, but they had no sympathy for the young people, selected by the Jewish Agency for reasons military rather than humanitarian, who were arriving by the shipload and threatening to 'swamp' their country. (Martin Charteris reported that all the 1014 immigrants disembarked from the *Fede* and *Fenice* were healthy youngsters between the ages of fifteen and thirty-five.) They felt no guilt or responsibility for what had been done to the Jews during the war. That guilt lay squarely on European shoulders, they believed, just as it had in previous centuries, when Jews were regularly persecuted in Christian Europe but lived for the most part secure and prosperous lives under the protection of Islam.

The British, the third point in the triangle of conflict, carried on searching for the impossible – a way out of the confusion that would give both Arabs and Jews something, while at the same time preserving something of their own interests. They understood neither the ingratitude of the Arabs, whom they had liberated from Turkish rule in 1917 and protected from the racist ravages of Nazism, nor the ingratitude of the Jews, all of whom owed their survival to Britain's steadfast stand in 1940.

The Commission had failed. Moderation and compromise showed no result. The Jewish leaders decided to arm themselves for the struggle, to step up illegal immigration and tolerate the judicious use of terrorism. The Arabs of Palestine, still without physical strength or political leadership, knew nevertheless that their cause was a symbol of Arab unity and purpose, that it would never be abandoned. They too prepared for battle. The British were now under a new GOC, Lieutenant-General Evelyn Barker, a tough soldier who would not be blackmailed or coerced by violent men. Under his command they would crush the illegal organizations. These three ingredients of a tragically powerful mixture were flowing together, seething and bubbling their way to the point of explosion.

8

The King David Affair

'I WAS in Palestine from March 1946 until the end of the year, ten hellish months,' says James Cassels: 'I got appallingly rude letters from America, saying that I was much worse than Hitler, addressed to me personally. We nearly had seizures every time we read a newspaper. The general line was that we were anti-semitic beasts and murderers. I don't think they realized that many of my men parachuted into Normandy in June 1944. Large numbers of them were killed and wounded fighting to remove Hitler from the face of the earth.'

'The wages of the British Foreign Office are war,' wrote Ruth Gruber in the *New York Post* on May 20th. The next day she continued in the same vein on the subject of the Palestine police: 'These men who loathed the idea of fighting their friends, the Nazis, embraced with passion the idea of fighting Jews. They walked around the streets of Jerusalem and Tel Aviv, the city built by Jews, singing the Horst Wessel song. They marched into crowded market places giving the Heil Hitler salute.'

British troops who entered Jewish settlements found themselves being spat on and showered with abusive names, usually 'Gestapo' or 'Nazi sadist' or 'English bastard'. The paratroopers were known in Hebrew as 'kalanioth' or 'anemones', because of their distinctive red berets, and a song about them referred to 'the red anemone with the black heart'. The alleged similarity between Britain and Nazi Germany was a serious theme of Jewish political writing. Haganah intelligence chief Efraim Dekel writes of Athlit detention camp: 'The camp itself was not very different from the hundreds of concentration camps in Nazi Germany, where defenceless Jews and non-Jews had been herded together under the most cruel conditions.'[1]

Major Dare Wilson writes that the average British soldier was 'intensely mystified' by the Jewish attitude. 'If he had expected to find an atmosphere of friendliness and hospitality, he was disappointed. Indeed, such was his reception that soon he was asking himself what he had been fighting for during the past five years.'[2]

The soldiers knew little or nothing about the politics of the matter. Many of them had seen the sufferings of Jews in Europe. Lieutenant-General Evelyn Barker, for instance, commanded a unit which liberated Belsen concentration camp. But they did not take in the extent of the slaughter or the marks it had made on the Jewish soul. They did not understand the depth of Jewish feeling against British policy and therefore against the soldiers whose job it was to enforce it. They felt that they were enforcing the law impartially between Arab and Jew. And if their general attitude to the Jews was more aggressive and suspicious than to the Arabs, this merely reflected the fact that, whereas the Arabs were quiescent, armed Jewish groups were bombing British buildings and shooting British soldiers.

Lieutenant-General D'Arcy told the chiefs of staff on his return to London: 'Our forces were under extreme tension. They were veterans of battles in Europe in the last war. They were taught to kill and were now placed under irritating restrictions.' His superior officer in the Middle East, General Bernard Paget, agreed with him about the effect of the Tel Aviv car park killings. 'If nothing is done, there is risk that troops will take law into their own hands.' D'Arcy gave a similar warning: 'If similar Jewish attacks occurred, he did not believe that it would be possible to restrain our troops as they had now reached breaking point. In his position as Commander-in-Chief he could not condone such action, but he had sympathies with their feelings.'[3]

At the same time Chaim Weizmann's wife Vera was one of the many to complain of troops entering settlements with shouts of 'Heil Hitler!' and scrawling swastikas or anti-semitic slogans on walls. Cunningham replied that British soldiers and police 'are frequently greeted by Jews with provocative slogans likening them to the Nazis' and were constantly exposed to 'relentless and malignant propaganda'.[4] He admitted that a few soldiers or policemen might well have retaliated in the way suggested. But, like all his colleagues, he was outraged at the continual repetition of this odious comparison.

Sergeant A. Bruce says: 'I went out there without any anti-Jewish feeling at all, but after a few months we were all very angry with the Jews, I admit it.' Part of his job was to check documents in the continual search for terrorists and illegal immigrants. 'Our general rule was to detain on suspicion any male between the ages of 18 and 35 who acted in a surly manner. It was a bit stupid, because I dare say that a real terrorist would have been as polite as he could. But at least it gave us a chance to get our own back for what we had to put up with.'

Late one night Captain Davidson and Lieutenant Benjamin Woodworth were walking down Ben Yehuda Street, Tel Aviv, on their way home to the officers' club, when they passed a group of Jews on the pavement. According to the British weekly report, one of the Jews jostled Davidson: 'For some time past the citizens of Tel Aviv have been in the habit of barging into British military personnel in the streets.'[5] According to the Jewish version, Woodworth pushed his way through the group, while Davidson picked on one member, Avram Rosenberg, calling him a 'Jewish bastard' and attempting to trip him up. Anyway, the result was that Woodworth drew his revolver and shot Rosenberg dead.[6] He was subsequently charged with the killing and removed from Palestine, suffering from a nervous breakdown.

Such incidents showed how sharp was the tension, how deep the mutual suspicion between the Yishuv and the army. During May there was generally a lull in the violence, as the world waited to see whether Britain would still be persuaded to admit the hundred thousand. It seemed to the Yishuv such an obviously just first step. They saw no reason for refusing it. Bernard Joseph replied scathingly to Cunningham's suggestion that it would produce a violent reaction from the independent Arab countries: 'They might shout a lot and possibly also give the Arabs of Palestine help in terms of money and permitting a few hundred terrorists to go across the frontier to Palestine, but we did not see them sending their armies into Palestine to take up battle. Nor were we worried about it.'[7] Joseph explained that he had known the Arabs for twenty-eight years, he understood their psychology. Once the Arabs were confronted with a fact, they accepted it.

Undeterred by Attlee's discouraging statement on May 1st, the United States applied continuous pressure on Britain over Jewish immigration. On May 8th, 1946, Truman advised the Prime Minister that the Report provided a basis for talks between Britain, the United States, Jews and Arabs. He referred to the 'urgency' surrounding the proposed entry of the hundred thousand. Attlee replied with a touch of irony: 'Thank you very much indeed for your message of yesterday about Palestine and for your kindness in consulting me.'

On May 27th Attlee sent another telegram, several pages long, listing numerous administrative and financial problems raised by such massive movements. Truman's reply promised that the United States would transport the hundred thousand to Palestine, temporarily house them and perhaps provide further long-term assistance. Again he referred to 'the urgency of the problem of the 100,000 Jews'.[8] On June 10th Attlee cabled again, re-emphasizing Britain's stated position that the Report must be considered as a whole and pointing out with regard to the hundred thousand: 'It is necessary to consider not only the physical problems involved, but also the political reactions and possible military consequences.'[9]

But in his reply Truman said that in his opinion the problems involved in admitting the hundred thousand, 'whose situation requires such urgent attention,' were 'purely technical'. The new British ambassador, Lord Inverchapel (Archie Clark Kerr), advised Bevin on June 13th: 'I had a short talk with Byrnes about Palestine yesterday and it was quite apparent that, despite all we have said, he takes for granted admission of 100,000 as an immediate step . . . He was alive to our difficulties, but wanted you to know he was under very strong pressure from Congress and outside it.'[10]

So by the end of May 1946 the tide had once again turned against the Zionists. An article by Arab Legion commander John Glubb in the *Daily Mail* declared that Palestine outweighed all other Arab considerations, that the result of a Zionist victory would be murder, sabotage, severed communications, convoy attacks and pogroms.[11] It seemed to many Zionists no coincidence that such views should be expressed in a leading London daily at such a time.

Then the Mufti, supposedly a prisoner of the French outside Paris, turned up in Damascus. Martin Charteris wrote: 'The protracted *fantaseeya* in Palestine which commenced with news of his flight from France on 9 June is proof of his popularity. During the three-day celebration in his honour, Arab towns and Arab districts were beflagged and plastered with his photograph.'[12] Ten days later he flew to Egypt, where Prime Minister Sidky welcomed him as a great Arab chief, though publicly inviting him to abstain from political intrigue. Sections of the Jewish press and two US Congressmen, John McCormack and Thomas Lane, immediately announced that Haj Amin's fifth miraculous escape had been arranged by Ernest Bevin so as to forestall Jewish immigration.

On June 12th Bevin added fuel to these flames with another tactless speech. He told the Labour Party Conference at Bournemouth that, if a hundred thousand Jews entered Palestine immediately, he would have to send another division of British troops to keep the peace and that this he was not prepared to do. He also took the chance to relieve some of his frustration against the United States: 'I hope I will not be misunderstood in America if I say that this was proposed with the purest motives. They did not want too many Jews in New York.'

This barbed remark had a devastating effect throughout America. Inverchapel cabled his boss the next day, choosing his words as diplomatically as possible: 'Your criticism of New York has, of course, not only hit the nail on the head but driven it woundingly deep.'[13] It had also, the ambassador explained, advertised British-American discord at the outset of joint expert discussions and made the President look foolish. Bevin was in no way contrite. 'It seems clear that judgements have been formed on a few sentences of my speech torn from their context,' he replied, inviting Inverchapel to send the full text to members of Congress, who were about to vote on the British loan.

But the damage was done. Mayor William O'Dwyer of New York was asked whether he had read Bevin's remarks and answered: 'I certainly did and I am astounded. What right has he to say what New York City thinks of the Jewish people?'[14] Stephen Wise referred to Bevin's 'offensive vulgarity'. Rabbi Louis Newman said at a memorial service; 'Any stick, even if it be tarred with anti-semitism, is good enough for the spokesman of the ineffective British Labour Government to beat the already tormented Jewish survivors in Europe.'

Attempting to cool the situation, Inverchapel asked Bevin at least to reassure Washington and Truman personally, since the President's prestige was involved, that Britain had not prejudged the question of admitting the hundred thousand. But Bevin replied: 'I am not sure that this is a wise thing to do. I am getting upset with this Jewish agitation. We have made our position clear.'

In Palestine a further crisis erupted on June 13th when Yosef Shimshon and Itzhak Ashbel, captured during the Irgun raid on Sarafand army camp on March 6th, were sentenced to death by a military court. They would be the first Irgun men to be executed in Palestine since Ben-Yosef in 1938. The Irgun was determined to act. Begin says: 'I went to my colleagues from Haganah and Lehi and explained that we would not tolerate the hanging of our men. We considered that our men were fighters, not criminals, fighters for the liberation of our people. If they were captured, they should be kept in a camp or prison. We did not recognize the emergency regulations. We did not recognize British rule in our country. We made this clear as early as 1944 and we said that, if our men were hanged, there would be retaliation.'

Pleas for clemency poured into British offices from Chaim Weizmann and others. But a Jewish guard had been killed and a British woman canteen worker, Jean Marjoribanks, seriously wounded in the Sarafand raid.[15] General Barker's view of such action is a thoroughly simple and straightforward one: 'I am in favour of the death penalty for murder, political or otherwise. The one strict law we had was against carrying arms. And it's no good having a law like that if you don't enforce it. So if anyone was caught carrying arms, he was up before a court martial, he could state his case, but if he was found guilty that was it. And, subject to Alan Cunningham's final say, I would confirm the death sentence.' It remained to be seen what the Irgun would do in reply.

As if this was not enough, the situation was then aggravated by the Haganah's discovery of detailed British orders to the army and police, providing for the disarmament of the Jewish community and the arrest of a 'blacklist' of key Haganah men. Israel Galili explains that a British officer at Sarafand army camp, not a Jew, read the orders and divulged their contents to his Jewish girl friend who, like many girl friends of British officers at that time, was a member of the Haganah. Arrangements were then made to infiltrate the camp more deeply. Eventually the Haganah were able to remove the documents from the safe, photograph them and replace them.

The British authorities knew nothing of this massive security leak until suddenly the text of their demands was being plastered over Tel Aviv on posters and broadcast by Haganah radio. The *Kol Israel* announcement on June 15th concluded: 'The document is now public property. Let the Yishuv, the diaspora and the whole world know what Bevin, Attlee and their henchmen are preparing for us. And let the world know that we shall fight.'[16] Galili, who was shortly to assume command of the Haganah, explains that this was done, if not to avert, at least to stultify the expected operation. Meanwhile his key men went into hiding and deepened their disguises. Weizmann told Cunningham on June 19th how shocked he was by the revelation of such a plan. He was sure that the details would find their way to the United States and do Britain damage there.

These five events – the two death sentences, Bevin's Bournemouth speech, Glubb's *Daily Mail* article, the discovery of the documents and the Mufti's escape – induced the Jewish resistance to end their semi-truce and strike further heavy blows against Britain. On June 10th the Irgun stopped three trains at a prearranged spot by pulling the communication cord, ordered the passengers to alight, then destroyed the trains by driving them over mines on the track.[17]

During the night of June 16/17th, 1946, the Haganah mounted a massive show of strength, unusual in that it had no connection with illegal immigration, destroying or damaging eight bridges around Palestine's frontiers with Transjordan, Syria and Lebanon. About thirty Haganah men attacked the Allenby Bridge, fought off the Arab Legion guard on the Transjordan side and blew it up. 'The bridge is impassable and will take some weeks to repair,' noted Gyles Isham. Only at the Az-Zib railway bridge did the Haganah plan fail. Yigael Yadin explains: 'The need to avoid British casualties was a very important factor in planning our operations. The objection was partly moral, partly practical. We realized that, if the Haganah caused British casualties, it would give the British a legitimate reason to take action against the whole Yishuv, or at least its leaders. The Zib railway bridge, for instance, was guarded by British sentries. But instead of just shooting them, which they could have done quite easily, the Haganah team tried to crawl towards them and overpower them. They were spotted and killed.' According to the British report, the police post opened fire when they saw the Haganah men placing charges under the bridge. This rifle fire killed two of the raiders and caused an explosion that killed four others.

The June 17th Lehi raid on the Kishon railway workshop in Haifa was a disaster. The party of thirty-five arrived in a truck, opened fire and bombed their way through the gate. Once inside they set off numerous explosions, destroying a locomotive, some small buildings and a fire engine, but also killing two of their own men. The army were alerted and roadblocks established. An hour before midnight the Lehi truck ran into one of these at Kfar Ata. The driver tried to burst his way through, but was brought to a halt. Immediately troops lining the ditch opened fire, killing seven Lehi men and wounding eleven more, including three women. The twenty-six survivors, armed with Sten and Tommy guns, were all captured.[18]

The Irgun, ostensibly still in alliance with the Haganah and Lehi, were preoccupied with the fate of their two condemned comrades. Begin says: 'I ordered our men to capture as many British officers as possible. We went for officers deliberately, because we believed that this would help us to save our men. By the way, we never took any hostages, civilian or military, to *free* our men. We only did it to save their lives.'

Accordingly at lunchtime on June 18th twelve Irgun men drove up to the officers' club in Tel Aviv's Yarkon Hotel. Seven kept watch outside, while five entered the dining-room with sub-machineguns. The officers had all handed in their revolvers at the cloakroom by the entrance. They were unarmed and helpless. The raiders herded them into a corner, inspected their shoulder tabs and removed four of the senior men, one of whom, Captain D. T. Rae, they clubbed with a piece of lead piping. An RAF officer, Flight Lieutenant Thomas Russell, was also abducted when he tried to slip down a corridor and raise the alarm. They were transferred to a truck ingeniously fitted with coffin-like secret compartments under the floorboards, to enable the prisoners to be passed through roadblocks undetected, and taken to a cellar prison.

Russell and Rae were correctly treated. They were guarded night and day by three or four men with .38 revolvers, their hands and feet were chained, but they had good food – chicken, melons and beer – and straw palliasses to sleep on. Rae, who was a Plymouth Brother, was given a Bible and a replacement for his bloodstained shirt. Several times they were visited by a hooded Irgun leader, who explained to them that they would be released as soon as the death sentences were commuted. He made it clear, though, that if the sentences were carried out, they would take the consequences.

Russell says: 'The guards were very well disciplined. They never relaxed their vigilance and every time their leader came in – I think it must have been Menachem Begin – they stood up and came smartly to attention. They seemed to be looking forward to open warfare between Britain and the Jews. One of them asked me, "When is the RAF going to start bombing us?" I told him not to be silly, the RAF would never bomb Tel Aviv, but he didn't believe me, he didn't want to believe me. Several of my airmen were killed fighting the Irgun, so I have no great affection for them, but I'll say this – they were brave and dedicated to their task.'

Weizmann told Cunningham on June 21st how deeply shocked he was by the kidnappings and agreed with him that the Haganah's bridge-blowing 'was a senseless and useless thing to do'.[19] Cunningham tried to explain that continuing violence was rapidly turning a political problem into a purely military problem. Did the Jews wish to see everything they had done in Palestine lost in a welter of bloodshed and desolation? Weizmann pointed out that the Jews had endured five clear acts of provocation in recent weeks. He would do what he could to calm things down. But Cunningham noted: 'I am afraid that his influence with the extremists is small and I do not believe that he knows most of what is going on, though quite possibly he intentionally avoids doing so.'

On June 22nd the Irgun leader came again with good news for Rae and Russell: 'He gave us a pep-talk, explained again why we'd been kidnapped and asked us to pass the message on to our superiors. Then he stuffed a pound-note each into the top pocket of our shirts. It was for "wear and tear" on our uniforms, he said. We tried to refuse, but he insisted and in the circumstances we thought it best to accept.' According to Rae's report, the Irgun leader promised to take disciplinary action against the man who had hit him and remarked in parting that he hoped to see them again, either in a café or in a pitched battle. They were then blindfolded, driven in circles for twenty minutes and released in Tel Aviv.[20]

General Bernard Montgomery, by then Chief of Imperial General Staff, returned from his June visit to Palestine much perturbed by what he had seen: 'The High Commissioner seemed to me to be unable to make up his mind what to do. Indecision and hesitation were in evidence all down the line, beginning in Whitehall. A policy was required and then decisions. The Palestine Police force was 50 per cent below strength . . .' In his view the answer to the problem was a new 'get tough' policy and he was fully prepared for 'a war against a fanatical and cunning enemy who would use the weapons of kidnap, murder and sabotage'.[21]

On June 20th he attended the Cabinet meeting and advised that the time had now come to break the illegal organizations. A telegram from Bevin, who was still in Paris, advised the Cabinet: 'We should make it clear that no action can be taken to implement it [the Report] as regards the 100,000 until terrorism has stopped. HMG will not submit to terrorism.'[22] He too was in favour of Monty's plan, which he wanted accompanied by a publicity campaign to make clear to British and American public opinion why it had become necessary. The Cabinet generally agreed: 'We could no longer tolerate a position in which the authority of government was set at nought.' Cunningham was there and then given authority to crush the 'more extreme elements' who, in Britain's view, had obtained control of the Jewish Agency and were, through the Haganah, controlling the terrorism.

On June 23rd Barker revealed to his divisional commanders that the operation would begin at 4.15 a.m. the following Saturday, June 29th, 1946. Great efforts were made to keep this fact secret. Conferences were held away from army headquarters and senior officers attending them minimized the impression of undue bustle by removing their distinctive red headbands. All letters about the operation were sent in an outer envelope and marked with a codeword, indicating exactly who was to open them. The American government, clearly a potential source of leaks to Zionist bodies, would be informed only at the last minute. The Jerusalem horse show, already fixed for June 28th and 29th, was allowed to continue.[23]

Dare Wilson writes that these measures 'did enable complete tactical surprise to be achieved'. But this is hardly the full truth. The Haganah already had the original contingency plan, though not the date of the operation, and they had made their preparations, improving hiding places and filling settlement areas with scrap iron to confuse British metal detectors. Also many Jewish clerks who worked in government offices gave information to the Haganah. Efraim Dekel recalls a noticeable increase in postal correspondence, the cancellation of police leave and orders placed with Jewish firms for three-day ration packs and quantities of buses. It all indicated that something important was being cooked up by the army and it needed no genius to guess what this was.

Attlee cabled Truman only at 1.15 a.m. on June 29th, 1946: 'In view of the continuance of terrorist activities in Palestine, culminating in the recent kidnapping of six British officers, HMG have come to the conclusion that drastic action can no longer be postponed.'[24] Three hours later a hundred thousand troops and ten thousand police occupied the Jewish Agency headquarters in Jerusalem, various other official Jewish buildings and twenty-five Jewish settlements. By the end of the first day 2659 men and 59 women were detained. Shertok, Joseph, Hacohen, Remez, Fishman and various other so-called 'VIJs' (Very Important Jews) were interned in a special compound in Athlit. Golda Meir was not arrested – a strange British omission which caused Ben Gurion's wife Paula to telephone several times to express her surprise. Mrs Meir writes that some people were later to say unkindly that it was the worst thing the Mandatory ever did to her.[25]

The troops faced widespread passive resistance from the settlers, who locked their gates, blocked the entrances with tractors and their own bodies, refused to cooperate in identification and fingerprinting, shouted insults and occasionally threw missiles at the soldiers. According to Jewish witnesses, some soldiers retaliated by shouting Nazi slogans, looting property and using unnecessary violence. Efraim Dekel writes that the troops and police behaved brutally, carrying out a virtual pogrom, but this is generally seen as an oversimplification. British retaliation varied in intensity, but was generally moderate, as was Jewish provocation.[26]

Meshek Yagur near Haifa, described in the British report as 'a truculent settlement', provides a vivid example of what took place that day. A battalion and a company of the 1st Infantry Division arrived at 9.30 a.m. to find all entrances blocked. The troops fired teargas shells, which the settlers at once rendered harmless with wet sand and manure bags. Water cannons were then used more successfully to disperse the human barriers.

Men, women and children then crowded around the central building and refused to move. Eventually the soldiers got into the central dining-room. whereupon the women threw dishes and boiling water at them. By 11 a.m. seventy-five men, eighteen women and eleven children were arrested.[27]

By 2 o'clock the number of men detained had risen to 250 and the troops were in a position to begin the arms search. Divisional commander Major-General Richard Gale says: 'I saw a piece of farm machinery and I said, "What's that?" They said it was a disused tractor. I said, "Don't be so bloody silly, there's a pipe coming up out of the ground." So we dug down and found half a mile of tunnelling and an underground arsenal, a factory making rifles and two-inch mortars.'

Golda Meir says: 'What they did in the Histadrut building was terrible. They didn't hurt people, because there was no one there on a Saturday. But they could have *opened* the doors of the rooms, instead of breaking them down. They did that everywhere. They behaved as if they were going into enemy territory.' She also complains that the troops caused 'wanton damage' in the settlements, that in Meshek Yagur 'they tore the kibbutz apart'.[28] The reason for this was the large quantity of arms that were concealed there. According to Dare Wilson, thirty-three arms caches were found all over Meshek Yagur, mainly underground.[29] The total find included 325 rifles, 94 two-inch mortars, 800 pounds of explosives and nearly half a million rounds of ammunition.[30]

The remnants of the Jewish Agency leadership publicized a series of complaints at a press conference and listed them in a memorandum. Three Jews were killed during the day's operations and many more injured. Perhaps the most emotive incident of all was the arrest of sixty-nine-year-old Rabbi Yehuda Fishman. 'Bastards!' says David Hacohen: 'They made him travel in a car. And he was so religious!' Weizmann alleged in a letter to John Shaw that the old rabbi had been struck in the face by a soldier for refusing to violate the Sabbath.[31] This was denied in an official statement, explaining that a minimum of force was used to lift him from a chair and carry him to a vehicle, but it in no way stilled the outrage felt by Jews at the mounting of the operation on the Sabbath, especially as it involved an old man being manhandled into breaking the laws of his religion.

Attlee wrote in his telegram to Truman: 'It is proposed to raid the Jewish Agency and to occupy it for a period necessary to search for incriminating documents.'[32] On June 29th police entered the empty building in Jerusalem and collected every available scrap of paper. But then they faced a problem – most of the documents were in Hebrew.

Richard Catling says: 'This was a major problem in our work, the problem of Hebrew. I can only think of five men in the whole British detective force who spoke it.' Arabic was always an asset to a good policeman and was widely studied during the Arab revolt. But hardly anyone learnt Hebrew. Most of the Yishuv spoke English and for decades very few of them fell foul of British law. Hebrew seemed unnecessary.

Catling quotes this as an example of Britain's amateurish approach to the problem of Jewish terrorism: 'We used microphones to listen to conversations of men in custody. But it was soul destroying. Firstly, there was so much interference and background noise. Secondly, hardly anyone could understand the Hebrew.' They could, of course, give the work to Jewish policemen, but then the translation might be deliberately distorted and a copy would find its way to the Haganah. C. A. Wade recalls that several policemen, British as well as Jewish, were brought under the Haganah's influence: 'They used money, drink, women – whatever they thought was a man's weak point.'

The volume of Hebrew documents removed from the Jewish Agency was so great that it would have taken qualified British policemen several years to check it all. The officer in charge, John Cockett, therefore formed a team of seven Jewish policemen, one of whom was Bobby Lustig: 'They had nobody else, so they had to use people like me, whose loyalty was to the Haganah, to work against the Haganah. We went through all the papers, but anything we found that was incriminating or might have harmed the Jewish Agency, we flushed down the lavatory. After two days all the drains at CID headquarters were totally blocked.'

Consul-General Pinkerton advised Washington that six confidential documents were found in the Jewish files, including a letter from Truman to Eisenhower on Harrison's report and a top-secret American document about oil in the Middle East. There was also a quantity of Egyptian material, enough to indicate that there were Zionist spies in the Egpytian Foreign Office. (This fact was kept secret for fear of anti-semitic reaction in Cairo.) But, Pinkerton noted: 'British express surprise that there was so little in view of known widespread activity of Jewish agents.'[33] Catling says: 'We found next to nothing. The search was really a washout, a damp squib.'

The police therefore handed the building back and concentrated their efforts on what they already knew from the coded messages. On June 20th Cunningham had already advised George Hall: 'We have more than ample evidence to justify proceeding against them.'[34] The messages clearly linked Shertok and Joseph with the Haganah and proved that the Haganah was in alliance with the terrorists. No further evidence was necessary, although the authorities had hoped to find additional material in the Jewish Agency files, to make their forthcoming disclosure more dramatic.

Under attack on July 1st, 1946, from a number of pro-Zionist Members of Parliament – Richard Crossman, Sidney Silverman, Robert Boothby, Michael Foot, Barbara Ayrton Gould and Barnett Janner – Prime Minister Attlee replied: 'We have evidence – I will produce the evidence in due course – of a very close link between the Jewish Agency and Haganah . . . We also have evidence of the close connection between the Haganah and the Irgun . . . The Jewish Agency cannot be a cover for running an illegal army in illegal actions.'

Dare Wilson writes that the operation, codenamed 'Agatha', achieved all its objects.[35] But this is wishful thinking. It added little to the already known fact of various Jewish leaders' complicity with illegal armies. It achieved the arrest of these political leaders – an easy task – but not the arrest of senior Haganah men like Israel Galili, Itzhak Sadeh or Moshe Sneh, who had gone into hiding or were never identified. 'I was one of the people unseen by the British,' says Galili. A British report claimed that half the mobilized members of the Palmach were arrested, about eight hundred men, thus dealing it 'a crippling blow'.[36] But it soon emerged that the Haganah's efficiency was hardly impaired. Most of its arsenals remained intact. Meshek Yagur was an exception. The British Cabinet's June 20th order 'to break up the illegal organizations' was not achieved.

The operation received no American support, rather the contrary. On July 3rd Truman told Jewish Agency representatives in Washington that he regretted what had happened, that he had not been consulted about it in advance and that he hoped the arrested leaders would soon be released. It provoked an embarrassing emergency debate in the House of Commons, revealing a deep split on the issue in the government party's ranks.

Most important of all, it failed to drive a wedge between the 'illegal organizations' and the 'vast law-abiding majority' of the Jewish community. The views of Ben Gurion, seen in London as out-and-out extremism, for instance his readiness to use limited violence to further illegal immigration and preserve Jewish armaments, were in fact the foundation stones of Yishuv consensus. Cunningham's announcement that the operation was aimed only against 'those few' taking an active part in the campaign, not against the Yishuv as a whole, was meaningless, because the vast majority of the Yishuv was in favour of violence, within certain limits.

Those who opposed it on principle, even the limited violence of the Haganah, were invisible. The Cabinet's order to break up the illegal armies amounted to an order to break up the Yishuv as a whole.

It is thus clear, in retrospect, that British forces had no chance of breaking the Haganah other than by the use of Nazi or Soviet methods against the whole Jewish community. Richard Gale remembers telling his Commander-in-Chief Miles Dempsey: 'If you want me to go to war against all the Jews in Palestine tomorrow, I can do so and sweep the whole lot into the Mediterranean. I've got the force to do it, if that's what you want. If it's not what you want, the only answer is to make a political deal, to cooperate with them.' Galili supports this view: 'In order to break the Haganah, they would have to use drastic mass violence, something that they were unable to do because of the nature of British democracy.'

Golda Meir, one of the few leaders still at liberty, recalls the reaction to 'Black Saturday': 'We all felt that something had to be done. Thousands of Jews had been picked up. The Haganah had ordered them to refuse to give fingerprints and many of our men were beaten up when they refused. I told Weizmann that the Yishuv would not just pass it over. I suggested a campaign of civil disobedience. I told him that if we did nothing, the Irgun and Lehi would do something, something far more serious.'

At this point the Irgun produced a plan worked out by their operations chief Amihai Paglin to blow up the army and Secretariat headquarters in Jerusalem's King David Hotel. Galili recalls himself and Haganah commander Sneh discussing the idea with the two dissident commanders, Begin and Yalin-Mor, and deciding that it would be an appropriate reprisal for the raids of June 29th. It might also, incidentally, succeed in destroying various dangerous documents taken there from the Jewish Agency building. On July 1st they brought the idea before the Haganah's Committee X, which had to approve all proposals of the united resistance, and gained their consent for an Irgun assault on unspecified 'government offices'.

Begin was thereupon given authority in writing to go ahead. The official Haganah history makes it clear, though, that the usual rule applied, every precaution was to be taken against loss of life.[37] And, according to Galili, it was made clear by Palmach chief Itzhak Sadeh that the explosion must take place outside office hours.[38]

But then the plan was postponed, because of a personal intervention by

Chaim Weizmann. On July 6th he received at his house in Rehovot some thirty of the Jewish leaders still at liberty, including Golda Meir, Mayor of Tel Aviv Israel Rokach, *Palestine Post* editor Gershon Agronsky and Agency Executive members Dobkin and Schmorak. He asked them to arrange for the suspension of all Haganah activity until the August meeting of the Jewish Agency in Paris. Continuing the armed struggle, he said, would be a declaration of war on Britain and would spell the doom of the Zionist enterprise. He then argued, in the words of the Haganah history: 'In all states it is the custom for the President to be the supreme commander of the armed forces. I have never needed this authority and have never considered interfering in your affairs. But this time, for the one and only time, I use this right and demand that you cease all activities.'[39] He did, however, according to Golda Meir, approve her proposal for a campaign of civil disobedience.

Meyer Weisgal, sent to convey this message to Sneh in hiding, explained that, if the demand was refused, Weizmann would resign his presidency and make known the reasons for his resignation. This ultimatum was then conveyed by Sneh to Committee X and, after some discussion, approved by a majority. The Committee cancelled the Haganah's parallel operation, a proposed raid on the British arms depot at Bat-Galim, and instructed Sneh to arrange for the postponement of the King David operation also, through the machinery of the united movement.

Exactly how this message was conveyed to the Irgun is still a matter of dispute. Begin writes that he received only a series of requests for postponement, all of which were very dangerous, because orders had been given and tasks assigned, and that eventually July 22nd was agreed as the date.[40] Shay writes that Sneh's final request for postponement was unclear and arrived too late. Galili says that Sneh twice asked Begin to postpone the operation. Begin writes that in the end, after Sneh's final request for a postponement on July 19th, the Irgun decided to go ahead with the King David operation alone. In any case, it is clear from Galili's evidence that this Irgun decision to carry out the operation independently on July 23rd was a surprise and a shock to the Haganah, as was their decision to act during office hours. Galili says clearly that Haganah orders stipulated otherwise.

Meanwhile Jewish opinion was further inflamed by one of the most terrible events of 1946. On July 5th a pogrom took place in the small town of Kielce, 120 miles south of Warsaw. A rumour had swept the town that Jews were murdering gentile children and using their blood for ritual purposes. (This false allegation about the practices of the Jewish religion, known as the 'blood libel', was widely believed in Europe of the Middle Ages. In certain primitive areas the belief persisted right up to the middle of the twentieth century.) A mob of enraged Poles, incited to homicidal fury by deliberate falsehood, besieged the headquarters of the Jewish community and then, with the connivance of various army and police officers, beat some forty Polish Jews to death.

It would be an exaggeration to say that the Yishuv blamed Britain directly for this atrocity. But many of them drew the conclusion that, if Britain had opened the gates of Palestine to the surviving one tenth of Polish Jewry, the forty murdered people would have left Kielce and survived. Gerald Keith, on the staff of the US embassy in Warsaw, explained that virulent anti-semitism was still rife in Poland, in spite of the collapse of Nazi rule.[41]

There was resentment against Jews who returned from deportation and reclaimed their property. There was even greater resentment against the Jews who formed a large part of Poland's new communist administration: 'When the Jews in government have by their being there linked themselves with the Russian influence, which is unquestionably not desired by at least 85 per cent of the Poles, it is not surprising that feeling against the Jews is extremely strong in many quarters.' Keith concluded that without doubt almost all Jews would wish to leave Poland. Bevin's belief that the Jews of Europe should help to rebuild their countries of origin was again thrown severely into question.

On July 7th Weizmann gave John Shaw a full account of his previous day's meeting as well as a 'solemn assurance' that there was no contact between Haganah and the terrorists, except for an occasional attempt to exercise restraint. (This was true as regards the date in question, but not as regards previous months.) Shaw replied that Weizmann's advisers were misleading him. There *had* been contact for evil purposes.[42] Weizmann was at pains to point out that he spoke as a firm friend of Britain. By her recent actions, he told Cunningham on June 29th, Britain had joined battle not only with the Yishuv, but also with world Jewry, including the five million Jews of the United States. In his opinion the British Empire could not stand up to such a war.

As the day came for the US Congress to consider the \$3750m. British loan, it seemed that Weizmann might well be right. When the debate opened in the House of Representatives on July 8th, several congressmen announced that they would vote against it because of British policy in Palestine. Representative Adolf Sabath advised Britain to raise money by selling her overseas investments. The United States had twice saved

Britain, he said, and what had Britain ever done for America in return? The press carried advertisements from pro-Irgun committees under the slogan 'Kill that Loan'. By July 11th the loan was reported in serious danger.

Had this happened, Britain would have faced bankruptcy and near-starvation. Butter, sugar, meat, petrol and clothing were still rationed as strictly as during the war, eggs were almost unobtainable and plans were being drawn up for the introduction of bread rationing. Mediterranean and tropical foods, for instance citrus fruit and rice, were non-existent and reserves of almost every staple commodity, including fuel, were at crisis level. British industry and manpower were depleted and exhausted by six years of war.

Various leaders of American Jewry then came to the rescue. Rabbi Stephen Wise said in a statement read to the House on July 9th: 'I shall not permit my abundantly justified indignation against the Palestine government and its lawless practices to change the fact of my support as an American of the British loan.' Representative Sol Bloom, chairman of the Foreign Affairs Committee, also promised support, in spite of Bevin's 'foolish, ridiculous and asinine' statements on the Jewish issue, even though (he said) this would displease many people who hated England. On July 13th the loan was approved by 219 votes to 155.[43]

This narrow escape made little impact on Britain's chiefs of staff, who on July 10th, in the midst of Congress's debate, signed a paper reiterating their view that good relations with the Arabs were a more important British interest. Implementation of the Report, they said, would be disastrous: 'There will be a general Arab rising in Palestine, more serious and more widespread than in 1936 and 1938–39.'[44] Massive reinforcements would be needed to deal with the situation.

John Glubb wrote that, if the hundred thousand were admitted, Syria and Iraq would make treaties with Russia. And any such Soviet advance would threaten the spinal cord of the Empire.[45] The Soviet press were already mounting an attack, accusing Britain of pouring oil on the flames of national strife.[46] British ambassador Stonehewer Bird cabled from Baghdad that any such decision would provoke extreme violence, denunciation of the Anglo-Iraq treaty and diplomatic rupture. All British and American nationals would have to be evacuated and Britain would have to intervene militarily.[47] Nor would the Jews cease their rebellion, the experts predicted. Britain would be saddled with a war on two fronts.

This was the evidence that convinced Attlee, in the words of his letter to Winston Churchill, that the Report clearly involved 'a burden beyond our resources to carry alone'.[48] The two rival leaders agreed, even at this early stage, that maybe partition would in the end turn out to be the remedy. But for the moment the British government was resolved, if possible, to retain with American agreement a large part of its Mandatory responsibility. The deputies of Truman's Cabinet committee, which consisted of the secretaries of State, Treasury and War, were on their way to London to see whether this agreement could be reached.

On July 10th Bevin explained to Norman Brook and Harold Beeley that his mind was not closed to the admission of the hundred thousand Jews. On the contrary, he said, he did not feel able to oppose it. And he no longer mentioned the precondition of Jewish disarmament. But Britain *would* require full American cooperation and some serious *quid pro quo* to offer the Arabs. For instance, he wanted the United States to accept a further large number of Jewish refugees. (Britain, he said, could not absorb any more, because of her commitment to shelter tens of thousands of Poles unwilling to return to communist Poland.) The Arabs must also receive provincial autonomy and their standard of living should be raised by an American subsidy.[49]

On July 11th, 1946, Ambassador Henry F. Grady arrived in London with the American deputies. Over the next two weeks they and the British team, under Herbert Morrison, reached agreement on the idea of a federal Palestine with provincial autonomy, divided into Zionist, Arab and central government districts – a variation on the 1944 partition plan. The hundred thousand would be allowed to enter the Zionist area, but it would cover only 1500 square miles and would remain, in the last resort, under British control. The United States would grant $50m. to develop the Arab area.

Meanwhile Menachem Begin and his organization, unaware of these political developments, were preparing their assault on the King David Hotel. Begin says: 'We carried out this very difficult operation at the request of the Haganah. The King David was a fortress in those days, surrounded by barbed wire and machineguns. For the Haganah the most important aim was to destroy the documents taken from the Jewish Agency. The British found documents which proved that the Jewish Agency knew about the operations of the Haganah. They found a report by Mr Shertok, who was then chief of the Political Department, which proved that he knew about the destruction of the railways. They were frightened that the British would declare the Jewish Agency illegal.'

Other Irgun sources, including the operation's coordinator Amihai

Paglin and historian Abraham Shay, confirm that this was the main purpose of the operation, that for this reason Palmach commander Itzhak Sadeh pressed Paglin to increase the quantity of explosives used and to minimize the warning period, to make sure that the documents were destroyed.[50] But Israel Galili, who was privy to the Haganah's role, states that, even though the June 29th events triggered the operation, the decision in principle to destroy the hotel had been taken by the Haganah weeks earlier, for purely political reasons: 'It is nonsensical to imagine that the explosion would destroy specific documents. It is nonsensical to assume that these documents were kept in only one copy. The question of documents was raised only as a by-product.' He dismisses as 'ridiculous' Paglin's whole account.[51]

Begin continues: 'We did not want to hurt one living soul. The ethics of the Irgun demanded every possible precaution to prevent civilian casualties.' For this reason, he says, a young Irgun girl, Adina Hay-Nissan, was ordered to telephone a warning to the hotel thirty minutes before the impending explosion, this period being a compromise between Paglin and Sadeh, the former having originally wanted to allow forty-five minutes for evacuation.

Several dozen accounts of what happened at the King David Hotel on July 22nd, 1946, have been written, but all of them give an incomplete picture, lacking as they do the benefit of British documents on the subject, especially the military investigations and the police report signed by Assistant Inspector-General J. P. I. Fforde, both released in 1978. The Irgun's day began at about 5.30 a.m. with the theft of a taxi and a truck in Tel Aviv. They were driven to Jerusalem where a further vehicle, a pick-up truck numbered 7022, was stolen around 11 o'clock. Seven milk churns containing explosives were loaded into this truck and then driven with the assault party, armed with Sten or Tommy guns and dressed as Arabs, down the sunken drive leading to the service entrance of the hotel and the kitchens of the Regence Café.[52]

The Irgun had picked on the weakest point in the hotel's meagre defences, which were, British witnesses claim, nothing like the picture of an armed fortress drawn by Begin and others. The main entrance to the building was undefended. It had to be, because it still functioned as a hotel and restaurant, Jerusalem's main social centre. The Secretariat entrance under the south-east wing was lightly guarded, but open to the public, who often called to see Secretariat members on matters of everyday administration. The Regence service entrance was not guarded at all.

At 11.45 a.m. three armed Irgun men held up the doorman, forced him into an office, then rounded up the rest of the basement staff and held them under guard in the kitchens. Other men unloaded the milk churns from the van and carried them along the corridor to the café, directly under the Secretariat offices. Israel Levi, leader of the party, began connecting detonator and timing devices, together with a booby trap to prevent any attempt at disarmament, then hung notices on the churns reading 'MINES – DO NOT TOUCH' in three languages.

Begin says: 'Then there was a pitched battle, because our men had to penetrate the cellar and there were armed British soldiers there. They probably saw something suspicious. There was shooting.' Again, British witnesses disagree. John Shaw, acting in Cunningham's absence as high commissioner, says: 'What happened was that the Irgun were challenged by a signals officer and they shot him dead. He was the only casualty. There was no pitched battle.'

The police report, which describes this incident in detail, makes it clear that the only British soldiers in the basement at the time of the Irgun's entry were women operating the army telephone exchange, some way along the corridor from the café. Around noon Lieutenant H. B. Chambers and Captain A. D. Mackintosh were in the headquarters Signal Office upstairs when the latter decided to go down to the basement to check the exchange. A few minutes later Sergeant Brown, the switchboard supervisor, telephoned Chambers to tell him that armed Arabs were chasing and grappling with Mackintosh in the corridor. She later testified that the fight lasted several minutes, as two Irgun men struggled to get Mackintosh into the kitchen with the other prisoners. Mackintosh had actually got as far as the service stairs, leading to the main lobby, when one of the Irgun men shot him in the stomach at pointblank range.

Mackintosh managed to stumble halfway up the stairs, where he was found by a hotel porter and helped back into the basement ladies' cloak-room. The porter then informed hotel manager Hamburger, who in turn informed the security post. Military police sergeant S. Petty writes: 'I then went to the basement by the stairs past the gentlemen's cloakroom. The Duty Officer (Captain Payne) came with me as far as the cloakroom, but then went off to telephone. Many people were moving about. The officer was lying on the floor. His shirt was off. He had a hole on the right-hand side of his stomach. I asked him what was the trouble. He merely said that there were some Arabs, that he went for one of them who shot him.'

At this stage, around 12.10 p.m., the security post knew only that an officer had been attacked and that some Arabs were acting suspiciously in the basement. Chambers and two other soldiers, warned by Brown that there were armed men in the basement corridor, went round the hotel and climbed into the telephone exchange through a window. Chambers writes: 'I looked through a grill which overlooks the Regence passage and two men in Arab Legion headdress immediately aimed their TSMG (Tommy guns) at me. I withdrew.'

Sergeant Petty returned to the hotel lobby to telephone Captain Payne and security officer Major Nicholls, then returned with another soldier to the basement corridor. He made his way some distance along the passage. As soon as he turned a corner and came within sight of the service entrance he was fired upon: 'I saw a man dressed in a white-and-blue check *gallabia* [Arab smock] standing in the doorway with a Sten gun. He said, "Halt! Halt!" I jumped back behind the corner. No more shots were fired. I then went back to the entrance. I saw a lorry and the man who had shot at me crouched down behind it on the far side. He got up and fired at me again with his Sten.' At about this time, 12.15 p.m., as the Irgun party was withdrawing, a clerk in the basement pressed the alarm bell, thus alerting Jerusalem police headquarters by the Jaffa Gate. Almost immediately a group of policemen led by Superintendent K. P. Haddingham set off by car for the King David.

The Irgun assault party abandoned their truck, since it was under fire, and made off on foot through the hotel garden towards their black taxi getaway car, standing 200 yards north-east of the hotel on the road running from King David Street to the French consulate. Gunner C. Buckle saw them and fired his Tommy gun. One of the 'Arabs' fell over, got to his feet and continued running. It later emerged that two men were hit, Aharon Avrahami and Itzhak Tsadok. Avrahami and about six Irgun men got into the taxi and were driven away. Others ran down the valley and across to the Jewish Quarter of the Old City. Avrahami and Tsadok were found there by police the next morning, the former already dead of his wounds.

Between 12.20 and 12.25 a small bomb, previously wheeled into position by another Irgun group on an Arab hawker's barrow, exploded a few yards south of the hotel outside a car showroom owned by Homsi Salameh, a Christian Arab firm. Begin says: 'The petard was meant to make a big noise and disperse the people. We achieved this goal, to disperse the passers-by without anyone being hurt.' The police record shows, however, that this bomb broke windows and damaged a passing Number Four bus, and that several Arabs were taken from the bus into the Secretariat to receive first-aid. Also many people working in the hotel ran to the windows and balconies of the south-west corner to see what was happening in the street, thus placing themselves right on top of the café and the churns of explosives.

Adina Hay-Nissan says: 'The petard was my cue to telephone the warnings. My boss Itzhak Avinoam ordered me to give three warnings – to the hotel, the French consulate and the *Palestine Post* – and he gave me three telephone numbers to memorize. I had to place myself by a public telephone and, as soon as I heard the petard, make the first call to the King David. I made this call from a pharmacy belonging to an Armenian, just across from the hotel, past the YMCA. I called the King David a few seconds after the petard. I said, "This is the Jewish Resistance Movement, we have planted bombs in the hotel. Please vacate it immediately. You have been warned." I repeated it in Hebrew and hung up.'

Adina Hay-Nissan says that she then ran to a telephone box in King George Street, called the French consulate and gave them the same message in English only, telling them to open their windows, so that they would not be shattered. She then ran to a hotel in Jaffa Road, opposite the bus station, and passed the message to the *Palestine Post* in Hebrew only. She estimates that she made the third call ten minutes after the petard went off. She does not, however, know which of the three hotel switchboards – the Secretariat, the army or the hotel proper – covered the number she was given: 'I don't know who I actually spoke to at the King David. I don't know if it was a man or a woman, an Englishman or a Jew. I was the one who did the talking. I wasn't there to have a chat. I was given an order and I carried it out.'

The first explosion, which happened just as the police were arriving to answer the alarm, triggered the wartime air raid system. All over Jerusalem sirens wailed, traffic came to a stop and people retired indoors to observe the automatic curfew. For most people in the hotel it was the first indication that something strange was afoot. Richard Catling and his friend Robert Musgrave went out on to a balcony which overlooked the road. 'We saw a lot of people running about and I said to Musgrave, "I'm going down to see what cooks." ' John Shaw also walked across to look, then walked back to his office in the south-east corner of the hotel, overlooking the Old City. Haddingham and his men began to investigate the cause of the explosion.

Soon they discovered a second bomb on another Arab barrow in the street to the north of the hotel, outside a shop called Deen's Indian Tailor. The police report makes it clear that the bombs were not what Begin describes – harmless petards, designed merely to clear the street of passers-by:

'These trolleys were designed apparently to carry incendiary bombs with the object of firing the road to prevent police and military obtaining access to the King David area. The bomb outside Homsi Salameh's shop exploded but failed to set the road on fire. That outside the Indian tailor's shop failed to explode and when dismantled by the police was found to contain TNT and inflammable material. Four tins of petrol were found along with the inflammable material on top of the explosives.'

The girls on the army switchboard, who knew about the shooting in the basement as well as about the first bomb, came out into the garden. But the investigating police still knew only about the bomb, nothing about anything elsewhere. After a few minutes they concluded that the bomb had caused only minor damage and that it was safe to give the 'all clear', a differently toned siren indicating that normal life could proceed. This was sounded at 12.31. The girls went back to the switchboard. The basement staff, unaware that the Irgun party had left more than ten minutes earlier, emerged apprehensively from their kitchen prison.

Haddingham made a few unfruitful inquiries, then walked up to the main entrance of the hotel: 'Hamburger, the Swiss manager, came out and talked to me. Everyone was baffled. Then, just after we walked in through the main door, several kitchen staff ran into the lobby from the basement stairs, telling us that they'd been held up by Jewish terrorists and that there were milk churns in the basement. I went down the stairs and was about halfway along the corridor, when the whole place exploded. I was blown about 30 feet back along the corridor.' This time, 12.37 p.m., is known exactly, because the explosion stopped every electric clock in the building.

The explosion turned the whole south-west corner of the hotel to dust and rubble. All six floors, a section of twenty-eight rooms, dropped to the ground in a heap, leaving the building without one of its corners, like a cake with a large rectangular slice cut out of it. Robert Newton, a member of the political Secretariat, was sitting typing when the ceiling fell and his desk was smashed by flying bricks: 'Instead of the wall behind my chair, I found that I was on the brink of a drop of five storeys. The lift well and staircase on the other side of the destroyed wall had gone, and with them the typists' room I had just visited and the adjacent room of one of my colleagues, who was sharing my house in the absence of our respective wives. He, of course, was somewhere under the rubble, dead, and with him the loyal and cheerful girls who had worked for us.'

John Shaw's first impression was of a muffled thump and a lot of vibration: 'The chandelier fell down on to my desk and the room filled with dust and smoke. I went out into the corridor and it was black as soot. You couldn't see your hand in front of your face. I walked long the corridor, with one hand to guide me, when suddenly I saw a yawning chasm under my feet, almost the whole depth of the building, from the fourth floor to the ground.'

A total of ninety-one people were killed – forty-one Arabs, twenty-eight British, seventeen Jews and five others. The police report explains that the number of dead was increased by the first explosion, which caused people to gather in the south-west corner of the building to see what was happening and also caused a number of Arabs to be brought into the Secretariat from their damaged bus for first-aid. It thus had the opposite effect to that intended by Begin and the Irgun. Haddingham recalls, as he was being carried injured out of the hotel, seeing the silhouettes of his friends Assistant Secretary E. W. Keys and Postmaster-General G. D. Kennedy printed in blood on the YMCA building opposite the hotel, fifteen feet above the ground. They had been standing by the entrance to the Secretariat, almost directly above the milk churns.

It therefore seems that only in the dying minutes of Israel Levi's timing device, between the 12.31 'all clear' and the 12.37 explosion, did any British soldier or official learn about the explosives in the basement and the threat to the lives of those in the south-west wing. This is the burden of the controversy that has lasted more than thirty years, in which Menachem Begin and other former Irgun leaders steadfastly maintain that they gave competent officials in the Secretariat ample warning of the impending blast, a full thirty minutes, more than enough time to evacuate the building and save everybody's lives.

The Irgun's version is supported by the direct evidence of Adina Hay-Nissan, who has explained exactly how she made the three warning telephone calls. There is also hearsay evidence, quoted in numerous versions of this story, to the effect that the telephoned warning was passed personally and in good time to John Shaw. Begin says: 'A police officer called Shaw and told him, "The Jews say that they have placed bombs in the King David." And the reply was, "I am here to give orders to the Jews, not to take orders from them." ' Begin says that he was told this by Israel Galili at a meeting between the two leaders on July 23rd, the day after the explosion.

The Irgun pamphlet *Black Paper*, published in 1947, also claims that thirty minutes' warning were given: 'For reasons best known to himself Shaw, the Chief Secretary of the Occupation administration, disregarded the warning. That is, he forbade any of the other officials to leave the building, with the result that some of his collaborators were killed, while he himself slunk away until after the explosion . . . Shaw thus sent nearly 100 people to their deaths – including Hebrews, including friends of our struggle.'[53] Irgun leaflets posted in Tel Aviv the day after the explosion claim: 'This tragedy came through the fault of British tyrants who played with human life.'

It is also supported by the obvious fact that the Irgun suffered severe political damage from the loss of so many innocent lives. Furthermore, it was contrary to the Irgun's practice to cause casualties on such a scale or in such a manner. The Irgun always envisaged casualties, both British and their own, when they attacked the army or the police. But after the heat of the battle, having placed their bombs, they customarily gave those within range, civilian or military, a chance to get clear.

On the other hand, in 1948 both John Shaw and his secretary Marjorie King made sworn statements denying the above allegation, after it was repeated by a London newspaper and became the subject of a libel action. The newspaper did not defend the case and apologized to Shaw unreservedly. Shaw says: 'Begin used to say that I received the warning and made good my escape at the expense of the lives of my colleagues and friends. It's about the worst thing that anyone could say about any man. I flatly deny it. And I flatly deny that I said, "I'm here to give orders to the Jews." I would never have made a statement like that and I don't think that anyone who knows me would regard it as in character. I would never have referred to the Jews in that way.'

Shaw's denial is confirmed by every one of the British witnesses in or near the hotel at the time of the explosion. None of them has any knowledge of any warning received in time to make evacuation possible. No one blames Shaw for failing to act. They all agree that he, like themselves, had no knowledge of the milk churns in the basement, that the allegation that he recklessly and cynically put colleagues' lives at risk is quite false. The only criticism sometimes made is that Shaw committed an error of judgement weeks earlier in not closing the café and placing guards on the service entrance. Shaw himself, with hindsight, admits that this was a mistake. But it was a difficult decision. Everyone was under orders to preserve the semblance of normality in Palestine. Social life had to be allowed to continue. And no one ever imagined that the Irgun would endanger the whole Secretariat, which had many Jewish employees.

This is the hitherto available evidence, much of it circumstantial, incomplete and vague enough to leave the question naggingly open for more than thirty years. Who was to blame for the loss of life, the Irgun or the Secretariat? Were the British in the hotel given enough warning to make their evacuation?

The secret police report, in three paragraphs directly answering the Irgun's claims, at last provides a conclusive answer: 'The telephone operator of the King David Hotel was interrogated and states that he received the warning two minutes before the main explosion and that this warning was communicated immediately to Mr Hamburger, the manager of the King David Hotel. This was corroborated by Mr Hamburger, who states that as he was informed, the explosion took place.

'The telephone operator at the French Consulate states that he received a warning five minutes after the main explosion. He reported this to the secretary to the French Consulate who corroborates his story.

'From investigations carried out at the *Palestine Post* offices it transpires that a girl rang up the *Palestine Post* and in the name of the "Jewish Resistance Movement.' stated that bombs had been placed in the King David Hotel. According to the editor's statement, this call was not received until after the second explosion. This was confirmed by the Duty Officer, Police Headquarters, to whom the information was passed on by the *Palestine Post*, who states that he received the call at 12.50 p.m.'

Furthermore, the Irgun's claim in their July 23rd leaflets were at once denied by Commander-in-Chief Miles Dempsey. The Irgun's explanation was misleading, he cabled the War Office the next day: 'It is stated ample warning was given by telephone for evacuation of hotel, but no official warning was in fact received.'[54] Five months later, after all inquiries were complete, Cunningham amplified the explanation of why nothing was done to evacuate the hotel or disarm the charges in the fifty-two-minute period between the Irgun's arrival and the main explosion. The shooting of Mackintosh and the invaders' Arab disguises, he writes, confused the security authorities, leading them away from the idea that the building was under attack from Jewish terrorists.[55] This confusion was deepened by the timing of the attack, noon on a Monday. Chosen by the Irgun because the service entrance would then be open and the café empty, it was the busiest hour of the busiest day of the week.

Also, the first explosion, happening as it did just as the police were arriving to answer the alarm bell, distracted British attention to the roadway outside the hotel and away from the Regence basement. The result was that no one in authority knew that the bombs were there until the last moment. It was then too late to mount any evacuation. In any case, if the telephoned warning, which reached the hotel two minutes before the main explosion, had been acted upon immediately, the death toll would have been even higher, because the entire Secretariat would have rushed to the stairs in the south-west corner, which were about to disintegrate.

It seems clear, therefore, that the Irgun did not intend to cause the ninety-one deaths in the King David Hotel that afternoon. They had nothing to gain politically or militarily from such an uncharacteristic act of wilful mass murder, rather the contrary, and there seems no reason to disbelieve the main substance of Adina Hay-Nissan's testimony. Nor was it their custom to cause loss of life on such a scale. Menachem Begin undoubtedly speaks the truth when he says that he did not intend to harm a single living soul.

On the other hand, it must be taken as proved that the Irgun failed to get their message through to anyone in authority until two minutes before the explosion. Begin's often repeated claim that John Shaw caused the death toll by disregarding a clear warning has been analyzed in detail. Israel Galili confirms that he repeated these words to Begin on July 23rd, 1946. But in 1978 Galili revealed that it was based on third-hand information, or perhaps fourth-hand, and could only be judged as hearsay evidence. His actual informant was Boris Guriel, a senior Haganah intelligence officer, who said that he had heard it from Associated Press correspondent Carter Davidson. But why Davidson, an American reporter who died in 1958, should have been privy to conversations taking place that morning in the Chief Secretary's office is in no way explained. In the face of Marjorie King's and John Shaw's sworn testimony, corroborated by many other circumstances, this is flimsy evidence indeed. The theory can be safely dismissed as myth.

Why the warning did not arrive in time must remain a matter for speculation. The police report explains that three telephone calls were made, but that they all arrived too late to make any difference to the outcome. Conceivably, other warnings were given, but not taken seriously by the hotel operator and not passed on to higher authority. Robert Newton, always in close touch with Secretariat security, says: 'I accept the assurance of the lady who says that a warning was given, but clearly no serious attempt was made to ensure that it was effective.' The Irgun used no code word, as do the IRA and other terrorist groups nowadays, to distinguish genuine warnings from hoaxes.

Begin says: 'This tragic event, with its many casualties, is an additional proof of our ethics. We did everything according to our ethics. We took every precaution humanly possible to avoid civilian casualties.' For more than thirty years he and the Irgun have refused to accept any moral responsibility for the loss of life and have shifted the blame to others. But the new evidence exonerates John Shaw. It shows too that the Irgun primed two serious incendiary devices to explode in King David Street, thus increasing the death toll, and that they did not succeed in making their warning effective. It may now cause them to re-evaluate the incident and admit that in this case they did overstep the self-imposed limits of their struggle. Their operation was boldly executed, it was not a deliberate act of mass murder, but its wretched combination of efficiency and negligence was clearly the main cause of the killing.

Army commander Barker has more than one reason for remembering July 22nd: 'My office was in the middle of the building, overlooking the Old City. When I heard the explosion, I walked across the landing and I couldn't see anything, only dust. I was so angry when I found out what had happened that I went straight to my office and wrote an order to the troops, putting all Jewish establishments out of bounds. It was a rotten letter, written on the spur of the moment. I ought to have restrained myself for an hour or two before putting pen to paper.'

It was, indeed, one of the most publicly embarrassing documents ever issued by a senior British authority. 'The Jewish community of Palestine cannot be absolved from the long series of outrages,' he began, then went on to point out that 'the general Jewish public' must bear a share of the guilt of terrorist acts, since without their active or passive support the gangs would be unable to operate. 'I am determined that they will suffer punishment and be made aware of the contempt and loathing with which we regard their conduct,' continued Barker. Therefore, no British soldier would be allowed to have any social or business intercourse with any Jew. 'I appreciate that these measures will inflict some hardships on the troops, yet I am certain that if my reasons are fully explained to them they will understand their propriety and will be punishing the Jews in a way the race dislikes as much as any, by striking at their pockets and showing our contempt for them.'

It is true that the General had reason to be angry when he wrote this letter, that in many books his words are worsened by substituting the word 'most' for 'as much as any' in the last sentence,[56] that it was a mistake by his staff Brigadier Walter Sale that gave it wide distribution under the heading 'Restricted', the lowest security classification, and that he now openly admits that he was wrong to write it.[57] But this is small mitigation for an act which not only gave serious personal offence to Jews everywhere, but also caused Britain great political damage at a crucial moment. Within a few hours of issue its text was in the hands of the Irgun and posted in English and Hebrew all over the cities of Palestine – vivid support for the Irgun's allegations about the vicious nature of British rule.

For Abba Eban, then an instructor with the British school of Arab studies in Jerusalem, the letter was a catalytic shock: 'Of course the British soldiers disliked being shot at and disliked the people who were shooting them. And the people who were shooting them were Jews. So inevitably this dislike spilled over sometimes and became anti-semitism. This was epitomized by Barker's letter, with its references to "race" and to "hitting them in their pockets". It was also the test of my conflict of identities. I decided at that moment that this conflict had to be resolved and that I could no longer remain in British employment.' He resigned his post and went to work for the Jewish Agency.

In the United States the letter caused Britain even more damage. A *Washington Post* editorial saw it as a Nazi line of argument to blame the entire Jewish race for the King David outrage: 'The whole farrago, with its smears and its intimidation, was written in bile and malice and was the work of a weak rather than a strong man.' The same view was reflected in other American newspapers and in letters to the British Embassy. Ambassador Inverchapel reported: 'Implicit in much of this comment, which in some instances links General Barker's remarks to Mr Bevin's words about Jews not being wanted in New York, is the idea that the British government is really anti-semitic.'[58]

The letter put paid to Ernest Bevin's hope on the day of the explosion that at least it might initiate a reaction in the United States against Jewish propaganda.[59] By the end of the month, on balance, the main reaction was against Britain. And for this Barker's letter was to blame. It aroused fierce arguments in the British Cabinet, several of whose members demanded Barker's immediate dismissal. Randolph Churchill (Winston's son) too suggested Barker's transfer to another place 'where his duties will not force him into contact with a race for whose genius he has so little appreciation'.

But, in spite of the damage he inflicted on Britain, probably greater than the damage inflicted on the Zionist cause by the King David explosion, the government felt itself obliged to retain Barker, to rebuke him privately but defend him publicly. It would have been unacceptable to British public opinion and especially to morale in Palestine to humiliate the leader of a British force engaged in mortal conflict with an implacable enemy.

Cunningham saw this as his main concern, the loss of British prestige, and he asked London for permission to take 'some immediate and striking action' to maintain British morale and to pacify the Arabs 'who are now in a particularly ugly mood'. He wanted to impose a fine of £500,000 on the Jewish community and to end Jewish immigration completely. 'It is *essential* to do something drastic and to do it quickly,'[60] he wrote, adding however that in his view a political solution was the only real remedy and that this would probably have to be partition.

The British government took some action. It brought forward the publication date of its pamphlet about Jewish Agency leaders' links with terrorism. Martin Charteris remembers being sent to London with a Haganah two-inch mortar unearthed at Meshek Yagur, his orders being to show it to the Lord Chancellor, William Jowitt, and convince him of the Haganah's military strength. Rushed through the printers and published on July 24th, it was a disappointment to many who had hoped to find dramatic revelations in seized Jewish Agency documents. Cunningham was simultaneously given permission to launch 'Operation Shark', a full-scale search of Tel Aviv. But his other requests were refused. Hall advised him on July 24th that the discussions with the American team were going well. Formal agreement was expected that very day, so nothing drastic could be done.[61]

On July 26th Ambassador Grady sent Byrnes an optimistic telegram about the agreed plan. He had spoken again to Norman Brook, he said, and there was no doubt at all that Britain would give the green light on the hundred thousand. They did not expect formal approval of the plan by either Arabs or Jews, but they did expect 'a measure of acquiescence'. On July 29th Byrnes sent Truman a list of the plan's advantages. Apart from the admission of the hundred thousand, it would nearly treble the area in which Jews could buy land. The Jewish province would contain the best land in Palestine, eighty-five per cent of the entire citrus-growing area, as well as the main water supplies, most of the coastline and the only deep water port. Byrnes also observed that, since eighty-two per cent of Palestine's Jews were living in an area of ninety square miles, the proposed 1500-square-mile province would give them large scope for expansion. To support the plan he mentioned only those factors which in his view would favour the Jews.[62]

The idea was then for Herbert Morrison, scheduled to speak for the government in an important House of Commons debate on July 31st, to use this diplomatic success to quieten members' strong feelings about the King David explosion. But by July 28th the outline of the plan was known and Weizmann rejected it as worse than Lord Peel's plan of 1937, while Abba Hillel Silver called it 'a conscienceless act of treachery'. On July 30th it was attacked in the US Senate as a betrayal of the Jewish homeland, an attempt to strangle the Yishuv by confining them inside an economically non-viable ghetto.

Truman therefore decided on July 30th, 1946, that, although the plan had been worked out and approved by his own nominees, he would have to reject it. It was, in the words of Ambassador Inverchapel that night, a deplorable display of weakness, solely attributable to reasons of domestic politics.[63] State Department official Loy Henderson explained to the ambassador that the two main American Jewish leaders, Wise and Silver, belonged respectively to the Democratic and Republican parties and that neither could afford by approving the plan to give advantage to the other party in the November congressional elections. Otherwise, said Henderson, there was nothing in the plan that would not have been acceptable to the United States.

Truman explained to Attlee that American opposition to the plan had become so intense that there was no hope of rallying effective support for it. Attlee replied: 'I feel bound to express my great disappointment that you have not yet been able to accept the plan worked out with so much goodwill by the American and British agents as the best solution to this very difficult question.'[64] He made it clear to the President that, if the plan failed, British consent to the admission of the hundred thousand would be withdrawn. This consent was on offer only as a 'package deal', not in isolation. Once again British-American discord on the issue had erupted and once again the Jewish refugees of Europe were denied their wish, when apparently on the brink of being granted it.

Meanwhile James Cassels was in Cairo taking part in an exercise. One afternoon he was woken from his siesta in Shepheard's hotel by a call from his commander-in-chief: 'It was "Bimbo" Dempsey. He said, "Get on a 'plane immediately with General Barker and go back to Palestine." I got on the 'plane and got my orders from "Bubbles" Barker. He said, "Jim, I want you to search Tel Aviv, every single room and attic and cellar in Tel Aviv. Is that quite clear?" I gulped a bit and he said, "Any questions?" Anyway, that was Operation Shark.'

A Dodge truck, numbered M 543 and stolen early in the morning of July 22nd in Tel Aviv, was believed to have transported explosives and men to Jerusalem. The Irgun getaway car, a black six-seater Plymouth taxi numbered 1493, had also been stolen in Tel Aviv and driven to Jerusalem, where, thirteen minutes after the explosion, it was stopped by a traffic policeman in Jaffa Road, abandoned by its driver, searched and found to contain eight revolvers, four grenades, a Tommy gun, Arab clothing, a suitcase of medical equipment and various documents belonging to its owner, Isaac Sandler of Achael Street, Tel Aviv. It all tended to show that the operation had been planned and mounted from there, not from Jerusalem. Cassels says: 'We knew that the King David chaps had legged it to Tel Aviv and our job was to find them.'

But it was like looking for a few needles in a haystack of 170,000 people. Four army brigades, about twenty thousand soldiers and police, established an outer cordon round the city in the early hours of July 30th. The citizens were then required to remain in their houses, while the army divided Tel Aviv into sectors with barbed wire and guard posts. The curfew was maintained for four days, except for two hours allowed each evening for essential shopping, while the army searched every house and escorted every inhabitant to improvised screening points. The police, armed with their rifles and books of photographs, then interviewed each person individually, at the end of which they marked each forehead with a special dye to indicate whether or not he or she was 'clean'. Nearly eight hundred were detained and sent to Rafah detention camp.[65]

Lehi second-in-command Itzhak Shamir (Yzernitzky) was taken for identification to a school where he saw with alarm that behind the desk sat Sergeant T. G. Martin, a particularly astute detective whose photograph he had seen in Lehi files: 'I knew at once that I was in trouble. I had a beard and I was disguised as a rabbi, but Martin had a special gift for recognizing people. Several times he had spotted Lehi men in the street and arrested them. When I got to the desk, he looked through his papers and said, "You are Yzernitzky." ' The Lehi leader, betrayed by his distinctive eyebrows, was arrested and spent two weeks in the cells, before being flown to a detention camp in Eritrea.

But this was the only significant British success. Of the hundreds arrested the police eventually identified only a few minor Irgun men. The army found several Haganah caches, including one in the main Tel Aviv synagogue,[66] but they missed the greatest prize of all, Menachem Begin, who spent the days and nights of the search without food or water in a secret compartment of his house, while a lance-corporal and three men camped in his garden, oblivious to what lay within their grasp.

Barker says: 'We should have caught him, but the men did not search his house properly. This is one of the problems of search operations. You have to rely on very junior people and, if they make a mistake, the whole operation can be damaged.' By the end of August almost all the arrested men were released, much to the annoyance of Cassels and some of his fellow-officers, who as usual felt that weak politicians were sabotaging their effective military approach to the problem of terrorism.

As the prospect of a hundred thousand certificates receded, the Jewish Agency increased their efforts to bring Jews to Palestine illegally. By the end of July, after the *Haganah* had been escorted into Haifa with 2678 immigrants and the *Hathayal Haieri* with 550, the situation was at crisis point. There were already 2252 in Athlit, waiting their turn in the quota, and three thousand more were known to be at sea on their way. On July 29th Cunningham reported: 'We are quite unable at the moment to guard any more illegal immigrants in this country. I would urge that any other ship on the sea is diverted. Otherwise the situation here may become completely impossible.'[67]

The British Cabinet discussed the matter on July 30th and 'were much impressed by the danger of serious Arab reactions to continued illegal immigration'. The funerals of the forty-one Arabs killed in the King David had been taking place all week, adding to the tension, and the Arab community was in mourning. Miles Dempsey reported that they blamed the tragedy on Britain's 'kid-glove'[68] treatment of the Jews as compared with her behaviour towards them during the Arab revolt. On August 1st Cunningham again raised the spectre of a war on two fronts, if immigration was allowed to continue. On August 2nd five hundred children and 170 expectant mothers were allowed to land from the two ships in Haifa harbour.[69] In London urgent consideration was being given to Cunningham's request to divert all future new arrivals to Cyprus.

Cunningham agreed that this idea, if approved, 'would unquestionably produce an immediate and hysterical Jewish reaction'[70] and Attlee too recorded his fears 'that it would lead to incidents which would seriously embarrass the government'.[71] But on August 3rd Bernard Montgomery advised the Prime Minister quite simply: 'If the Cabinet so decides, the armed forces in the Middle East can and will stop illegal immigration.'[72]

Chief of the Imperial General Staff Montgomery pointed out that accommodation for two thousand was available immediately in Cyprus, which would relieve the short-term problem of the two ships in Haifa harbour, and that more places could be made available shortly. During the transhipment in Haifa there would be unpleasant scenes and minor injuries, but it would be done in the most humane manner possible and fatal casualties could probably be avoided: 'There will undoubtedly be strong Jewish reaction. This can and will be dealt with . . . I am prepared to put this plan into operation as soon as His Majesty's Government give me the order. In view of the urgency of the matter, you may not wish to wait until next Wednesday's Cabinet meeting.'

On August 7th, 1946, the Cabinet generally agreed that Montgomery's plan 'was the only effective way of stopping illegal immigration'.[73] They therefore approved it. For several days rumours abounded in Palestine and two more immigrant ships arrived, the *Yagur* with 758 and the *Henrietta Szold* with 450. On August 12th a third ship arrived, the *Katriel Yaffe* with 615 immigrants, and late that evening units of the 1st Infantry Division moved secretly into the port area.[74]

At dawn the passengers on the *Yagur* and the *Henrietta Szold* were escorted or carried to two British ships, specially fitted with wired-in hulls, and shipped to a hastily prepared camp near Famagusta. Radio listeners that morning heard the official announcement that, while the three thousand from the two July ships would be transferred to Athlit, all the rest and all future arrivals above the 1500-a-month limit would be deported to Cyprus. Immediately mobs of demonstrators, ignoring the curfew, poured into the streets and attacked the troops guarding the port. Three Jews were shot dead during the subsequent mêlée.

It was a serious escalation of the conflict. The Jewish authorities, of course, found intolerable the idea of any Jew being deported from Palestine. The passengers from the *Yagur* and *Henrietta Szold* had offered only passive resistance to the forcible move. But, once the implications of the new British order were clear, a new tactic was developed. It was decided that in future Jewish refugees, under the guidance of their Haganah organizers, would resist the Royal Navy boarding parties and would use violence, within certain limits, to prevent their ships being diverted from the Palestine shore.

Yigal Allon had now taken over from Sadeh as Palmach commander: 'I gave the order for the immigrants to resist British boarding parties and to refuse to be transshipped. This was to make it more painful, more disturbing for the British, and to show them up as cruel people to be treating in this way survivors of the Holocaust, having fought against Hitler so gallantly. There was some opposition to this order. Some said, "These are poor people. Why should they have to fight? Let *us* do it." But I knew that, if they were transferred without resistance, the moral effect would be diminished by more than 50 per cent.'

To increase the moral pressure, it was decided that women as well as men would fight, not with firearms or any lethal weapons, but with fists, bottles, fingernails, knees, sticks or any other weapons that they could muster. The Haganah crews would do their best to beach their ships in spite of the Royal Navy, to allow the refugees to wade ashore and mingle with the local people. And if they failed, they would make sure that the process of boarding and transshipment was made as difficult and embarrassing as possible for Britain.

One of the first ships to use the new tactic was the *Fede II, renamed the Four Freedoms*, which was spotted by British aircraft close to Palestine waters on September 2nd. Lieutenant-Commander Tony Bailey, captain of the destroyer HMS *Childers*, was ordered to intercept it and capture it within the three-mile limit. But he was not allowed to use the ship's guns or firearms, except in self-defence. There were few precedents for such an operation in naval history. It would be no good to order the *Fede* to heave to under threat of sinking. The refugees would know that the threat was an idle one and would disregard it. Bailey and his officers considered several methods – fouling the *Fede*'s screw with lines and wires, using the depth charge thrower to sling an anchor on her like a grappling iron, lowering the boarding party on her by a system of ropes and poles. Eventually they decided to use the old-fashioned method, to bring the *Childers* so close alongside the *Fede* that the boarding party would be able to leap on board.

At 3.30 p.m. Bailey spotted the *Fede* on his radar, making only eight knots, and half an hour later he brought the *Childers* within a few yards of her: 'As the ship steamed up past the 500-ton auxiliary wooden schooner, a 1000-odd passengers burst into song with "John Brown's Body" and other less familiar dirges. The Star of David flag was flying at the masthead. Displayed in the well-deck were banners which read – "Do not stop us – we are unarmed," "We are 1000 Jewish refugees seeking peace," "If you want to stop us you will have to sink this ship – will you do this? Remember we have no lifebelts," "All we want is a peaceful life in our home PALESTINE." '

Bailey reported that the decks of the *Fede* looked like Brighton beach on a Bank Holiday. Not only were the men and women squashed shoulder to shoulder, but some of them were also in bathing suits and lifebelts, ready to swim ashore. They were promptly warned through a loudhailer that if necessary depth charges would be used to 'discourage' them. About 6 p.m. Bailey's ship crossed the three-mile limit. He exploded a depth charge, fired his Oerlikon and Bofors guns over the other ship's bows and brought the *Childers* in alongside, using high-pressure firehoses to clear a way for the twenty-one-man boarding party.

The hoses produced only an initial shock. Once they were thoroughly soaked, the Jews simply ignored them. So Lieutenant A. Stein and his party failed in their first assault. One man was knocked out, two more were injured and several others were bruised or scratched or suffered the indignity of having their weapons thrown overboard. The rest fought their way through to the poop, but they were unable to capture the key point, the wheelhouse, which was guarded by tough young men with two-foot iron bars. Bailey reported that they were 'severely mauled and forcibly ejected'. Another party of eleven men reached the *Fede* and launched a second attack on the wheelhouse, which also failed.

Stein reported that his men were nonplussed, and reluctant to use extreme violence, especially against the women. Bailey radioed for reinforcements and at 6.33 p.m. he signalled: 'Ship has stopped. Have secured wire to her stern. My men in charge aft, but Jews very truculent. In fact there is a hell of a banyan going on.' The continuous uproar was hushed only after the *Childers* fixed her line and began towing the *Fede* stern-first away from the Promised Land. At this emotionally pregnant moment eleven refugees jumped into the sea, but were soon picked up by the British launches.

The British sailors still did not control the *Fede* wheelhouse or poop. Stein and his men, shaken by the violence of their reception and uncertain how to deal with such an unusual problem, were making no progress against the refugees. Bailey therefore sent for his ship's cricket and hockey teams: 'They boarded the stern of the *Fede* and literally walked across the solid mass of Jews, using their shoulders as stepping stones. Anyone who resisted got hit with a stick or bat.'

At the time he wrote in his report: 'With both ships' companies yelling encouragement the boarders counter-attacked at 2025 (8.25 p.m.). Hitting out, regardless of sex, they cleared the poop and had control of the ship within fifteen minutes.' The *Fede* was then escorted by two destroyers, *Childers* and *Chivalrous*, to a point two miles out of Haifa and during the afternoon of September 3rd the 985 refugees, half of them women and children, were transferred amid scenes of gloom and occasional violent hysteria to the *Empire Heywood* and removed to Cyprus.

The British naval officers of the 'Haifa patrol' studied the episode and drew conclusions from it. They realized, for instance, that at one stage the *Fede* operation had been in danger because of the sailors' reluctance to use violence against women. Bailey says: 'After that we had to talk to them about this problem, indoctrinate them, if you like, and make it clear that any woman who opposed them would have to be treated in the same way as a man.'

Lieutenant G. A. Kitchen, Bailey's second-in-command, says: 'We felt sorry for the refugees, especially the women. It was before the days of "woman's lib" and there was great reluctance to use force against them.

But when a strapping young or middle-aged woman hits you over the head with a bottle or knees you in the groin, you don't feel sorry for her at that particular moment. Maybe you feel sorry for her later, but not then.'

Bailey personally believed that British policy was right. He had been in Palestine in the late 1930s, he says, and had been struck by the Arabs' violent resentment towards Jewish immigration. Other naval officers supported the Jewish side and felt abhorrence at the task assigned to them. But the majority were ignorant or indifferent to the politics of the matter. Their attitude was governed by the needs of the moment, especially training and morale, both of which required serious attention, if the 'Haifa patrol' was to prove effective. They were professional men, concerned mainly to carry out their task efficiently and with a minimum of fuss.

The Royal Navy, spearhead of the fight against illegal immigration, was now the main target of the Haganah. Yigal Allon says: 'I was dying to blow up a British destroyer. It was my greatest dream of those days.' During August the refugee-carrying ships *Empire Heywood* and *Empire Rival* were both damaged, the latter by a limpet mine attached to her hull by Haganah frogmen. The ships were forced to stay away from the Palestine shore, putting into Haifa only for the shortest possible time, to refuel or take people on board. The destroyers hardly ever approached the dock and the men had no shore leave. An attempt to mine a refuelling destroyer was thwarted by the vigilance of Lieutenant-Commander Lionel Crabb, who disappeared in April 1956 while inspecting the hull of the Soviet cruiser *Ordzhonikidze* in Portsmouth harbour.

Even when they anchored in Haifa Bay, they were in danger and forced to take inconvenient, nerve-racking precautions. Sentries patrolled the upper deck continuously, looking for bubbles or for divers surfacing to see where they were going. Men in small boats circled the ship, watching its hull with glass-bottomed boxes, known as 'shufti-scopes'. If they reported anything suspicious, the propellers were run slow astern, to create a wash under the hull and sweep frogmen away. At night-time the ship and water-line were well lit, with special lights shining on the water, and two or three times an hour charges strong enough to kill or deafen any nearby frogman were exploded under the water. William Jones, a telegraphist on HMS *Brissenden*, says: 'It made it very uncomfortable for us at night, because every explosion was like someone hitting the side of the ship with a sledgehammer. We didn't get much sleep.'

A school was set up at Ghain Tuffieha in Malta to teach the strange skills required by officers and men of the 'Haifa patrol'. A system of assault courses and 'pep-talks' toughened the boarding parties, preparing them physically and morally for the task. Kitchen says: 'You needed a lot of psychological strength to leap across a yawning gap in the middle of the night, with the water rushing past and the danger of being crushed between the two ships, knowing that there were violent men and women waiting for you at the other end.' The courses also taught them to avoid timidity, to look self-confident and menacing, to develop a general appearance stern enough to crush the commitment and desperate resolve of the refugees and their Haganah guides.

'We had great *esprit de corps*. It was nothing to do with being anti-Jewish. It was simply that we were fulfilling a task and wanted to do it well,' says Bailey. He and other captains divided their boarders into teams and every week put them through a competition of various physical skills. Each team would vie for the Number One position. After the *Fede* incident Bailey reported that his sailors 'seemed to have enjoyed their scrap and are already looking forward to the next.' This contrived spirit of competition and team rivalry was necessary, he believes, because without it his sailors' morale might have succumbed to the anticlimax of peace.

In Palestine, even though the world war had been over for more than a year, the whiff of mortal danger remained as a stimulus to the efforts of both sides. On August 16th a military court sentenced to death eighteen Lehi men, captured during their abortive attack on Haifa railway work-shops two months earlier. Eleanor Roosevelt wrote to Lady Reading, a member of a famous British Jewish family: 'I hope and pray that they will not actually put to death these young terrorists.'[75] A few days later, much to the fury of the soldiers who had captured them, they were all reprieved.

On September 9th Lehi men took revenge on Sergeant T. G. Martin, who had arrested Shamir during 'Operation Shark', by killing him on a tennis court in Haifa. Shamir says: 'Of course I was not consulted about the decision to kill Martin. But if I had been, I would have approved it. Martin was one of the most active men of the CID, emotionally involved in the fight against us. It was even published in the newspapers that Martin had recognized me. So it was like a challenge. It was very important from the morale point of view for us to do something about it, to make a demonstration to the Jewish people. You could say he signed his own death warrant.'

Shamir, Speaker of the Israeli parliament, still stoutly defends Lehi's tactic of individual assassination: 'There are those who say that to kill Martin is terrorism, but to attack an army camp is guerrilla warfare and to bomb civilians is professional warfare. But I think it is the same from the moral point of view. Is it better to drop an atomic bomb on a city than to kill a handful of persons? I don't think so. But nobody says that President Truman was a terrorist. All the men we went for individually – Wilkin, Martin, MacMichael and others – were personally interested in succeeding in the fight against us.

'So it was more efficient and more moral to go for selected targets. In any case, it was the only way we could operate, because we were so small. For us it was not a question of the professional honour of a soldier, it was the question of an idea, an aim that had to be achieved. We were aiming at a political goal. There are many examples of what we did to be found in the Bible – Gideon and Samson, for instance. This had an influence on our thinking. And we also learnt from the history of other peoples who fought for their freedom – the Russian and Irish revolutionaries, Garibaldi and Tito.'

The Palestine Conference opened in London on September 9th with no Palestine delegates, neither Arab nor Jewish. The Jewish Agency had decided in Paris to reject the Morrison–Grady plan and not to take part in formal talks while their leaders were detained in Latrun. The Palestinians stayed away because of Britain's refusal to receive Haj Amin al-Husseini. Only three Arab states sent delegates – Hafez Ramadan of Egypt, Faris el-Khoury of Syria and Nuri es-Said of Iraq. Azzam Pasha represented the Arab League.

Bevin put forward the British-American plan, but was unable to convince the Arab representatives, who all replied that the proposed system of provincial autonomy would inevitably lead to partition, that once there was a Jewish state in Palestine, however small, it would become a bridgehead for Jewish political and economic penetration of the area. The Jews would fill their state with immigrants from Europe, until they had the basis of a justifiable claim for greater living space, and would then expand their state by force. They proposed instead a unitary Palestinian state with a legislature elected by all citizens, the Jewish representation being limited to one third. All Jewish immigration would cease and the land restrictions would remain intact. A treaty would be signed under which Britain would receive military facilities.[76]

The Jewish Agency had meanwhile let Britain know informally that they would accept a solution that gave them a viable Jewish state in an adequate area of Palestine. On September 15th Weizmann wrote to Ben Gurion suggesting the submission of this plan to the London conference,

but a majority still opposed participation while their leaders were detained. They also made it clear that little would be achieved so long as
General Barker, described by Weizmann in letters to Whitehall as 'a
self-confessed enemy of our people', remained in charge of the army. The
British delegates spent the rest of September trying to bring the Arabs
within reach of partition and trying to persuade the Jews to send such
delegates as were free – Weizmann, Kaplan and Meir.[77] Not surprisingly
(although Cunningham was told reliably that King Abdullah at least
favoured partition privately) they failed in both objectives. The Arab
delegates left for New York and the conference was adjourned until
December 16th. Bevin and Hall noted that Jewish representation would
never be available until Britain could find an adequate reason, in terms of
law and order, to justify releasing all the Jewish leaders from Latrun.

John Shaw was recalled from his post and promoted to the governorship
of Trinidad. Apart from a short wartime gap, he had served in Palestine
since 1935: 'It wasn't really a promotion. We used to say to one another
in those days, "There is no promotion from Palestine." Once you've been
there, you don't really want to go anywhere else.' He recalls being told
to his amazement by Cunningham and police chief Nicol Gray that he
must leave for London immediately, at the end of September: 'I rounded
on Nicol Gray, who was one of my subordinates, and asked him what
stories he'd been telling. He said that there was firm information that I
was on the terrorists' death list.' The real reason, Pinkerton cabled Washington, was the Chief Secretary's nervous state after the King David
affair.[78] His sudden departure strengthened unfair rumours of his
responsibility for the disaster.[79]

The collapse of the plan brought further deterioration in British-
American relations. The American press carried Irgun advertisements and
was loud in its criticism of Britain. The *New York Herald Tribune* called
the Palestine administration 'utterly tyrannical' and 'as perfect an example
of the absolute police state as can be found anywhere on earth'.[80] The
New York Post printed the Irgun's reaction to the death of a Jewish
refugee during the boarding of the Haganah ship *Palmach* on September
22nd: 'The fact that the marines who pumped lead into refugees salute the
Union Jack instead of the Swastika does not alter the fact that another
Hebrew has been killed in cold blood for no other reason than that he
is a Hebrew.' Readers were invited to send cheques in support of 'the
heroic Hebrew fighters in Palestine'. The British embassy made constant
complaints about these advertisements, pointing out that the American
League for a Free Palestine enjoyed charitable status and substantial tax

advantages,[81] whereas in fact it was soliciting funds for the violent subversion of the administration of a friendly power. The State Department was sympathetic, but could do nothing.[82]

On October 15th the London *Evening Standard* reported: 'Forty-four thousand, eight hundred people have already flocked into a Broadway theatre to see the most virulently anti-British play ever staged in the USA. Every one of them has been handed a blank cheque along with his programme at the door.' The play was Ben Hecht's *A Flag is Born*, a lyrical portrayal with music by Kurt Weill of the efforts of a group of survivors from Treblinka extermination camp to reach sanctuary in Palestine in the face of British obstruction. Tevya, the main character, says: 'The English have put a fence around the Holy Land. But there are three things they cannot keep out – the wind, the rain and a Jew.'

Judah Magnes, president of the Hebrew University at Jerusalem, a pacifist and ardent supporter of bi-nationalism, wrote to Eleanor Roosevelt protesting against her sponsorship of the play, drawing particular attention to its climax, the appearance of a group of young Palestinian Jews with guns, followed by an open appeal for funds for the purchase of such guns. Magnes asked Eleanor Roosevelt: 'Are you in favour of supplying money and arms for the terrorists who are destroying life here and many of the achievements of the Jewish pioneers, who are poisoning the minds and souls of the younger generation?'[83]

The British as a whole were outraged at the vilification of their country in New York. But a few Englishmen, General Barker prominent among them, apparently ignorant of or insensitive to the consequences of their actions, went out of their way to encourage such criticism. 'It wasn't so much our actions that I objected to, it was our attitude,' says Martin Charteris. 'There was a lot of loose anti-semitic talk among army officers at parties.' He particularly had in mind Katie Antonius's evening dances, at which Barker was a frequent guest.

A gross example of this 'attitude' was revealed on October 24th, after terrorists had placed bombs in or near a number of British roadblocks around Jerusalem. The subsequent explosions killed two men and injured ten others of the 1st Battalion, Argyll and Sutherland Highlanders. Their commanding officer, Lieutenant-Colonel Richard Webb, immediately summoned thirteen journalists of various nationalities and read them an anti-Jewish diatribe. 'These bloody Jews – we saved their skins in Alamein and other places and then they do this to us,'[84] he said – a feeling then widespread among British troops, but not usually expressed so crudely, at least not in public.

The colonel then told the journalists, all busily making notes, that as a reprisal for the bombings he had pulled one thousand Jews out of their beds and was going to make them stand in line all night waiting to be identified, and that the purpose of this exercise was to cause the Jews so much trouble that they would turn against the Stern gang. After several references to the Jews as 'a despicable race', whose men ate too much carp and whose women bulged in all the wrong places, Webb told his amazed audience flamboyantly: 'Print everything I've said. Use my name. I don't care if I'm out of the army tomorrow.'[85] George Cassidy of the *New York Post* duly did just this and a scandal ensued, convincing many Americans of the incurable anti-semitism of the British army and administration.[86] Many other Americans were disgusted at the idea of a senior British officer behaving in such a way, whatever the provocation. Webb was relieved of his command.

This mood of anger and mutual mistrust finally reached the highest level of all, the heads of the two governments. On October 3rd Truman approved a statement insisting yet again on the immediate admission of the hundred thousand and giving his approval in principle to the Jewish Agency's partition plan. That evening Under-Secretary of State Dean Acheson gave the statement to Inverchapel, explaining that its aim was to stave off an attack which all the Republican candidates nominated for New York in the November 5th elections were preparing to launch upon him. 'I fear that we must be prepared for something like a whirlwind here,' reported the ambassador.[87]

Around midnight (London time) an American embassy official took the text to 10 Downing Street. The Prime Minister read it and immediately wrote a reply: 'Dear Mr President, I have received from Mr Gallman a copy of your proposed statement on Palestine. The Foreign Secretary is in Paris and I should like to have time to consult him. You are, I am sure, aware that we are in consultation with members of the Jewish Agency at the present time. I would therefore earnestly request you to postpone making your statement at least for the time necessary for me to communicate with Mr Bevin.'[88] This reply was at once cabled to Washington and taken to the White House at 9.35 p.m.

Early in the morning of October 4th Attlee cabled Bevin for advice on how best to change or delay Truman's statement. He doubted whether he would dissuade the President completely, he wrote, but at least they should explain the 'unfortunate effect' of any such statement on the forthcoming negotiations. They were on the verge of getting Jewish Agency representatives into consultation. The statement would pre-empt any

British concession on Jewish immigration and would infuriate the Arabs, who had already challenged the United States's right to intervene in the matter at all. Perhaps Truman could be persuaded at least to modify his remarks.

Bevin and Hall had, in fact, received Weizmann, Fishman, Goldmann and four other Jewish leaders at the Foreign Office on October 1st. The meeting was quite friendly, although Fishman reminded Bevin that Palestine had been given to the Jews by God, that Britain must therefore be seen as God's envoy in the matter, whereupon Bevin replied that God moved in mysterious ways.[89] Several further meetings of this type were scheduled to take place in the next two weeks. It seemed to Bevin and Attlee to be a crucial stage in the talks. When, therefore, totally ignoring the Prime Minister's urgent request of the previous evening, Truman went ahead and issued his statement on October 4th, it seemed to the British leaders the height of irresponsibility and personal discourtesy.

Attlee therefore sent the President a most furious message: 'I have received with great regret your letter refusing even a few hours grace to the Prime Minister of the country which has the actual responsibility for the government of Palestine, in order that he may acquaint you with the actual situation and the probable results of your action. These may well include the frustration of the patient efforts to achieve a settlement and the loss of still more lives in Palestine . . . I shall await with interest to learn what were the imperative reasons which compelled this precipitancy.'[90]

Truman replied that he was sorry if his statement had caused Attlee embarrassment, but the postponement of the conference had brought such depression to the Jewish refugees in Europe and their American sympathizers that he could not even for a single day delay speaking out. He reminded Attlee that October 5th was Yom Kippur, the Jewish Day of Atonement, when it is the Jews' custom to contemplate the lot of their people, and expressed his conviction that one of the main purposes of Britain's Mandate was the development of the Jewish National Home, which had no meaning in the absence of Jewish immigration and settlement on the land. There should therefore be 'immediate and substantial'[91] Jewish immigration and it was unthinkable to force the refugees to spend another winter in Europe without any clear idea of their future.

The British leaders, recognizing Truman's genuine concern for the refugees, saw nevertheless a certain hypocrisy in his remarks. They suspected, on the basis of what Acheson had told Inverchapel, that the timing of the statement was dictated not by the October 5th Day of Atonement, but by the speech which Thomas Dewey, governor of New York and future presidential candiate, was to make on October 6th. Dewey did indeed belabour the Truman administration over Palestine, calling for Jewish immigration 'not of 100,000 but of several hundreds of thousands'. Irving M. Ives, Republican candidate for a New York senatorship, demanded that Palestine become a refuge for 'millions'[92] of distressed Jews. The parties were outbidding one another for Zionist votes. Truman's statement seemed mainly designed to pre-empt such speeches and to promote his party's prospects in the November 5th elections.

Pinkerton reported from Jerusalem on October 8th: 'Hebrew press unanimous in approving President's statement on Palestine and Arabic press equally unanimous in condemning it.'[93] The Baghdad newspaper *Al-Yaum* wrote: 'The Arabs must prepare armed resistance to Truman's schemes.' The Palestinian Arab historian Walid Khalidi says that it was this statement that gave Zionist leaders the extra confidence they needed to strike in favour of their maximum demands.[94] Goldmann said that 'as a great sacrifice in the cause of peace' the Jewish Agency would accept a state within the frontiers proposed by Lord Peel, plus the Negev.

On October 28th Ben Gurion explained his position in a long letter to Weizmann: 'I would accept a Jewish state in a sufficient section of the country instead of a British Mandate and *paper* rights in the whole country.' The Zionist position vis-à-vis Britain should therefore be to demand either a state or else a return to the pre-1939 position, with immigration based on Palestine's economic absorptive capacity. In the light of Britain's and the Labour party's past promises, the Attlee government's position was 'to all intents and purposes illegal'.[95] Jewish honour had been raised by the rebellion against it, even in the eyes of the Arabs. And if a Jewish state was set up, the Arabs would be its best friends.

This was one of the keystones of the Zionist approach to the problem, the belief that the Arabs would not fight, provided that Britain was firm with them, that they were by nature inclined to bow to the *fait accompli* and accept solutions imposed from outside. On November 14th Silver told Bevin in New York's Waldorf-Astoria Hotel that no troops would be required to impose a settlement agreed between Britain and the United States, since Arab military strength was 'illusory and purely a matter of propaganda'. At a second meeting on November 20th, 1946, he told Bevin 'that the Arabs would agree, if it were known that HMG and the US government supported partition'.[96]

Dean Acheson told Inverchapel on November 26th that the United States would 'go along with' a British partition proposal. He was sure that the President's mind was working in this direction.[97] Zionists and

Americans hoped therefore that Britain would put this before the next session of the London conference on January 21st. (It had been held over, because of the Zionist Congress, due to begin in Basle on December 9th.) Provided that Britain made a gesture in favour of partition, the Jewish Agency would attend the conference. Otherwise they would probably not attend, although the final decision would be taken at the Congress. This told Britain the price that she was being asked to pay – her agreement to an imposed solution by partition. If she agreed, she would have Zionist and American support. Otherwise she would take the consequences.

Britain's choice was plain: should she or should she not submit to the pressure and change her policy yet again? The Foreign Office posed its usual questions and emerged with its traditional answers. Partition was anathema to the Palestinians and the whole Arab League. A few Arab leaders, for instance Nuri es-Said and King Abdullah, had flirted with partition in private talks, but they all knew that to urge it publicly would mean political and perhaps physical suicide.

In the same way Mustafa Nahas, former Egyptian premier, disliked Haj Amin al-Husseini most intensely, but in public he felt obliged to support him. On November 13th he referred to him as 'Egypt's cherished guest' and invoked God's aid for 'his glorious battle for the good of Palestine'.[98] Arab leaders felt the constant need to show the purity of their patriotism on the Palestine issue, the one issue that united them. None of them would be able to compromise over it and survive.

The Foreign Office did not accept the view that Arab hostility to a Jewish state was a mere chimera, that it would wither away in the face of *force majeure*. On the contrary, they saw it as something very real indeed, something furious and lasting. Five British divisions would be needed to quell the blaze that would result and it would destroy Britain's valuable treaties with Egypt and Iraq.

British experts were also beginning to take into account the Soviet reaction. On September 22nd the Moscow newspaper *Trud* demanded the referral of Palestine to the United Nations: 'Only by this course can Palestine be rescued from the proposed plan of partition.' On November 1st *Pravda* likewise took a pro-Arab line, quoting various angry Arab reactions to Truman's October 4th statement and concluding: 'Small Arab countries demand freedom, independence and the inviolability of their frontiers. They do not want their fate to be decided without them and against their will.'

Harold Beeley mentioned this article in a talk on November 4th with

Waldemar Gallman, minister at the American embassy. He thought that its aim must be to pave the way for Soviet support of the Arab case, if and when the Palestine problem was handed over to the United Nations. For this was the idea that Bevin was mentioning more and more often in his talks with Zionist leaders, much to their distress, the possibility that Britain would decide that the Mandate was too heavy a burden and would abdicate it, perhaps to the United States, more probably to the United Nations.

Robert Howe summarized the Foreign Office's departmental view in a note to Bevin. There were only three possible final solutions: partition, surrender of the Mandate to the United Nations, or a solution along the lines of the Arab proposals of September 30th. Which was it to be? The Foreign Office concluded that partition 'would so antagonize the Arab states that we should no longer be able to count on their goodwill, which we have hitherto regarded as vital to the maintenance of our position in the Middle East'. Surrender to the United Nations, on the other hand, would be interpreted as a sign that Britain had decided to withdraw from the Arab world: 'The Middle Eastern states would feel that they could no longer rely on British interest and support, and our influence would rapidly decline.'[99]

These were days when many educated people – and not only in Britain – thought of the Empire as an important civilizing power, a force for good which would probably last for centuries. John Glubb, writing to the Foreign Office in July 1946, provides a vivid example of such thinking: 'The sufferings (however much to be lamented) of a few hundred thousand Jews cannot be weighed in the balance with the future of the British Commonwealth, which numbers hundreds of millions . . . If, as a result of ill-advised action on our part, Russia were to establish herself in the Middle East, the premature collapse of the British Empire within a generation or two might well result.'[100]

The Foreign Office therefore confirmed their original belief that 'disastrous consequences' would be the result of choosing either of the first two options and that 'the third policy of negotiation with the Arabs on the basis of their proposals is undoubtedly the most advantageous'.[101] True, this was only the view of one government department, not that of the British government as a whole, but it played a vital part in the decision-making process.

It ensured, for instance, that there could be no question of approving partition before the Zionist Congress. On November 29th Attlee warned Bevin not to give Silver or Goldmann any such assurance. If it were given, it would undoubtedly leak out and give Arabs the impression of British double-dealing.[102] They would then boycott the January conference, rebel in Palestine, overthrow Nuri's moderate government in Iraq and demonstrate against Britain everywhere else.

Abba Eban, passing through London on his way to Basle and helping Weizmann with his speeches, got the impression that British public opinion was rebelling against the Palestine commitment. It was the coldest winter in living memory and frequent power cuts were forcing people to work by candlelight in their overcoats: 'A feeling of indignation was growing against 100,000 British troops being kept there months and years after the war was over. And then there were the casualties. Five or six deaths often make more impact than five or six thousand, especially when added to all the rationing and fuel shortages of post-war Britain.'

The great issue to be decided in Basle was whether or not to attend the London conference. Britain had made a few concessions to Zionism, replacing General Barker, releasing all the Jewish leaders from Latrun and allowing a number of refugees in Cyprus to enter Palestine. But she had not moved on the central issue of partition. Weizmann believed that a Jewish delegation should nevertheless attend and he made a decision along these lines a condition of his candidacy for re-election as president of the Zionist Organization.

Another crucial issue was terrorism. And on this Weizmann's emotions were close to breaking point. Eban says: 'Weizmann accepted the use of violence only as a controlled calculation to achieve a political end. He probably thought that the Haganah had it about right. He was certainly surprised and indignant when he finally learnt about the link with the other two organizations. He was afraid that terrorism would get out of control and create an ideology of violence, which would destroy the liberal and humane element in Zionism, thus leading to a chauvinistic lack of realism.'

The conference went badly for Weizmann. From the beginning there seemed to be a majority against taking part in the conference. Blanche Dugdale wrote: 'But I don't believe they will dare to be such fools. For if not, then what?' The next day Abba Hillel Silver spoke out against partition and in favour of 'resistance'. It was like a call for the renewal of Haganah violence. On December 16th Weizmann confronted these advocates of rebellion, especially those from the United States, far from the firing line: 'Moral and political support is very little when you send other people to the barricades to face tanks and guns.'

Then Emmanuel Neumann, one of Weizmann's opponents in the Jewish Agency, at last pushed his fabled oratory to its greatest peak by interrupting him from the floor. Weizmann paused and, as the shock of what had happened reverberated round the hall, launched into his famous final words: 'Somebody has called me a demagogue. I do not know who. I hope that I shall never learn the man's name. I – a demagogue! I who have borne all the ills and travail of this movement! The person who flung that word in my face ought to know that in every house and stable in Nahalal, in every little workshop in Tel Aviv or Haifa, there is a drop of my blood . . . If you think of bringing the redemption nearer by un-Jewish methods, if you lose faith in hard work and better days, then you commit idolatry and endanger what we have built. Would that I had a tongue of flame, the strength of prophets, to warn you against the paths of Babylon and Egypt. Zion shall be redeemed in Judgement – and not by any other means.'

This remarkable speech has gone down in history, but it did not achieve its object in December 1946. The vehemence of it irritated the Revisionists, Silver's supporters and Weizmann's other opponents, strengthening their resolve to remove what remained of his political power. Golda Meir's proposal to allow the Zionist executive to attend the conference was defeated by a small majority. Weizmann's candidacy automatically lapsed.

9
Abdication

YALIN-MOR and his men of Lehi, now largely independent of Haganah influence, decided to step up the killing of British soldiers: 'You see, we were in a political dilemma. There are advantages in killing individually selected people. You eradicate some of the people responsible for the policy you are fighting. But it was a big empire and these people could be replaced. More effective, perhaps, were our attacks on the rank and file, ordinary soldiers and policemen.

'We adapted the practice of the Irish Republican Army. If you remember, in the 1920s the IRA put wires across the road where British motorcyclists passed. They could not see the wire in the night, so their heads were cut off. We adapted this a bit. We planted mines disguised as milestones on both sides of the road and exploded them by electricity when British vehicles came between them.

'Later I read that this kind of action broke the nerves of the British army. It meant that instead of their imposing curfew on the Jews, we imposed curfew on them. They were afraid to leave their barracks, so they had to stay there night after night, month after month. It was very bad for morale. And the casualties spread unrest among British families in England. They started demanding the evacuation of British troops. It had a political effect. That was the purpose.'

A British quarterly report of October 1946 records: 'The morale both of officers and other ranks is particularly low, the reason being that Tel Aviv has been under curfew and out of bounds for some considerable time. And owing to numerous incidents men are confined to their quarters.'[1] The road mine, which began killing soldiers in September, was a packet of steel rivets enclosed in plaster of Paris or painted white as a disguise. Similar in style and effect to the 'bowler hat' bombs taught by British instructors in kibbutzim in 1942, they would be placed beside the road with the tough side of the casing towards the verge and the soft side towards the tarmac. An explosive charge, wedged between the tough casing and the rivets, would blast the latter across the road like a shower of machinegun bullets.[2]

Lieutenant D. J. Haslip remembers five or six of his men being killed by these mines: 'None of our vehicles were proof against them. You could sandbag the base of your machine. But this restricted your movement, which made things very difficult, and I never did it myself. I just trusted to luck and made a point of never patrolling the same road at the same time of the day.' Some drivers drove everywhere at high speed, hoping to confuse the man on the trigger by reducing to a split second the time spent in the danger area. Other drivers rejected this advice, preferring to face the steel rivets than to be thrown out of control by a near-miss into the prickly cactus that lined the roads.

On October 30th an Irgun party planted a suitcase bomb in Jerusalem railway station. The police knew about the plan from an ex-Irgun informer and were lying in wait. Constable R. W. Smith carried the case out into the open and was killed when it blew up. The police opened fire on the raiders' cars, wounded several men, pursued them and captured four. The next day another Irgun team, commanded by Eli Tavin, wrecked the British embassy in Rome with another suitcase bomb. The Vaad Leumi passed a resolution warning the Yishuv of 'the grave dangers inherent in such acts of madness', adding that those who kill innocent soldiers and policemen 'stain the purity of our creative work and frustrate the justice of our fight'.[3]

Private T. C. Foley recalls: 'When things were calm, we were allowed out in a party of four. We carried rifles at all times, with fifty rounds in a canvas bandolier round our necks. If we went into Nathanya, it had to be a party of ten. We might sit in an open-air café with two or three men detailed off to keep watch while we drank our beer. When we went to the beach, it was a party of thirty. One section mounted guard while the rest bathed.' Ralph Capenerhurst, an army baker stationed in Haifa, says: 'It was a depressing time altogether, it was the boredom, the heat, the lack of mail and the general feeling that there was no reason for us to be where we were. I remember that I had a metal cigarette case. I took it to a jeweller and had a Star of David engraved on it. I thought it might help me, if ever I was kidnapped by the Irgun or the Stern gang.'

Above all this collapse in morale persuaded army chiefs that the time had come to 'take the gloves off' and so regain the initiative against terrorism. Inspector-General Nicol Gray remembers being asked again and again: 'Why don't you get tough?' He used to reply that even Hitler, the toughest of them all, had been unable to stamp out resistance in Poland or France. Nevertheless on November 20th Bernard Montgomery and Miles Dempsey made a determined effort to gain Cabinet consent for the use of harsher measures, collective fines and punitive searches, in no way concealing their view that the High Commissioner's soft approach was largely to blame for the deterioration. What the army and police found most incomprehensible was that none of the death sentences imposed on Jewish terrorists were being carried out.

Dempsey cabled War Minister Frederick Bellenger: 'We know that terrorism is tacitly accepted by all and sundry. Were this not so these murderers would soon be apprehended. The people must therefore take the consequences.'[4] Montgomery told the Defence Committee that since October 1st seventy-six soldiers and twenty-three policemen had been killed or wounded.[5] After gaining the initiative on June 29th, he said, the army had been forced (presumably by Cunningham) to adopt a defensive role. This, together with the Administration policy of imposing light sentences and never implementing the death penalty, was the reason for the poor morale. Bellenger agreed with his CIGS that enforcement of the death penalty would most effectively remove any impression of British weakness in the face of terrorism. There was particular resentment about the reprieve granted to all the Lehi men captured after the Haifa railway workshop raid on June 11th.

Cunningham advised strongly against Dempsey's ideas: 'I do not believe it would have the slightest effect in reducing terrorism and might well increase it. I should say, with the example of Ireland and even the Arab rebellion before me, I am dead against reprisals as such.' Attlee reminded Montgomery that the Cabinet had been assured in June that Operation Agatha would seriously cripple the illegal organizations: 'It appeared now that the action had not achieved its object, insofar as terrorist activity was in fact increasing.' He did, nevertheless, while rejecting the demands for collective punishment, set in train a process that would allow the army and the military courts to strike the terrorists harder.

In December 1946 two sixteen-year-old Irgun boys were convicted of carrying arms during a bank raid three months earlier and, too young to be condemned to death, were sentenced to eighteen years' imprisonment. They were also sentenced to eighteen strokes of the cane. Begin says: 'This again was absolutely intolerable to us. Our men were fighters and it was a humiliating punishment.'

Begin writes in *The Revolt*: 'Certain elements in the machinery of British government seem to have a special affection for the use of the whip . . . Was an oppressor now to whip us in our own country? Would the rebels of our generation, ready and willing to sacrifice their lives for the liberation of their people, tolerate this new humiliation? What was the purpose of this bestial punishment? Did the regime want to demonstrate that it regarded us as natives, that it would teach these impudent Jews in the orthodox fashion how to behave towards their benevolent masters?'[6] Begin himself wrote the text of the public warning, in English he had learnt from BBC radio, and had it pasted up in Tel Aviv: 'If it is put into effect – every officer of the British occupation army in Eretz Israel will be liable to be punished in the same way: *to get 18 whips*.'[7] However, on December 27th Benjamin Kimchi was duly flogged.

Two days later Major Brett of the 2nd Parachute Brigade was taken from the lobby of the Hotel Metropole in Nathanya, where he was sitting with his wife, bundled into a car and taken to a quiet road, where he too was given eighteen strokes, and in other parts of Palestine three sergeants suffered the same pain and indignity. Within a few minutes Nathanya was cordoned off and a huge search operation began. The *Palestine Post* records: 'Before the search had got well under way, however, the Major reappeared at the hotel, dishevelled and without his uniform, about an hour after he had been kidnapped.'[8] He at once set off with the police and tracker dogs to try to find the place where he had been taken. District Commissioner W. V. Fuller reported: 'The story of his flogging is well known and I must say that Major Brett personally has taken it extremely well. He behaved as a real sportsman throughout.'[9]

But Major Brett's sportsmanship was not enough to eradicate the humiliation inflicted on the whole British nation by this incident. And when Cunningham remitted the flogging sentence on the other young Irgun prisoner, it only seemed to make matters worse. It was the sort of decision that showed all the vices of overcaution, Churchill told the House of Commons: 'This is the road of abject defeat. And though I hate this quarrel with the Jews and I hate their methods of outrage, if you are engaged in the matter, at least bear yourselves like men.'[10] For Begin it was a notable moral victory: 'There were no more floggings in this country. A few weeks later a young Arab was sentenced to be flogged and the army commander cancelled it. We were glad that neither Jewish boys nor Arab boys would be flogged any more in this country.'

Beeley told Gallman that the effect of the floggings on British public opinion would be greater even than the King David bombing, because it went 'right down through the ranks'.[11] He feared a general rise of anti-semitism. A synagogue in Dollis Hill, London, was broken into and vandalized. But, in the midst of their triumph, the Irgun suffered a misfortune. One of their cars was stopped by a roadblock near Wilhelma on the Lydda road. In the ensuing gunfight one Jew was fatally wounded and three were captured – Yechiel Drezner, Mordechai Alkochi and Eliezer Kashani. Firearms and rawhide whips found in the car convinced the British soldiers that some at least of the perpetrators of the great indignity were in their hands. Enraged by what their comrades had suffered, it is said, they exacted summary revenge on the Jewish prisoners.[12]

This unsavoury event boded ill for the new year, which all sides anticipated as the year of decision. The fear that the Zionists would boycott the London discussions turned out to be unreal. On January 2nd, 1947, Ben Gurion explained to Arthur Creech-Jones, who had succeeded Hall as colonial secretary on October 4th, that the Basle resolution in no way prevented him and his colleagues from taking part in the conference informally. In practice, this differed little from formal participation. Cunningham arrived in London the next day, partly to discuss the army's request for a freer hand against terrorism, but also to give his views about a political settlement.

But at this stage there seemed little to decide. Attlee and Bevin had made up their minds to follow the Foreign Office's advice, outlined by Robert Howe in December, and impose a variation of the plan submitted by the Arabs on September 30th. On January 13th Montgomery advised them that it was 'essential to retain the right to station forces in Palestine'. Most of Egypt was being evacuated, though not the Canal Zone, and there was no other area that could accommodate Britain's Middle East reserve. This reserve was needed to ward off any threat to the Canal, the pipeline and the oil installations themselves. And air bases were needed for imperial communications.

Lord Tedder, Chief of Air Staff, said: 'Our whole military position in the Middle East depended upon the cooperation of the Arab states.'[13] Two days later he explained to the Cabinet that retaining her existing position of influence in the Middle East was one of the three vital props of the British Empire's defence. They were all interdependent. And if any one were lost, the whole structure would be imperilled. Attlee recalled the Palestinian Arabs' promise that, once they were put on the way to independence and majority rule, they would grant Britain military facilities. Only by this solution, it seemed, could these requirements be fulfilled.

Bevin gave perhaps the clearest indication of his priorities in the matter at a meeting of the Defence Committee on January 1st. Agreeing with the argument that Palestine was strategically essential to Britain's Middle East position, he told the service chiefs and the Prime Minister: 'Without the Middle East and its oil and other potential resources, he saw no hope of our being able to achieve a standard of living at which we were aiming in Great Britain.'[14]

By January 14th Bevin had distilled his ideas into a Cabinet paper. And here his first concern was to dispose once and for all of the idea of partition. He had received legal advice, he wrote, that Britain could only impose partition with United Nations consent. The League of Nations, the fount of British power in Palestine, had been wound up in April 1946, but not before transferring all its mandates to the control of the new international body. The United Nations would thus have to approve any basic departure from the original Mandate. A British proposal to partition Palestine would be opposed by the whole Arab bloc. And, concluded Bevin: 'There can be little doubt that in this event the Soviet group would align itself with the Arabs.' He was convinced that this forecast was right: 'I cannot conceive of the British government, even aided by the United States, being able to carry partition with the requisite majority.' Beeley says: 'This was a unanimous view in the Foreign Office, that even if we wanted partition, we would never get the UN to approve it.'[15]

Bevin proposed therefore to merge the 1946 British and Arab proposals into a plan that would give independence to the Arab majority. But the Arabs would have to pay a price. They would have to grant 'a substantial number of [Jewish] immigration certificates'. A system of local government would then emerge and there would be a number of Jewish cantons. But, apart from this final batch, there would be no further Jewish immigration without Arab consent.

He predicted that the announcement of this policy would lead to 'a major rebellion' by the Jews in Palestine, which would gain some sympathy in the United States government and fill the American press with abuse of Britain: 'It is however doubtful whether American hostility towards us on this account would be either widespread or lasting.' A further advantage was that this Jewish rebellion would take place during the period of transition to Arab majority rule, while Britain was still responsible for law and order. The British army would be able to bring the situation under control.

This paper was circulated to members of the Cabinet only a few minutes before they met on the morning of January 15th. Perhaps it was this that annoyed them, because Bevin's ideas ran into unusually strong opposition. Chancellor of the Exchequer Hugh Dalton, Minister of Health Aneurin Bevan and Minister of Fuel Emmanuel Shinwell all joined Creech-Jones in urging a return to partition.[16] The meeting adjourned without reaching a decision.

The next day Creech-Jones produced an impassioned Cabinet paper explaining his views in detail. He agreed that the Arab plan conformed with normal democratic principles and with Article 76 of the United Nations Charter, which demands self-government for every country according to 'the freely expressed wishes of the people concerned'. But, in his view, while the plan could be defended in theory, there was not the slightest hope of its proving workable in practice.

The simple fact was that even the most moderate Jew in Palestine would resist it tooth and nail: 'It would spell the cessation of immigration, the arrest of Jewish development in Palestine, and the permanent subjugation of the national home, with its highly organized European population and its extensive commercial and industrial interests, to a backward Arab electorate, largely illiterate and avowedly inimical to its further progress.'[17]

Creech-Jones considered that it would be a gross betrayal of Britain's and the Labour party's commitments to the national home to hand the Jews over to the mercy of an Arab-ruled state, of which Haj Amin al Husseini would probably be the head. It would mean disorder and bloodshed on a scale which Britain could not contemplate. He attached a note from Cunningham in support of his and other Cabinet ministers' belief that partition was the only remedy: 'This solution possesses an element of finality which is elsewhere absent.'

At the end of January Dean Acheson told Inverchapel that his Administration stuck by Truman's October 4th statement: 'The American government, for domestic and other reasons, would find it easier to support in the United Nations and elsewhere the solution of the Palestine problem calling for partition and the setting up of a viable Jewish state . . .'[18] Jewish Agency representatives also offered to support this idea during several meetings at the Colonial Office, beginning on January 29th.[19]

Partition was now the approved policy of the Zionist majority. But it was seen by them as a concession, a reasonable withdrawal from their basic (and justifiable) demand for a Jewish state in the whole of Palestine. And a minority of Zionists, including the whole Revisionist party, saw the concession as quite unreasonable. Menachem Begin argued this point strongly on the Irgun's clandestine radio: 'We shall fight these plans, even if the majority of the Jewish Agency sees them as the solution of the Palestine issue. We shall never acquiesce in the partitioning of our homeland.'[20]

Of course the Arabs of Palestine were the spearhead of the battle against a Jewish state of any size. Jamal al-Husseini, their delegation's leader, made clear in his opening speech to the London conference on January 27th his view that partition was futile, unjust and impracticable. At the moment, he said, the Arab world was racially homogeneous and territorially continuous: 'The creation of an alien Jewish state in Palestine means the destruction of this territorial continuity and national homogeneity and the creation of a running sore that will undoubtedly become a permanent source of trouble in the Middle East.'[21]

Nevertheless it seemed briefly that Creech-Jones had collected enough support to win the day for partition. Major-General 'Windy' Gale recalls: 'Weizmann came to see me early in February, just after his return from London, and said, "General, this is the greatest day in my life. Creech-Jones has promised that we will have partition." He had come to tell me this gladsome news.' Beeley was busy denying reports in the New York press of a British government split. 'He knows of no Cabinet disagreement,'[22] reported Gallman on February 3rd.

Bevin spent his time making spirited forays into both camps, receiving the Arabs at Lancaster House, the Jews at the Colonial Office, but it was soon predictably clear that neither plan would do, that partition would provoke an Arab rebellion, the Foreign Office plan a Jewish rebellion. By now he was no longer looking for a plan which both sides would approve. That was far too much to expect. But he still had hopes of finding a formula in which both sides would acquiesce, reluctantly and perhaps angrily, but without violence, and which would incidentally neutralize the opposition centred around Creech-Jones. He would make one final attempt. Beeley says: 'I remember the genesis of that last plan. I wrote it, on the basis of Bevin's ideas. I remember he sent for me one morning early in February. He said he had been lying awake since five o'clock thinking about Palestine and he gave me a list of ideas in rather jumbled form, telling me to go away and make what I could out of it. I worked entirely within the framework he had given me.'

The result was the 'Bevin plan', which allowed Jewish immigration at four thousand a month for two years, nearly a hundred thousand in all, followed by further immigration only with Arab consent or, failing that, by United Nations arbitration. It provided for immediate local autonomy under British trusteeship and independence after five years, with certain safeguards for the Jewish minority.[23] Bevin discussed the plan with Creech-Jones and, though there is no record of what was said, clearly impressed him with its merits. The clinching argument, in Beeley's recollection, was Bevin's and the Foreign Office's firm conviction that partition would never be approved by the United Nations, that the Soviet bloc was bound to join with the Arabs in opposing it. (The Soviet press had always made this opposition clear.) Bevin's will prevailed over that of Creech-Jones, as it usually did. Creech-Jones abandoned his impassioned advocacy of partition and joined Bevin in signing the 'plan', which was presented as a Cabinet paper on February 6th.

Creech-Jones, who a few days earlier had spoken up so strongly for Jewish rights, now agreed with Bevin that partition 'would be demonstrably unfair to the Arabs', would 'have little chance of securing the necessary two-thirds majority' and would 'involve us in a heavy military liability'. He was totally converted away from the idea of a Jewish state. He also agreed with Bevin that, if this last plan failed, they should carry out the threat put to the Zionists by Bevin in a 'thinking aloud' session on January 29th.[24] They would lay the problem before the United Nations without any recommendation.

The plan was put before the Zionists on February 10th and the Arabs on February 12th. Both rejected it outright. Deprived of their partition goal, the Zionists reverted to their second option, first conceived by Ben Gurion, demanding a return to the pre-1939 Mandate. The Arabs, or some of them, asked Britain to evacuate Palestine immediately. In the resulting clash, they said, they would end the problem once and for all. The Cabinet rejected the Zionist idea, on the ground that it would gradually but inevitably lead to a Jewish takeover, and also rejected the Arab idea, which Bevin and Creech-Jones described as 'this humilitating course'.[25]

The Zionists made a last effort to avert what they knew was coming. On February 13th, at a meeting arranged by the British-Jewish businessman Simon Marks, Ben Gurion spent three hours trying to persuade Lord Chancellor Jowitt to keep the situation fluid, to continue the Mandate, even with some limits on Jewish immigration.

Ben Gurion made it clear that he would accept the four-thousand-a-month limit, which formed part of Bevin's plan, provided that after two years the principle of economic absorptive capacity was restored. And he would agree to accept the British High Commissioner as arbiter. Then, provided that the land regulations were also repealed, the Yishuv would respond to his call to eradicate terrorism and illegal immigration.[26]

But it was too late. Bevin had made up his mind. The next morning he showed the Cabinet a Jewish Agency map assigning, in his view, a far larger area to the Jews than Britain could ever contemplate, even conceding the principle of partition. When Jowitt repeated his conversation of the previous night, Bevin replied that Ben Gurion's object in suggesting such a plan was quite clearly to enable the Jews to attain a majority in Palestine under British protection. Any such policy would excite the active hostility of the Arabs.[27]

The only possible remedy was therefore, as Churchill had suggested on August 1st and again on November 12th, to hand Palestine back to its original guardian – the United Nations, the League's successor. On February 18th Bevin duly told the House of Commons that this would be done. He hoped that this announcement 'might bring them [Jews and Arabs] to a more reasonable frame of mind'. Britain would try to hurry the United Nations processes, so as to have the matter decided by the General Assembly in September, and in the meantime she would not cease her efforts to find a solution. If a solution was found, she could withdraw the matter from the UN agenda.

In Palestine security continued to deteriorate. Armed clashes with Jews (including the King David explosion) led to the death of 212 people in 1946: sixty Arabs, forty-five British soldiers, thirty-seven unarmed Jews, twenty-nine British police, twenty-six armed Jews, fourteen British civilians and one other.[28] On January 7th, after an Irgun attack on Citrus House, the Tel Aviv military headquarters, troops of the 6th Airborne Division rounded up some sixty or seventy men from the Montefiore district, took them to the Sarona police compound and made them run the gauntlet between lines of soldiers and police, who beat them with sticks and rifle butts. The next day Inverchapel read detailed accounts of this incident in the New York press, one story alleging that twenty-nine men were injured, seven seriously enough to require hospitalization.[29] He asked for clarification and word came from Cunningham that the stories were based on fact.[30]

The story of Dov Gruner was also approaching its climax. Captured during a raid on Ramat Gan police station on April 23rd, 1946, he was too severely wounded to be brought to trial and it was January 2nd, 1947, before he was convicted and sentenced to death. At once the British embassy in Washington began receiving telegrams and telephone calls urging clemency for the Irgun fighter, mentioning particularly his years of service in the British army in the war against Hitler. Senator Robert

Taft advised Inverchapel that Gruner had only been in the vicinity of the raid because he was applying for a job as an electrician nearby.[31] Inverchapel asked London how he should reply to these inquiries: 'His execution will undoubtedly cause an outcry among Zionists and their sympathizers.'[32]

Barker says: 'This was a cut-and-dried case. Gruner had been caught redhanded, armed and shooting up British troops. His political views were nothing to do with the matter. It's nonsense to say that he was a prisoner of war. There was no war. Even if there had been, the Irgun were not obeying the rules of war. He was a criminal, a murderer. So I took it up to Alan Cunningham and I said, "This is an absolutely definite case of carrying arms and I propose to sign the death warrant. Do you agree?" He said he did. It wasn't political. It wasn't referred to London. It was a decision taken by me on the spot.' Barker confirmed the death sentence on January 24th and the date of execution was set for January 28th.

Henry Gurney, Shaw's successor as Chief Secretary, told Pinkerton that Gruner was captured with an automatic weapon in his hands.[33] Tests showed that the weapon had been fired. An Arab policeman was killed in the raid and two others injured. These were aggravating circumstances. Also, it was Gruner's misfortune that his case came to crisis point at a time when the British public's hearts were hardening against Jewish terrorism, especially after the flogging incident, when the army were demanding the right to 'take the gloves off' in the fight and when the government were being taunted by press and Parliament for their faintheartedness as well as by the Arabs for their frequent willingness to hang Arab terrorists or criminals, but not Jews. During the 1936–9 disturbances, Parliament was told, 107 Arab terrorists had been hanged and only one Jewish terrorist, Ben-Yosef, in 1938. No Jewish terrorist had been hanged in Palestine since then.[34]

If Gruner had come up for trial six months earlier, he would almost certainly have been sentenced to death and reprieved, as were all Jewish terrorists in the years 1939 to 1946, even those caught redhanded. But at the end of the year Britain's reluctance to enforce the death penalty had been mentioned in Cabinet meetings as one of the reasons why the security forces were failing. Therefore, although Barker's and Cunningham's decision was taken independently of the political centre, it was certainly influenced by the political background of a British public unable to understand why their young men's murderers were not being hanged.

So once again the Irgun looked for hostages. But soldiers and policemen, especially officers, expected this move and were on their guard. The Irgun then turned to civilians. Their first acquisition was a retired officer, Major H. A. Collins, who later described on Palestine radio what happened to him that Sunday afternoon, January 26th: 'It was rather strange to be just finishing your tea, to hear a knock on the door, then suddenly to find yourself talking to a woman who said she had a message and then, the next instant, to find yourself facing three automatic weapons and within another minute to find yourself with your face to the wall and chloroform being poured over you.' At this point Collins turned round, not to resist, but because the chloroform was burning him. Immediately his abductors hit him on the head, pushed him into a sack, carried him to a car, drove him some distance and locked him up in a dark and damp cellar, lit only by a candle. A doctor sewed up his head and told him why the Irgun wanted him. He spent the next twenty-four hours in the cellar, gagged and bound. On the morning of January 27th the Cabinet in London was told of the kidnapping and that, if Gruner was hanged, Collins's life might be in danger. They recorded their view that 'even if such threats were made, Gruner's execution should not be put off on that account'.[35]

That same morning Judge Ralph Windham was trying a 'rather boring succession case' in his court in Tel Aviv. 'Suddenly, without the slightest warning, I was seized by the elbows and wrists by two young terrorists who must have crept in from behind me. They were armed with revolvers, so I didn't resist. They hustled me down the stairs and I could see the terrified faces of my court officials staring helplessly at me as I was hurried out of the building, all of them prevented at revolver point from trying to rescue me.

'The whole building had been quietly invaded by terrorists carrying out a swift and perfectly coordinated plan. All telephone wires had been cut. I was frogmarched over a low wall behind the court, still wearing my wig and gown, into a car waiting there in Lilienblum Street. I was made to crouch down in the back of the car, a coat over my face so that I could neither see nor be seen. My captors wore black eye-masks, like highwaymen. The shock and speed of events left me no time to think or reflect. I was simply whirled along like a twig in a torrent.'

Windham was driven at breakneck speed for half an hour to a settlement near Givat Shmuel, where he was kept in rather better conditions than Collins was. He was given good cold food, though with a little too much garlic for his taste, and a copy of Arthur Koestler's *Thieves in the Night*. He writes, contrary to the account in Begin's book, that he had no idea where he was and that his captors were always masked.

The next day, January 28th, the day set for the execution, Windham read 'with a personal interest' in the *Palestine Post* that Gruner had been given leave to appeal his sentence to the Privy Council in London. The Cabinet that morning, after expressing 'surprise' that a British judge had been abducted with such apparent ease, was told of the postponement of the execution, since Gruner 'intended to apply for leave to appeal to the Privy Council'. In fact he had indicated no such intention.

Begin says: 'It was Judge Windham who really counted, because he was a member of your class, Lord Bethell. He was an aristocrat.' He writes in his book: 'Windham is a member of a fine old English family and it was undoubtedly his detention that had decided the British Labour government to postpone Dov's execution.'[36] The strange fact of the last-minute change of mind, a few hours after the Cabinet's decision not to intervene on Collins's account, lends some weight to Begin's theory, although it was probably Windham's position as a judge, rather than his collateral connection with the Bowyer-Smyth baronetcy, that induced the Palestine authorities to pause. And, contrary to what Begin writes, the decision was not taken by the British Cabinet. The record makes it clear that they were told of it only after the time set for the hanging.

That same afternoon, when he was halfway through Koestler's book, Windham was blindfolded, taken for a long walk and released by a roadside near Ramat Gan. He subsequently became Chief Justice of Tanzania, where in 1963 he received a letter from his former chief Irgun guard Yesheyahu Zamir, inviting him to be his guest in Beersheeba. Collins was not so lucky. He too was released by the Irgun, but his wife Irene Collins says: 'Soon after the incident he started developing chest trouble. Various doctors said it was because of all the chloroform that he inhaled, when it was poured over him. Finally it turned into emphysema. He was in and out of hospital the whole time and he died in 1960.'

In Britain these bizarre events aroused two sorts of emotion. The first was an unwilling admiration for the sheer courage of Dov Gruner, who had faced the hangman's noose rather than acknowledge British authority. 'The fortitude of this man, criminal though he be, must not escape the notice of the House,' said Churchill on January 31st. Dare Wilson wrote: 'Although it might be described as fanaticism, his conduct throughout his year in custody, four months of which was spent in the condemned cell, was that of a very brave man.'[37]

The second feeling was one of fury against a government which had once again allowed itself to be blackmailed and humiliated. Churchill taunted the government with cowardice. How would Britain ever have won the war against Hitler, he asked, if this attitude had prevailed in recent years? What were Britain's hundred thousand troops doing in Palestine? What good was Britain getting out of it? Finally he asked the government 'to divest us of a responsibility which we are failing to discharge and which in the process is covering us with blood and shame.'

'Rule or quit' was the heading of the *Sunday Express* editorial, approving the Churchill line and remarking unkindly that Creech-Jones was not the sort of man to be in charge when his country was under fire: 'During 1946 seventy-three British subjects were brutally murdered.[38] How many culprits paid the supreme penalty? None . . . Hang the murderers. Be strong. Visit crime with stern, relentless justice. And above all, no more surrender.' The British authorities, visibly stung by this criticism, decided to take the sort of action that their people clearly wanted.

At the end of January they therefore instituted 'Operation Polly', the evacuation of British civilians and dependents, some three thousand in all. Cunningham explained to Pinkerton that this was done 'to give government free hand for any preventive measures necessary without possible embarrassment of having hostages seized'.[39] The Foreign Office advised Washington that, since civilians could not be protected effectively, they must be removed so as to permit 'any action which the Government might think necessary to enforce the law'. Cunningham added that 'further action in his [Gruner's] case would not be taken until after evacuation measures had been completed'.[40]

The results of this decision, the appearance of an undignified scramble for safety, provoked criticism from the civilians themselves. Cunningham replied: 'In regard to the accusations of panic, they presumably arise from the fact that we acted quickly. You of course realize that this was due to a desire to get the Gruner case out of the way as soon as possible. It was not then evident that legal action which is being taken could delay it as it has.' The execution had again been delayed by two appeals to the Privy Council, one by the Tel Aviv municipality and one by the prisoner's American uncle, Frank Gruner. 'It is somewhat difficult to explain this to the press,' noted Cunningham.[41]

Chief Secretary Henry Gurney then invited the Jewish Agency to state 'categorically and at once' whether they were willing within seven days to begin cooperation with Britain against terrorism. Certain districts of Jerusalem were designated as security areas, which meant the evacuation of Jewish families to provide safe accommodation for British troops. The *New York Herald Tribune* saw this as 'the first in a series of collective punishments of the Jewish community'.[42] Golda Meir told a meeting that it was not the task of the Yishuv to be spies, watching every friend, fellow-worker or neighbour.[43] The Jewish Agency rejected Gurney's ultimatum on February 7th.

On February 10th Drezner, Alkochi and Kashani, captured during the night of the floggings, were sentenced to death. Palestine was swept by rumours that these were to be the first in a series of hangings, that the British were preparing a massacre. Barker was supposed to have boasted at one of Katie Antonius's parties: 'I will hang a hundred Jews and there will be peace in Palestine.' He denies that he ever said such a thing, but his generally favourable attitude to the use of the death penalty in that situation is shown by his confirmation of the three latest sentences two days after they were passed, on the actual day of his departure. This act, wrote the *Palestine Post*, carried out with the ink on the sentences scarcely dry, was a Parthian shot worthy of Barker's record.[44]

That same day, February 12th, Assistant Inspector-General Bernard Fergusson submitted his plan for a new type of police activity. It was to be based on the countergang principle, a system of special squads trained to make contact with terrorist groups by infiltrating their community, to create situations likely to result in armed clashes. This scheme, if it worked, would have an important effect on British morale. Rather than waiting in their besieged garrisons, wondering when the next attack would come, the police and army would themselves go on to the offensive and search the enemy out. It was an early attempt at a now well-established and effective counterterrorism technique.

Fergusson wrote: 'There is in the army a small number of officers, who have both technical and psychological knowledge of terrorism, having themselves been engaged in similar operations on what may be termed the terrorist side in countries occupied by the enemy in the late war.'[45] Today he says: 'We planned to be unorthodox, but not illegal. The idea was to provoke contact, to look for a confrontation, but not to fire the first shot. It's wrong to say that we were assassination squads. If we'd seen Begin, we'd have held him up, hoped he'd shoot first and then anticipated him.'

Fergusson knew several young officers of this type, graduates of Special Operations Executive and MI6, experts in sabotage and espionage: 'Ran Antrim was going to come, but his farm manager died. He'd been in SOE. I asked David Smiley, who'd been dropped into Albania twice and then into Yugoslavia and Thailand. But he'd just got married and his wife wouldn't let him. The two I finally got were Alistair MacGregor, an ex-regular soldier at one time in MI6, and Roy Farran, who had fought brilliantly behind the lines in occupied France. Alistair and Roy had operated behind enemy lines with great success and I thought that their minds would work like terrorists' minds.'

It was a daring plan. Farran says today, 'Fergusson was right in the basic principle that an underground war can only be fought by counter-terrorist forces, who are prepared to mix with the enemy in his own environment. Small groups can counter other small groups.' The technique of the 'countergang' was later to be used by Britain with some success in Malaya, Kenya and Northern Ireland.

But, Farran complains, the British authorities seemed uncertain in their own minds whether they were mounting a limited police action or suppressing a full-scale rebellion by the local population as a whole. From his present vantage point as a political figure, Solicitor-General of the Canadian province of Alberta, he has reached the conclusion that unorthodox police activity must be combined with some indication of the political end in view: 'Despite a few little successes, I regard my operation as a failure. I would have done better not to have tried and to have appreciated that the conditions were hopeless.'

Furthermore in 1947 Roy Farran was a young war hero, a highly trained guerrilla fighter with years of experience in the utterly ruthless world of resistance to Nazi-German occupation. He was no politician then and he was not suited to play any important part in the sensitive balancing act of British policy in Palestine. He and his special squad were ordered by Fergusson to trail their coats, to look for trouble actively, but not to be the first to open fire. Such orders brought the squads close to the borderline with illegality and seemed to some members a 'green light' for the use of methods similar to those of their enemy. If ever that borderline was crossed, a lurid picture would emerge in the vigilant American and Jewish press, causing Britain's already cracked reputation another heavy blow.

The final measure, the imposition of martial law on the whole Tel Aviv area, was conceived at the end of January and planned in detail through February. Appropriately called 'Operation Elephant', it was far bigger than 'Operation Shark' the previous summer, involving as it did the isolation of a ten-mile-by-five continuous built-up area and 300,000 people, nearly half the Jews of Palestine. On March 1st the Irgun executed a number of especially destructive operations, including an attack on the Jerusalem officers' club. Twenty British soldiers were killed.

Begin says today, 'There was never a decision by the Irgun to kill the British. There was a decision to fight the British. Of course there were casualties, but all caused during the operations. This is the difference between what is called terrorism and what is called a fight for liberation.' But the men in the Jerusalem officers' club knew only that a bomb had been placed by the Irgun under one section of their building and had gone off without warning, killing a dozen of their friends. They were not inclined to understand Begin's fine distinction.

The next morning martial law was proclaimed and the whole Tel Aviv area came under the control of Major-General Richard Gale's 1st Infantry Division. But after two days he had to lift the curfew. He simply did not have enough men to enforce it. His searches led to the arrest of a few minor suspects, but their main result was unemployment and the paralysis of Tel Aviv industry, but not of the Irgun, who again made a successful attack on Citrus House. Gale reported: 'Unemployment may lead to demonstrations and thence on to rioting. This can be overcome by decrees, by curfews and by force. I deplore this line of approach, because I think it leads nowhere save to increased bitterness. It doesn't hit the right people. And it is the one way of forcing those who would be on the side of law and order into the ranks of the lawless elements.'

On March 13th Gale advised Lieutenant-General Gordon MacMillan (Barker's replacement) that the operation had achieved its object and should be discontinued: 'It has sealed off the "Elephant" area with incalculable loss to the Jewish community. Business on a large scale is hamstrung, contracts have been broken, banking operations with all their complications are virtually impossible. Small and large-scale businesses are coming to a standstill. Insurance companies are affected. For eleven days no one has had a letter from the outside world. 2300 mail bags lie piled up unopened and the valuable packages amount to a quarter of a million pounds.'[46]

Gale concluded that the reimposition of martial law was a terrible threat: 'They do not want "Elephant" again. If my assessment is correct, they will therefore continue their endeavours to eradicate the evil.' Creech-Jones reported to the Cabinet after the lifting of 'Elephant' on March 17th: 'The Jewish community have been given a taste of the consequences of their continued passive attitude towards terrorism.'[47] There had been more than sixty arrests, including twenty-four known members of the Irgun and Lehi.

But on March 20th the Cabinet as a whole took a less rosy view. Most ministers felt that the results were disappointing. In spite of the restrictions, serious outrages had continued, with the loss of twenty-four lives, including thirteen British soldiers and one British civilian. True, the cordon damaged the Jewish community, but it also damaged the Administration by disrupting the economy, preventing the collection of taxes and tying up manpower.[48] And the lifting of martial law after only fifteen days gave the impression of weakness. The system imposed seemed needlessly drastic. Perhaps the answer lay in the use of a more flexible style of martial law, involving fewer troops in the streets and permitting commercial life to continue. Such a regime could cover the whole country and remain in force for several months, in fact until the Jewish community found it convenient to bring terrorism to an end.

On March 26th, 1947, the chiefs of staff made a further drastic suggestion, the establishment of summary military courts in areas under martial law: 'The existence of such courts would in our view be a substantial contribution to the maintenance of law and order, particularly if their powers could be extended to the death sentence for specified offences . . .'[49] Such death sentences, they proposed, should be executed without the possibility of legal delays. On March 27th Creech-Jones and Jowitt were asked to consider this dangerous idea and report back to the Cabinet, but British documents suggest that in the end it was not pursued. And the Hitlerian proposals for eradicating terrorism, attributed to a British general in Leon Uris's semi-factual book *Exodus*, belong purely to the world of fantasy.

On March 17th the four Jews under sentence of death in Palestine were joined by Moshe Barazani, a Lehi man caught with a hand-grenade during a raid a few days earlier, and on April 3rd by Meir Feinstein, an Irgun man wounded and captured during the October 31st attack on Jerusalem railway station. Dov Gruner was begged again and again to appeal to the Privy Council, since without his signature the two appeals already lodged were unlikely to be seriously considered. At one point he gave a power of attorney to Max Seligman, a lawyer sympathetic to the Irgun, but he withdrew it within twenty-four hours. Seligman visited him several times and begged him to renew the authority: 'I told him that this was an English court, not a Palestine court, so there was no reason for not recognizing it. He said, no, he was a prisoner of war and he wouldn't sign. I said that in that case he would probably go to the gallows. He just replied, "Well, I'm not the first and I probably won't be the last." '

The tension of the impending executions affected all three communities, not least the British, who kept themselves closely guarded for fear of being taken hostage. On March 21st a Lehi team turned the Haifa oil refineries into an inferno. The fire was still burning on April 16th when Gruner, Drezner, Alkochi and Kashani were hanged in Acre fortress.

As Cunningham explained to the Cabinet on March 27th, special precautions had been taken to meet the situation. No announcement of the impending executions was made. The prisoners themselves were not told what was to happen until the evening before they were hanged.[50] Rabbi K. N. Magrill, resident Jewish chaplain at Acre, who had previously agreed to attend the executions, was persuaded by his family to decline at the last minute because of possible terrorist reprisals. The authorities thus had no time to find a replacement and the four men died without the consolation of a rabbi. The purpose behind this unseemly haste and sub-terfuge was, of course, to deny the Irgun the chance of another desperate effort to avert the executions, either by hostages or by straight rescue. An Irgun rescue attempt was, in fact, already being planned.

Begin says: 'The first I knew of it was an announcement on the radio at seven o'clock that morning. The announcer was a young woman, Leah Porat, and when she spoke about the executions, suddenly her voice broke down and she cried. It was one of the most bitter days of our lives. Dov Gruner's sister, Helen Friedmann, had come from America to see her brother and been told that she would see him. They misled us and they would not allow a rabbi to visit the cells. The men were singing as they were taken to the gallows. Other prisoners woke up in the middle of the night, realized what was happening and joined in the singing. They sang the Hatikvah until their very last breath. They died heroically.'

A US congressman, Joseph Baldwin, who had recently interviewed Begin in hiding, referred to the execution as 'murder' and called on his Political Action Committee 'to implement countermeasures' against Britain. Ex-Senator Guy Gillette accused Britain of throwing away all pretence of justice. In New York on April 18th, while Acting-Mayor Vincent Impellitteri was hosting a reception in honour of crew members of the Irgun immigrant ship *Ben Hecht*, some fifty Betar youngsters infiltrated the British consulate and demonstrated noisily for two hours. Their combination of youthfulness and rabble-rousing discipline, reported Consul-General F. E. Evans, was such as to put the Hitler Jugend to shame.[51] Ben Hecht made a statement: 'As an American giving alms to Britain, I would like to know how much Dov Gruner's gallows cost.'

The Irgun radio broadcast on April 20th: 'At dead of night, like miser-able cowards, hiding behind the armour of their cars, the officers of murder arrived in Acre to watch the spectacle of the death of captive Hebrew soldiers at the hands of an intoxicated British hangman ... Hurry, hangman, hurry. Tighten the noose, there is no time, there must be no delay, we want this blood, we want to hear the death rattle of the son of this hated people on the gallows ...' There would now be reprisals, they warned. Irgun units would be accompanied by military courts to try British prisoners and hang or shoot those condemned.

On April 21st, on the eve of their execution, Feinstein and Barazani blew themselves up in their cell with a hand-grenade smuggled to them inside an orange. The next day the Irgun bombed the Cairo–Haifa train near Rehovot, killing five British soldiers and three Arab civilians. On April 24th they abducted M. M. Collins (no relation to H. A. Collins) from the Park Hotel in Tel Aviv and would have hanged him, but he convinced them that he was a Jew, whereupon they escorted him back to his hotel.

There was one man above all others against whom the Irgun sought revenge, Lieutenant-General Evelyn Barker, the man who had written of his contempt and loathing of the Jewish community and been described by Weizmann as 'a self-confessed enemy of our people', the man who had confirmed the death sentences on Gruner and three others. Begin says: 'Barker was the one case when we went for an individual British soldier. He behaved like a Nazi Gauleiter in our country. He tried to crush our resistance with hangings.' Therefore, even though Barker had left Palestine, Begin and his colleagues decided to make him pay the penalty, to deter his successor from continuing his policy. They would hunt him down in England.[52] And the man they chose for this mission was Ezer Weizman, Chaim's nephew, who in 1977 became Israel's Minister of Defence.

Ezer Weizman, who had been recruited into the Irgun by Eli Tavin after four years' service with the Royal Air Force, planned the operation from his flat in London with a colleague he knew only by the codename 'Joel': 'We got to the point of finding Barker's house and our idea was to mine the road and blow him up. But various snags got in the way. Somehow we attracted the suspicion of Scotland Yard. One day an Inspector knocked on my door and said, "You so-and-so, when are you planning to leave England?" I said in a couple of days. He said, "Bloody good idea!" I thought it wise to take his advice and leave the country, so that was the end of the operation.'

Barker remarked, after hearing about this attempt on his life for the first time in 1977: 'I expect he's glad that he failed in his mission. What good would it have done to kill me? It wouldn't have helped the Jewish cause or the Irgun or anyone else. At least General Weizman has been able to go through the last thirty years without a murder on his conscience.'

There were other operations in Britain, mostly the work of Lehi, planned by their explosives expert Yaacov Eliav (Levstein), who today manages an Israeli security company. He planned, for instance, the attempted bombing of the Colonial Office in London on April 16th. That morning Elizabeth Hart, a Colonial Office cleaner, discovered a large parcel in a ladies lavatory, opened it and found that it contained twenty-six sticks of gelignite. The police announced later that the time fuse had failed. Otherwise it could have wrecked the entire building.[53]

In Palestine Lehi were more successful. They took their customary revenge for the death of Moshe Barazani against Assistant-Superintendent A. E. Conquest, chief of CID in Haifa, where Barazani had been captured. C. A. Wade remembers visiting Conquest at his house: 'I went into his room and he was holding an automatic pistol. There was another one hanging behind the door and hand-grenades all over the place. I asked him what on earth was the matter. He said, "They're after me." I said, "Who?" He said, "The Stern gang." I told him that in that case he had no business staying in Haifa. If they were after him, they were going to get him. He ought to telephone CID headquarters and explain the situation. He said, "But they'll think I'm afraid." I said, "Well, it's quite obvious from the state of your house that you *are* afraid. And there's nothing to be ashamed of in that.' But he wouldn't listen to me, he stayed where he was and on April 26th they got him.'

On May 4th, 1947, the Irgun mounted one of their most daring and successful operations, originally planned to save their comrades from the gallows, the famous rescue raid on Acre fortress. By skilful timing and by building up a network of communications with their captive comrades, they were able to blast holes in the thick prison walls and extract twenty-nine key men. For several minutes one whole section of the prison was open to the outside world and 214 Arab convicts also seized the opportunity to escape, though many were soon recaptured. Eight Irgun and Lehi men were killed and five arrested.[54]

This exploit inspired Ben Hecht to another brilliant piece of propaganda rhetoric, a semi-poetic Letter to the Terrorists of Palestine, published as a full-page advertisement in several New York newspapers. 'My brave friends,' it began: 'You may not believe what I write you, for there is a lot of fertilizer in the air at the moment. But, on my word as an old reporter, what I write is true. The Jews of America are for you. You are their champions. You are the grin they wear. You are the feather in their hats. In the past 1500 years every nation in Europe has taken a crack at the Jews. This time the British are at bat.' The advertisement continued with a paragraph still well remembered and often quoted in Britain:

'Every time you blow up a British arsenal, or wreck a British jail, or send a British railroad train sky high, or rob a British bank, or let go with your guns and bombs at British betrayers and invaders of your homeland, the Jews of America make a little holiday in their hearts.'[55]

Immediately the Foreign Office complained vigorously to American ambassador Lewis Douglas.[56] Bevin cabled New York: 'This advertisement is the most disgusting one that has appeared so far to my knowledge in the US press . . . It is in fact nothing more or less than an appeal for funds to aid Jewish terrorist activities in Palestine, which are resulting almost daily in the loss of lives, British, Arab and Jewish, for which we as Mandatory are responsible. You should impress upon the State Department that it is intolerable that such advertisements should appear in the press of a country friendly to Great Britain and that I expect that now at last the administration will be able to take effective measures to put a stop to them . . .'[57]

But by this time the United States was not inclined to fulfil British requests or answer British protests on the Palestine issue. The decision to refer it to the United Nations was taken against America's advice. On February 17th Secretary of State Marshall told Bevin of his country's 'regret' that this had been done.[58] On February 25th Bevin made another long extempore statement, reaffirming his belief in a cantonal solution, rejecting partition as an economic and moral impossibility, referring to the Jews as a religion rather than as a nation. It all sounded like an attempt to influence the United Nations, in spite of the previous week's promise that there would be no British recommendation. But the most controversial part of Bevin's speech was a personal attack on Truman for issuing his October 4th statement about partition and the 100,000.

Bevin said: 'I begged that the statement be not issued, but I was told that if it was not issued by Mr Truman, a competitive statement would be issued by Mr Dewey. In international affairs I cannot settle things if my problem is made the subject of local elections . . . I know what it involves. It can lead to civil war before you know where you are. However, the statement was issued. I was dealing with Jewish representatives at the time and I had to call it off because the whole thing was spoilt.' He cabled Inverchapel: 'I recognize that certain passages in this speech may give offence in the United States and may temporarily add to your difficulties. But it was necessary to show the House of Commons how we have striven for American cooperation and how the attitude of the United States has in fact complicated our problem.'[59]

Bevin may well have had good reason to complain about what Truman did on October 4th, 1946. But it is hard to see how this bitter public expression of the complaint months later achieved anything but a worsening in mutual British-American irritation and suspicion. 'I feel bound to inform you of the reactions which your remarks have provoked here,' replied Inverchapel on February 27th. The White House called the speech 'most unfortunate and misleading'. The columnist Walter Lippmann accused Bevin of making the President a scapegoat for his own failure. Senator Alben Barkley found it 'almost astonishing' for Britain, in effect, 'to charge the President of the United States with working a cheap political trick.'[60]

The Zionists believed that Bevin was the one playing tricks. They did not believe in the sincerity of his proposal to hand the problem to the United Nations. It seemed to them no more than a manoeuvre and a bluff, an attempt to blackmail them into yielding their basic demands. They knew, or they thought they knew, that Britain would never willingly give up the strategic advantages she enjoyed in Palestine. What Britain wanted, they believed, was the right to retain these privileges without the obligation to build the Jewish national home. And this was the aim of Bevin's plan.

Although they could not predict how the General Assembly would decide the fate of Palestine, they shared the then British view that a two-thirds' majority in favour of partition was inconceivable. Again and again the Soviet Union had declared its opposition to their aims. Bolshevism and Zionism were enemies. So much had been clear ever since the two ideologies began. The Russians would never permit the emergence of a Jewish state. With their East European allies and the Arab and Moslem countries, they would be more than enough to block any such idea.

The Zionists believed that they would be unable to overcome the arithmetic of the United Nations, that as the months passed and the vote approached they would find themselves under greater and greater pressure. What would they do? They could allow themselves to be outvoted, thus abandoning the Yishuv to whatever fate the General Assembly chose to inflict on them. Or, as the price of saving the Yishuv's existence, they could acquiesce in granting Britain the kind of Mandate she wanted. Jewish immigration would end and Britain's imperial interests would be preserved on the basis of Arab friendship.

Beeley wrote on March 1st: 'It was evident at the London talks with the Jewish Agency representatives that they thought up to the last possible moment that the Secretary of State was bluffing when he said that he would go to the United Nations.'[61] Having been proved wrong, they were of course plunged into gloom. Cunningham reported: 'Not since 1939 has greater despondency prevailed. And contrast with the high hopes of two years ago has brought added bitterness.'[62] Robert Howe reported on March 3rd that the Arab delegates in London were 'reasonably happy' about the referral to the United Nations.[63]

On March 31st Beeley reported a widespread Zionist allegation that Britain had only referred the matter in order to gain time and respectability, that in fact she had no intention of bringing her rule to an end.[64] On April 3rd the *New York Times* confirmed, on the basis of 'an authoritative quarter', that Britain would never give up the Mandate. And this was the general view outside Britain, that the retention of control of Palestine, or at least of strategic facilities in Palestine, was Britain's first priority, something that whatever happened would never be put at risk.

This suggestion is worth examining in detail. Firstly, there is the evidence of Bevin's January 14th Cabinet paper that he was sure that partition would not be the United Nations' choice. Bevin had good reason for this belief. Communist representatives all over the world, even Jewish communists in Palestine, had again and again declared their opposition.[65] In early 1947 partition was rejected by delegates to the communist British Empire Conference in London. As late as April 27th an article in the Moscow *Red Fleet* called for an independent Arab Palestine and dismissed partition as an aspiration of the Jewish bourgeoisie.

Partition, therefore, was not one of the possibilities that Bevin and his colleagues envisaged. But what did they envisage? Did they imagine, as many Israelis now claim, that the UN would return the Mandate to Britain under conditions that she would accept, without the obligation to build the Jewish national home? British documents show nothing to indicate that this was in Bevin's mind, or even at the back of his mind.

Beeley says: 'Neither Attlee nor Bevin can realistically have expected such an outcome. It is true that some American interests, especially in the State Department, were anxious to maintain British influence in the Middle East, mainly so as to prevent the problem being handed over to *them*. But the Zionist lobby was always strong enough to overcome this idea. The United States was firmly committed to the Jewish national home and strong enough to block any plan that would have brought its further development to a close.'

Bevin's internal memoranda also indicate a determination to relinquish British control, though maybe not British influence. On March 30th he wrote: 'We have reached a point where the Mandate can no longer continue. We have examined and exhausted with the two parties all the possibilities of a peaceful settlement under the Mandate.'[66] For this reason, he said, Britain had asked the United Nations to consider and choose one of the three options put forward in his February 25th speech – an Arab state, a Jewish state or a unitary Palestinian state – or to choose some other course. He was determined to rid Britain of the problem and it was only with difficulty that officials dissuaded him from committing Britain in advance to acceptance of the UN recommendation.

Abba Eban was now a Jewish Agency negotiator: 'I told Zionists in America that Britain was prepared to surrender the Mandate, not necessarily determined to, but prepared to. Some British officials may have hoped for the return of the Mandate, without obligations to facilitate Jewish immigration, but they must have realized that there was a risk that the United Nations would vote for a different solution. The fact was that Palestine's strategic value was decreasing. And the British military realized this. India was gaining independence. Palestine was a stepping stone to India, a stepping stone to something that no longer existed. I think that in early 1947 the balance shifted for Britain and Palestine became more of a liability than an asset.'

The evidence therefore suggests that Britain's first priority was no longer to maintain her privileges in Palestine, let alone British rule. She *hoped* to retain something, but was prepared to risk losing everything, bases and influence as well as control. The first priority now was to rid herself of the burdens imposed by the Mandate. If the United Nations would help her to do this and to remain in Palestine also, she would accept. Otherwise she would withdraw and concentrate on salvaging what she could of her treaties and interests elsewhere, in other parts of the Middle East.

Britain therefore decided to expedite this inevitable process. On April 2nd she asked the UN Acting Secretary General to summon a special session of the General Assembly, in order to appoint a special committee, which would prepare a report in time for consideration at the regular session in the autumn. By April 13th a majority had approved Britain's request and Secretary General Trygve Lie announced that this session would take place at Flushing Meadows, New York, on April 28th.

Britain did not foresee that the Soviet Union was planning a diplomatic volte-face, a dramatic change of policy carefully calculated as the best way to crush once and for all Britain's privileged Middle East position. Up to the end of April, when the special session began in New York, the Soviet press maintained its usual hostility to Zionism and partition. Then on May 14th Soviet delegate Andrey Gromyko addressed the General

Assembly in words that struck his British and Arab listeners like lightning from a clear sky. He suddenly put forward the novel Soviet argument that Western Europe's failure to guarantee the elementary rights of Jews was the reason behind their present aspiration to found their own state.

He went on: 'It would be unjustifiable to deny this right to the Jewish people, particularly in view of all they have undergone during the Second World War.' Perhaps the solution then lay in turning Palestine into a unitary state, he said, with equal rights for Jew and Arab. But, if the special committee decided that this was impossible, it might be necessary to consider a second plan 'for the partition of Palestine into two independent autonomous states, one Jewish and one Arab'.

The Palestine Arab press reacted with unbelieving fury. *Ad-Difa'a* accused Gromyko of selling his country's principles[67] and the United Nations at a cheap price and of speaking 'exactly like the representatives of imperialism'.[68] The British were taken quite aback. Bevin's bald forecast that a decision to partition Palestine was impossible was quite suddenly thrown into serious doubt. Gromyko had not yet committed his country to partition, but the fact that he was even considering it was enough to open a whole new range of possibilities for the United Nations Special Committee on Palestine, known as UNSCOP, which came into being on May 15th, 1947.

This decision in no way lessened Britain's two main problems in Palestine, terrorism and illegal immigration. Between July 1945 and the end of 1946 some thirty ships entered Palestine waters with Jews from Europe. The Royal Navy intercepted eighteen of them, interning their 17,992 passengers either in Palestine or Cyprus. Twelve of the smaller ships broke through the patrol, adding an estimated 1225 to the Jewish community.

During 1947 the ships kept coming. On February 8th the motor sailing vessel *Mercia* was spotted on her way to Palestine with 664 immigrants. Richard Catling reports that early the next morning she was approached by the destroyer *Chieftain* on the high seas nine miles west of Caesarea. The immigrants threw broken bottles at the British sailors, causing five of them to be treated for cuts.

The Royal Navy replied with teargas canisters, which were promptly thrown overboard, and then with small-arms' fire over the resisters' heads. The boarding was then accomplished, after one Jew was wounded in the thigh by a ricochet bullet and three others by stick blows to the head, one fatally.[69] The rest were transferred to Cyprus on the *Empire Heywood*. A similar fate befell the 807 immigrants of the *San Miguel* on

February 16th, the 1416 of the *Haim Arlosoroff* on February 27th and the 601 of the *Abril* on March 8th.[70]

On March 9th Cunningham advised London that, according to secret information, there were another twenty-five thousand Jews ready to leave Europe for Palestine at short notice. The threat was such as to stretch British resources beyond breaking point. The Cyprus camps could accommodate only another seven thousand. There were not enough aircraft to do the spotting, not enough destroyers to do the intercepting. Unless the 1500-a-month quota was increased the deportation scheme would collapse and terrorism would be nourished by the unavoidable sharpening of military repression.[71]

Once again, therefore, the Foreign Office circularized its embassies in six Arab capitals to ask whether an increase to four thousand a month might take some of the heat out of the situation, especially now that the United Nations was to consider the whole matter. And once again the answer came back at high speed, a thoroughly predictable, unanimous and uncompromising negative.

Grafftey Smith reported from Jedda that any such concession would have 'disastrous effects' on public opinion. The foreign minister had spoken to him severely about Britain's failure to check Jewish terrorism, mentioning particularly the 'unavenged outrage' of the flogging of British soldiers. Ronald Campbell referred to the same incident in a cable from Cairo. The Egyptian press was suggesting that the Jews were the only people who knew how to deal with the British, that the British Empire was rapidly crumbling.

Stonehewer Bird wrote from Baghdad: 'It cannot be too often repeated that the Arabs regard immigration as a foreign invasion and the additional immigrants not as homeless victims of Hitlerism, but as valuable reinforcements for the Zionist forces.'[72] Bevin read all these reports and minuted on March 18th: 'In view of the answers I feel we had better stick to the present quota. We are doing our best to speed up the hearing.'[73]

The Jewish Agency, of course, were doing their best to speed up the immigration. On March 12th a Haganah crew successfully beached the *Susanna*. And although the army rounded up 350 of the immigrants, another 350 escaped into the Jewish community and three British sailors from the *St Bride's Bay* were drowned while pursuing immigrants in a small boat that overturned in the surf. On March 30th another 1750 immigrants from the *San Felipe* were caught and diverted to Cyprus.

On March 13th Cunningham cabled Creech-Jones: 'As you know, I have continually stressed that there is a real human issue involved in this problem, which has not yet been met.' Unless the quota was increased, he wrote, 'there is no way of stopping terrorism other than by outright war with the Jews'. But, as usual in the Palestine issue, one man's basic right was another man's intolerable injustice. William Houstoun-Boswall, British minister in Beirut, saw Cunningham's telegram and commented: 'The humanitarian issue which the High Commissioner stresses might have had some appeal, had Zionists not seen fit to use it as a means to secure sovereignty. And that is just what puts the Arabs off.'[74]

Therefore, although the Royal Navy were largely successful in intercepting the Haganah ships and diverting their passengers, the organizers of Aliya B were winning the battle politically, filling the Cyprus camps to bursting point, overtaxing the resources of the British army, navy and air force in the eastern Mediterranean, imposing unbearable pressure on the Palestine administration and branding Britain as inhuman in most of the world's press. And still they had not played their trump card, a 1814-ton four-deck river steamer, the *President Warfield*, soon to be renamed the *Exodus*.

10

The Honey and the Sting

IKE ARANNE, the Palmach captain of *Exodus*, went on
board for the first time in November 1946 in Norfolk,
Virginia: 'I could see that in many ways she was particularly suitable to
run the blockade. First of all there was her speed. She could do 17 knots
and short bursts of 20 knots. Then there was her size. She was by far the
biggest ship we had ever managed to get. Most important of all, she
was very flat bottomed, she drew only eight feet, which meant that she
could run where no destroyer could run. She offered us our best ever
chance of landing several thousand immigrants in Palestine in one operation.'

She had disadvantages too. She was not designed to sail in rough waters.
Although she had been pressed into US government service in 1942, taken
across the Atlantic and used as a British training ship off Devon, then in
1944 as a store ship off Normandy, she was designed as a ferry on the
Baltimore–Norfolk run in the calm waters of Chesapeake Bay. Shortly
after leaving Norfolk and venturing into rough seas on February 25th,
1947, she began shipping water through her hawsepipes, the holes for the
anchor chain, which were only a few feet above the water level, and her
heavy superstructure swayed from side to side. She radioed for help and
was escorted ignominiously back to Norfolk.

Repairs were necessary and money was short. Aranne and his forty-man
crew had to sell the ship's copperwork to pay the workmen who
strengthened the superstructure and cemented up the hawsepipes. They
also built two metal pipes right round the ship, one connected to the
boilers, the other to the fuel supply, the first designed to squirt intending
boarders with hot steam, the second with hot oil. At the end of this work,
on March 29th, the *President Warfield* put to sea again. This time the

weather was kind and the structure held. On April 10th she reached Marseilles.[1]

Two weeks later she anchored at Portovenere, a few miles from La Spezia, for the rest of the detailed fitting-out work. The main job was the construction of beds for 4500 people, beds of a quite extraordinary type. Micha Peri was the Haganah commander assigned to the ship in Europe: 'We needed to carry as many immigrants as possible. But this meant terrible conditions for their journey. The compartments were stacked up with 18 inches of width and two feet of headroom for each person and just enough room between the stacks for one person to pass. They had to stay in these bunks day and night like sardines in a tin, hardly moving, with only half an hour in every 24 hours for exercise on deck.'

By early June the bunks were ready and the ship was also equipped with barbed-wire defences, an elaborate radio system and a reserve steering gear below decks, in case the wheelhouse was captured. On June 12th she put to sea again with a certificate entitling her to sail only in coastal waters. An Italian gunboat followed her part of the way down the Italian coast-line, but after a few miles she turned sharply north-west back towards Marseilles. Already the 4500 passengers, mostly Jews from Poland, had been earmarked by Haganah officials.

Peri says: 'We had prepared papers, identity cards for each person, showing that we were going to Colombia in South America. The names were false, but the papers were genuine. We bought them from Colombian officials.' Using these documents, the Jews travelled by train from camps in Germany to Marseilles, where they were met and escorted to a Jewish Agency camp nearby, recently acquired from the French government, in preparation for their uncomfortable journey.

Meanwhile the Jewish Agency, in view of the UNSCOP investigation and the partial transfer of the conflict to the diplomatic arena, was looking for better relations with Britain. Inevitably this meant a worsening of their relations with the Irgun. On June 12th, the birthday of King George VI, almost all the Haganah men in Palestine jails were amnestied and released, the Agency flew the Union Jack next to the Star of David outside their Jerusalem headquarters and the Haganah blew up an Irgun arms dump.[2]

The inter-Zionist conflict spread to New York. The main Jewish bodies took great exception to the pro-Irgun advertisements of Peter Bergson and Ben Hecht, especially to being labelled in Hecht's Letter to the Terrorists as mere 'respectable and wealthy Jewish personalities'. The American League for a Free Palestine, they riposted, was a small group which spoke for itself alone. And terrorism was hostile to the spirit of Jewish religion and tradition.[3]

The Jewish Agency could nevertheless not ignore the fate of Alexander Rubowitz, a seventeen-year-old Lehi member who had disappeared without trace and whose fate remains officially unknown, even to this day. The *New York Herald Tribune* suggested that he might have been kidnapped by a police strongarm squad, tortured to death and handed over to a Bedouin for disposal.[4] The government announced that intensive efforts were being made to find Major Roy Farran, who had been held for questioning in connection with the case, had escaped from Allenby barracks and was rumoured to be in Syria. Farran was behaving in a most peculiar fashion. He held talks with Syrian leaders and was offered a senior post in the Syrian army. Fergusson was sent to Syria to talk to him and to persuade him to return. It was all very mysterious and undignified. A further source of tension was the imposition on June 16th, the actual day of the eleven-country UNSCOP team's arrival, of death sentences on three Irgun men captured after the Acre raid – Avshalom Haviv, Yaacov Weiss and Meir Nakar.

Clear evidence of a Haganah–British reconciliation emerged on June 18th, when an explosion in a building near Citrus House showed the existence of an Irgun tunnel, already 45 feet long, almost ready to blow the British military headquarters sky high. It emerged that the Haganah, having tried unsuccessfully to halt the Irgun operation by written and oral warnings, had sent a team to seal off the tunnel's opening. Zeev Werba, the team leader, had touched off a booby trap and been killed. His funeral was attended by twenty thousand people, including high-ranking British representatives, as Cunningham explained, 'in view of the fact that he lost his life while engaged in an operation which saved the lives of a number of British soldiers'.[5] The Irgun reacted scathingly to such obvious evidence of Jewish collaboration with the British oppressor.

But this collaboration in no way extended to the two cornerstones of Haganah activity, arms acquisition and illegal immigration. On the contrary, they believed that, while terrorists would discredit their case before UNSCOP, a demonstration of massive Jewish resolve to return to the Promised Land would reinforce it. On June 14th Aranne and his crew reached the small harbour of Port-de-Bouc, near Marseilles, and took on 315 tons of fuel oil, redoubling their efforts to bring about the great exodus, the landing in Palestine of one shipload of 4500 Jewish immigrants.

A crew member's diary, subsequently confiscated by British police, explained what was to happen: 'The ship must arrive in daylight, since the shores will be packed with crowds of Jews from Tel Aviv. We will then try to escape the escort by going between two ships, to enter territorial waters and then: full speed ahead! We shall attempt to beach the boat on the shore . . . Once we reach the shore our passengers will disperse in the crowd and it will be difficult to find them again.'[6]

Aranne says: 'I did very careful calculations to find out what would happen when we beached. When you beach a ship, there is an upthrust. And if you don't have buoyancy, you can capsize, especially with a lot of weight on the upper decks. First I did theoretical tests, then I checked them empirically by inclining the vessel and working out how much weight it took to incline it so many degrees. I was able to work out the metrocentric height and evaluate the ship's stability. In the end, after we'd stripped all excess weight off the upper decks. I was able to convince the crew that we could beach the ship without anything horrible happening.'

The British did their best to interfere with this inexorable process. On April 15th UN representative Alexander Cadogan pointed out to Trygve Lie that for illegal immigration to continue in parallel with the UNSCOP inquiry was dangerous and inherently unjust: 'I am therefore instructed to request you to appeal to all member states to take the strictest precautions in so far as they are concerned to prevent the transit through their territory and the departure from their ports of Jews attempting to enter Palestine illegally.'[7] Lie passed on the appeal, but with little result.

On July 7th High Commissioner Noel Charles complained to Dr Migliore of the Italian Interior Ministry about the intensive Zionist activity in his country – Haganah camps and truck depots, document forgers and teams of couriers helping Jews across the border from the French zone of Austria. Migliore replied that his police force was undermanned and that he was generally baffled by the problem. When they caught illegal entrants, they returned them across the border to Austria, but the French did nothing and the Jews simply came back into Italy by another route.[8] Charles's other diplomatic approaches were equally unsuccessful: 'The US Embassy here run away hard whenever the word "Jews" is said and the French are certainly not going to get involved.'[9]

James Cable of the Foreign Office was advised that the ship's certificate of seaworthiness, issued in Baltimore, allowed her to proceed only in fine weather and without passengers: 'I think we might inform Marseilles of this. If the local authorities are at all willing to collaborate, this might well serve them as an excuse for detaining ship.' Bevin wrote a personal letter to Foreign Minister Georges Bidault asking France to refuse oil.

coal, provisions, clearance, repair facilities or harbour facilities to the *President Warfield* and five other named ships.[10]

During the evening of July 9th the *President Warfield* slipped out of Port-de-Bouc and entered the small harbour of Sète, 65 miles to the west. British Consul Sydney Kay at once informed Paris that about five thousand Jewish passengers were being embarked and that he had complained to the Prefect of Montpellier, who had promised to investigate. Duff Cooper complained to the Foreign Ministry and was reassured that the ship was being held and the passengers forced to disembark. This detention was quite legal, since her certificate of seaworthiness did not allow her to carry passengers.

The *President Warfield* was now guarded and needed a pilot to take her from Sète through a narrow channel to the open sea. Micha Peri says that they paid a million francs for a pilot, but he never appeared and they had to set sail without him. John Grauel, an American Baptist minister accompanying the crew, spent the evening of July 11th talking and drinking whisky with the guards. At six o'clock the next morning they cut their cables, started their engines and moved off along the channel. Peri says: 'First the ropes got mixed up in the propellers. Two of the American boys dived down and removed them. Then we went aground in the channel, but we got off and by the morning we were in the open sea. The first thing we saw was a British aeroplane and a few hours later we were joined by a British ship.'

Bevin was quite furious when he received this news in Paris on July 12th. Visiting Georges Bidault at the Quai d'Orsay that same day, he took with him a stiff letter of complaint, pointing out the frequent British requests and equally frequent French promises on the subject of illegal Jewish immigration. He drew attention to the treaty between Britain and France, recently signed at Dunkirk, to the fact that Palestine was *sub judice* at the United Nations, to the 'extreme misery' of the immigrants themselves, encouraged by the controllers of 'this infamous traffic' to sell their possessions in order to buy 'at extravagant rates' their passage to Palestine.

What would be the feelings of the French government, he continued, if Britain were to facilitate the arrival of 'elements calculated to disturb the peace' in some French territory? He wrote in his report: 'I stated that we intended to make an example of this ship by obliging her to return to a French port with all her passengers and I counted on the French to cooperate by receiving her back and disembarking passengers. Mr Bidault agreed to this.'[11]

Irgun barrel bomb used in an attack on a Jerusalem police compound, October 1947.

h Officers' Club, Jerusalem, a few minutes after an explosion which killed eleven and injured people, March 1st, 1947.

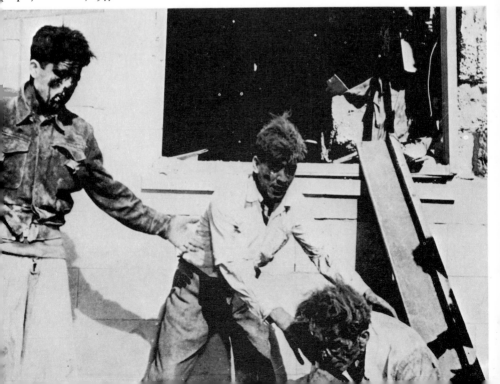

Brigadier George Johnson, commander of Operation Polly, at Lydda station during the evacuation of British wives and dependants, February 1947.

Jewish refugees from *President Warfield* walking to trains shortly after their return to Hamburg.

... of the Mandate: a photograph from the *Illustrated London News*, May 1948, with its orginal caption.

Azzam Pasha, Secretary-General of the Arab League.

David Ben Gurion, first Prime Minister of Israel

Ernest Bevin, British Foreign Secretary 1945–51.

Harry S. Truman, President of United States

Later that day Bevin called on Prime Minister Paul Ramadier to reinforce his complaint: 'I said that in the exercise of our responsibilities under the Mandate for Palestine we had received rather shabby treatment from other countries.' France should understand that her indulgence to Jewish 'unauthorized persons and troublemakers' might well cause alarm and dismay among the Arabs of French North Africa. He himself had taken drastic steps to make sure that British subjects caused no trouble in areas of French interest: 'Was it too much to ask that the French government should reciprocate in the matter of this illegal Jewish traffic, which was in any case largely a financial racket controlled from New York?'[12]

But it was too late, the bird had flown and none of Bevin's harsh words would bring her back to French territory – until, at least, she could be boarded off Palestine and escorted back by the Royal Navy. Creech-Jones communicated this decision and the reasons for it to Cunningham: 'It will be most discouraging to the organizers of this traffic, if the immigrants in the first ship for some weeks to evade the British "blockade" end up returning whence they came.'[13]

The Royal Navy knew nothing about this. Their job, they assumed, would be like all previous jobs – observation, interception, transhipment and internment in Cyprus. The frigate *Mermaid* was the first to shadow the *President Warfield*, then the destroyer *Cheviot*. Aranne remembers: 'Your King and Queen were visiting South Africa at the time and I remember saying that we must be getting a better naval escort than they had. I recognized some of the British sailors. We had met in the same bars and the same whorehouses in Marseilles.'

On July 13th Midshipman John Lawson of the *Ajax* saw her for the first time: 'The *PW* was a typical-looking river steamer – hard chine, high superstructure, a very tall, black conspicuous funnel and a bridge like a summer house.' On July 15th she stopped twice to re-cement her hawse-pipes. *Cheviot* offered assistance, which was politely refused, inquired her destination and received no answer. That same day the *Cheviot* was relieved by another destroyer, the *Childers*.

Captain Dymock Watson, appointed to command the operation from the destroyer *Chequers*, told *Childers* to make contact with the Jewish ship and to report as much as he could discover of her anti-boarding preparations. 'Intelligence reported that a strong force of Irgun terrorists had been put on board,' he writes. He was misinformed, of course. The 'strong-arm men' on board were strictly Haganah. But Tony Bailey, George Kitchen and the other *Childers* officers did not take long to observe the strength of the *President Warfield*'s defences. The boarding operation was going to be far more difficult than any previously carried out by the Royal Navy.

The unusual Jewish ship presented many special problems. Her rubbing strake – a six-inch-wide band of iron-coated wood running round the ship six feet above water level, a normal protection for river boats that have to bump against jetties – was strong enough to stove in the side of any small warship coming against her in choppy conditions. On the other hand, like all merchant ships she had no internal sub-divisions. If a destroyer were to ram her, she might easily sink her in a matter of minutes or else cause her to list right over, with consequent panic and loss of life among the over-crowded passengers. All destroyer captains were warned to avoid the slightest risk of any such accident, the consequences of which would have been politically disastrous.

Bailey says: 'The first thing we noticed was that all ladders except one leading from the promenade deck to the boat deck had been removed. I thought to myself, "Aha, this man has done his homework. No doubt his other preparations will be equally thorough." ' He realized that the boarding parties would not be able to board in the normal way from the destroyers' fo'c'sle. With the help of sextant angles taken from a position on the beam, he worked out on the basis of the *President Warfield*'s known length, 320 feet, the height of each of her decks above water level. The height of the fore deck and poop was sixteen feet, that of the promenade deck twenty-four feet, that of the boat deck thirty-two feet.

The problem was that the destroyers' fo'c'sles were only nineteen feet above water level and so would give boarders access only to the lowest deck of the Jewish ship, the fore deck. The boarders would then be stuck in a 'killing area', unable to move while immigrants bombarded them from above with cans of food and other missiles. The middle deck, the promenade deck, was blocked off with life rafts and sealed from the boat deck above with barbed wire and chicken wire. Boarders would have no chance whatever of climbing from the lower decks up to the boat deck. And it was this deck that was the primary objective and the key to the problem, since it housed the control centre of the ship – the wheelhouse.

Bailey therefore concluded that some means must be found to board directly on to the boat deck. But how could this be done? The boat deck was level with the highest point of each destroyer's superstructure, the bridge, which was more than six feet inboard of the ship's side. The gap was too wide for a heavily equipped man to leap. Bailey and his men came up with the answer – a special wooden boarding platform, complete with guard rails and protective netting. Within a day they had designed and built the platform at bridge level on their starboard side. Its potential was studied and reported to Watson on the *Chequers*, as a result of which he had a similar platform built himself and ordered his other destroyer captains, Commander G. C. Fardell of the *Chieftain* and Lieutenant-Commander R. H. C. Wyld of the *Charity*, to do the same.

Meanwhile the Irgun's main concern was to save the lives of their three condemned comrades. The UNSCOP team pointed to 'the possible un-favourable repercussions' of executions carried out during their investiga-tion. Encouraged by this intervention the Irgun asked UNSCOP to call the three prisoners as witnesses 'in order to establish the charges of mal-treating prisoners and killing wounded'. The British authorities rejected such suggestions. In their view, UNSCOP was in Palestine to work out a final political settlement, not to interfere in the day-to-day affairs of Mandatory rule, which would continue until that settlement was imple-mented.

Once again, therefore, the Irgun looked for hostages. But they found this a much harder task than they had in June 1946 or January 1947. The remaining British community was carefully protected in guarded com-pounds. Judge Windham, who in January had walked across fields to his Tel Aviv courtroom, was later taken there by armed escort. John Briance remembers Teddy Kollek joking to him as the British withdrew more and more behind their barbed wire, 'Congratulations! You have finally suc-ceeded in rounding yourselves up.'

Begin writes: 'We tried to find officers. Several times in Jerusalem and Herzlia we almost had within our grasp Very Important Persons, but were prevented by something or other from consummating their capture.' Only on July 12th did the Irgun achieve some modest success. Clifford Martin and Mervyn Paice, two intelligence corps sergeants, spent that Saturday evening in a Nathanya café with a Jewish army clerk. They then left the café and walked with him through the town. They were in civilian clothes, they were unarmed, they were out of camp after permitted hours and they were two men rather than a group of four – all serious breaches of army regulations. As they reached the middle of Nathanya, an Irgun team drew up in a car beside them, clubbed them, bundled them in and chloroformed them.

The two sergeants were taken to a specially built cell under a Nathanya diamond factory, an almost perfect hiding-place, a three-metre cube totally sealed from the factory floor by a thick layer of sand, airtight and soundproofed, with only a tiny well-insulated entrance hatch. Amihai Paglin had equipped the box with the barest requirements for his prisoners' survival – a canvas bucket, a week's food supply and two oxygen cylinders, which they were taught to turn on at regular intervals, to keep the air breathable.[14]

Paice and Martin could sense no fresh air, light or sound from the outside world. Every few days they were taken out, the bucket changed, the cell aired and the food replenished, but always at great speed, because thousands of troops had sealed Nathanya and every building was being combed, some again and again. In these grim surroundings they spent their indistinguishable days and nights, deprived of all senses except their own conversation and nightmare thoughts of what would happen if the three Irgun men were executed.

UNSCOP, the UN Palestine Committee, spent most of July hearing the Jewish case from Shertok and other Agency witnesses. On July 8th Weizmann gave evidence in his private capacity, advocating partition as the only remedy that combined finality, equality and justice.[15] Henry Gurney gave evidence in camera. Then very soon, to his fury, a full summary of his remarks appeared in the Jewish press. The Arab Higher Committee and other Palestinian groups, shattered by their recent diplomatic failures, especially the apparent defection of the Soviet Union, boycotted UNSCOP's entire proceedings. And all this time the Committee's work was complicated, if not overshadowed, by rumours about the *President Warfield* and fears for the lives of the three condemned Jews and the two British hostages. On July 13th Brigadier Rodney Moore summoned Mayor of Nathanya Oved Ben Ami, warning him that the army 'would take action which might cause inconvenience to the population as a whole' if the sergeants were not released at once. Ben Ami, the *Palestine Post* and other official Jewish spokesmen described the kidnapping as a provocative act, which would in no way encourage the High Commissioner to exercise his prerogative of mercy.[16]

The *President Warfield* was making her way across the Mediterranean towards Palestine. On July 14th naval Commander-in-Chief Algernon Willis cabled the escorting vessels *Ajax, Childers* and *Cheviot*: 'Now that *Warfield* is well clear of Malta you should start the verbal softening up process on her, having first asked where she is bound. The softening should be along the lines that passengers will not be allowed to land in Palestine, that no one wishes passengers any harm, but it is the duty of the Royal Navy to see that the law is carried out and H.M. ships will if necessary use overwhelming force to carry out this duty, and that resistance is useless and can only lead to injury. This should be passed in as many languages as you have available.' The order ended significantly, 'Nothing is to be said about the destination of the passengers after the ship has been seized.'

By July 17th the *Cheviot* had dropped away and the British escort consisted of four 'CH' class destroyers – *Childers, Chequers, Charity* and *Chieftain* – as well as the *Ajax* and the *Cardigan Bay*. The boarding parties, toughened by the Malta assault courses and constant physical training, were practising their leaps and climbs, sometimes in gas respirators, preparing for the split second when their skills would be required. Watson reported that morning, 'All ships have been examining *Warfield*. Large nameboard showing and flying flag of Honduras. Large number of people on deck, all quiet and peaceful. Propaganda being passed and understood in both English and German. Replies in American.' Later he added, '*Chequers* was treated to a fine vocal rendering of "The Yanks are Coming" by a male voice choir.'

The Jewish ship briefly entered Egyptian territorial waters off Cape Brulos. This caused the British some concern. 'With her shallow draught she was capable of hugging the coastline right round to the Palestine border in waters where the destroyers could not enter. But, to general British relief, she merely fixed her position and then altered course to the north-east towards Tel Aviv, where the Haganah were preparing to clear the beaches and receive her. The British army was also out in force 'hopping up and down the coastline', as Watson recalls, waiting anxiously for his radio signal that the ship had broken the blockade, in which case it would be their job to try to round up the immigrants in the face of serious resistance from the Haganah.

Watson's final orders to his ships explained, 'My object is to ensure the quick arrest of *President Warfield* by getting over the greatest number of men in the shortest possible time.' They set out times for the destroyers to 'close, illuminate and otherwise wake up' the Jewish ship during the night. The cruiser *Ajax* was to stay between her and the coastline, to prevent any dash for the beaches. The destroyers were to position themselves on either side of her, making sure that none of her passengers or crew could see the boarding platforms, some of which had been built to port of the bridge, others to starboard.

Watson's orders, marked 'secret – to be destroyed by fire when complied with', were passed across to the ships by heaving line, to avoid possible interception of radio signals, and details were then clarified by ship-to-ship loud hailer. The boarding parties, under the command of Lieutenant R. J. G. McPherson of the *Chieftain*, were to jump, seize the wheelhouse and establish it as a citadel, then launch a sortie into the bowels of the ship to gain control of the engine room and steering gear. To help them they had sketches of the ship, made when she was off Britain in 1944.

At nightfall the flotilla passed the Suez Canal and the British ships increased their pressure with feint attacks and so-called 'annoyance runs'. Aranne says, 'They kept shouting at us in German, "Your leaders have deceived you" and "Turn back". We shouted back, "Speak English." ' The loudspeaker din and searchlight glare, applied at regular intervals by each destroyer in turn, was designed to keep the Jews awake and jar their nerves, to lower their resistance and effectiveness in the forthcoming battle.

During the early part of the night Watson noticed women and children being moved up to the promenade and boat decks, leaving the young men ready for action down on the fore deck. The boarding-platform trick seemed to be working. The wheelhouse was almost unguarded. At 2 a.m. he radioed his superior officer Commodore de Salis, 'There is some prospect that resistance will be slight.' Forty-five minutes later he recorded that the *President Warfield* was 'approaching territorial waters' west of Gaza. She was, in fact, still on the high seas about twenty miles from the Palestine coast. He nevertheless gave the order to board.

Childers and *Chieftain* closed up alongside their quarry. Aranne says: 'They suddenly put their horrible searchlights on us and shouted, "You are now entering the territorial waters of Palestine." We shouted back that it was a complete lie. We were twenty miles from the coast. We hadn't expected anything to happen until morning. We were quite staggered.'

Aranne sounded his ship's siren, which stuck and blared continuously for the next half hour, rang full speed and turned hard to port, leaving *Chieftain* standing. *Childers* tried to come alongside, but the highly manoeuvrable Jewish ship, whose turning circle was half that of a destroyer, turned away to starboard and escaped. It was several minutes before *Chieftain* was able to catch up, but once she did so the destroyers had the *President Warfield* in an ideal position, squeezed between the two of them.

She would have to touch a destroyer now, whichever way she turned. In the event she turned to port again, enabling *Childers* to sidle in at the correct angle by reversing the outer screw, and bring the new boarding platform within a few yards of the wheelhouse door. As the two ships converged, Lieutenant K. P. Shallow stood poised on his platform with his team of fifteen men in two flights equipped with helmets, truncheons, wire cutters, a crowbar and battering tam, teargas grenades and semi-inflated lifebelts. Officers and petty officers only carried pistols. Their orders were to use such physical force as was necessary to seize the ship, but to use firearms only in self-defence. The immigrants likewise were ordered to resist tooth and nail, but wherever possible to avoid fatal casualties, as was the Haganah rule. During the run-in, Shallow's petty officer's arm was broken by a bully beef tin, so he did not jump.

At 3.05 a.m. the gap closed between the boarding platform of the *Childers* and the boat deck of the *President Warfield*. But, to achieve this momentary contact halfway along the length of the two ships, Bailey had to steer a course parallel to that of his opposite number. Then, as soon as the ships touched, the water pressure between the two bows, cutting through the water at considerable speed, increased to such an extent that it bounced the two ships apart. The boarders had only a few seconds in which to make their jump, but that moment of contact was long enough for Shallow and five men to leap across to the other ship's deck only a few yards from the wheelhouse.

Bailey says: 'We had two secret weapons. The first was our platform. The second was our Chinese crackers. The immigrants hadn't come across these before. They make a very loud noise, they deafen you for a moment, but do no permanent damage.' The Haganah crew were used to blinding searchlights and high-pressure hoses, which they ignored, and to teargas grenades, which they threw either overboard or back at the British ships. But they were taken aback by the platform and the Chinese crackers.

'I could never understand how those sailors got on to my boat deck. I thought they must have swung across on ropes,' says Aranne, who was in the wheelhouse at the time. This element of surprise, combined with the stunning effect of the crackers, which brought the Jews in the vicinity to their knees, gave the six boarders their chance. The immigrants' missiles, mainly cans of food, bounced off the sailors' tin helmets as they burst into the wheelhouse and ejected the four Jewish crew members, including Aranne and his American mate Bill Bernstein, whom they coshed severely over the head when he refused to leave the wheel.

The British had gained a success and were able to turn the ship's head to seaward, but had by no means won the battle. Aranne took Bernstein down to his cabin, then went immediately to the steering room above the rudder and disconnected the rudder from the wheelhouse. This was something the British had not expected. Although they had captured a valuable defensible citadel, which was later to become a rallying point for other boarders and a bridgehead for sorties into the bowels of the ship, the initiative passed to the Jews. For twenty minutes the boarders choked on teargas and smoke canisters left by the crew, while they feverishly

defended themselves against continuous assaults. *Childers*'s other boarding party, on the deck below the special platform, found itself confronted
by wire netting and had been unable to jump, so the six were on their
own, with little hope of immediate reinforcements. Aranne says: 'They
were very brave. I take my hat off to them. To jump into a sea of people
under these conditions is no picnic.'

Aranne took a compass with him to the emergency steering room, but
it worked badly because of the large quantity of metal surrounding it in
the bowels of the ship. Several times he went up on deck to check his
ship's direction from the stars. He then tried to work out to what degree
his compass in the room below deviated from magnetic north. But it was a
rough-and-ready means of navigation, especially with his ship zigzagging
to left and right like a snake, and he could not maintain his course towards
Tel Aviv.

His violent and skilful manoeuvring nevertheless made the destroyers'
task very difficult. For half an hour no men could be got across to reinforce
Shallow and the others. Jewish crew members spent the time hacking at
the roof with axes. Aranne says: 'We made a hole and I shouted through
it. I told them that we were a long way from territorial waters, that they
were guilty of an act of piracy and they ought to clear the wheelhouse.'
He then returned below to the engine-room and steering gear. An
American crew member fired two rifle shots through the hole. One of
Shallow's men returned the fire. But no one was hit.

The Jewish defenders brought some of their Haganah men up to the
boat deck and, as other destroyers converged on them, operated their
steam and oil jets. The steam was ineffective, Watson reported, because of
insufficient pressure. Its heat could just be felt by sailors on *Chieftain*'s
fo'c'sle. The boarders, high up on their platforms, were not affected at all.

The oil weapon was more successful. Large amounts of it were pumped
on to *Chieftain*'s decks, making them slippery and unpleasant to work on.
Watson writes in his report: 'Attempts were made by Jews to fire this oil
by throwing over seaboots filled with oily waste and ignited, suitcases
filled with wood shavings and ignited and by distress flares. Fire was
averted by prompt action in ditching these objects.'

Lieutenant MacPherson boarded at about 3.20 a.m. with three other
Chieftain men. At once they were attacked by Jewish defenders with
assorted missiles – cans of food, buckets, bottles, crowbars and scaffolding
poles – and driven into a cabin, where they were held prisoner by an
angry mob. He remembers two immigrants from Poland, each with a
number tattooed on one arm, telling him 'in no uncertain terms' that they

did not intend being put back in another concentration camp by the British. Lieutenant G. Pearse also boarded with four men from *Charity*. They too were driven into cabins by hails of missiles.

Bailey's second successful run was not until 3.32 a.m., three-quarters of an hour after the first. Lieutenant Stein and four others jumped from the platform and made it to the wheelhouse, where they joined Shallow and the original team. Five minutes later he got *Childers* alongside again and another eight men jumped, but suddenly *President Warfield* altered speed and part of her lifeboat equipment banged against the boarding platform, causing it to collapse. While he was extricating his ship, his bows swung round and smashed into the wooden side of his adversary. He remembers his searchlights picking out the startled faces of Jewish immigrants lying in their bunks a few feet away.

Under cover of this incident Lieutenant D. G. Gill and three others took the opportunity to leap from the flag deck and claw their way up the Jewish ship's protective chicken wire with their fingers. They too reached the wheelhouse. A few minutes later, around four o'clock, Mac-Pherson and his team escaped from their cabin and also reached the wheelhouse. There was now a considerable British force in what had once been the ship's control centre. But apart from what MacPherson described as 'a stream of blasphemous exhortations to quit', no action was being taken against them. Control had passed an hour earlier to the Haganah officers below.

Bailey writes in his report, 'The *PW* certainly presented a fantastic spectacle as she steamed at full speed through the night, keeled under rudder, with two enormous Star of David banners streaming from her mastheads and illuminated by our 20-inch searchlights. Her wailing siren gave the impression of a wounded cow bellowing through the night, as it fled from some unknown terror.'

W. J. Williamson, a petty officer on the *Chequers*, writes: 'Our job was to hurl teargas grenades and fearsome pyrotechnics into every opening in the ship as we drew alongside. This was "to wear the buggers out", we were told. I can assure you that I now often cringe at the memory, considering that the below-deck spaces were packed with women and children.'

But the *President Warfield* was no passive or helpless victim. All night the immigrants and crew kept up a radio commentary on the battle, which thousands of the Yishuv heard with admiration and enthusiasm. At 3.47 a.m. Bailey had to report minor hull damage: 'This chap launched a liferaft from the *PW* straight on to my fo'c'sle. I saw him do it. And I remember how thoroughly pleased with himself he looked after he'd done it.'

Williamson recalls that the same happened to the *Chequers*: 'First of all they dropped an anchor and a boat on us. Then we were heavily pelted with iron stantions and canned food. (We used the food later to supplement our Navy rations.) The men we got on board were attacked with bottles and clubs. They all wore cricketers' abdominal protectors, because the women used to kick them between the legs. I dare say that our men were pretty tough. They had to be, otherwise they'd just have been thrown off.'

The battle was going badly for the British flotilla. A teargas grenade thrown by a Jewish immigrant landed in Captain Watson's jacket, temporarily blinding everyone on the bridge and putting *Chequers* out of action for several minutes. The wind was force six and conditions quite unsuitable for bringing destroyers alongside a large ship. In spite of using every single fender they possessed, both *Chieftain* and *Charity* had their sides buckled by the Jewish ship's rubbing strake.

The destroyers managed to get forty men on board, twenty-three of them from *Childers*, and by four o'clock most of these were in the wheelhouse. A few were thrown into the sea by the immigrants. A few others were still locked in cabins. Aranne now came up with an original and ruthless plan to ensure the fulfilment of his mission: 'I suggested taking these chaps out of the cabins and hanging them over the side of the ship on ropes, like fenders. If we'd done that, the destroyers would have kept away. They wouldn't have risked crushing their own men.'

Now that the wheelhouse no longer controlled the ship, the second part of MacPherson's orders became doubly important. Keeping about half the party in the wheelhouse, he sent a team out under Shallow and Pearse to seize the emergency steering gear and stop the engines. But they found the engine room and boiler room behind locked steel doors and the steering engine protected with a barbed wire screen. They had no means of breaking through these barriers.

Just before four o'clock *Chieftain* signalled, 'It appears that the boarding party is being overwhelmed.' This was not the case. The wheelhouse was well manned and the sailors taking part in the sortie were walking between groups of Jews without opposition. By 4.30 it seemed to them that the Jewish immigrants and crew had 'had enough'. But they still had no way of gaining control of the ship and turning her away from the coast.

At this point political disagreement arose among the Jewish leaders on board. Ike Aranne and Micha Peri, both Lalmach men, believed that their passengers could and should be landed. They had lost the wheelhouse, but they could still steer the ship from below. Even if they missed the planned Tel Aviv beaching area, they would certainly be able to run the ship aground at some point on the Palestine coast. They had hundreds of lifebelts and thousands of feet of three-inch cord with cork floats. American crew member Bernard Marks explained to Watson later: 'It had been intended for one thousand people to swim ashore and the remainder to get ashore with the assistance of buoyed ropes.'

Aranne believed and still believes that such a landing was possible. It would involve some risk of loss of life by drowning in the surf, but thousands would get ashore and be spirited away into Jewish settlements. For the immigrants themselves it would be the end of their journey, the crown of their hopes. It would also be a massive political success, a proof to the world that the British were incapable of keeping Jewish immigrants out of Palestine. Mass illegal immigration, which by mid-1947 was the whole basis of the Haganah's struggle against Britain, would become a feasible possibility.

Also, although Aranne and Peri did not know it at the time, Captain Watson was coming to believe that the battle was lost, that it might be impossible to prevent the *President Warfield* from beaching. He had no prospect of capturing the below-decks control centre and he believed that his boarding parties were being overwhelmed. He told Bailey later that he was thinking of reporting failure and warning the army to be ready to arrest the immigrants as they landed.

But Aranne, although captain of the ship, was subject to orders on policy from Yosi Har-El, the senior representative on board both of the Haganah and of the organizers of illegal immigration (Mossad le-Aliya). And they believed that the landing of the immigrants in Palestine was only a second priority. The first priority was the political effect of the operation on world public opinion. Aranne says: 'Mossad le-Aliya not only suggested, they gave us orders that this ship was to be used as a big demonstration with banners to show how poor and weak and helpless we were, and how cruel the British were. I was told to make as much of a demonstration as possible, but not to let the fight go too far.'

Bailey points out that by 4.30 a.m. the Jewish passengers and crew were in a sad and battered state. Their ship was holed on both sides, was taking water and could have been in danger of sinking. Two hundred Jews were in urgent need of medical attention. Two had been killed and Bernstein was dying. And, although in theory they still controlled the ship, the effect of the metal surroundings on their compass below decks would not allow them to steer an accurate course. The sight of British sailors walking up and down the ship unmolested was a further blow to Jewish morale.

Bailey believes, therefore, that the technical success of the boarding operation, especially the first assault on the wheelhouse, was the main factor in inducing the Jewish leaders to 'call it a day' and start negotiating surrender terms. Aranne, on the other hand, maintains that the decision to negotiate was a political one, based on Mossad le-Aliya's primary propaganda aim. His own advice was to continue the fight, but the political leaders felt the overriding need, especially during the UNSCOP visit, to show the refugees to the world in the most pitiable state possible.

MacPherson writes that chaplain John Grauel made one final attempt to achieve victory, imploring him in the name of humanity, since the ship was sinking, to evacuate the wheelhouse and hand control back to the Jewish crew, who would then make for the nearest land. These pleas were reinforced, he writes, by a hysterical American shouting that babies were dying and women drowning in the bilges. He refused, insisting instead on a hand-over of command by the Jewish captain. He would then send for a medical team and sail the ship to Haifa.

Unwillingly, therefore, and to the great relief of Captain Watson, who was beginning to sense the possibility of failure, Aranne surrendered command to his American 'shadow' captain Bernard Marks and at about five o'clock the latter agreed with MacPherson to place the ship under British control. A medical team under Surgeon-Lieutenant D. C. S. Bett came on board to find three Jews dead or dying and twenty-eight in need of hospitalization. The rest of the two hundred received first-aid. Most of the British boarders also needed medical attention, twenty out of twenty-three in the case of *Childers*. In view of the declared policy of both sides in the conflict to avoid the use of firearms and other lethal weapons, these were heavy casualties.

Both sides nevertheless felt that they had won a victory. The Royal Navy were glad to have maintained the efficiency of their blockade, overcoming with courage and ingenuity the fierce resistance of the Jewish passengers and crew. Bailey believes that it can be claimed that the arrest of the *President Warfield* was technically the most difficult boarding operation ever carried out in peace or war. Both he and Watson, speaking (they believe) for all the British officers involved, express their admiration for the skill and imaginative approach of Aranne and his crew, as well as for their resolution in defence against the largest and most highly trained squadron ever employed to arrest a single ship.

Aranne and his crew failed to land the immigrants in Palestine. But, as Har-El had predicted, they won a stupendous victory in terms of world public opinion. The crew and immigrants continued their radio broadcasts throughout July 18th. John Grauel spoke to the eagerly waiting corps of American correspondents. Aranne and Peri spoke in Hebrew. A choir of immigrant children sang the 'Hatikva'. All this was received on radio sets in Palestine and carefully reported in the world's press.

As they approached Haifa around 3 o'clock that afternoon, Aranne asked for one last chance to turn his ship hard to starboard at full speed and run it on to a convenient beach. But once again he was overruled. He and a few other key Palestinian Jews then withdrew to secret hiding places in the ship, where they would wait for a day or two, until there was a chance to sneak ashore. A strong military force awaited the *President Warfield* on the Haifa quayside as she steamed in at 4 o'clock.

Emil Sandström and Valado Simič, the UNSCOP delegates from Sweden and Yugoslavia, watched her arrive, preceded by the *Ajax* and followed by two destroyers, gashed open on both sides, her decks black with fuel oil squirted at the boarders. Railings were ripped off, liferafts lay all askew and cables dangled from the bridge. There were children looking out of the portholes, British sailors with bloodstained clothes and head bandages. The whole scene was filmed and photographed.

The women and children disembarked first. The stretcher cases were removed to hospital. The rest were searched and relieved of fountain pens, water bottles, tins of food and any sharp object that could be used for self-mutilation, in readiness for embarkation in the three cage ships. Husbands and wives were reassured that they would not be separated. Every few minutes depth charges were exploded in the harbour to discourage Haganah frogmen. By 9 p.m. the open wired-up hull of the *Ocean Vigour* was full and she sailed out of Haifa back across the Mediterranean. By the early hours of the next day, July 19th, the other two ships sailed. But no one on board – immigrants, soldiers or crew – knew the destination that Bevin had decided in Paris on July 12th, the fact that all but a handful of the 4554 immigrants who had left Sète – 1600 men, 1282 women, 1017 teenagers and 655 children – were on their way back to France. On July 20th the *Palestine Post* headed its account of their departure: 'Expected in Cyprus this morning.'

Major M. C. Gray and 170 soldiers were in charge of security on board the *Empire Rival*. Only after he had been at sea for six hours was he allowed to open his sealed orders and discover his destination. He called the Jewish representatives and told them that they were not going to

Cyprus: 'They told me they knew this already. They'd worked it out from the stars. I told them that my orders were to take them back to Port-de-Bouc. They said that in that case they were going on hunger strike. I told them they could do as they pleased. They treated me coldly, with reserve, not with hostility. From time to time they talked to me about the persecution of Jews, tried to make me see their point of view. But I had my orders and there was nothing much I could say in reply.'

Bevin had not realized at this stage what a Pandora's box he had opened by his July 12th decision 'to make an example of this ship', or the fact that the boarding operation, although brilliant from the purely technical point of view, was a political failure. 'It is of course most undesirable that any admission should be made that vessel was boarded on high seas,'[17] noted Cunningham. But everyone knew that this was the case. The New York daily *P.M.* wrote that, since the ship was seized outside territorial waters, the killing of Bernstein was murder. At a twenty-thousand-strong meeting in New York's Madison Square Park on July 24th there was talk of arresting the British naval officers involved on charges of piracy.[18]

Ambassador Duff Cooper, close friend and wartime colleague of Winston Churchill, warned Bevin what was likely to happen as early as July 18th: 'Forcible removal from British ships at a French port is likely to provide lurid anti-British propaganda, to which French public opinion may well be receptive in view of memories of German persecution of the Jews under occupation. Man in street is totally ignorant of Palestine problems and sees only in these illicit immigrants survivors of a persecuted race seeking refuge in their national home.'[19] Nevertheless Bevin replied to Paris the next day, the day of the three ships' departure from Haifa: 'Guards have been instructed to use whatever force may be required in order to deliver immigrants into French hands.'[20]

The Foreign Office hoped that the 4554 Colombian visas, improperly supplied by the consul-general in Marseilles, would nevertheless be honoured, in which case Britain would arrange with France to transport the immigrants to South America. A circular was sent to British missions overseas to anticipate the unfavourable publicity, comparing the large number of passengers carried by the tiny *President Warfield* with those accommodated in a normal passenger ship and pointing out her clear breaches of various international conventions on the protection of life at sea.

On July 23rd the French Council of Ministers spelt out the exact meaning of Georges Bidault's July 12th agreement to the return of immigrants. The three British ships now at sea would be admitted to a French port.

If the Jews then disembarked willingly, they would be fed and cared for and eventually freed, either to live in France or to go elsewhere. But, said Minister for ex-Servicemen François Mitterand, no measures would be taken to force or pressurize them into landing.[21] This was not what Bevin had expected or understood from his French colleague's earlier assurance.

Duff Cooper therefore issued another warning: 'The forcible carrying ashore of 4500 people of all ages and both sexes will not only be a very severe strain on the endurance of those charged with the task, but will also afford a most unedifying spectacle, of which full advantage will doubtless be taken by journalists and photographers.'[22] The French authorities would refuse to cooperate in the task and might even refuse the British soldiers permission to carry it out. The latter would then be exposed to charges of brutality as well as to ridicule. Cooper suggested that, if the immigrants insisted on staying on board, the three ships would have to put back to sea.

Bevin replied on July 25th that, while he understood Cooper's anxiety, there could be no question of accepting his proposal: 'If the transports were to leave France with some of their passengers on board, they would have to land them in Cyprus. There is no alternative destination. To carry these illegal immigrants to Cyprus after all would certainly expose us to ridicule. It would also amount to acknowledging defeat . . .'

On July 29th the three ships reached Port-de-Bouc. René Colaveri of the local prefecture was taken by launch to the *Runnymede Park* and received by Lieutenant-Colonel M. L. Gregson, the officer in charge of the convoy. He was then taken to the edge of the grille that enclosed the immigrants, where he read the French government's offer of asylum: 'They will be given asylum on the national soil, where they will enjoy all the liberties which France traditionally bestows on those who fight for human freedom.'[23]

Micha Peri was one of the Haganah men who stayed with the immigrants on the return voyage: 'Our people in France were very well organized. They sent us messages in small boats, asking us not to go ashore. But imagine what the French offer meant to someone who had been in a concentration camp – work, money, somewhere to stay. And imagine the conditions on board – 1500 people all living in the hold of a steel ship in mid-summer in the Mediterranean. It was like an oven. We were given food and water, but some of the immigrants were almost naked. They'd lost everything in the fight off Palestine. It was a temptation.'

Aranne says that administrative pressure, the threat of ostracism, was enough to dissuade the immigrants from accepting the French offer. Physical pressure was not necessary. A handful of immigrants accepted the offer, thereby opting out of the Zionist enterprise for ever. The rest refused it outright. Reuters correspondent Boyd France spoke to the immigrants on the *Ocean Vigour* from a launch and asked them whether they intended to land. They answered with shouts of 'Nein, nein,' and a chorus of the 'Hatikvah'. They put up Star of David flags and one enterprising group raised a British naval ensign with a black swastika sewn on to the red background.

Duff Cooper reported: 'The French press are making the most of the situation that now exists at Port-de-Bouc, which is as I ventured to foretell most unedifying.' The communist *Humanité* described the three ships as 'a floating Auschwitz', *Combat* as 'cages for wild beasts'. *Figaro* reported that the incident had brought more tension into British-French relations than had existed since 1945. The arrogant British, it seemed, were for their own imperial designs forcing France to participate in acts of obvious brutality. The rights of the Arabs and the other nuances of the Palestine problem were not being discussed. Once again Cooper begged Bevin to withdraw the ships from French waters and once again, on July 30th, Bevin refused, insisting that the local police be given instructions 'to cooperate in disembarking volunteers and non-volunteers alike'.[24]

It was an unfortunate coincidence, to put it mildly, that the day of the three ships' arrival in Port-de-Bouc was also the day when the three Irgun men were hanged in Acre prison. 'Do not grieve too much. What we have done we did out of conviction,' was the message they passed to their families through Chief Rabbi Nissim Ohana.[25] Supporters of the Zionist cause, while deploring the hangings, immediately pleaded with the Irgun to spare the lives of the two sergeants. The Vaad Leumi declared that any act of reprisal would be 'a bloodthirsty deed contrary to all human standards'. Mervyn Paice's father wrote to Begin that his son was an innocent caught up in a tragic political situation and had never been anti-Zionist. At the United Nations in New York Alexander Cadogan described the reprisal principle, under which his two fellow-countrymen's lives were at risk, as one of the most evil features of the recent common enemy.

But the Irgun had made up their minds. 'We had nothing against the two boys personally. We just wanted to stop the hangings,' says Haim Landau, then Irgun chief of staff. Samuel Katz writes: 'The decision to apply retaliation had been taken months earlier, after we had warned the British to observe the prisoner-of-war convention.' Already the Irgun had held a trial of the two men, allegedly following an inquiry into their criminal anti-Hebrew activities, in which they were charged with 'membership of the British criminal-terrorist organization', the British army of occupation, which was responsible for torture, murder, espionage and illegal entry into the Jewish homeland. A notice posted on the walls of Haifa announced: 'The court has found the two guilty of all charges and sentenced them to hanging on their necks until their soul would leave them.'[26]

On hearing the news of the Acre executions, Amihai Paglin drove to Nathanya with some fellow Irgun men, opened the prison box under the diamond factory and extracted the first sergeant. The man was dazed by the light and confused by lack of oxygen. He was hooded, placed on a chair and tied by the wrists and ankles. He asked his unseen escorts whether they were going to hang him, then whether he could leave a message. Paglin told him there was no time. They placed a noose around his neck, Paglin gestured and one of the men kicked the chair away. The Irgun team then hanged the second sergeant, placed the bodies in a jeep, drove them three miles to a eucalyptus grove in the government forestry station of Tel Zur, suspended them from a tree and placed a mine in the ground underneath the spot where they hung, between the two bodies.[27] (In 1977 Paglin was appointed the Israeli government's anti-terrorism adviser. A few months later he was killed in an automobile accident.)

On July 30th the Irgun notices announced: 'The request of the condemned men for clemency has been rejected. The sentence has been carried out.' The execution, it continued, was not a reprisal, but an ordinary legal act by the Underground court, liable to be applied to all 'who belong to the criminal Nazi-British army of occupation'. But the day passed and the bodies were not found, in spite of intensive searching by British and Jewish forces. There were still many who could not believe that the Irgun had done it. At the end of the day, fearful of the danger to themselves if their mine was set off by a Haganah patrol, the Irgun telephoned the Nathanya Municipality, warning them about the mine and giving them the map reference of the spot where the bodies hung.

They were found at seven o'clock the next morning (July 31st) by a Jewish police patrol, who touched nothing, merely reported their find to headquarters. Shortly afterwards a party of troops, police, civilian officials and journalists made their way to the eucalyptus grove and, advancing gingerly behind sappers with mine detectors, made their way through the trees. After five minutes a voice called out: 'Here they are.' Captain D. H. Galetti of the Royal Engineers then asked all civilians to withdraw while his men thoroughly checked the area around the bodies.

The area was pronounced safe and the party reassembled around the grisly scene. Photographers took pictures of the two hanging hooded men and one of these, labelled 'Picture that will shock the world', appeared the next day across the front of the London *Daily Express*. Galetti then cut the first rope with a knife fastened to the end of a pole. The rope parted and he jumped clear, but the falling body set off the mine in the ground underneath and was blown to pieces, uprooting the nearby tree from which the second body was suspended and injuring Galetti in the face and shoulder.[28]

Begin writes: 'We repaid our enemy in kind. We had warned him again and again and again. He had callously disregarded our warnings. He forced us to answer gallows with gallows.' Recently he said: 'It caused great pain in our hearts, but the decision of the high command was unanimous. We had to save our men. We intended to carry on military operations and we knew that some of our men might be taken prisoner by the British. In fact, many men of the Irgun were captured. Eighteen members of Lehi were captured and sentenced to death. But all the sentences were commuted. Why was this possible only after our retaliation? Why was it possible to refrain from executing Irgun and Lehi men for nearly a year after the two sergeants were killed? I think that by what we did we must have saved the lives of several dozen men of the Underground. It was a cruel deed to hang the two sergeants, but it was inescapable.'

But the reaction to the deed at the time, among Jewish Agency supporters almost as much as among the British, was of unparalleled ferocity and horror. 'If there were such a thing as a Streicher Medal, the Irgun leaders would surely deserve it for services rendered to anti-semitism,' wrote Haganah supporter Jon Kimche. The Jewish Agency and Vaad Leumi spoke of 'the dastardly murder of two innocent men by a set of criminals'.[29] *The Times* of London wrote: 'They were kidnapped unarmed and defenceless. They were murdered for no offence. As a last indignity their bodies were employed to lure into a minefield the comrades who sought to give them a Christian burial. The bestialities practised by the Nazis themselves could go no further.'[30] Various journalists in New York telephoned Ben Hecht to ask him whether the hangings had caused him to have a little holiday in his heart.

Many other public men and journals drew a contrast between the three Irgun men and the two sergeants. The former, it was suggested, had of their own will taken up arms as members of an armed underground group. They claimed, although this was a matter of debate, to be fighters in a just cause, a war of liberation. But the nub of the matter was that they had knowingly and voluntarily taken part in acts of violence, against the orders of their community's elected body. And in days when opposition to the death penalty on principle was not widespread it was assumed that such men, if caught, must pay the supreme price.

The sergeants, on the other hand, were conscripts in a national army and in no way personally involved in the fight for Palestine. They were innocent bystanders, not active enthusiasts. And it was morally impermissible, although as Begin points out effective in the practical terms of the fight, to carry out a cold-blooded killing of the former in order to avenge, or even to deter, a similar killing of the latter.

Immediately the news became known, anti-semitic riots broke out in parts of Liverpool, Manchester, Glasgow and London. A synagogue in Derby was burnt down. In Birkenhead fifty slaughterhouse workers refused to handle kosher killings. For a few days, although no one was killed or seriously hurt, Jewish shopowners had bricks thrown through their windows and other Jewish premises were in danger of attack. The Soviet press described all this in detail as evidence of the vicious nature of British society, but without mentioning the death of the sergeants. After a few days these hooligan elements, often on the lookout for loot rather than revenge, faded away into obscurity, unanimously condemned by the British police and press.

The riots in Palestine were more serious, especially as various policemen were their ringleaders. On July 31st, according to the British report, gangs of soldiers and policemen began causing serious trouble around 8 p.m. in Tel Aviv: 'The depredations of these rioters consisted of shop-window smashing, smashing the windows of omnibuses, overturning vehicles and assaulting members of the Jewish community.'[31] Young Jews then retaliated by taking to the streets in gangs and stoning policemen on foot. At 9 p.m. twelve soldiers beat up a taxi driver and stole his vehicle. At 9.10 p.m., because of the deteriorating situation, all British police foot patrols were withdrawn from Tel Aviv.

The centre of attention now shifted to Citrus House security compound, the temporary base of mobile police units from Lydda district. Deputy Superintendent R. S. Hainsworth reports that tension and anger mounted all day among the men confined in the compound, who had heard that morning about the hanging of the sergeants. Then, around 9.15 p.m., their colleagues on foot patrol began returning to base under the protection of armoured cars with stories of how they had been stoned and abused by young Jewish men. They prepared themselves for action and around

10 o'clock there was 'a spontaneous movement towards armoured cars and vehicles'. Without waiting for orders, six armoured vehicles left the compound and headed for Tel Aviv in irregular formation.

Shortly after entering Allenby Road from Colony Square, one of these cars opened fire on a bus, killing a Jew and wounding three others. Hainsworth writes: 'This shooting was deliberate, felonious and entirely without justification.' At 10.15 p.m. police from an armoured car beat up a café in the Neve Shaanan quarter, then fifteen minutes later fired at another bus in the Hatikva quarter, killing three Jews. Five minutes later policemen raided another café, exploding a bakelite grenade in it as they left. The dead body of a Jew was later found a few yards away.

Hainsworth and his team of investigators made serious efforts to find those responsible. They examined each car's guns and ammunition supply. But the guns had been cleaned and the ammunition replaced. He was unable to pinpoint the guilty cars. He interrogated members of the regular mobile patrols in the area, men who must have known the truth, but without success: 'I have been met with little but evasions and untruths . . . The required evidence of identification is in the possession of certain British police personnel only and these decline to divulge it.'

A few police officers were disciplined. The Lydda mobile units were dispersed and reformed. But no criminal charges were brought against the policemen who caused the five Jewish deaths and committed the several dozen other violent acts listed in the documents. So strong was the feeling in the British police and army after the hangings that it would hardly have been possible to take harsh measures against the culprits. Neither British morale in Palestine nor public opinion at home would have tolerated such a step.

'Such conduct on the part of a disciplined force cannot be excused,' wrote Cunningham to Creech-Jones. But he still felt it appropriate to mention the extenuating circumstances: 'Most of them are young, without the benefits of long service. They have had to work in an atmosphere of constant danger and increasing tension, fraught with insult, vilification and treachery.' It was therefore understandable that Paice's and Martin's murder 'excited them to a pitch of fury which momentarily blinded them to the dictates of discipline, reason and humanity alike'.

The atmosphere of those few days was calculated to sharpen Bevin's already harsh attitude to the *President Warfield* passengers. On July 31st he had to inform the Cabinet that the French authorities had refused to cooperate in forcibly disembarking them. The question therefore was, what was to be done with them? There could be no question of sending them to Palestine or Cyprus. There were therefore only two possibilities, a suitable British colonial territory or the British zone of Germany. In due course they would decide which it was to be: 'No harm would be done by leaving the three transports at Port-de-Bouc for a few days. And there was a possibility that their passengers might decide eventually to go ashore peaceably.'[32]

And so the 'unedifying spectacle' continued, four and a half thousand Jews, almost all survivors of concentration camps, women and children as well as men, caged by British guards under the glare of the summer sun and under the gaze of the world's press. Britain redoubled her reproaches against France, for permitting the *President Warfield* to sail in the first place with unauthorized passengers and improper documents, for permitting Zionist representatives to approach the three ships and put pressure on the refugees not to go ashore, and for failing to cooperate in the refugees' return to their point of departure as provided by international law.

French public opinion replied with equal vigour, pointing to the essentail inhumanity of what Britain was doing. *Franc-Tireur* summed up the general view with its cartoon captioned 'Alert in the Mediterranean', showing eight great Royal Navy warships and flights of British aircraft all converging on one tiny sailing dinghy flying the Star of David. The reaction of the Arab press – approval of British firm handling of the 4500 at Port-de-Bouc, qualified by criticism of past British weakness in allowing quantities of usurping aliens to enter their country – was hardly noticed outside the Arab world.

On August 12th former Under-Secretary of State Sumner Welles argued the Palestine crisis in the *New York Herald Tribune* in exactly contrary terms from those of High Commissioner Cunningham. The hanging of the two sergeants, he wrote, was thoroughly wrong, but should be seen against its background – the 'judicial murder' of three young Jews who had helped their friends to escape from Acre fortress, the torturing to death of Alexander Rubowitz by a notorious British strongarm squad and the simple fact that the British administration in Palestine was 'shot through from top to bottom with anti-semitism', as shown by the July 31st pogrom in the streets of Tel Aviv. Cunningham had reported that, in all the circumstances, the Tel Aviv retaliation was understandable. Sumner Welles took the view that, given the nature of British rule in Palestine, the murder of the two sergeants was understandable.

By August 8th rumours of the British decision to divert the ships to

Hamburg reached Berl Locker and induced him to seek an interview with Creech-Jones. If this were done, said Locker, the repercussions would be tragic. The Colonial Secretary replied that the solution was in the Jewish Agency's hands. The refugees were not prisoners at Port-de-Bouc. They could go ashore whenever they wished. And most of them would probably already have done so, were it not for Zionist pressure. He urged Locker to see that they were now advised to disembark.[33]

A Reuter correspondent reported from the *Ocean Vigour* that the refugees seemed neither ill-nourished, miserable nor sick. The children played ball, the women seemed well dressed and they could all take sea-water showers.[34] Every day small boats brought them baskets of fresh fruit and vegetables, which they hauled over on ropes. Major M. C. Gray says: 'As far as Port-de-Bouc we ate the same rations. But after our stay in France they ate far better than we did.'

Micha Peri says: 'We used ropes to send down letters and messages to our friends. But Yigal Allon had told the Palmach that, if ever we had trouble with British ships, we were to sink them. So I asked for detonators and explosives to be sent over the ship's side with the food. Also two Haganah men came on board as doctors and ran into our part of the ship, where the British never came. They stayed and helped me make a large bomb.'

Britain's propaganda disaster was now almost complete. On August 16th Bevin explained to his Washington and Paris ambassadors, both deeply worried about rising anti-British feeling, that the refugees would now have to go to the British zone of Germany. There was no alternative. They could not be left indefinitely at Port-de-Bouc. To send them to Cyprus, let alone Palestine, would be a humiliating defeat for British policy. The British zone was the only place where it was politically feasible to disembark them. Everything possible would be done, he said, to mitigate the effect of this decision on public opinion. Embassies should point out, for instance, that the refugees were quite at liberty to go ashore in France. If, therefore, they continued to Germany, it was of their own free will.[35]

Trafford Smith conveyed the decision to Berl Locker in the Colonial Office on August 21st. The refugees would have until 6 p.m. the following day to disembark, failing which they would be taken to the British zone, the only place with facilities for housing and feeding such a large number of people.[36] The British government still hoped that the Jewish Agency would cooperate by sending a representative to Port-de-Bouc to advise the refugees to leave the ships. In Jerusalem the same message was passed to Golda Meir, who replied that no Jew could contemplate advising another Jew to proceed anywhere but Palestine.[37]

So by the evening of August 22nd, in spite of all Britain's persuasions, only thirty-one of the Jewish refugees had accepted the French offer. The ships therefore put to sea again and made for Gibraltar. After a month at sea the exhaustion and heat were beginning to take their toll on everyone's nerves. Gray recalls: 'My men were spat on the whole time and called "Nazi bastards". It was not the refugees, at least not originally. It was organized by the hard core of the Haganah. It was very unfair. Some of my men had been parachuted at Arnhem and lost their friends fighting against Nazi Germany. But I don't think they retaliated, even when men and women spat in their faces.'

At Gibraltar an offer was made to transfer all pregnant women to Palestine. But by now the refugees were determined to see the ordeal through to the end and they refused. On September 8th they reached Hamburg. The refugees from the *Empire Rival* disembarked quickly. Major Gray says: 'They went off like lambs. I thought it was pretty odd. Also my sentries had heard banging down in the hold. So I sent a bomb disposal team down. They discovered that an inspection cover in the hold had been tampered with and when they lifted it up they found a seven-gallon cooking oil tin with two wires coming out of it. It was so arranged that, as soon as the ship got out to sea, the bilge water would have sloshed across the contact and up the bomb would have gone.'

The refugees from the *Runnymede Park* and *Ocean Vigour* had no such reason to hurry off their ships. Some of them resisted fiercely, others walked off with resignation towards the trains that were to take them to Poppendorf camp, near Lübeck. The *Palestine Post* wrote: 'Some of the soldiers helped women across, led children by the hand and assisted with the refugees' packages – all that they had left, as one soldier said. In a number of cases the offer of assistance was refused by the deportees, who spat in the soldiers' faces and called them "dirty fascists".'[38]

Other refugees threw back the food and drink offered them on the trains by soldiers and Red Cross officials. All these scenes were reported and photographed, much to the detriment of Britain's reputation. It seemed an act of calculated inhumanity to send Jewish survivors of concentration camps back to the country where these horrors had been perpetrated and where their relatives had died. Far from 'making an example' of the *Exodus* and rallying the world against the organizers of illegal immigration, Bevin succeeded only in shocking the world community into deeper sympathy for the Zionist enterprise.

This great Haganah success was nevertheless overshadowed by the result of the UNSCOP team's inquiry. After their month in Palestine they visited refugee camps in Germany and Austria, then retired to Geneva to write their report, much as the American and British investigators had done a year earlier. The report, signed just before midnight on August 31st, contained a unanimous proposal to end the British Mandate as soon as possible.

But the most important section was the majority recommendation, approved by seven countries with three opposed and one abstaining, to partition Palestine into an Arab state and a Jewish state. The idea was for the two states to conclude a treaty of economic union, for Jerusalem to be under direct United Nations administration and for 150,000 Jewish immigrants to be admitted in the transitional period of two years, during which Britain would retain her Mandatory responsibilities.

The General Zionist Council, meeting in Zurich, at once passed by fifty-one votes to sixteen a resolution describing these ideas as 'an earnest effort to bring the problem to a just conclusion'. Secretary of State George C. Marshall announced that the United States 'puts great weight' not only on the unanimous recommendations, but also on the majority ones. But the political committee of the Arab League, meeting in Lebanon, declared UNSCOP's partition proposal a violation of the natural right of Palestine Arabs to independence and a threat to security in all Arab countries.[39] There was a general Arab view, reported Cunningham, that any attempt to impose partition would be met by a repetition of the 1936 revolt.

For Bevin and the British government the UNSCOP majority proposal was an advance towards an idea which until May 14th had seemed quite impossible and which in September seemed no more palatable for the fact that seven men from countries quite unfamiliar with Palestine's problems had for reasons best known to themselves voted in favour of it. Bevin wrote on September 18th: 'The majority proposal is so manifestly unjust to the Arabs that it is difficult to see how, in Sir Alexander Cadogan's words, we could reconcile it with our conscience.' Although Bevin had originally wanted to, Britain had not committed herself to accepting, still less to enforcing, any recommendation at all. So what should Britain do if, as now seemed likely, the General Assembly confirmed UNSCOP's view and voted for partition?

Bevin observed that the UNSCOP majority's Jewish state was far larger than that proposed by Lord Peel in 1937 or by the Cabinet Committee in 1944. It would contain 500,000 Jews and almost as many Arabs, about 450,000. It would contain most of the citrus orchards, the mainstay of Palestine's economy, about half of which were Arab-owned. The Arab

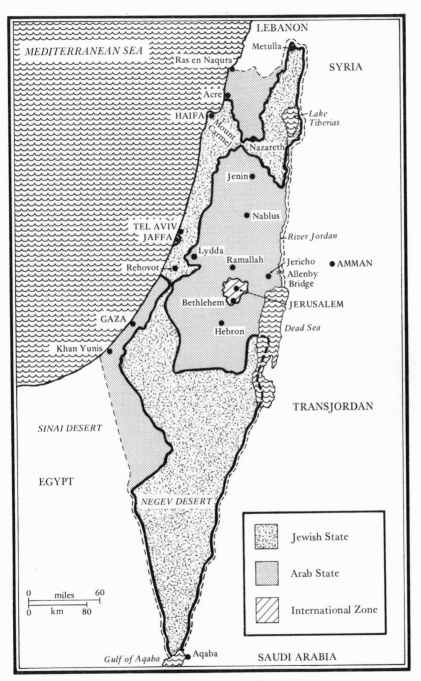

United Nations Partition Plan, 1947

area would be far less fertile. It was also larger than the Jewish state discussed at the conference in February.[40] The Arabs had said to him then: 'If it is wrong for the Jews to be in a minority of 33⅓ or 40 per cent in the whole country, what justification is there for putting 380,000 Arabs under the Jews? What is your answer to that?' As he explained in his February 25th speech, Bevin had no answer to that and he had even less of an answer to Arab objections to the UNSCOP proposal.

The chiefs of staff estimated that at least one further British division would be required to enforce the UNSCOP plan and that any such action would be seen by all Arab states as a breach of faith. Arab goodwill, which was of 'overriding importance to our strategical position', would be shattered. And this view was shared by the Foreign Office. Beeley says: 'As the year wore on, the decision boiled down more and more to one question, was Britain to be responsible for partition or not? After the Soviet volte-face and the UNSCOP report, it looked more and more as if partition was going to happen. So what were we to do about it? We decided that, if we helped to impose it, the fury of the Arabs would be such that our position in the Middle East would be destroyed. Therefore we must simply slide out of the problem.'

There were others who felt keenly the indignity and humiliation of such a policy. The Colonial Office in particular were dismayed at the idea of abandoning their three decades of work, of leaving in anarchy a country where they had served and which they had helped to build. There were senior army officers too who felt that the chiefs of staff were over-estimating Arab military potential. Major-General Richard Gale says: 'It was always my view that we could impose partition with the troops we had, without reinforcements. The Arab armies were not worth much on the ground. I mean, of course, at that time. But Monty and the others took a different view.'

Beeley says: 'Maybe we were wrong. Maybe we should have put troops along the partition frontiers and made sure that partition was carried through. I agree that this would have been a more dignified posture. But, in the Foreign Office's view, it would have involved a serious injustice to the Arabs. And it would not have been in Britain's national interest. All through 1947 Bevin was negotiating with prime ministers Nokrashi and Saleh Jabr of Egypt and Iraq to preserve British facilities, for the protection of the Suez Canal and our oil concessions, and to integrate the two countries into the Western alliance. All this would have been ruined if we had played a part in creating the state of Israel.'

Bevin was not in favour of pressing for a smaller Jewish state in line with previous British proposals. 'Now that the appetite of their followers has been whetted by the majority plan,' he wrote, the Zionist leaders would accept nothing less. He was therefore drawn inescapably to the idea of unconditional British withdrawal. Britain could reconcile the proposed plan neither with her conscience nor with her national interest. She would therefore refuse to enforce it.

That same day (September 18th, 1947) the figures of those killed as a result of terrorism since August 1945 were received from Jerusalem. Not counting the ninety-one killed in the King David explosion, they included 141 British, forty-four Arabs and twenty-five Jewish non-terrorists. Jewish terrorists suffered thirty-seven killed in fighting, seven executed and two who committed suicide while awaiting execution.[41] The figures seemed a clear demonstration of Britain's gentle approach to the Irgun and Lehi. Usually, when elements of a local population rebel against a foreign occupying power, the guerrilla fighters and their supporters are killed in greater numbers than the occupying forces.

Bevin's heart was thus hardened to the point where he wanted British withdrawal even, as he wrote, 'at the cost of a period of bloodshed and chaos'. This policy would have two important advantages. British interests in the area would not be destroyed and British lives would no longer be at risk. And while it was true that Britain might then be accused by both Jews and Arabs of failing to fulfil her obligations, she could at least plead in mitigation that she had tried to bring both sides to a compromise and that she was even now ready to accept a mutually agreed solution: 'We cannot permit ourselves to be kept in Palestine indefinitely by the fear of this accusation.'

During September a further twelve British policemen were killed by terrorists in Palestine, four in a Lehi raid on Barclays Bank in Haifa, three by a tar barrel bomb, which an Irgun team rolled from a truck with a cleverly designed sloping ramp over the security fence and up against the wall of Haifa police headquarters.

On October 1st Roy Farran, having been persuaded to return from Syria, stood trial for the murder of Alexander Rubowitz. Melford Stevenson, later a well-known High Court judge, was the Judge Advocate, the court martial's legal adviser: 'I recollect that the prosecution collapsed because Farran, having escaped from custody, left in his tent an army exercise book containing what the prosecution described as "a full confession", intended for the attention of his defending officer. I had to advise the court that this "confession" was the subject of legal professional privilege and the court could not rely on it.'

The prosecution was further weakened when Bernard Fergusson, who had followed Farran to Syria and discussed the case with him in some detail, declined to give evidence on the ground that he might incriminate himself by so doing. Again the court accepted this and excused Fergusson from giving testimony. After this the only serious piece of evidence was a hat allegedly found at the scene of Rubowitz's abduction and inscribed with a name that looked like Farran's. This was purely circumstantial, not nearly enough to convict the British officer.

There was no case to answer, and Farran was acquitted amid the derision of American correspondents and the fury of the Jewish community. Fergusson's special squads, whose whole existence depended on secrecy, were blown wide open. Hastily they were disbanded and their officers removed from Palestine.

Rubowitz's commander Yalin-Mor waited a few months, then had one of his men send Farran a parcel bomb in England. But it was opened by his brother Rex. Rex Farran's stomach was torn to pieces and he died. Ten years later, at a bizarre conspiratorial meeting in Paris, Yalin-Mor said to Fergusson: 'Tell Farran that we are satisfied to have had our revenge in this way. Tell him that he has nothing more to fear from us.' In 1979 Roy Farran was Solicitor-General of the Canadian province of Alberta. The whereabouts of Rubowitz's body is still not known.

As British rule in Palestine became daily more confused, British officials made haste to mend their bridges with Arab leaders. Perhaps, in spite of Arab threats, it might be possible to avert an armed clash. In any case it was important to make clear Britain's neutrality, should the conflict come, the fact that, whatever the United Nations decided, she would not be enforcing the partition plan that the Arabs so hated.

In September two top policemen, Arthur Giles and John Briance, travelled to Cairo with orders to approach Haj Amin al-Husseini informally about partition. The Mufti explained through a British intermediary why his answer was an uncompromising no. Quite simply, Palestine was Arab and not a suitable subject for bargaining. It was like a robber trying to make conditions on which he would return stolen property. Furthermore, the proposed partition would not satisfy the Zionists. It would merely be a springboard from which they would leap on to more. Several times he repeated to the British intermediary in French: 'The appetite grows with eating.'

Haj Amin continued: 'Put yourself in the Arabs' place. Remember yourselves in 1940. Did you ever think of offering the Germans part of

Britain on condition that they let you alone in the rest? Of course not and you never would. To start with you would have preferred to die defending it. In the second you know that they would never have kept their word to have remained in the one part.'[42] He then explained that there was no fundamental Arab enmity towards Britain. Their quarrel was purely political: 'They hate the policy that has founded and nourished the Zionists' national home.' They now wanted Britain to refrain from doing any more for the Jews, to stop supporting political Zionism. The Arabs would then solve the problem themselves, with their own armed forces.

On October 7th Haj Amin left Cairo, illegally as usual, turning up at Beirut airfield without passport or visa. Prime Minister Riad at once took him in as a house guest. The British no less than the Zionists were once again outraged at the sight of responsible Arab leaders welcoming with honour a leading Nazi collaborator. Azzam Pasha had to explain that the Mufti 'had captured the imagination of the Arab masses' and that the Arab League could not afford to drop him. Azzam added that, since the Jews had their Irgun and Stern, he supposed that the Arabs must have theirs also.

The Arab leaders were divided only by the degree of their dislike of the Yishuv, the newcomers from Europe who now threatened to deprive the Palestinians of their birthright. Haj Amin, while he spoke more liberally to British emissaries, made it clear to other Arab leaders that, as soon as British forces were withdrawn, the Arabs should with one accord fall upon the Jews and destroy them.[43] Bevin had expressed the hope that the prospect of British withdrawal would bring the two sides together. The Mufti's followers, on the other hand, looked forward to withdrawal with keen expectation as the moment of final reckoning. (Haj Amin died near Beirut in 1972.)

But even the more moderate Arabs, while they did not speak of the Jews' physical destruction, were as vehement as Haj Amin in their refusal to contemplate Jewish statehood. 'No Arab will ever be ruled by a Jew,' said Iraqi Foreign Minister Jamali. Azzam Pasha, invited to open informal talks with Zionist leaders, replied that, so long as they maintained their claim for a Jewish state, negotiation was useless: 'The gap between the two sides at present was too great and he thought nothing could be gained by talk.'

So what was to become of the plan, the economic union between the two states, the United Nations administration of Jerusalem? As early as October 8th Cunningham expressed his worries. Unless the Arabs co-operated, he reported, and it seemed most unlikely that they would, there would be many areas of administration where it would not be possible to transfer power. What was to happen to railways, ports, prisons, mail, telegraph and customs? Presumably a Jewish government would take over its allotted area, but what was to happen in the Arab areas? The result would almost certainly be a disaster and a tragedy for the people of Palestine.[44] He told the foreign press that it would be physically possible for Britain to leave Palestine without any administration, but only at the cost of misery and chaos.[45]

On October 17th Creech-Jones told the United Nations what the Cabinet had decided: 'His Majesty's Government would not accept responsibility for the enforcement, either alone or in cooperation with other nations, of any settlement antagonistic to either the Jews or the Arabs or both, which was likely to necessitate the use of force.' Gradually the significance of British policy sunk in. British forces in Palestine were not going to enforce the plan. They were not even going to contribute to a United Nations force entrusted with the same task. If the General Assembly approved the plan, they would accept the decision, but passively, giving no help or comfort to any organization attempting to implement it.

On November 5th Cunningham sent an even more alarmed cable: 'The question is, are we prepared to face the Christian world with complete abandonment of the source and centre of their religion? I must repeat therefore again that I cannot be associated with leaving Jerusalem in a vacuum. We could probably put in as many as 2000 British police . . .' But this was exactly what Britain had decided not to do. The withdrawal must be total, to show the Arabs convincingly that Britain was playing no part whatever in enforcing the plan and dividing their country.

During November the fate of Palestine was decided in the lobbies of the United Nations. Thailand, Haiti, Iceland, Peru, Costa Rica and the Philippines – these were some of the countries whose votes lay in the balance, whose delegates would decide whether or not a Jewish state was to come into existence. On November 12th British police surrounded a Lehi weapon-training centre near Raanana and five young Jews were shot dead. The Lehi retaliated immediately, killing three British Shell Oil employees outside a Haifa café and throwing grenades into another café in Jerusalem. In a few days they killed eleven British subjects and injured twenty-three.[46] They also abducted and killed five Arabs suspected of denouncing their hideout.

On November 27th, 1947, the Chief Rabbi of Jerusalem asked the

Yishuv to pray at the Wailing Wall. Two days later they sat by their radio sets, listening as the delegates in New York voted for or against their future state. The thirty-three in favour included the United States, the Soviet Union and France. The thirteen against were Cuba, Greece and the eleven Moslem countries. Britain, even though her government had labelled the plan as hostile to her interest and irreconcilable with her conscience, voted among the ten abstentions. The two-thirds majority was achieved and the Jews of Palestine danced in the streets.

On December 4th Bevin's policy of non-participation was again approved by the Cabinet. British rule was to end on May 15th, 1948, and total military withdrawal would be completed by August 1st. Until May 15th undivided British rule would continue. The United Nations Commission, whose job it would now be to police the plan, would therefore be admitted to Palestine only on May 1st, since it would be 'intolerable' to have to share authority with them at a time of probable Arab rebellion.

In this, his last important paper on the Palestine issue, Bevin explained that this apparently self-contradictory policy, an insistence on retaining authority combined with an unwillingness to exercise it, was amply justified. Britain had undertaken the Mandate to establish a national home for the Jewish people on the clear understanding that nothing must prejudice the civil and religious rights of existing non-Jewish communities. Britain had not undertaken to create either a Jewish or an Arab state by force or to coerce either party in the interests of the other. But this was exactly what the United Nations now wanted her to do.

Britain's position was especially delicate. She was the only power in Palestine with forces capable of taking effective action. She was also being accused of harbouring ulterior movies. If she were now to use these forces to impose a solution acceptable to one side but hateful to the other, she would incur a grave responsibility and damage her own national interest. There was only one way of remaining faithful to all her obligations, to the Mandate and to the United Nations, and that was by doing nothing. For the next five months she would rule Palestine in name alone, using her forces only in self-defence, involving herself as little as possible in the war that was about to erupt.

The events of these five months make dismal and familiar reading. Although thirty more British police were killed between December 1st and the withdrawal, the main battleground was no longer between the Jews and the British. The violent Arab protests that greeted the decision to set up a Jewish state escalated within a few days into a series of killings and counterkillings that would continue for decades. On December 19th a communiqué was issued: 'The High Commissioner now gives warning that communal disorders must cease . . . Should these disorders continue, he will have no option but to direct the security forces to adopt severe measures against all those, Jew and Arab alike, who are breaking the law.'

But he knew that he was bluffing. The British had neither the means nor the will to stamp out the violence. On December 13th he cabled London: 'Unless there is a police force in effective operation in Jerusalem on the date [May 15th], bloodshed and destruction cannot be prevented and will be laid at our door . . . It must surely be difficult to reconcile with our consciences a proposition which we know will endanger the holy places of Christianity, namely that Jerusalem should be taken over by a body with no force at its disposal.'[47]

Jerusalem District Commissioner J. H. Pollock reported in December: 'The political situation has deteriorated throughout the district and inter-community strife may now be said to be in full swing.'[48] By December 16th roadblocks made of barbed wire and barrels were manned by Arabs in various parts of the city. By the following day the countrywide death toll since the end of November amounted to 106 Arabs and 96 Jews.[49] On December 28th a Jewish convoy was ambushed ten kilometres along the Jerusalem–Jaffa road and suffered seven casualties, two of them fatal. These convoys would soon be the centrepiece of the war. On the same day a party of twenty Jews attacked two Arab villages. On December 30th bombs were thrown at a hundred Arabs standing in line for work outside a Haifa factory. Arab employees immediately rioted against their Jewish fellow-workers and by the time troops and police restored order forty-one Jews and six Arabs were dead.

Cunningham reported that the Haganah was aggravating the situation by savage reprisals, typical of past Irgun tactics. By their own admission they were attacking villages suspected of harbouring armed Arabs, blowing up houses (as the British had done during the Arab revolt) and killing the ordinary people, including women and children. They had also turned their weapons on British police and troops attempting to restore order.[50] On the other hand, Golda Meir complained to him on December 17th: 'The main activity of the government has been directed at weakening the standing force of the Jews through searches of arms and almost daily arrests . . . Policemen and soldiers were standing around while shops were set on fire and Jews were being attacked, behaving as if it had nothing to do with them.' Other soldiers and policemen, she hinted, were actually helping or equipping the Arab fighters.[51]

This was the burden of frequent Jewish complaint during the early months of 1948. The British administration was withering away and, in spite of Cunningham's personal concern and requests for more positive action, they were doing nothing to discharge their elementary duty of keeping the peace. Their orders were to withdraw from the Arab-Jewish conflict, to concentrate on self-protection, not to get involved in any police action which could be interpreted as an attempt to enforce the United Nations decision. This policy is seen by many still as a serious dereliction of duty. Cunningham, it is said, acted in the same way as a previous colonial governor in the same area some 1900 years previously – he washed his hands of the problem.

However unfair this may be to Cunningham personally (he continued to bombard London with requests for action), this harsh accusation bears some relation to the disorderly scene of Britain's last and least glorious months as Palestine's ruler. Its full story remains to be told – some British documents are still kept closed – but some of its more glaring and unsavoury features are known in general terms. There was, for instance, the Ben Yehuda Street explosion of February 22nd, in which fifty-two people died, mainly Jews. This was the worst of a number of incidents in which a few British policemen and soldiers, hardened against Jews as a whole by their experience of terrorism and demoralized by the general disintegration, committed random acts of violence against Jewish civilians.

A few others deserted their units, joining either the Arab Legion or the growing Arab irregular armies. British stores were being liquidated, money was available and there was good opportunity for the unscrupulous to line their pockets. For a time, in certain Arab areas, British rifles, pistols, ammunition and hand-grenades were on sale in local markets side by side with oranges and melons. Generous bribes were available to any official ready to turn a blind eye to Haganah arms smuggling.

Former Inspector-General Rymer-Jones was deeply shocked by what he saw on his return to Palestine in January: 'I found all the urban areas divided into small security zones. Syrian roving bands infested the countryside. As we returned by cars to Jerusalem one evening, the irregulars stopped us at a roadblock, thrusting their rifles in the windows. A police superintendent was turned out of his car and made to walk home. Control of the country was visibly lacking. I won't describe the situation further. It's too shaming.'

For Menachem Begin, about to bring his underground army into open battle with Arab forces, the withering away of British authority was important only because it was a step forward in the inevitable progress towards Jewish statehood. He had no doubt whatever that the Jewish people were entitled to this statehood – and not only within the boundaries set by the United Nations: 'My greatest worry in those months was that the Arabs might accept the United Nations plan. Then we would have had the ultimate tragedy, a Jewish state so small that it could not absorb all the Jews of the world.' He wanted to create the Jewish state, then to extend its territory throughout the whole original area of Mandatory Palestine.

Today, as Prime Minister of Israel, he says: 'What is clear is one thing. This land belongs to us. We were born here, we built our culture here, our state here. We had our two Temples. They were destroyed. Every prayer was connected with this land. We used to turn to Jerusalem when we prayed. Palestine lived within us, even there in my home in Brest-Litovsk. We saw it with our mind's eye. We always spoke about it. We never doubted that we would return to Palestine. It is our land.'

Begin feels no guilt towards the Arabs of Palestine: 'The grudge is there, I have to admit it. But they shouldn't feel that grudge. We don't do any wrong to the Arabs. They will live with us. They will be a minority, it is true, but today the Arabs have twenty-two states. And if they want a twenty-third state to use to make life hell for us, then we say in good conscience that we are not going to agree to that. It is unjust.'

As for the methods he used as Irgun commander, there is not one single instance – the King David hotel, the Jerusalem officers' club or anywhere else – where he will admit to a sense of remorse, or even that an error was committed, He maintains that the Irgun's 'fight for liberation' was the most just, or the least unjust, in the whole history of such struggles, and he is insulted by comparisons between his Irgun and today's PLO or IRA, both of whom regularly attack and kill civilians.

Arthur Koestler asks us in *Promise and Fulfilment* to see the Irgun's struggle as part of the dilemma of ends and means, which is the core of the human predicament. Without the rebellion of the English barons, he points out, there would be no Magna Carta, without the storming of the Bastille no proclamation of the Rights of Man. Violence should not therefore be ruled out as a political weapon in all circumstances. But when it is justifiable, it is justifiable only within very narrow limits. It is like arsenic. Injected in very small doses it can be a stimulant to the social body. In large doses it is deadly poison. A surgeon is justified in cutting, if his cuts will heal and if their results are reasonably predictable. But very soon the point arrives where the surgeon's scalpel becomes the butcher's cleaver.[52] This passage was read to Begin at the end of 1978. He replied that he agreed with Koestler's argument and that he was satisfied that the Irgun's operations stayed within these morally permitted limits, without exception.

Koestler believes that there *were* exeptions, two of them, the hanging of the British sergeants and the killing of some 250 Arab civilians during an attack on Dir Yassin village on April 9th, 1948. The effect of the latter event still reverberates around the Arab world, where it is seen as one of the cruellest atrocities ever perpetrated by the soldiers of political Zionism.

But even in this, the most controversial Irgun operation of them all, Begin will not agree that his men were at fault: 'Loudspeakers were brought there – this is a very interesting fact about the ethics of the Irgun – to warn civilians to leave Dir Yassin before the battle started, so that none of them would be hurt. Now the houses were of stone, like in all those villages built on the mountainside. Our men could not overcome the fire coming from the houses. So what did they do? They threw hand grenades into the houses. So those civilians who did not escape as a result of the warning were injured and killed, it is true. And we regret it very deeply. But what I would like to explain to you is that none of our men of the Irgun and Lehi carried out a massacre. It was very tragic, but there was no massacre. And I do not agree with Mr Koestler.'

Most historians, in Israel as well as outside it, reject this account. Both the International Red Cross and the British reported the incident in terms strongly critical of the Irgun. A British document quotes the defiant words of an Irgun-Lehi spokesman, uttered on the evening of the operation: 'We intend to attack, conquer and keep until we have the whole of Palestine and Transjordan in a greater Jewish state . . . We hope to improve our methods in future and to make it possible to spare women and children.'[53] The Jewish Agency immediately expressed their 'repugnance' at the methods used, alleging that many civilians had indeed been massacred out of hand, and this version remains the one most widely believed.

The immediate result of Dir Yassin was the headlong flight from the allotted Jewish area of two-thirds of its Arabs, about 300,000 people who even more than thirty years later are not allowed to return to the homes and land they left behind. Begin acknowledges therefore that the attack, or in his view the legend of it, was of military and political help to the embryo Jewish state. On the other hand, the words 'Dir Yassin' are still perhaps the most emotive of all to the ears of every Palestine Arab and have survived as a symbol of their deep feeling of resentment at being driven out of their country. This was the operation's long-term result.

Begin also maintains that the Irgun deserve most of the credit for forcing Britain to leave. He quotes Abba Hillel Silver: 'The Irgun will go down in history as a factor without which the state of Israel would not have come into being.'[54] He also quotes a former senior official of the Palestine secretariat, Colonel Archer Cust: 'The hanging of the two British sergeants did more than anything to get us out.' (He does not quote the next line of Cust's article, which refers to 'the hideous massacre of Dir Yassin' which 'got the Arabs out and started the refugee problem'.[55])

Veterans of the Haganah and Jewish Agency reject these and other ex-Irgun or ex-Lehi claims. In their view, Israel was created not by minority military units or by attacks on police stations, still less by street assassinations, but by their three decades of work spent organizing settlements, armed forces and institutions of government. Thus, when the day of British withdrawal drew near, the Yishuv was ready with a parallel state apparatus to fill the vacuum.

Some of them are ready to admit that the Irgun made a significant contribution to the pressure on Britain, that they hastened the decision to withdraw. And if this is the case, if the Irgun and Lehi brought forward Britain's abdication by as much as a year, they may indeed have affected the subsequent course of history. The events of 1948 – the communist takeover in Czechoslovakia, communist victories in China, Stalinist purge trials in Hungary, the Berlin blockade and Stalin's quarrel with Tito – effectively converted American policy-formers away from the belief (which many held) that the world's future would be based on cooperation with the Soviet Union. Had Palestine's year of decision been 1948 rather than 1947, the United States Congress and President might have felt it necessary to stabilize the British Empire along the lines suggested by the State Department. And this would have meant supporting Britain over Palestine, switching over to an anti-Zionist policy.

Former Haganah leaders believe nevertheless that they were right to avoid terrorism by limiting the violence they used, except in a few instances, to the fulfilment of their programme of illegal immigration. This, they feel, was an effective and well-judged combination of the humanitarian and the political. It gave hope to the survivors of the holocaust. It increased the numbers of the Yishuv. It put pressure on Britain, causing her particular embarrassment in the United States. And it demonstrated to the world how deep was the motivation of European Jews to find safe refuge in their Promised Land. Haganah leader Noah Klieger says, 'We think the *Exodus* was the most important event on the way of the Jewish people to an independent state.'

They feel that this motivation and the political support of the United States had by 1947 made the Yishuv an irresistible force, had made a Jewish state inevitable. The methods used by Irgun and Lehi were, therefore, not only very dangerous in that they risked dragging the Yishuv into the ultimate abyss of civil war, but they were also improper and un-Jewish, a discredit to their just cause, a stain on Zionism's record.

Thirty years have passed and most of these inter-Israeli wounds have healed. For instance, former Haganah leader Yigael Yadin, who now serves as deputy Prime Minister under his old adversary Menachem Begin, states his retrospective opinion that the two types of resistance in fact complemented one another: 'It was not planned as such and it was not understood. At the time the Irgun and Lehi were known as "porshim", the ones outside the camp. But now I would say that the Irgun were helpful. They were a complement to the main activity, which was ours.' The really intense mutual dislikes, such as the one between Ben Gurion and Begin, fade with the passage of time and the passing of the main characters.

The Palestine Arabs, as they fled from their homes and fields in April and May, knew only that they had been beaten by a stronger and out-witted by a cleverer enemy. In 1947-8, even with the help of their fellow-Arabs, they were no match for the Zionists either on the battlefield or in the United Nations. Disorganized and leaderless, compromised by their lukewarm attitude to the Allied struggle against Hitler and by the Mufti's flight to Berlin, they were outmanoeuvred in almost every non-Moslem diplomatic arena. But as they felt themselves losing the battle, they re-tained their belief, as their sons believe, that Palestine is their birthright, an Arab country turned slowly but inexorably into a Jewish country by a combination of outside forces, and they vowed that one day they would win the war and return home.

The First World War, the Balfour Declaration, the British Mandate, the skills and successes of the early Jewish immigrants, the rise of Hitler, the upsurge of Jewish immigration, the mass murder of European Jewry, Zionist lobbies in British and American political circles and their influence over poorer, less developed United Nations members – it all seemed to have conspired to inundate their country with European newcomers and ultimately to drive them out of it.

Britain had done her best (or worst) to prevent this outcome. Since the mid-1930s her Foreign Office had pursued a consistent policy of opposi-tion to a Jewish state. And, apart from a brief period in 1943-44 when Churchill brought his pro-Zionist views to bear on the problem, this policy dominated British action in Palestine right to the end. On one level, it was a successful policy. By abdicating her rule, she was able to rid herself of her obligations to Zionism and at the same time avoid the odium (in Arab eyes) of having assisted in the creation of Israel. She was able to preserve her influence in the Middle East through treaties and ties of friendship with Arab nations, in the short term.

She kept control of the Suez Canal until 1956 and bases in Iraq until the fall of Nuri in 1958. She had troops in Libya until the 1969 revolution and in the Gulf until the early 1970s, after which she was forced out by her own economic weakness, rather than by local opposition. Judged by these results, the Bevin policy was a moderately successful salvage operation.

But in terms of national morale and world prestige, it left Britain deeply wounded. The disintegration of her rule in Palestine was a dismal and well-publicized drama revealing the shaky foundations of a seemingly impregnable empire and indicating to national leaders in other colonies how vulnerable the British lion really was, and how effective urban guerrilla warfare can be against an imperial power, especially against one which accepts certain civilizing self-restraints.

In the three years of post-war conflict 338 British subjects were violently killed[56] by Jewish groups. Compared to the number of Jew and Arabs killed in the five months of civil war that followed the United Nations decision, an estimated total of 5014,[57] this is a low figure, a miniscule figure if compared with the number of Jews murdered in Nazi Germany. But since each of the 338 was killed in a personal way, either singly with bullets or in a small group with a bomb, their deaths made as much impact on British public opinion, perhaps more impact, than the heavy British casualties of the Second World War, which were endured with fortitude and resolution. The 338, it seemed, had died quite unnecessarily. Political pressure to bring the killings to a halt was therefore all the stronger.

Britain had suffered a defeat. None of Bevin's explanations could disguise this fact. Churchill, the former enthusiastic Zionist, felt particularly keenly the humiliation of the David-and-Goliath outcome, the British Empire of hundreds of millions succumbing to the puny Yishuv of a few hundred thousand. In 1948 he rebuffed his old friend Weizmann's efforts to make peace with a cold verbal message: 'The Palestine position now, as concerns Great Britain, is simply such a hell-disaster that I cannot take it up again or renew my efforts of twenty years. It is a situation which I myself cannot help in, and must, as far as I can, put out of my mind. But send Weizmann himself my warm regards.'[58]

Churchill understood the effect of the defeat on Britain's imperial interests. Like many politicians of his generation – and not only British politicians – he saw the Empire as a force for good, a most valuable civilizing influence and a boon to the whole world. Now, amid a glare of publicity, one of its props was cut away, and in the Holy Land of all places, cradle of the three great religions. It was a terrible omen, perhaps the beginning of the end. This was the reason for his distress.

Other leading statesmen, of a younger generation or of a different political hue, welcomed the fact that Britain had surrendered a thankless task, though deeply regretting the way in which this was done. They looked back on the record – the conflicting promises of 1917, the changes of policy, the commissions of enquiry, the white papers, and now the bloodshed and the chaos. Where had they gone wrong?

Some felt that the fault lay not in the administration or formation or policy, but in the whole concept of the Mandate, with its built-in contradictions. There was only one solution to the task – not to have embarked upon it in the first place. Others felt that somehow, somewhere along the line, some golden opportunity must have been missed. Something should have been done differently.

Perhaps Britain should have imposed partition, in 1937 or in 1945 or in 1948? Perhaps a different foreign secretary, less prone to tactless remarks and more understanding of Jewish suffering under Hitler, would have made Britain's post-war task a little easier? Perhaps Britain should have chosen one side, either the Jews or the Arabs, not both, and awarded Palestine to this nominee quite firmly?

As it was, Britain chose the most thorny path of all, trying to bring the two sides to a compromise agreement consistent with her own essential interest. This was like trying to square, or triangularize, a circle. The more she tried, the more vicious the circle became. And when finally the whole construction snapped, she was too weary and disillusioned even to try to pick up the pieces.

On May 1st former Jerusalem council chairman Robert Graves announced, 'The present state of Jerusalem is untenable. There is no law and order in certain parts of the town. Cars are being stolen daily. The whole of the Municipal fire brigade plant and cars were stolen and they are not likely to be returned. My own car was stolen a few days ago.'[59] Inmates of prisons and mental hospitals were released and allowed to wander away. On May 3rd the *Palestine Post* estimated that in five months of fighting more than 10,500 people have been killed or wounded.

Robert Newton, a British official who did his best to serve Palestine, which he loved, writes today, 'Palestine was indeed a tragedy. It moved to its fated conclusion like the Oresteia of Aeschylus. We who worked there could do no more than attempt to mitigate the operation of fate, in a sense the consequences of the creation of sin by sin as Aeschylus put it. I am afraid that the tragedy has not yet reached its end and that the teeth of the children will still be set on edge.'

On May 14th the Zionist leaders proclaimed the State of Israel in Tel Aviv. The same day General Sir Alan Cunningham left Government House for the last time. He inspected a guard of honour from the Highland Light Infantry, then was escorted by armoured cars and police outriders, with RAF aircraft flying overhead, through Jerusalem to Kalundia airstrip: 'I was in my bullet-proof Daimler, a huge car with glass an inch thick. Originally it had been made for the King, to protect him from bombs during the London blitz. He lent it to me, because of my job. We drove through Jerusalem with Jews on one side and Arabs on the other, all pointing guns, but they let me through.'

He left the car at the airstrip with General MacMillan, was flown to Haifa, then driven to the port, where the cruiser *Euryalus* was waiting to take him away. The troops were lined up in his honour. In the early evening he went on board the cruiser. Precisely at midnight the British flag was lowered and the *Euryalus* slid out of the port. It was the end of Britain's moment as ruler of the Holy Land.

Exhausted by the war against Germany, harassed by the first truly successful manifestation of urban guerrilla warfare, branded as inhumane by the public opinion of her closest allies, accused (justifiably) by both Jews and Arabs of the breach of solemn promises, at odds with the American President and Congress (though not with the State Department), pinpointed as the primary target of Soviet diplomacy, confused and trapped in the mire of the transitional stage between imperialism and decolonization, half-anxious to preserve the Empire, half-willing to discard it, embroiled in a dozen equally pressing problems, Indian independence, famine in Germany, bread rationing at home and national bankruptcy, Britain had shown herself unable to master the Sisyphean task of solving the conflict between Jews and Arabs in Palestine.

Notes

In the following references to documents available in the Public Record Office, London, the prefix 'FO' indicates Foreign Office records, 'WO' War Office records, 'CO' Colonial Office records, 'CAB' Cabinet Office records and 'PREM' Prime Minister's Office records. One British Admiralty document, known as ADM 1/20685, is used as a source on the boarding of the *President Warfield* or *Exodus* ship. The prefixes 'Z' or 'S' indicate a document from the Central Zionist Archives, Jerusalem. Documents prefixed with a number, in the case of Palestine usually '867N', are from the National Archives, Washington. Publication details of books cited can be found in the Select Bibliography.

Unless otherwise indicated, page references to books listed in the Bibliography refer to the first edition given.

CHAPTER ONE: The First Four Thousand Years

1 Palestine Royal Commission Report, July 1937, p. 24.
2 FO 371 24565.
3 CAB 24 282.
4 Samuel, p. 121.
5 Marlowe, *Rebellion in Palestine*, p. 167.
6 Gilbert, *Sir Horace Rumbold*, p. 421.
7 Royal Commission, p. 141.
8 ibid., p. 131.
9 Gilbert, pp. 425–6.
10 *New York Times*, May 30th, 1937.
11 *Jewish Chronicle*, July 9th, 1937.
12 Royal Commission, Minutes 5648.
13 *Jewish Chronicle*, July 16th, 1937.
14 Documents on German Foreign Policy, Series D, Vol. VI, No. 566.
15 *The Future of Palestine*, p. 43.
16 Rose (Ed.), *Baffy*, October 1st.
17 *The Times*, November 25th, 1937.
18 *New York Times*, February 2nd, 1938.
19 Foot, p. 48.
20 Marlowe, *Rebellion*, p. 193.
21 Foot, p. 51.
22 *The Times*, January 27th, 1938.
23 *Baffy*, March 10th.
24 *Jewish Chronicle*, May 13th, 1938.

CHAPTER TWO: The Arab Revolt and the White Paper

1 FO 371 21870.
2 Marlowe, *Rebellion*, p. 206.
3 FO 371 21863.
4 ibid.
5 CAB 24 278.
6 FO 371 21863.
7 *The Times*, October 8th, 1938.
8 *The Times*, October 3rd, 1938.

CHAPTER TWO—*continued*

9 *New York Times*, October 26th, 1938.
10 Marlowe, *Rebellion*, p. 206.
11 CAB 26 96.
12 *The Times*, October 27th, 1938.
13 *New York Times*, October 27th, 1938.
14 CAB 24 279.
15 CAB 23 96.
16 Marlowe, *Rebellion*, p. 209.
17 *The Times*, November 21st. 1938.
18 FO 371 21868.
19 FO 800 321.
20 CAB 23 96.
21 FO 371 21868.
22 CAB 23 96.
23 *The Times*, December 3rd, 1938.
24 *The Times*, December 28th, 1938.
25 867N. 4016/97.
26 CAB 67 4.
27 FO 371 21868.
28 CAB 24 282.
29 FO 371 23221.
30 Antonius, p. 411. This book was reviewed in *The Times* on January 20th and the *New York Times* on February 5th, 1939.
31 FO 371 23221.
32 FO 371 23221.
33 *Palestine Post*, December 8th, 1938.
34 *Palestine Post*, December 11th, 1938.
35 867N. 01/1425.

36 124.90G3 35.
37 *Palestine Post*, February 1st, 1939.
38 CAB 24 282.
39 Weizmann, p. 244.
40 CAB 23 97.
41 *Baffy*, February 11th.
42 *Palestine Post*, March 1st, 1939.
43 867N. 01/1482.
44 867N. /9111/216.
45 FO 800 321.
46 *Baffy*, March 8th.
47 867N. 01/1472.
48 FO 371 23232.
49 867N. 01/1556.
50 *The New Palestine*, March 17th.
51 FO 371 23232.
52 867N. 01/1550.
53 S.25/7563.
54 S.25/7563.
55 *Palestine Post*, May 19th, 1939.
56 FO 371 23241.
57 Parliamentary Question, March 23rd, 1938.
58 867N. 01/1556½.
59 *Manchester Guardian*, August 18th, 1939.
60 Weizmann, p. 250.
61 FO 371 23237.
62 FO 371 23239.
63 WO 216 46.
64 867N. 01/4016/97.
65 Weizmann, p. 253.
66 FO 371 23239.

CHAPTER THREE: The Little Death-Ships

1 S25/7563.
2 Weizmann, p. 256.
3 FO 371 23013.
4 Nuremberg Document PS-3363.
5 FO 371 23242.
6 S25/7563.
7 S25/7563.
8 FO 371 23242.
9 FO 371 23240.
10 S25/7563.

11 FO 371 23239.
12 FO 271 24565.
13 Dayan, p. 35.
14 CAB 67 4.
15 Z4/14847.
16 S25/7563.
17 *Baffy*, November 15th.
18 FO 371 23242.
19 FO 371 23239.
20 CAB 67 4.

21 FO 371 24565.
22 *Jewish Chronicle*, November 3rd, 1939.
23 CAB 65 5.
24 S25/7563.
25 S25/6286.
26 FO 371 24563.
27 FO 371 24240.
28 FO 371 23240.
29 FO 371 24568.
30 FO 371 24565.
31 FO 371 27124.
32 *New York Times*, October 13th, 1939.
33 FO 371 24565.
34 S25/7563.
35 FO 371 25242.
36 CO 733 429.
37 CO 733 429.
38 ZA/14632.

39 CAB 65 7.
40 PREM 3 348.
41 CAB 65 8.
42 FO 371 23234.
43 *Baffy*, September 13th.
44 FO 371 25242.
45 CAB 65/10.
46 FO 371 25242.
47 Steiner (Ed.), *The Two Eliahus Return Home*, p. 8.
48 Z4/14734.
49 FO 371 29161.
50 CAB 65 10.
51 PREM 4 52/5.
52 FO 371 29162.
53 FO 371 29161.
54 CO 733 430.
55 FO 371 29161.
56 FO 371 29162.

CHAPTER FOUR: Nazi Invasion

1 Dayan, p. 42.
2 *Documents on German Foreign Policy*, Vol. XI, No. 680.
3 Hirszowicz, p. 135.
4 DGFP, Vol. XII, No. 293.
5 CO 733 439.
6 Churchill, Vol. 3, p. 228.
7 DGFP, Vol. XIII, No. 494.
8 Churchill, op. cit., p. 236.
9 DGFP, No. 568.
10 FO 371 27124.
11 ibid.
12 DGFP, No. 399.
13 DGFP, No. 452.
14 FO 371 52585.
15 *Baffy*, p. 261.
16 Weisgal and Carmichael (Eds.), *Chaim Weizmann*, p. 262.
17 CAB 66 15.
18 FO 371 29163.
19 FO 371 29162.

20 *New York Times*, March 29th, 1941.
21 *Chaim Weizmann*, p. 257.
22 WO 193 67.
23 *Foreign Relations of the United States*, 1941, Vol. II, p. 860.
24 *Palestine Post*, December 2nd, 1941.
25 819.8591/118.
26 FO 371 29207.
27 Samuel Lubell, 'War by Refugee', *Saturday Evening Post*, March 29th, 1941.
28 CO 722 445.
29 FO 371 32661.
30 FO 371 32661.
31 Z4/14645.
32 FO 371 32662.
33 FO 371 32663.
34 FO 371 32662.
35 FO 371 32663.

CHAPTER FIVE: Partition and Terror

1 FO 371 31378.
2 CO 733 455.

3 Morton, p. 144.
4 CO 733 445.

CHAPTER FIVE—*continued*

5 CO 733 445.
6 FO 371 31567.
7 Meir, p. 133.
8 Ainsztein, p. 231.
9 *Trials of War Criminals before the Nuremberg Military Tribunals*, XII, pp. 210–19, 1951–2.
10 Ainsztein, p. 234.
11 Morse, p. 8.
12 *New York Times*, February 13th, 1943.
13 *New York Times*, April 20th, 1943.
14 *New York Times*, April 20th, 1943.
15 FO 371 36676.
16 FO 371 36747.
17 Morse, p. 54.
18 Yad Vashem Archives.
19 FO 371 36747.
20 FO 371 35034.
21 867N. 01/2011.
22 *Palestine Post*, September 26th, 1943.
23 *Palestine Post*, September 7th, 1943.
24 867N. 00/648.
25 Shirer, p. 974.

26 FO 371 35033.
27 *Chaim Weizmann*, p. 261.
28 FO 371 41039.
29 FO 371 35033.
30 FO 371 35032.
31 FO 371 35033.
32 FO 371 35034.
33 FO 371 35033.
34 WO 32 10260.
35 FO 371 35034.
36 FO 371 35036.
37 FO 371 35037.
38 FO 371 40139.
39 FO 371 35034.
40 WO 32 10260.
41 FO 371 40139.
42 *Chaim Weizmann*, p. 267.
43 FO 371 40129.
44 *Chaim Weizmann*, p. 268.
45 FO 371 40129.
46 WO 32 10260.
47 CO 733 461.
48 PREM 4 52/5.
49 CO 733 461.
50 FO 371 40125.

CHAPTER SIX: The Rise of the Irgun

1 867N. 01/2011.
2 Haber, Chapter Nine.
3 Begin, p. 48.
4 Morse, p. 85.
5 Begin, p. 32.
6 Katz, *Days of Fire*, p. 8.
7 Begin, p. 28.
8 *Palestine Post*, March 24th, 1944.
9 *ad-Difaa*, March 26th, 1944.
10 *Falastin*, March 26th, 1944.
11 S25/5601.
12 867N. 00/666.
13 Begin, p. 101.
14 FO 371 40125.
15 867N. 01/2324.
16 *Palestine Post*, March 24th, 1944.
17 CO 733 461.

18 ibid.
19 FO 371 40136.
20 Morse, p. 353.
21 CAB 95 15.
22 Morse, p. 358.
23 Z4/15202.
24 *Chaim Weizmann*, p. 273.
25 Morse, p. 357.
26 Weissberg, p. 167.
27 CAB 95 15.
28 ibid.
29 FO 371 42817.
30 Weissberg, p. 167.
31 Begin, p. 45.
32 CO 733 457.
33 CAB 66 56.
34 *Palestine Post*, October 12th, 1944.

35 CAB 95 14.
36 Shavit, p. 101.
37 CO 733 457.
38 Shavit, p. 88.
39 CO 733 461.
40 FO 371 41516.
41 Shavit, p. 88.
42 CO 733 457.
43 CO 733 461.
44 FO 371 41516.
45 ibid.
46 *The Answer*, December 1st, 1944.
47 Begin, p. 150.

48 CO 733 461.
49 Shavit, p. 102.
50 FO 371 40128.
51 CO 733 457.
52 CAB 66 59.
53 WO 169 19758.
54 Begin, p. 147.
55 CO 733 457.
56 Bell, pp. 129–33.
57 CO 733 457.
58 Pedazur, Vol. 2, p. 25.
59 Begin, p. 309.

CHAPTER SEVEN: Churchill's Legacy to Bevin

1 890F. 00/1-2645.
2 867N. 01/10-945.
3 CO 733 461.
4 867N. 01/2-2145.
5 *Chaim Weizmann*, p. 277.
6 Churchill, Vol. 6, p. 349.
7 FO 371 45378.
8 CO 733 461.
9 PREM 4 51/1.
10 PREM 4 52/5.
11 Trevor, p. 141.
12 *Chaim Weizmann*, p. 277.
13 CO 733 461.
14 Churchill, Vol. VI, p. 491.
15 Churchill, Vol. VI, p. 528.
16 CO 733 461.
17 *Chaim Weizmann*, p. 278.
18 FO 371 45378.
19 Wheeler Bennett, p. 636; see also *Observer*, August 23rd, 1959.
20 867N. 01/7-3145.
21 CO 733 461.
22 ibid.
23 FO 371 45378.
24 FO 371 45379.
25 FO 371 45378.
26 Meir, p. 164.
27 CAB 129/2.
28 FO 371 45378.
29 *New York Times*, August 17th, 1945.
30 FO 371 45379.

31 CO 733 461.
32 Crossman, p. 210.
33 FO 371 45380.
34 CAB 129 2.
35 PREM 8/89.
36 WO 169 19744.
37 S25/33.
38 FO 371 45380.
39 WO 169 19758.
40 *Palestine: Statement of Information Relating to Acts of Violence*, p. 4.
41 FO 371 45380.
42 PREM 8/89.
43 *Palestine Post*, September 16th. 1945.
44 CO 733 457.
45 Z4/15202.
46 PREM 8/89.
47 CO 733 461.
48 FO 371 45419.
49 S25/7566.
50 *Palestine: Statement of Information Relating to Acts of Violence*, p. 5.
51 WO 169 23021.
52 S25/7689.
53 FO 371 45387.
54 S25/7689.
55 WO 169 22956.
56 Wilson, p. 28.
57 ibid., p. 29.
58 Trevor, p. 162.
59 867N. 01/1445.

CHAPTER SEVEN—*continued*

60 867N. 01/1945.
61 FO 371 45387.
62 *New York Times*, December 1st, 1945.
63 867N. 01/10–445.
64 CO 733 461.
65 867N. 01/12–745.
66 FO 371 45387.
67 WO 169 19745.
68 *Palestine Post*, January 1st, 1946.
69 *New York Times*, January 3rd, 1946.
70 *Palestine Post*, January 3rd, 1946.
71 *Mid-East Mail*, December 30th, 1945.
72 FO 371 52503.
73 ibid.
74 Crossman, p. 43.
75 *New York Herald Tribune*, November 22nd, 1945.
76 Crossman, p. 45.
77 WO 169 23021.
78 CO 537 1710.
79 FO 371 52504.
80 FO 371 52506.
81 FO 371 51507.
82 Crum, p. 70.
83 Crossman, p. 66.
84 Crum, p. 90.
85 FO 371 52505.
86 Koestler, *Thieves in the Night*, p. 214.
87 FO 371 45421.
88 Hirszowicz, p. 312.
89 FO 371 52585.

90 FO 371 45421.
91 CAB 128/2.
92 FO 371 52511.
93 CO 537 1710.
94 FO 371 52511.
95 WO 169 23031.
93 CO 537 1710.
96 FO 371 52511.
97 WO 169 23031.
98 Crossman, p. 139.
99 ibid., p. 156.
100 ibid., p. 146.
101 WO 169 23053.
102 WO 169 23022.
103 FO 371 52515.
104 FO 371 52516.
105 FO 371 52515.
106 FO 371 52616.
107 FO 371 52524.
108 Crum, p. 76.
109 ibid., p. 35.
110 FO 371 52524.
111 Crossman, p. 200.
112 WO 169 22978.
113 WO 169 23022.
114 WO 169 23031.
115 WO 169 22978.
116 FO 371 52519.
117 CAB 129/9.
118 FO 371 52521.
119 FO 371 52519.
120 FO 371 52521.
121 *ad-Difa'a*, May 1st, 1946.
122 867N. 01/5–1446.

CHAPTER EIGHT: The King David Affair

1 Dekel, p. 93.
2 Wilson, p. 15.
3 FO 371 52525.
4 FO 371 52537.
5 WO 169 22957.
6 Trevor, p. 215.

7 S25/7706.
8 867N. 01/6–546.
9 867N. 01/6–1146.
10 FO 371 52529.
11 *Daily Mail*, May 27th, 1946.
12 WO 169 23022.

13 FO 371 52529.
14 *New York Times*, June 13th, 1946.
15 Wilson, p. 41.
16 Trevor, p. 212.
17 WO 169 23022.
18 WO 169 23031.
19 FO 371 52532.
20 WO 169 22978.
21 Montgomery, p. 423.
22 FO 371 52530.
23 Wilson, p. 58.
24 FO 371 52535.
25 Meir, p. 159.
26 Dekel, p. 45.
27 WO 169 22957.
28 Meir, p. 159.
29 Wilson, p. 61.
30 Trevor, p. 221.
31 S25/7703.
32 FO 371 52535.
33 867N. 01/8-646.
34 FO 371 52532.
35 Wilson, p. 59.
36 Dekel, p. 149.
37 Slutsky, p. 898.
38 Begin, p. 216.
39 Slutsky, p. 897.
40 Begin, p. 218.
41 860C. 00/7-1546.
42 FO 371 52538.
43 *New York Times*, July 10th, 1946.
44 FO 371 52538.
45 FO 371 52542.
46 *Izvestia*, July 4th, 1946.
47 FO 371 52539.
48 FO 371 52536.
49 FO 371 52538.
50 Shay, p. 9.
51 *Yediot Aharonot*, September 16th, 1977.
52 CO 537 2290.
53 *Black Paper*, p. 13.
54 CO 537 1726.
55 CO 537 2290.
56 Begin, p. 221.
57 Bell, p. 174.
58 FO 371 52548.
59 FO 371 52543.
60 CO 537 1726.
61 CO 537 1726.
62 867N. 01/7-2946.
63 FO 371 52546.
64 PREM 8/627.
65 Wilson, p. 66.
66 Trevor, p. 232.
67 FO 371 52545.
68 CO 537 1726.
69 FO 371 52549.
70 ibid.
71 CAB 128/6.
72 CAB 129/12.
73 CAB 128/6.
74 Trevor, p. 239.
75 FO 371 52556.
76 CAB 129/13.
77 CO 537 2317.
78 841. 01B67N/9-346.
79 *Eschnab*, October 11th, 1946.
80 *New York Herald Tribune*, August 1st, 1946.
81 867N. 01/10-246.
82 FO 371 61799.
83 FO 371 52571.
84 Trevor, p. 273.
85 FO 371 52562.
86 S25/6910.
87 FO 371 52560.
88 867N. 01/10-446.
89 S25/7566.
90 CAB 127/280.
91 FO 371 52561.
92 *New York Times*, November 1st, 1946.
93 867N. 01/10-846.
94 Thames Television (London), July 4th, 1978.
95 Weizmann Archives.
96 FO 371 52565.
97 CO 537 1787.
98 883. 00/12-646.
99 FO 371 52567.
100 FO 371 52547.
101 FO 371 52567.
102 FO 371 52565.

CHAPTER NINE: Abdication

1 WO 261 129.
2 Wilson, p. 113.
3 *Palestine Post*, November 1st, 1946.
4 CAB 127/280.
5 WO 32 10260.
6 Begin, p. 231.
7 Bell, p. 185.
8 *Palestine Post*, December 30th, 1946.
9 CO 537 2280.
10 January 31st, 1947.
11 867N. 01/12-3046.
12 Bell, p. 192.
13 CAB 127/281.
14 CAB 127/281.
15 CAB 129/16.
16 CAB 128/11.
17 FO 371 61764.
18 867N. 01/2-1247.
19 S25/7567.
20 *The Answer*, January 17th, 1947.
21 867N. 01/2-347.
22 ibid.
23 CAB 129/16.
24 867N. 01/2-447.
25 CAB 129/17.
26 PREM 8/627.
27 CAB 128/9.
28 Written Parliamentary Question, February 4th, 1947.
29 *New York Herald Tribune*, January 8th, 1947.
30 FO 371 61763.
31 FO 371 61763.
32 FO 371 61764.
33 867N. 01/1-2747.
34 Parliamentary Question, February 4th, 1947.
35 CAB 128/9.
36 Begin, p. 257.
37 Wilson, p. 121.
38 *Sunday Express*, February 2nd, 1947.
39 867N. 01/1-3147.
40 FO 371 61765.
41 CO 537 2334.
42 *New York Herald Tribune*, February 7th, 1947.
43 CO 537 2294.
44 *Palestine Post*, February 16th, 1947.
45 CO 537 2270.
46 *Operation Elephant*, unpublished report, p. 9.
47 CAB 129/17.
48 CAB 128/9.
49 CAB 129/18.
50 *New York Herald Tribune*, April 17th, 1947.
51 FO 371 61753.
52 Weizman, p. 48.
53 *Evening Standard*, April 16th, 1947.
54 Bell, pp. 204–17.
55 *New York Post*, May 14th, 1947.
56 *New York Herald Tribune*, May 15th, 1947.
57 867N. 01/5-1547.
58 CO 537 2313.
59 FO 371 61768.
60 CO 537 2313.
61 FO 371 61751.
62 CO 537 2281.
63 FO 371 61873.
64 FO 371 61771.
65 Krammer, p. 12.
66 FO 371 61771.
67 *ad-Difa'a*, May 16th, 1947.
68 *ad-Difa'a*, May 20th, 1947.
69 FO 371 61802.
70 Bailey Journal.
71 FO 371 61802.
72 FO 371 61903.
73 FO 371 61905.
74 ibid.

CHAPTER TEN: The Honey and the Sting

1 Derogy, p. 53.
2 *New York Herald Tribune,* June 13th, 1947.
3 *New York Herald Tribune,* June 5th, 1947.
4 *New York Herald Tribune,* June 26th, 1947.
5 CO 537 2294.
6 CO 537 2280.
7 CO 537 2345.
8 FO 371 61814.
9 FO 371 61813.
10 FO 371 61814.
11 FO 371 61815.
12 FO 371 61816.
13 FO 371 61815.
14 Bell, p. 227.
15 *Chaim Weizmann*, p. 297.
16 *Palestine Post*, July 13th, 1947.
17 FO 371 61816.
18 FO 371 61758.
19 FO 371 61816.
20 FO 371 61817.
21 *Palestine Post*, July 24th, 1947.
22 FO 371 61818.
23 *Palestine Post*, July 30th, 1947.
24 FO 371 61819.
25 *Palestine Post*, July 30th, 1947.
26 Wilson, p. 133.
27 Bell, p. 237
28 *Palestine Post*, August 1st, 1947.
29 ibid.
30 *The Times*, August 1st, 1947.

31 CO 733 477.
32 CAB 128/10.
33 S25/7567.
34 Derogy, p. 310.
35 CO 537 2313.
36 Derogy, p. 318.
37 CO 537 2294.
38 *Palestine Post*, September 9th, 1947.
39 CO 537 2281.
40 CAB 129/21.
41 CO 733 477.
42 FO 371 61835.
43 FO 371 61836.
44 FO 371 61960.
45 Koestler, *Promise and Fulfilment,* p. 170.
46 CO 537 2281.
47 FO 371 61893.
48 CO 537 2280.
49 S25/22.
50 CO 733 477.
51 S25/22.
52 Koestler, *Promise*, p. 252.
53 CO 733 477.
54 Begin, p. 316.
55 *United Empire,* November/December 1949.
56 *The Times*, May 14th, 1948.
57 *Palestine Post*, May 3rd, 1948.
58 *Chaim Weizmann*, p. 335.
59 *Palestine Post*, May 2nd, 1948.

Select Bibliography

Adams, Michael, and Mayhew, Christopher: *Publish It Not . . .* The Middle East Cover-up. London, Longman, 1975.

Ainsztein, Reuben: *Jewish Resistance in Nazi-occupied Eastern Europe.* With a Historical Survey of the Jew as a Fighter and Soldier in the Diaspora. London, Paul Elek, 1974.

Antonius, George: *The Arab Awakening.* The Story of the Arab National Movement. London, Hamish Hamilton, 1938. New York, G. P. Putnam's Sons, 1946.

Arendt, Hannah: *Eichmann in Jerusalem.* A Report on the Banality of Evil. London, Faber and Faber, 1963. New York, Viking, 1964.

Attlee, Clement Richard: *As It Happened.* London, William Heinemann, 1954.

Avriel, Ehud: *Open the Gates.* A Personal Story of 'Illegal' Immigration to Israel. New York, Atheneum, 1975.

Barbour, Nevill: *Nisi Dominus.* A Survey of the Palestine Controversy. London, Harrap, 1946.

Bauer, Yehuda: *From Diplomacy to Resistance.* A History of Jewish Palestine 1939–45. Philadelphia, Jewish Publication Society of America, 1970.

Begin, Menachem: *The Revolt.* Story of the Irgun. New York, Henry Schumann, 1951.

Bell, J. Bowyer: *Terror Out of Zion.* Irgun Zvai Leumi, LEHI and the Palestine Underground, 1929–1949. New York, St Martin's Press, 1977.

Ben-Gurion, David: *Rebirth and Destiny of Israel.* New York, Philosophical Library, 1954.

Bentwich, Norman and Helen: *Mandate Memories 1917–1948.* London, Hogarth Press, 1965. New York, Schocken Books, 1965.

Birkenhead, F. W. F. S., 2nd Earl of: *Halifax.* The Life of Lord Halifax. London, Hamish Hamilton, 1965.

Black Paper. The British Terror in Palestine. New York, American League for a Free Palestine, 1947.

Blum, John Morton: *From the Morgenthau Diaries.* Boston, Houghton Mifflin Company, 1959.

Churchill, Winston: *The Second World War.* 6 vols. London, Cassell, 1948–53.

Cohen, Gavriel: *The British Cabinet and Palestine.* April–July 1943. Tel Aviv, kibbutz Hameuchad, 1976.

Cohen, Gavriel: *Churchill and Palestine 1939–1942.* Jerusalem. Yad Izhak Ben-Zvi Publications, 1976.

Cohen, Geula: *Woman of Violence*. Memoirs of a Young Terrorist 1943–1948. London, Rupert Hart-Davis, 1966.

Cohen, Michael J.: *Palestine: Retreat from the Mandate*. London, Elek, 1978.

Crossman, Richard: *Palestine Mission*. A Personal Record. London, Hamish Hamilton, 1947. New York, Harper & Brothers, 1947.

Crum, Bartley C.: *Behind the Silken Curtain*. A Personal Account of Anglo-American Diplomacy in Palestine and the Middle East. New York, Simon and Schuster, 1947.

Dalton, Hugh: *High Tide and After*. Memoirs 1945–1960. London, Frederick Muller, 1962.

Dayan, Moshe: *Story of My Life*. London, Weidenfeld and Nicolson, 1976. New York, Morrow, 1976.

Dekel, Efraim: *Shai*. The Exploits of Hagana Intelligence. London and New York, Thomas Yoseloff, 1959.

Derogy, Jacques: *La Loi Du Retour*. La Secrète et Véritable Histoire de l'Exodus. Paris, Fayard, 1969.

Documents on German Foreign Policy 1918–1945. Series D Vol. V. Poland, the Balkans, Latin America, The Smaller Powers June 1937–Mar. 1939. London, Her Majesty's Stationery Office, 1953.

Documents on German Foreign Policy 1918–1945. Series D Vol. VI. The Last Months of Peace March–August 1939. London, Her Majesty's Stationery Office, 1956.

Documents on German Foreign Policy 1918–1945. Series D Vol. XII. The War Years Feb. 1–June 22, 1941. London, Her Majesty's Stationery Office, 1962.

Documents on German Foreign Policy 1918–1945. Series D Vol. XIII. The War Years June 23, 1941–Dec. 11, 1941. London, Her Majesty's Stationery Office, 1964.

Drummond, Ian: *Imperial Economic Policy 1917–1939*. Studies in Expansion and Protection. London, Allen and Unwin, 1974.

Foot, Hugh: *A Start in Freedom*. London, Hodder and Stoughton, 1964.

Gilbert, Martin: *Sir Horace Rumbold*. Portrait of a Diplomat 1869–1941. London, Heinemann, 1973.

Gilbert, Martin: *Exile and Return*. The Emergence of Jewish Statehood. London, Weidenfeld and Nicolson, 1978.

Gitling, Jan: *Conquest of Acre Prison*. Tel Aviv, Hadar, 1962.

Haber, Eitan: *Menachem Begin, The Legend and the Man*, New York, Delacorte Press, 1978.

Hersey, John: *The Wall*. New York, Alfred Knopf, 1950.

Hirst, David: *The Gun and the Olive Branch*. The Roots of Violence in the Middle East. London, Faber and Faber, 1977.

Hirszowicz, Lukasz: *The Third Reich and the Arab East*. London, Routledge and Kegan Paul, 1966.

Jefferies, Charles: *The Colonial Police*. London, Max Parrish, 1952.

Joseph, Bernard: *British Rule in Palestine*. A Timely Study by the Military Governor of Jewish Jerusalem. Washington D.C., Public Affairs Press, 1948.

Joseph, Bernard: *The Faithful City*. The Siege of Jerusalem, 1948. London, The Hogarth Press, 1962.

Kayyali, A. W.: *Palestine: a Modern History*. London, Croom Helm, 1978.

Katz, Samuel: *Days of Fire*. London, W. H. Allen, 1968.

Katz, Samuel: *Battleground*. Fact and Fantasy in Palestine. New York, Bantam, 1973.

Kimche, Jon: *Seven Fallen Pillars*. The Middle East 1945–52. London, Secker and Warburg, 1953.

Kimche, Jon and David: *Both Sides of the Hill*. Britain and the Palestine War. London, Secker and Warburg, 1960.

Koestler, Arthur: *Thieves in the Night*. Chronicle of an Experiment. London and New York, Macmillan, 1946.

Koestler, Arthur: *Promise and Fulfilment*. Palestine 1917–1949. London and New York, Macmillan, 1949.

Krammer, Arnold: *Forgotten Friendship*. Israel and the Soviet Bloc, 1947–53. Urbana, University of Illinois Press, 1974.

Lucas, Noah: *The Modern History of Israel*. London, Weidenfeld and Nicolson, 1974.

MacDonald, Malcolm: *Titans and Others*. London, Collins, 1972.

Marlowe, John: *Rebellion in Palestine*. London, The Cresset Press, 1946.

Marlowe, John: *The Seat of Pilate*. An Account of the Palestine Mandate. London, The Cresset Press, 1959.

Martin, Kingsley: *Harold Laski (1893–1950)*. A Biographical Memoir. London. Victor Gollancz, 1953.

Meir, Golda: *My Life*. London, Weidenfeld and Nicolson, 1975. New York, G. P. Putnam's Sons, 1975.

Monroe, Elizabeth: *Philby of Arabia*. London, Faber and Faber, 1973.

Montgomery of Alamein, Field Marshal Viscount: *Memoirs*. London, Collins, 1958. Cleveland, World Publishing, 1958.

Morse, Arthur D.: *While Six Million Died*. A Chronicle of American Apathy, New York, Random House, 1968.

Morton, Geoffrey: *Just the Job*. London, Hodder and Stoughton, 1957.

Newton, Frances E.: *Searchlight on Palestine*. Fair-play or Terrorist Methods? Some Personal Investigations. London, The Arab Centre, 1938.

Palestine Royal Commission Report. Presented by Secretary of State for Colonies to Parliament July 1937. London, His Majesty's Stationery Office, 1937.

Palestine: Statement of Information Relating to Acts of Violence. London, Her Majesty's Stationery Office, 1946.

Palestine. A Study of Jewish, Arab and British Policies. Vol. II. New Haven, Yale University Press, 1947.

Pedazur, Elazar: *The History of the Irgun Zvai Leumi*. Jerusalem, Department of Education, 1959.

Ro'i, Yaacov: *From Encroachment to Involvement*. A Documentary Study of Soviet Policy in the Middle East 1945–1973. New York, John Wiley and Sons, 1974.

Rose, N. A. (Ed.): *Baffy*. The Diaries of Blanche Dugdale 1936–1947. London, Valentine, Mitchell, 1973.

Samuel, Maurice: *What Happened in Palestine?* Boston, Stratford, 1929.

Sharef, Zeev: *Three Days*. London, W. H. Allen, 1962.

Shavit, Yaakov: *Open Season*. The Confrontation Between the 'Organized Yishuv' and the Underground Organizations (Etzel and Lehi) 1937–1947. Tel Aviv, Hadar, 1976. (In Hebrew.)

Shay, Abraham: *The Milk Churns Roared*. Tel Aviv, Hadar, 1977. (In Hebrew.)

Shirer, William L.: *The Rise and Fall of the Third Reich*. A History of Nazi Germany. Book Club Associates, 1973. (Secker and Warburg. 1959.) New York, Simon and Schuster, 1960.

Slater, Leonard: *The Pledge*. New York, Simon and Schuster, 1970.

Slutsky, Yehuda: *History of the Haganah*. Vol. III: 'From Resistance to War'. Tel Aviv, Am Oved Publishers, 1973. (In Hebrew.)

Steiner, Yosef E. (Ed.): *The Two Eliahus Return Home*. Tel Aviv, Hanhaga Olamit of Betar, 1975.

Sykes, Christopher: *Cross Roads to Israel*. London, Collins, 1965. Cleveland World Publishing, 1965.

Taylor, Alan R.: *Prelude to Israel*. An Analysis of Zionist Diplomacy 1897–1947. London, Darton, Longman and Todd, 1961. New York, Philosophical Library, 1959.

The Future of Palestine. London, The Arab Office, 1946.

Townsend, Peter: *The Last Emperor*. Decline and Fall of the British Empire. London, Weidenfeld and Nicolson, 1975. New York, Simon and Schuster, 1976.

Trevor, Daphne: *Under the White Paper*. Some Aspects of British Administration in Palestine from 1939 to 1947. Jerusalem, The Jerusalem Press, 1948.

Weisgal, Meyer W., and Carmichael, Joel (Eds): *Chaim Weizmann*. A Biography by Several Hands. London, Weidenfeld and Nicolson, 1962.

Weissberg, Alex: *Advocate for the Dead*. The Story of Joel Brandt. London, André Deutsch, 1958. (Published as *Desperate Mission*) New York, Criterion Books, 1958.

Weizman, Ezer: *On Eagles' Wings*. The Personal Story of the Leading Commander of the Israeli Air Force. London, Weidenfeld and Nicolson, 1976.

Weizmann, Chaim: *Trial and Error*. London, Hamish Hamilton, 1949. New York, Harper, 1949.

Wheeler-Bennett, John: *King George VI: his life and reign*. London, Macmillan, 1958.

White, John Baker: *Sabotage is Suspected*. London, Evans Brothers Ltd, 1957.

Williams, Francis: *Ernest Bevin*. Portrait of a Great Englishman. London, Hutchinson, 1952.

Wilson, Major R. D.: *Cordon and Search*. With 6th Airborne Division in Palestine. Aldershot, Gale and Polden Limited, 1949.

Index